Dynamics of Interorganizational Learning in Learning Alliances

Schriften zur Unternehmensplanung

Herausgegeben von Franz Xaver Bea, Alfred Kötzle und Erich Zahn

Band 74

PETER LANG
Frankfurt am Main · Berlin · Bern · Bruxelles · New York · Oxford · Wien

Florian Kapmeier

Dynamics of Interorganizational Learning in Learning Alliances

PETER LANG
Europäischer Verlag der Wissenschaften

Bibliographic Information published by the Deutsche Nationalbibliothek
The Deutsche Nationalbibliothek lists this publication in the Deutsche Nationalbibliografie; detailed bibliographic data is available in the internet at <http://www.d-nb.de>.

Zugl.: Stuttgart, Univ., Diss., 2006

Umschlagabbildung:
Erich Zahn

D 93
ISSN 0175-8985
ISBN-10: 3-631-56150-4
ISBN-13: 978-3-631-56150-8
US-ISBN 0-8204-8794-5

www.peterlang.de

Foreword

A core question in strategy research is why firms differ in their performance. In answering this question, researchers have traditionally chosen the single firm as a unit of analysis. According to this research, firms strive for competitive advantage either through favorable industry conditions or idiosyncratic internal resources and capabilities. More recently researchers have found that a firm's performance may be strongly influenced by its interfirm ties. This finding supports an extension of the unit of analysis to a firm's strategic alliance, strategic networks etc., and suggests complementing the conventional "atomistic view" with a "relational view". Thereby, competitive advantages and abnormal economic rents can be explained on both the firm level and the alliance level. So far, alliance research has focused on isolated aspects such as motives and pitfalls of alliances, but has neglected interactions and feedback mechanisms. These are important for understanding alliance dynamics.

With his thesis, Florian Kapmeier offers an original contribution to alliance research. In order to gain deeper insights into the "dynamics of interorganizational learning in learning alliances" he uses a system's perspective, formalizes findings from literature and an in-depth case study, and designs a System Dynamics simulation model. The model is used to analyze various aspects of common and private learning in alliances, such as gatekeeper openness, free riding, differing aspirations as well as perceived fairness and trust. Managers' trust formalized on the basis of behavioral game theory turns out to be a critical aspect of the performance of a learning alliance. Trust between partners certainly supports common learning. But trust is a rather fragile concept because changes in trust can easily shift behavior from a virtuous to a vicious cycle. This is clearly demonstrated by a tipping point policy analysis, which is an exceptionally innovative part of the study.

Some outcomes of the policy analyses offer new insights and suggest modifications to propositions in the current alliance literature. But it is not only for this reason that the study will certainly be of interest to academics. The research approach itself proves appropriate for improving our understanding of the dynamics of learning alliances. Moreover, the study offers practical recommendations for policy makers who are interested in building and managing successful learning alliances.

Stuttgart, August 2006 — Prof. Dr. Erich Zahn, Universität Stuttgart

Foreword

This thesis offers an original model-based treatment of learning alliances and opens-up a broad and important new area of application for system dynamics modelling in the policy and strategy area. Alliances are conceived as knowledge-generating engines whose success depends on collaboration among scientists. The organizational environment in partner firms either supports or thwarts collaboration depending on partners' attainment of common and private goals as well as the atmosphere of trust among managers responsible for the alliance. The research usefully contributes to both academic and practitioner understanding of alliance performance.

There is a thorough review of the academic literature about why firms enter alliances and some of the pitfalls they face. The review spans classical approaches such as organizational economics, resource-based theory and game theory as well as softer contemporary approaches such as dynamic capabilities, behavioural game theory and the knowledge-based view. From this review come important constructs for the model such as common and private learning, absorptive capacity, openness and trust. The conceptual model is then effectively applied to an in-depth case study.

The case model is lucidly presented in terms of its main feedback loops and stock accumulations. There is a well-documented equation description covering not only tangibles such as scientists active in the alliance but also intangibles such as trust and scientist openness. Policy analysis reveals potential sources of underperformance in learning alliances caused by free-riding and by various misleading intentions and actions of partners. Simulations compare the organizational conditions that lead to successful inter-organizational learning versus premature termination. This analysis is certainly of interest to academics. There are also practical recommendations for policymakers on how to promote common learning, limit private learning and prevent opportunism.

London, August 2006 Prof. Dr. John Morecroft, London Business School

Acknowledgements

The past years of conducting research on alliances with the System Dynamics method and writing this thesis have been intense and rewarding. System Dynamics has had a bigger impact on my academic career and private life than I could have imagined when I began to work for Prof. Erich Zahn at the Universität Stuttgart. This particular work has benefited greatly from the ideas and perspectives of many people whom I would like to thank in the following.

I am grateful to Prof. Erich Zahn for guiding the focus of my research in the captivating fields of System Dynamics and alliance research. He provided me with generous freedom to plan and conduct my research and many other activities at the Chair autonomously. He supported my ideas, provided direction, motivated me with his enthusiasm for research questions, and always had an open ear for issues of importance to me. I am highly indebted to him for initiating my first research stay with the System Dynamics Group at the MIT Sloan School of Management in Fall 2001. I am deeply indebted to Prof. John Sterman at MIT for inviting me to spend a semester with his group and allowing me to return for continuing research at any time in the future. He shaped my System Dynamics education, asked the right questions at important crossroads of my research and urged me to narrow the problem focus and hone my views.

I would like to thank the German Academic Exchange Service, DAAD, for supporting me with the PhD scholarship "DAAD Doktorandenstipendium im Rahmen des gemeinsamen Hochschulsonderprogramms III von Bund und Ländern" for the stay at MIT in 2001.

I thank Prof. John Morecroft of the London Business School for thoughtful comments and suggestions which proved immensely helpful. I also thank him for co-refereeing my thesis. I would also like to thank Prof. Michael Reiß of the Universität Stuttgart for co-refereeing my thesis.

I thank Prof. Paul Carlile, now at Boston University School of Management, for fruitful discussions and feedback. I deeply thank my (former) fellow PhD students of the MIT System Dynamics Group for welcoming me so warmly during my stays at MIT between 2001 and 2005. Brad Morrison, Gökhan Dogan, Hazhir Rahmandad, Jeroen Struben, Laura Black, Mila Getmansky, Paulo Gonçalves, and Timothy Quinn were constant sources of support and valuable advice. Jeroen gave especially helpful and constructive feedback on my work and I benefited immensely from his thoughts and ideas. I am grateful for his unique friendship during those years.

A wider community of System Dynamicists provided constructive feedback – first, the members of the MIT-SUNY at Albany System Dynamics PhD Colloquium. Besides the MIT group members, Aldo Zagonel, Ignacio Martinez, Roderick MacDonald, and Prof. George Richardson from SUNY have followed my alliance modeling work from the very beginning. I am deeply grateful to Prof. David Andersen, SUNY, for opening the doors to my research field site. Second, I thank the members of our System Dynamics Colloquium Series in Germany with scholars from the universities of Stuttgart, Mannheim, and Karlsruhe, and especially Andreas Größler from the University of Mannheim.

I would like to thank everyone at my field site. They generously gave their time and shared their expertise with me. For reasons of confidentiality, I will mention them solely by their initials. SC, DF, GW, BB, HG, and DM gave me insight into real world alliances. I would especially like to thank SC for supporting my research with tireless effort and making it possible to conduct the case study with the two firms. I thank BB for his patience and the efforts he made to help me understand the production processes.

I am grateful to my colleague Meike Tilebein, Universität Stuttgart, who listened and asked pertinent questions about my research from the very start. She was a very important research companion with whom I had fruitful discussions and shared creative ideas. I thank Birgit Kopainsky, ETH Zürich, and Jörg Sandrock, Universität Karlsruhe, for carefully reading chapters and for valuable feedback. I thank my assistants Stefan Grösser and Verena Krauer for ensuring a thorough literature database. I thank Rachel Teear for her perseverance in proofreading.

I especially thank my family for their enthusiasm and endless encouragement, particularly during the final writing phase. I also thank my friends who were there when I needed them. Finally, I am especially grateful to Susan Klemm, who has given up much of our time together to coaching and encouraging me in continuing with and finishing my thesis. Susan was always there for me – either for discussing System Dynamics based topics and alliance-related topics or for the wide variety of important issues outside of research.

Stuttgart, 29 August 2006 Florian Kapmeier

Table of Contents

List of Figures

List of Tables

Abbreviations

B .... balancing feedback loop
CL .... common learning
Eq. .... equation
G1 .... Partner firm 1's scientist group
G1 .... Partner firm 2's scientist group
GA .... goal attainment
i .... index i
j .... index j
max .... maximum
min .... minimum
NUMMI .... New United Motor Manufacturing Company
Op .... openness
P1 .... Partner firm 1
P2 .... Partner firm 2
p. .... page
PL .... private learning
pp. .... pages
R .... reinforcing feedback loop
R&D .... Research & Development
Sc .... scientists
SNECMA .... Société Nationale d'Étude et de Construction de Moteurs d'Aviation
T .... table function

Summary

In the 1970s, there was little tradition of firms entering alliances. In the meantime, alliances, even between competitors, have become an increasingly important strategic option for firms to achieve competitive advantage in all different kinds of business areas. Cooperation between competitors is of particular interest for alliances where the main motive is to learn with each other: single firms in research-intensive industries like biotechnology, chemistry, or information technology oftentimes lack the knowledge required to generate breakthrough innovations. They seek to overcome this shortage by sharing their knowledge to learn and generate new knowledge jointly. The jointly created knowledge may be used to generate joint innovations, for example.

As the outcome of such research-intensive learning alliances is oftentimes decisive for the long-term success of the parent firms, the participants involved in alliances mostly start out with great enthusiasm. Studies have shown, however, that most alliances are terminated early with at least one parent firm disappointed and without reaching the common goals. The literature identifies various reasons for alliance failure. Though providing valuable insight, most studies focus on specific aspects of failure while oftentimes neglecting a holistic and dynamic perspective. Yet, a dynamic perspective can lead to insight into how a cooperative venture between competitors might develop over time and why it might fail.

In this study, we chose a holistic approach, formalize literature and case study findings considering competitive and cooperative policies to analyze the dynamics of a learning alliance between two firms over time. We do so by designing a System Dynamics simulation model based on a dynamic feedback perspective. We use the model to analyze various dynamic aspects of learning alliances. For designing the model we use insight from an in-depth case study conducted with a learning alliance in the research-intensive chemical industry. Furthermore, we use insight from alliance-relevant theories. Apart from organizational economics, for example, related research entails static strategy approaches and their dynamic descendents, network theory, and behavioral game theory, that reveals insight into the perception of fairness and reciprocity – both of which are important in (learning) alliances characterized by the challenge of finding the balance between cooperation and competition. Policy-designers and decision-makers may transfer findings from the generic model with its fictitious data on real-world learning alliances as the model structure, with its elements and their interrelationships, and the basic dynamics are not only validated by latest alliance research but also by the in-depth case study. In learning alliances, cooperation and competition are represented by the two types of learning in alliances, common learning with the partner to obtain joint goals and private learning from the partner for areas unrelated to the alliance. While common learning is a desired objective of the learning alliance, private learning is an undesirable consequence of the alliance. The purpose of the simulation model is to identify policy implications to successfully manage common learning in learning alliances and to increase awareness in cases where the partner is doing private learning. The application of a dynamic, feedback perspective leads to a series of important managerial findings.

Model simulations and policy analysis concerning private learning suggest that private learning may only occur after common learning has taken place and with a time delay. Common knowledge is thus the basis for private learning. This insight contradicts the current learning alliance literature, which suggests that private learning is finished before common learning occurs. Furthermore, our findings question current alliance research when stating that private learning may be concealed from the partner firm. In other words, we learn from the model that the cheated partner firm does not necessarily perceive that its partner is using the jointly created alliance knowledge for its own purposes outside the alliance scope.

As private learning strengthens the cheating partner, we identify policies for how firms may protect themselves from being outlearned. One is, for example, to install formal contractual controls such as gatekeepers. At the same time, managers should support the building of social controls like trust to encourage effective knowledge exchange. Yet, they need to take care that trust does not completely substitute formal controls.

Whereas current alliance literature only identifies opportunistic behavior in alliances concerning private learning, we learn from our model that unfair behavior may also occur in situations which focus on common learning. Firms may have hidden agendas, for example, with the intention to free-ride. We learn from the model that in such a case, moderate unfair behavior is accepted by the partner. However, when a cheating alliance partner overacts, mutual trust may suffer and the alliance may be terminated early before the common goals are reached. We also found that partnering firms may be able successfully disguise their unfair intentions.

Although we do not find ways to prevent unfair behavior per se, we learn from the model about when alliance managers should be on their guard and analyze their partners' integrity. We find evidence for trust, driven by fair behavior and reciprocity, being a crucial determinant for learning alliance success. A trusting environment makes it easier for firms to collaborate. Yet, trust is a fragile construct. We identify a tipping point that determines the shift in trust from a virtuous to a vicious cycle. If the virtuous cycle kicks in, trust increases, resulting in a stable alliance relationship. Yet, if the vicious cycle kicks in, trust depletes and the alliance is terminated. This insight has implications for initial trust situations between partnering firms, for example. We show why, under certain circumstances, it may be important for firms to spend a considerable amount of time on building trust and paying attention to its long-term development.

Furthermore, we identify a number of implications for future research that we would not have been able to derive without applying a dynamic feedback perspective.

Firms considering our propositions in designing their alliance policies may increase the quality of their alliance outcomes and thus increase the share of successful alliances.

Zusammenfassung

Noch vor drei Jahrzehnten waren zwischenbetriebliche Kooperationen ein selten zu beobachtendes Phänomen. Inzwischen stellen Kooperationen selbst zwischen direkten Wettbewerbern eine zunehmend wichtige Option zur Erzielung von Wettbewerbsvorteilen dar. Besonders Wettbewerber in forschungsintensiven und innovationsgetriebenen Branchen wie Biotechnologie, Chemie oder Informationstechnologie gehen Kooperationen ein, da einzelne Firmen heutzutage oftmals nicht mehr allein über die für Innovationen erforderlichen (Wissens-)Ressourcen verfügen. Eine sogenannte Lernkooperation mit Wettbewerbern bietet diesen Unternehmen die Möglichkeit, ihr Wissen miteinander zu teilen und gemeinsam zu lernen, um auf diese Weise gemeinsam Innovationen zu generieren.

Obwohl oftmals gerade Kooperationen über den langfristigen Erfolg von Innovationsprojekten entscheiden und sie daher durchaus mit großem Engagement und hohen Erwartungen aller Beteiligten beginnen, scheitern sie häufig und werden beendet, bevor die gemeinsamen Ziele erreicht werden. Die unterschiedlichen in der Literatur hierfür identifizierten Gründe liefern zwar punktuelle Beiträge zum besseren Verständnis des Scheiterns von Kooperationen. Eine holistische, dynamische Betrachtung des Kooperationsverlaufs wird dabei jedoch meist außer Acht gelassen. Gerade eine dynamische Betrachtungsweise kann aber wertvolle Einsichten liefern, wie sich Kooperationen zwischen Wettbewerbern im Zeitablauf entwickeln und warum sie gegebenenfalls scheitern.

In der vorliegenden Arbeit wird ein ganzheitlicher Rahmen für die Untersuchung der dynamischen Entwicklung einer Lernkooperation aus zwei Unternehmen berücksichtigt. Hierfür wird ein auf der System Dynamics Methode basierendes Simulationsmodell erarbeitet, mit dessen Hilfe daraufhin verschiedene dynamische Aspekte von Lernkooperationen mit Simulationsexperimenten untersucht werden. Zur Modellerstellung wurde zum einen eine Intensivfallstudie einer Allianz aus der Chemieindustrie durchgeführt. Zum anderen wird im Rahmen der Arbeit auf kooperationsrelevante Theorieansätze zurückgegriffen. Erkenntnisse aus aktueller Kooperationsforschung beinhalten beispielsweise solche aus der Neuen Institutionenökonomik, der Strategieforschung, der Netzwerktheorie und der verhaltensorientierten Spieltheorie. Letztere untersucht bspw. das Verhalten von Akteuren in Bezug auf Gerechtigkeitsempfinden und Reziprozität – beide spielen gerade für die Analyse von Austauschbeziehungen in (Lern-)Kooperation eine wichtige Rolle. Das Simulationsmodell mit seinen Elementen und dessen Beziehungen bildet als ein allgemeines, generisches Modell eine Lernkooperation zwischen zwei Unternehmen in einer forschungsintensiven Branche mit fiktiven Daten ab. Erkenntnisse lassen sich auf die Realität übertragen, da die grundlegenden Verläufe anhand von Einsichten aus der Fallstudie validiert wurden. Kooperation und Wettbewerb in Lernkooperationen ist durch zwei Arten von Lernen charakterisiert: Gemeinsames Lernen für den gemeinsamen Erfolg und privates Lernen einzelner Partner für Unternehmensbereiche, die nicht direkt zu den expliziten Kooperationszielen gehören. Während gemeinsames Lernen ausdrückliches Ziel der Kooperation ist, gehört privates Lernen eines Partners zu den aus Sicht des anderen Partners unerwünschten Auswirkungen der Kooperation. Das Modell soll grundlegende Entscheidungsregeln identifizieren, die ein erfolgreiches gemeinsames Lernen ermöglichen und gleichzeitig privates Lernen zu verhindern versuchen. Die damit durchgeführten Simulationsexperimente führen zu einer Reihe von zentralen Erkenntnissen.

Bezüglich des privaten Lernens zeigen Modellsimulationsläufe und Analysen von Entscheidungsregeln, dass – entgegen gängiger Meinung in der Literatur – hierfür zunächst gemeinsames Lernen stattfinden muss. Weiterhin zeigen verschiedene Simulationsläufe, dass privates Lernen durchaus stattfinden kann, ohne vom Kooperationspartner bemerkt zu werden. Auch diese Erkenntnis stellt die herrschende Meinung in Frage, nach der sogenannte Lernrennen für alle Beteiligten offensichtlich und meist ein Grund für die frühzeitige Beendigung der Kooperation sind.

Erfolgreiches privates Lernen kann den Kooperationspartner entscheidend im Wettbewerb stärken. Modellsimulationen zeigen, wie sich die Partnerfirmen vor einem zu starken privaten Lernen des Partners schützen können, beispielsweise durch formale, vertragliche Vereinbarungen: Gatekeeper können den Wissensaustausch insofern effizient kontrollieren, dass kein Wissen aus dem Unternehmen abfließt, das nicht abfließen soll. Gleichzeitig müssen Kooperationsmanager darauf achten, dass informale Kontrollmechanismen wie Vertrauen aufgebaut werden, die den Wissensaustausch zwischen den Kooperationsmitarbeitern fördern. Es muss jedoch darauf geachtet werden, dass die formalen nicht völlig zu Gunsten der sozialen Kontrollmechanismen aufgegeben werden.

Opportunistisches Verhalten in Kooperationen wird zur Zeit in der Kooperationsliteratur ausschließlich in Form von privatem Lernen dargestellt. Jedoch bietet auch gemeinsames Lernen Optionen zum opportunistischen, unfairen Handeln. Nach dem sogenannten Trittbrettfahrer-Phänomen können Firmen Hidden Agendas verfolgen, mittels derer sie den Kooperationspartner ausnutzen wollen. Modellsimulationen zeigen, dass der ausgenutzte Partner unfaires Handeln in Maßen durchaus toleriert – übertreibt der sich opportunistisch verhaltende Partner jedoch, verliert der ausgenutzte Partner Vertrauen in die Integrität des Partners. Als Folge könnte die Kooperation vorzeitig beendet werden. Allerdings zeigen die Simulationsläufe in der vorliegenden Arbeit auch, dass der opportunistische Partner sein Verhalten verschleiern kann. Der Partner merkt erst davon, wenn der opportunistische Partner seine nicht gemeinsam abgestimmten Ziele schon erreicht hat.

Obwohl in der vorliegenden Arbeit nicht Möglichkeiten identifiziert werden, opportunistisches Verhalten im Bereich des gemeinsamen Lernens zu verhindern, können Entscheidungsregeln aufgezeigt werden, nach denen sich Partner davor schützen können. Dem fragilen Konstrukt des gegenseitigen Vertrauens fällt hierbei eine besondere Bedeutung zu. Modellanalysen identifizieren einen Tipping Point, der darüber entschiedet, ob sich gegenseitiges Vertrauen steigern lässt und die Kooperation in eine (relativ) stabile Partnerschaft übergeht oder Vertrauen verloren geht, was zur Auflösung der Kooperation führen kann. Hieraus lassen sich Erkenntnisse über die Bedeutung von vertrauensbildenden Maßnahmen in Lernkooperationen ableiten, die eine langfristige Ausrichtung einer Lernkooperation unterstützen kann.

Darüber hinaus hat die in dieser Arbeit gewählte ganzheitliche, dynamische Betrachtung von Lernkooperationen zur Aufdeckung weiteren Forschungsbedarfs geführt, der ohne diese Betrachtungsweise nicht hätte identifiziert werden können.

Unternehmen, die bei Eingehen von Lernkooperationen die in dieser Arbeit vorgeschlagenen Erkenntnisse berücksichtigen, können die Qualität ihrer Kooperationsergebnisse erhöhen und den Anteil erfolgreicher Kooperationen erhöhen.

1. Introduction

1.1 Problem Statement

During the past 15 years, the formation of alliances, of which joint ventures and licenses are frequent examples, has become a common element for firms in all kinds of business sectors to achieve competitive advantage.[1] DOZ AND HAMEL report that it was still unusual for firms to have alliances at the end of the 1980s.[2] CONTRACTOR AND LORANGE explain that up to that time, leading corporations prided themselves on being internalized.[3] Internal, hierarchical strategies based on competition stood in the foreground. One of the few economic reasons for entering alliances in those days was governments from socialist and developing countries requiring licensing and joint ventures to enter their markets.[4] Hence, US-based companies formed only 750 alliances in the 1970s.[5] Consequently, there was very little tradition and experience in cooperating with other firms at that time.[6]

Since then, socio-economic and political-legal environments have changed and technology has improved.[7] These and other changes have favored the rise of alliances over the years. Therefore, entering alliances has become increasingly a strategic option for companies to pursue their visions. Hence, the number of alliances between companies has increased at a high rate. According to a study by Booz, Allen & Hamilton the number of alliances grew at 25% per year from 1987 to 1997.[8] Scholars report similar growth figures. BÜCHEL, for example, states that the average number of joint ventures announced increased from 1,000 to 7,000 between 1991 and 2001.[9] Moreover, ANAND AND KHANNA explain that there were 20,000 reported alliances worldwide between 1998 and 2000.[10] On average, a company has between 50 and

1 See, for example, Inkpen and Tsang (2005), p. 148, Aloysius (2002), Dyer et al. (2001), Lane et al. (2001), Zahn (2001), Inkpen (2000a), Child and Faulkner (1998), Doz and Hamel (1998), Gulati (1995b), Ring and van de Ven (1992), Contractor and Lorange (1988b).

2 See Doz and Hamel (1990), p. xiii.

3 See Contractor and Lorange (2002b), p. 4.

4 See Contractor and Lorange (2002b), p. 4.

5 See Deering and Murphy (2003), p. 4.

6 See Jorde and Teece (1989), p. 32.

7 See Zentes and Schramm-Klein (2003), p. 259 and Zahn and Tilebein (1998), pp. 49-52. Duysters, Kok, and Vaandrager present an S-shaped graph indicating the number of newly established strategic technology alliances. At the same time, share of equity arrangements as a ratio of the total number of agreements has fallen. See Duysters et al. (1999), p. 344. An example of change in the political-legal environment is the enacting of the National Cooperative Research Act in the U.S. in 1984 and its extension of 1993 to relax antitrust regulations and encourage the formation of research and development cooperations by firms from the same industry. See Sakakibara (1997), p. 144 and Oxley and Sampson (2004), p. 746. Differently, there has been a long tradition of cooperation between competitors in Germany. See Teece (1992), p. 3. Contractor and Lorange identify three similar factors seeming to impact alliance formation, but name them differently: regulatory changes, for example, government policy changes, changes in the business environment that are independent of regulation, and changes in the industry practice. See Contractor and Lorange (2002b), p. 6.

8 See Harbison and Pekar Jr. (1997), p. 25.

9 See Büchel (2003), p. 91.

10 See Anand and Khanna (2000), p. 296.

60 alliances.[11] Given these figures, A.T. Kearney analyzed the alliances' impact on firms' financial performance. The analysis shows that alliances accounted for 26% of the average Fortune 500 company's revenues and for 6% to 15% of their market value by 1999. It also states that, in 2003, U.S. and European executives expected alliances to account for 30% and for even close to 40% of their revenues by 2004, respectively.[12] These figures indeed seem to be high. However, as CONTRACTOR AND LORANGE put it, "even if one were skeptical of such numbers, there is little doubt that the alliance phenomenon is here not only to stay, but is set to grow rapidly."[13]

Literature on alliance formation states various motives for companies to enter alliances.[14] One of the motives is interorganizational learning.[15] Alliances' parent companies share their knowledge bases and create joint or common knowledge. The new knowledge then serves as the nucleus for innovation. These days, innovations are increasingly based on interdisciplinary and interindustrial advances. LUBATKIN, FLORIN, AND LANE, for example, argue that without cooperating one single company would lack the required know-how for breakthrough innovations.[16] Hence, cooperating seems to be necessary for generating innovations that may then lead to competitive advantage.[17] This motive especially encourages companies in R&D intensive industries like biotechnology, chemistry, or information-technology to enter alliances.[18]

Although such specific interorganizational learning alliances and alliances in general are increasingly important and popular for companies' long-term success and value creation, most studies show that they suffer from a high failure rate or dissatisfaction of at least one partner.[19] Studies have shown that more than 50% of alliances have failed to meet partner expectations.[20] Dissolving failed alliances destroys billion dollars' worth of shareholder value each year.[21]

Hence, while alliances are getting increasingly important for firms' success, it seems to be difficult for decision-makers to find appropriate ways to manage an alliance

---

[11] See Deering and Murphy (2003), p. 5 and Dyer et al. (2001), p. 37, respectively.
[12] See Deering and Murphy (2003), pp. 4-5 and A.T.-Kearney (2003), p. 39.
[13] Contractor and Lorange (2002b), p. 4.
[14] Motives for companies to enter alliances will be discussed in depth in Section 3.3.
[15] See, for instance, Inkpen (1996), or Inkpen (2002).
[16] See Lubatkin et al. (2001), p. 1353 and also Reid et al. (2001), p. 80, Harrison et al. (2001), p. 680, Dussauge et al. (2000), p. 100 and Whipple and Frankel (2000), p. 22.
[17] See Inkpen (1996), p. 123 and Powell et al. (1996), p. 116.
[18] See Oxley and Sampson (2004), p. 723 and Grant and Baden-Fuller (2004), p. 63. See Hagedoorn and Osborn (2002), p. 524 for a comprehensive study on trends in interfirm R&D partnerships since 1960 and Schwerk (2000), pp. 183-190 for quantitative development and geographic distribution of alliances.
[19] See Kale et al. (2002), p. 747, Ireland et al. (2002), p. 414, Anand and Khanna (2000), p. 295, and Madhok and Tallman (1998), p. 326.
[20] The failure rates analyzed in empirical studies range from 50% of alliances formed (see Ho Park and Ungson (2001), p. 35 and Dyer et al. (2001), p. 37), to 50-60% (see Büchel (2003), p. 91), to even 70% (see A.T.-Kearney (2003), p. 40, Deering and Murphy (2003), p. 5, Whipple and Frankel (2000), p. 22), or 80% (see Gulati et al. (1994), p. 61). See Section 4.4 for further explanations.
[21] See Deering and Murphy (2003), p. 5. In Chapter 4.4 we discuss reasons for alliance dissolution. See also Kogut (1988a), for more information on dissolution of cooperations.

successfully and to achieve alliance success.[22] The literature suggests different reasons for alliance failure, including opportunism, poor management, poor communication, lack of trust, competitive rivalry, lack of top management commitment, lack of complementary resources, lack of cultural fit, changed priorities, quickly accomplished goals, one of the partners having won the learning race, or management's short-term view.[23] The wide range of reasons identified in the literature give an indication of the high complexity decision-makers are confronted with when managing an alliance.

Feedback structures consisting of the interaction between its components determine the dynamics of a social system, here of the alliance, and hence determine how the system, or the alliance, develops over time.[24] Looking at the dynamics of an alliance is of particular interest as most alliances start off with high expectations and enthusiasm of the people involved and then fail. Even though alliances are widely discussed in the literature, authors often tend to neglect such a feedback perspective.[25] This might happen when some of the aspects mentioned above are explained and discussed separately from each other. Excluding a variable might cut an important feedback loop that is actually significant for the dynamic development of alliances. This is because cutting a feedback loop via cutting a link between two or more variables might be critical as the interaction between the variables might be more important than the variable itself.[26]

Some authors use terms like 'feedback perspective' or 'positive' and 'negative feedback' but do not apply the underlying concept of intertwined loops or apply it but do not seem aware of its significance.[27] Others, however, consider a feedback perspective for explaining and underlining their arguments.[28] While asking for "the dynamics of partner cooperation in alliances"[29] to be fully understood, ZENG AND CHEN suggest three approaches that could help scholars and practitioners to gain deeper insight into alliance dynamics: simulation and modeling, in-depth case study, or empirical operationalizations.

---

22 See Gulati et al. (1994), p. 61 and Kale et al. (2002), p. 748.

23 The list provides a representative, but not exhaustive, catalog of reasons. See Kale et al. (2002), p. 748, Gebrekidan and Awuah (2002), p. 681, Ho Park and Ungson (2001), p. 38, or Larsson et al. (1998), p. 287 for overviews.

24 See Sterman (2000), p. 81.

25 See, for example, Aulakh and Madhok (2002), p. 28, Calantone et al. (2002), p. 516, Dussauge et al. (2002), p. 708, Griliches (1990), p. 1671, Inkpen (2000a), p. 1026, Lane et al. (2001), p. 1142, and Tsang (2002), p. 837.

26 See Forrester (1961), p. 14.

27 See Child (1998), pp. 247, 252, Goussevskaia and Swan (2003), p. 9, Ho Park and Ungson (2001), p. 51, Madhok and Tallman (1998), p. 333, Powell et al. (1996), pp. 121, 147.

28 See Ariño and de la Torre (1998), p. 308, Büchel (2003), p. 91, Büchel (2000), p. 637, Doz (1996), p. 64, Gulati (1995b), p. 623, Khanna et al. (1998), p. 193, Lubatkin et al. (2001), p. 134, Kumar and Nti (1998), p. 357, Olk (2002), p. 131, Zeng and Chen (2003), p. 601, and just recently Kapmeier (2003), Otto and Richardson (2004), and Kapmeier (2005).

29 Zeng and Chen (2003), p. 601.

1.2 Aim of the Study

As stated above, even though learning alliances have been subject to recent research, only some articles imply a dynamic approach.[30] The models being designed often concentrate on specific building blocks of the field of research on learning alliances and/or neglect a feedback-loop point of view.[31] The analysis of the dynamics of learning alliances requires simulation of the behavior of interrelating variables from a feedback perspective. For this purpose we combine two of the three research approaches suggested by ZENG AND CHEN in this work, simulation and modeling and case study research.[32] In contrast to other contributions to the field of study we do not demonstrate the existence of a new variable or test the strength of the correlation between two variables. Also, we do not report new data from another explorative study. Instead, we review the existing literature on interorganizational learning in depth and present a case study. We represent our findings in feedback loops and develop and analyze a quantified simulation model.[33] The result is an internally consistent approach providing new insight into the success or failure of interorganizational learning in alliances. We thus conduct case study driven experimental theory-building in a virtual world. In this work, the focus of attention is the dilemma between cooperative and competitive learning behavior in alliances. Insight emerges on the following two aspects: First, how firms may behave opportunistically in a cooperative venture. This should alert alliance managers to how their prospective alliance partner may take one-sided advantage of the originally cooperative alliance. Second, we refer on how alliance managers may design their policies in a way that ensures that both parties enter the alliance with cooperative objectives and then also behave fairly in the ongoing alliance.

1.3 Thesis Structure

The structure of this thesis follows the aim of the study. The thesis is divided into six main chapters, as illustrated in Figure 1-1. In the sections of Chapter 2 we describe the research approach that we apply to conduct the study. We first lay out the state of the art concerning interorganizational learning in learning alliances and then present the modeling and simulation approach. We further clarify how a simulation approach is helpful for an interorganizational learning analysis from a feedback perspective. To design the formal model we also apply information from a case study conducted with a research alliance. As the last section of Chapter 2 we present the case study design.

In Chapter 3 we look into the various theoretical concepts that explain competitive advantage. We show the basic ideas behind the concepts and then focus our discussion on their contributions to the existence of learning alliances. We discuss the inputs of organizational economics including transaction cost economics, agency the-

[30] See, for example, Lane et al. (2001), Khanna et al. (1998), Kumar and Nti (1998), or Doz (1996).
[31] See Kapmeier (2002), p. 2 and Kapmeier (2003), p. 9.
[32] See Zeng and Chen (2003), p. 601.
[33] We apply the System Dynamics methodology to develop the formal model. Concerning explanations on System Dynamics see Forrester (1961), Sterman (2000), and Section 2.3.4.

ory, and property rights theory. Findings from these theories refer to general opportunistic behavior in alliances and on the existence of hidden agendas. Then we continue with strategic management approaches. We begin with the static approaches, the outside-in perspective of the market-based view and the inside-out perspective of the resource-based view. The former highlights the firms' positions in the market place and the latter the firms' idiosyncratic internal characteristics as a source of competitive advantage. These explanations are the basis for discussing the dynamic descendents of the latter: competence-based view and knowledge-based view, dynamic capabilities, and the relational view. The relational view specifically integrates some of the insight of the discussed theories into one framework which specifically focuses on alliances. We then discuss the network approach that views cooperating firms as being embedded in a widely spanned network of firms. A firm's position and its reputation within the network are crucial for finding potential collaboration partners. When firms enter alliances for doing joint learning, the prospective partner oftentimes is a competitor. The dilemma between firms pursuing simultaneously collaborative and competitive strategies is widely discussed in game theory. We amplify the rational game theoretical approach with the latest findings from behavioral game theory. Among other things, behavioral game theory studies fairness and reciprocity in relationships, of which both are crucial determinants in learning alliances. The chapter concludes with a summary of the theoretical approaches explaining competitive advantage with learning alliances.

In Chapter 4 we lay out various factors determining the long-term development of learning alliances identified in the alliance literature. Where appropriate we add insight from the case study to support or qualify literature findings. In addition, we present how we transfer the findings into System Dynamics terminology. This way, the reader already becomes familiar with the representation mode of the formal model introduced at a later stage. We begin with defining organizational and interorganizational learning and continue with how the latter may influence alliance performance. Subsequently, we discuss the success and failure of alliances. According to the alliance literature, one reason for the high alliance failure rates is the cooperative and competitive dilemma between common and private benefits. Common and private benefits are of special interest for the rest of this thesis since the former may lead a firm to learn with the partner and the latter from the alliance and the partner. In the subsequent section we discuss selected factors that influence interorganizational learning. We present learning enablers and barriers, discuss the importance of absorptive and relative absorptive capacity for learning, and reveal that firms are required to be transparent for joint learning. Yet if they are too open, firms might be afraid that too much (competitively critical) knowledge might flow out of the firm. Therefore we discuss means to prevent unintended knowledge spillover. These could be formal controls, for instance, which the collaborating firms need to commit to in the contract. Alternatively, social controls like mutual trust may prevent firms from knowledge spillover. As trust is a crucial element in interorganizational collaborations, we discuss this concept in a separate section.

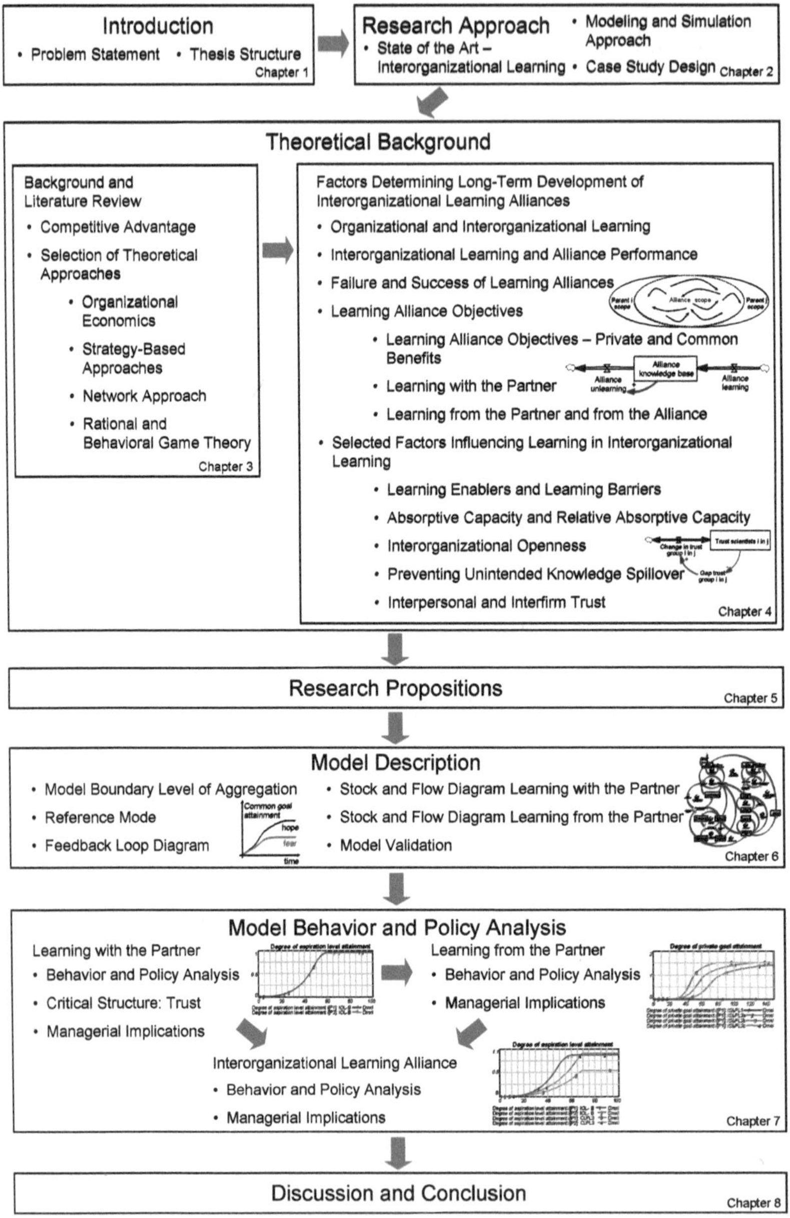

Figure 1-1: Thesis structure.[34]

[34] Source: authors' representation.

In the subsequent Chapter 5 we present our research propositions. They are based on the latest theoretical insight presented in the preceding chapters.

The findings from Chapters 3 and 4 provide the basis for formulating the formal simulation model which we describe in Chapter 6. We first define the model's boundary and its level of aggregation. Then we present reference modes and an aggregated feedback loop diagram that illustrates the main feedback loops driving system behavior. Subsequently, we describe the formal model. We divide the explanation into two sections: learning with the partner and learning from the alliance and the partner. Then we test the model to increase confidence in the model structure.

In Chapter 7 we analyze model behavior and test various policies in three sections: we first concentrate on learning with the partner, then on learning from the alliance and the partner, and finally on combining both learning modes. At the end of each section we present managerial implications that derive from the policy analyses. We also review the research propositions of Chapter 5.

Finally, we take up and summarize the central statements of the thesis in Chapter 8.

2. Research Approach

In this chapter we present the research approach that we apply to conduct our study. It therefore lays the theoretical foundation of our work. We begin by providing an overview of the state of the art concerning interorganizational learning in learning alliances. As we design a formal model on interorganizational learning we then discuss the suitability of the modeling and simulation approach in science in general. We also clarify how a simulation approach is helpful for an interorganizational learning analysis from a feedback perspective. Next we focus on the System Dynamics modeling approach that we apply for our study. The formal simulation model we design is based on two pillars: first, on insight from alliance and alliance-related literature, and second, on insight from a learning alliance case study that we conducted. As we refer to the interviews throughout the study, also in later chapters, we finally present the case study design and the case study alliance.

2.1 State of the Art Regarding Research on Interorganizational Learning in Alliances

With the advent of alliances and especially learning alliances as a means to sustain or enhance competitive advantage, publications on interorganizational ventures also emerged. HAGEDORN AND OSBORN examined major theories and trends in interfirm partnerships that focus on R&D. According to their study, existing theory ignored R&D alliances from the 1960s to the mid-1980s.[35] Since then scholars have focused on a wide variety of aspects of alliances. These aspects include research questions concerning stability and duration of alliances as well as alliance dynamics or evolution and alliance outcomes.[36] Since HAMEL, DOZ, AND PRAHALAD's seminal work[37] on cooperating with competitors, the subject of interorganizational learning with competitors has been increasingly discussed in the research community.[38] In the meantime, publications include longitudinal, empirical, and theoretical analyses of different kinds of aspects that might be of relevance for managing alliances. Empirical studies include INKPEN AND CROSSAN's study of 40 joint ventures between North American and Japanese automobile suppliers[39] or KALE, DYER AND SINGH's study of 78 U.S. firms reporting 1,572 alliances in industries "where alliances are generally considered an important aspect of firm strategy"[40], for example. Lately, several special issues[41] on

[35] See Hagedoorn and Osborn (2002), p. 517. With a different focus on international joint ventures, Reus and Ritchie III identify three influential publications from 1960 until the mid-1980s with 194 successive publications in ten major journals from 1988 to 2004. See Reus and Ritchie III (2004), pp. 370-371.

[36] This distinction in research streams is made by Dussauge et al. (2000), p. 100 and Doz (1996), p. 55. See these contributions for overviews.

[37] See Hamel et al. (1989).

[38] In the meantime, it has become impossible to give a quick review of relevant contributions to alliance literature. However, Chapter 3 covers an in-depth discussion on the learning alliance literature.

[39] See Inkpen and Crossan (1995), p. 604.

[40] Kale et al. (2002), p. 753.

[41] The 1995 Academy of Management Journal Special Issue focuses on intra- and interorganizational cooperation. The 1997 Academy of Management Journal Special Issue and the 1998 Strategic Management Journal Special Issue both focus on alliances and networks. The 1998 Organization

this topic have been published, including those of the Academy of Management Journal, Harvard Business Review, Organization Sciences, Organization Studies, and Strategic Management Journal. Additionally, CONTRACTOR AND LORANGE[42] and ZENTES, SWOBODA, AND MORSCHETT[43] have recently edited books on this topic.

The publications include contributions by leading scholars on alliances and related topics. Here and in other regular publications a major focus of interest lies in the aspect of interorganizational learning or knowledge transfer between the cooperating partners. One underlying theoretical motive for learning in alliances is embedded in the resource-based view and its dynamic descendents.[44] HAMEL, DOZ, AND PRAHALAD examine how easily knowledge can be transported, interpreted, and absorbed.[45] LANE AND LUBATKIN acknowledge that firms need to value, assimilate, and apply the partner's knowledge.[46] The learned knowledge can then either be used for exploration or exploitation.[47] According to KHANNA, this decision, among other things, depends on the partners' individual scopes.[48] Furthermore, KHANNA, GULATI, AND NOHRIA examine how an alliance develops over time in cases where both partners are interested in common learning or where one partner is only interested in outlearning the other.[49] If the latter happens, one partner uses its originally well-intentioned and trusting partner and exploits its knowledge base without reciprocating.[50] In this context, trust is widely acknowledged as an important driver for alliance success. Its contribution toward cooperational behavior in alliances is studied interdisciplinarily [51]

In conclusion, publications on alliance research provide a profound basis of information on the topic of interorganizational learning in alliances. However, so far, the information has stood more or less side by side. In Chapter 4, we put together, sort, analyze, and discuss the wide range of information. This information is the basis for a detailed and in-depth model-building analysis on learning alliance dynamics. In the following section, we discuss the modeling method that is applied for the analysis.

Science Special Issue focuses on interorganizational learning. Organization Studies' 1998 Special Issue's focus is on interorganizational relationships. Recently, the Harvard Business Review published a 2002 Special Issue on strategic alliances.

42 See Contractor and Lorange (2002a).

43 See Zentes et al. (2003).

44 See Combs and Ketchen (1999), p. 867, Khanna et al. (1998), p. 204, for example. The static resource-based view originated from Wernerfelt (1984), p. 172 and Barney (1991), p. 100. Its dynamic descendents encompass the knowledge-based view, the competence-based view, and dynamic capabilities. See Sections 3.4.2.3 and 3.4.2.4 for further discussion.

45 See Hamel et al. (1989), p. 133.

46 See Lane and Lubatkin (1998), p. 462.

47 See Rothaermel and Deeds (2004), p. 201 or Holmqvist (2003), p. 96.

48 See Khanna (1998), p. 340.

49 See Khanna et al. (1998), p. 193, Inkpen (2000b), p. 775, Inkpen and Currall (2004), p. 594, or Oxley and Sampson (2004), p. 723, who discuss the cooperating partners' scope, for instance.

50 In the 1980s, American companies were often outlearned by their Japanese partners. See Reich and Mankin (1986), p. 78 for further explanations.

51 See Currall and Inkpen (2002), p. 479, or Glückler and Armbrüster (2003), p. 279, Janowicz and Noorderhaven (2002), p. 3, Dengel and Milling (2002), p. 10, Child and Faulkner (1998), p. 293, Doz and Hamel (1998), p. 257, Granovetter (1985), p. 487, Das and Teng (2002), p. 449, Ring and van de Ven (1994), p. 93, Camerer (1997), p. 169, and Gulati (1995a), p. 91, for example.

2.2 Modeling Approach

As stated above, managers often have difficulty managing learning alliances successfully due to their complex underlying structure. Learning alliances can be regarded as complex systems.[52] An analysis of a learning alliance structure might provide decision makers with necessary insight for successfully managing alliances. To analyze the structure and behavior of such a complex system we apply the System Dynamics method. Hence, as systems stand in the focus, it is necessary to give an overview of the basic terms of systems. In the following we first introduce the systems terminology. Due to real systems' complexity, humans have difficulty examining in detail system structure which determines system behavior. Therefore, simplified models of such systems help us to gain deeper insight into the real system. For this reason, we focus further on modeling real systems. In System Dynamics, the models designed may be quantified and used for computer simulation. Conclusions from simulation runs give hints about possible redesigning of managers' policies.[53] For the special case of learning alliances, this means that the simulation model supports decision-makers in redesigning their policies to manage learning alliances successfully. We briefly present different approaches for computer simulation and discuss the System Dynamics method in more detail. This also includes a discussion of the validation and iterative modeling process.

2.2.1 Systems Theory and Systems

General systems theory covers both the theory of static and the theory of dynamic systems. As only the latter type of system exists in economic reality,[54] we focus on the theory of dynamic systems which is also called cybernetics.[55] System analyses based on systems theory and cybernetic findings serve to gain deeper insight into the behavior of systems as well as their underlying structures. Systems terminology can be attributed to general systems theory, founded by VON BERTALANFFY.[56] He tries to find an optimal level of abstraction for all disciplines applying biological examples. Other scholars like SHANNON AND WEAVER[57] and WIENER[58] focus on this challenge from an engineering perspective. In contrast to an atomistic perspective, general systems theory and cybernetics apply a holistic point of view. This involves thinking in interdependent contexts. Generally speaking, both systems theory and cybernetics can be understood as interdisciplinary approaches. They provide explanations for

---

52 See Inkpen and Currall (2004), p. 587.

53 See Keough and Doman (1992), p. 9. Policies are the rules that govern decision making. See Forrester (1961), p. 93 and Forrester (1994a), p. 13.

54 See Baetge (1977), p. 510.

55 Cybernetics, Greek: kybernetis = helmsman, navigator. There are different definitions of the term cybernetics. See Ulrich (1970), p. 100 for an overview.

56 See von Bertalanffy (1932), and von Bertalanffy (1949).

57 See Shannon and Weaver (1949).

58 Wiener, in particular, is regarded as the founder of cybernetics. See Wiener (1948). Yet, cybernetic thinking as the art of regulating and adjusting goes back to Platon whose ontology is closely related to a holistic perspective. See Zahn and Kapmeier (2002), p. 1921. For a comprehensive overview of the history of systems and feedback thinking see Richardson (1991a).

complex and dynamic phenomena of various disciplines which is why the term system is used and interpreted divergently in different fields.

Considering the aim of our study, we define the term system as referring to business administration. Generally, a system can be understood as a well-ordered totality of elements. Its elements are linked or could be linked via some kind of relationship.[59]

ACKOFF defines three different types of systems: mechanical, organismic, and social systems.[60] As firm constructs may be interpreted as open social systems, we only concentrate on the latter type here.[61] The behavior of a social system is determined by its underlying structure.[62] The structure consists of a set of interacting elements, or variables. They are called elements if it is not possible to divide them any further or if the system analyst would not gain any further insight by dividing them. Elements of the latter occurrence are called subsystems: they entail further elements whose structure is not of importance for the analysis.[63] The system itself is part of a comprehensive super system that it is interacting with.[64] Elements and the comprehensive system in turn could also be interpreted as a system in the above definition.[65] In other words, a system can be aggregated or disaggregated depending on the desired level

---

59 See Ulrich (1970), p. 105. For an overview of other definitions, also see Ulrich (1970), p. 105.

60 See Ackoff (1994), p. 175. For further information on mechanical and organismic systems, refer to Ackoff (1994), p. 175.

61 See Ulrich (1970), p. 166, Ackoff (1994), p. 176 or Zahn and Kapmeier (2002), p. 1920, for example.

62 See Richardson (1996), p. 659 and Richardson (2001), p. 809.

63 One example is the structure of a single firm which is not necessarily of importance for analyzing the world economy, as is described by Forrester (1971).

64 Ulrich and Ackoff define firms as being open social systems as they maintain relationships with their environment. Firms, as open systems, exchange matter, energy, and/or information as inflows or outflows (see Ulrich (1970), p. 112 and Ackoff (1994), p. 176). Forrester states that an open system is characterized by outflows that result after preceding inflows. The outflows are seen separately from the inflows and do not influence the inflows at all. According to his findings, open systems neither observe nor react to something (see Forrester (1972), p. 15). The dilemma between these definitions is that firms do react to certain inflows but also regulate themselves. Nevertheless, the openness of a system is a dimensional characteristic. Hence, openness may differ in extent with totally closed systems on the one side of the range and totally open systems on the other. The degree of openness depends on the extent of inputs and outputs. Ulrich states that living beings are open to some degree – and closed to another degree. He continues that artificially designed systems like machines have certain openings for humans to intervene in the system (see Ulrich (1970), p. 113). Forrester, on the other hand, states that open systems do not control themselves – like automobiles without a driver or mechanical clock movements that do not observe their own inaccuracy and hence do not regulate themselves according to a specific system purpose (see Forrester (1972), p. 15). Considering both points of view, a firm can be interpreted as a system that is indeed open toward its environment. Elements outside the system border may influence the system structure and vice versa. However, its internal structure and policies consist of self-regulating feedback loops that use information from preceding inflows which influence proceeding actions, for instance, such as the purpose of satisfying customers' needs. Following a more engineering perspective, Forrester acknowledges that the question of whether or not a system is open or closed depends on the system observer's point of view (see Forrester (1972), p. 16). Richardson underlines the difference in interpretation by stating that the closed system does not refer to the general system meaning, but more accurately to the attempt to view a system as causally closed (see Richardson (1996), p. 659 and Richardson (2001), p. 809).

65 See Ulrich (1970), p. 107.

of system analysis.[66] Moreover, the system boundary separates whatever lies within the system and its environment.

There are two different kinds of relationship between system elements: positive and negative link polarities.[67] Generally, and particularly in System Dynamics, such links are shown by arrows. A positive link has two ways of interpretation. On the one hand, it means that the effect increases with an increasing cause above what it would have been otherwise. On the other hand it stands for an effect decreasing below what if would otherwise have been if the cause decreases. The example of a positive link in Table 2-1 shows that an increasing birth rate leads to an increasing population and vice versa.

Symbol	Interpretation	Mathematics	Example
X $\xrightarrow{+}$ Y	All else equal, if X increases (decreases), then Y increases (decreases) above (below) what it would have been. In the case of accumulations, X adds to Y.	$\partial Y/\partial X > 0$ In the case of accumulations, $Y = \int_{t_0}^{t} (X + \ldots) ds + Y_{t_0}$	Birth rate $\xrightarrow{+}$ Population
X $\xrightarrow{-}$ Y	All else equal, if X increases (decreases), then Y decreases (increases) below (above) what it would have been. In the case of accumulations, X subtracts from Y.	$\partial Y/\partial X < 0$ In the case of accumulations, $Y = \int_{t_0}^{t} (-X + \ldots) ds + Y_{t_0}$	Death rate $\xrightarrow{-}$ Population

Table 2-1: Link polarity between variables.[68]

A negative link between two variables is interpreted in the following two ways. First, if the cause increases, the effect decreases. It decreases below what it would have been otherwise. Second, the effect increases above what it would have been otherwise if the cause decreases. The example of a negative link in Table 2-1 shows that an increasing death rate leads to a decrease in population and vice versa. It needs to be pointed out that such link polarities do not describe what actually happens in the system but what would happen if a change in one of the variables occurred – considering ceteris paribus conditions.

System elements and their interacting relationships form feedback loops. The basic concept of the latter is illustrated in Figure 2-1. A feedback loop is a closed path that connects a decision resulting in action, the real world (or state of the system), and the information that feeds back from the real world to the decision-maker.[69] The dynamic behavior of the system arises from the temporal sequence of information fed back from the real world that produces decisions and actions which in turn have consequences which generate further information. These phases may not follow immedi-

---

[66] See Coyle (1996), pp. 40-44.
[67] The following explanations are based on Sterman (2000), pp. 138-140.
[68] Source: Sterman (2000), p. 139.
[69] See Sterman (2000), p. 15 and earlier Forrester (1972), p. 19.

ately after one another. There may be time delays between cause and effect, procrastinating effects arising.[70]

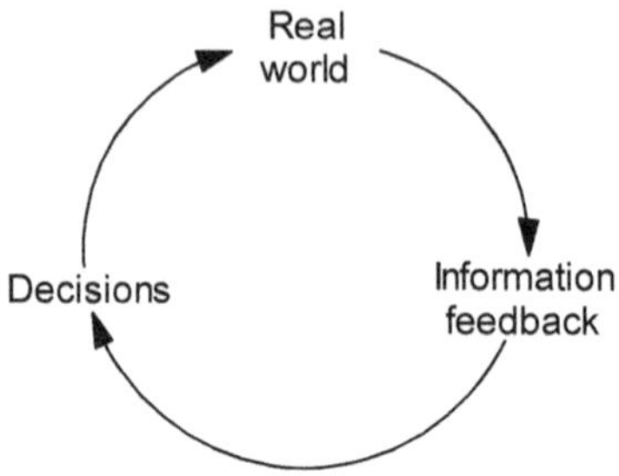

Figure 2-1: Feedback loop.[71]

The dynamics arising from a system structure are based on only two different kinds of feedback loop.[72] They either strengthen or weaken the state of the system. Reinforcing, or positive feedback loops amplify what is happening in a system. Balancing, or negative feedback loops tend to oppose the action in a system. When standing alone, the dynamics resulting from these structures should be straightforward.[73] However, real social systems usually consist of a number of such intertwined feedback loops. The increase in complexity makes matters remarkably worse: it confuses people when trying to understand the system and to estimate or even forecast its behavior. Moreover, the relationships between system elements are usually nonlinear.[74] Consequently, intertwined nonlinear feedback loops form patterns of shifting loop dominance. This means that under some circumstances one part of a system may be very active, and under other circumstances another set of relationships takes control and shifts the entire system behavior.[75] Generally, nonlinearity is fundamental to the dynamics of systems of all types. [76] To conclude, the system characteristics are the cause of insensitive reactions of complex systems toward human intervention. In ad-

[70] A situation (almost) without any time delay is when touching a hot stove with the hand. The heat can be (nearly) felt immediately. See Forrester (1994a), p. 14. Looking at the situation accurately, there is a small delay when the information about the burnt skin travels from the hand through the nerve system until it is finally felt.

[71] Source: Sterman (2000), p. 15, Sterman (1994), p. 293 and similarly Forrester (1961), p. 94.

[72] See Sterman (2000), p. 12. Further explanation regarding positive and negative feedback loops is given in Section 2.3.2.

[73] Sterman and Booth Sweeney have shown in experiments with students that even highly educated humans have difficulties grasping simple system structures. The experiments include graphical integration tasks like filling a bathtub or checking a bank account. See Booth Sweeney and Sterman (2000), p. 249 or Sterman (2002), p. 501. In the meantime, these results have been replicated at different universities or schools in the U.S. (see, for instance, Atkins et al. (2001), or Kainz (2002)) or in Europe (see, for example, Ossimitz (2002), or Kapmeier (2004)). See also Sterman (2000), p. 29.

[74] See Müller (2004), p. 54 and Sterman (2000), p. 551.

[75] See Meadows (1980), p. 33, Richardson (1996), p. 658, and Richardson (2001), pp. 808-809. Linear first-order systems can only exhibit three kinds of behavior: exponential growth, exponential decay, or equilibrium. Nonlinear first-order feedback systems can exhibit S-shaped growth with shifting dominant feedback loops as the system evolves. See Sterman (2000), p. 291 also Section 2.3.4.

[76] See Sterman (2000), p. 551 or Forrester (1980), p. 21.

dition, complex systems may show behavior that differs considerably from what is expected intuitively.[77] This is a typical phenomenon when dealing with complex systems. It is called counterintuitive system behavior.[78]

According to DÖRNER complexity is a subjective measure as some people might interpret situations as being more or less complex than others. However, variety might be a helpful measure for determining complexity objectively. Variety can be interpreted as the number of relationships between system elements.[79] SENGE calls this detail complexity.[80] However, he places more importance on dynamic complexity, describing situations in which cause and effect are distant in time and space while decision makers expect causes near the events.[81] Hence, consequences of interventions are not observable immediately. Because of this complexity, states of systems may result in a wide variety. This is the reason why complex systems cannot be entirely described.

Decision makers could gain insight into real systems when studying the system closely. Nonetheless, because of commonly focused short-term orientation they risk overlooking some (important) effects of their – or their predecessor's – decision that may only be revealed after a considerable time delay. Hence, the time given to study the real system might be too short. Another possibility would be to run experiments with the real system. Many systems, however, should not be experimented with. It can either be not possible at all, too expensive, too time-consuming, or too dangerous.[82] It could be too dangerous, for instance, because under some circumstances evolutions in real systems are irreversible. In other words, the initial situation cannot be reestablished in order to run a different scenario to look for different outcomes. Experiments also do not solve the time delay problem. For these reasons, humans may design models with many abstractions for a better understanding of systems and their behavior. In the following, we go deeper into discussing model characteristics.

2.2.2 Models

Generally speaking, models feature three main characteristics.[83] First, models are representations of natural or man-made original systems, and second, models are

---

77 See Milling (1984), p. 507.

78 See Forrester (1975b).

79 See Dörner (2002), p. 61 and also Ulrich (1970), p. 116.

80 See Senge (1990), p. 71. For further discussion on detail and dynamic complexity see also Espejo (1994), Sterman (2000), pp. 21-23, and Sterman (2001), pp. 10-15.

81 See also Sterman (2000), p. 22. He enlightens in depth the reasons why dynamic complexity in systems arises: dynamic complexity arises because systems are dynamic, tightly coupled, governed by feedback, nonlinear, history-dependent, self-organizing, adaptive, counterintuitive, policy resistant, and characterized by trade-offs.

82 Examples of the restrictions mentioned are crash tests, research on social systems, astronautics, effect of emission of CO_2 on composition of the world atmosphere, or safety of nuclear power plants.

83 See Stachowiak (1973), pp. 131-133.

simplifications and abstractions of things that could be models themselves.[84] Only those elements and relationships between elements that seem to be relevant for explaining its structure or dynamics from the model builder's perspective are selected from the real system.[85] This abstraction simplifies the system so that we are able to analyze the model. Third, models only replace systems for the time period necessary for certain mental or actual operations by individuals who want to gain insight into the system. Thus, models help people to understand systems better. However, due to the same reasons, one has to realize that the models humans base their decisions on are incomplete and incorrect; they are simply wrong.[86] This is explained in more depth in the following.

As mentioned above, decisions depicted in Figure 2-1 are made on the basis of models.[87] Every individual intuitively uses models. The question is not whether or not to apply a model but which model to apply.[88] More specifically, decisions are the consequence of applying a policy to information about the real world as the decision maker perceives it.[89] Policies, strategies, and structures are embedded in humans' mental models. Humans create mental models to reduce the complexity of real social systems. These models are suited for a gaining a better "understanding of obscure behavior characteristics more effectively than could be done by observing the real system."[90] Mental models contain intuitive and implicit knowledge.[91]

Even though widely acknowledged and used throughout science and philosophy, the term mental model is defined differently.[92] Yet, system dynamics scholars agree on the construct's advantages and disadvantages. Mental models are flexible in their structure. Or, as FORRESTER puts it, "within one individual a mental model changes with time and even during the flow of a single conversation."[93] A mental model can cover a broader scope of information than merely numerical data. It can be modified when supplementary information becomes accessible. To sum up, mental models

84 Stachowiak interprets models and systems as being nearly identical (see Stachowiak (1973), p. 131 as does Wyssusek (2004), p. 382). Yet, in this work we understand systems as the chosen part of the real world, and models as their illustration and representation. Therefore, we distinguish (real) systems from their (representative) models.

85 The relationship between system and model can either be homomorphism or isomorphic. The former type of relationship means that the system and the model both consist of the same number of elements and relationships. In the latter type the model has fewer elements and relationships than the system. This way, some attributes of complexity are excluded. See Wyssusek (2004), p. 384.

86 See Sterman (2000), p. 846 and Sterman (2002), p. 525.

87 See Forrester (1971), p. 14 or Keough and Doman (1992), p. 18. The following statements also refer to Figure 2-2.

88 See Forrester (1975b), p. 213.

89 See Sterman (2000), p. 16 and Forrester (1961), p. 97. A policy is a decision rule capturing institutional structures, organizational strategies, or cultural norms. See also Sterman (2000), p. 514.

90 Forrester (1961), p. 49.

91 Intuitive and implicit knowledge is also called tacit knowledge. Tacit knowledge covers soft knowledge skills (see Nonaka and Takeuchi (1995), for further revision). It is only revealed through its application. See Grant (1996), p. 111.

92 See Sterman (2000), p. 16 or Doyle and Ford (1998), pp. 3-29 for further insight.

93 Forrester (1975b), p. 213.

can be interpreted as the filters through which humans interpret the world on the basis of their personal experience.[94]

However, mental models also have shortcomings. According to FORRESTER, mental models are fuzzy, incomplete, and imprecise.[95] They are dynamically deficient and insensitive to nonlinearities. They ignore the feedback processes that the real world consists of and fail to acknowledge time delays between cause and effect.[96] In other words, mental models are ambiguous and unquantified.[97] This is why mental models are difficult for others to understand, for instance in conversations, and result in different interpretations. This occurs although structures of mental models are usually very simple. "Often these mental models are also flawed"[98] as humans often make mistakes in deducing the effects of underlying assumptions. Hence, humans make erroneous inferences about the dynamics of systems. Humans are not even able to mentally simulate the simplest possible feedback structure without error.[99] Keeping in mind that real social systems like learning alliances consist of multiple nonlinear feedback loops, it can be expected that managers will often fail to see long-term effects of their decisions which may lead to policy resistance.[100]

Formal models, like System Dynamics models, can support humans in their decision making to overcome mental models' drawbacks.[101] Information contained by mental models needs to be verbalized and translated into formal models. Formal models represent numerical values that were formally part of vague mental constructs.[102] As stated above, formal models are generally useful in situations that are too dangerous or unethical to experiment with in reality, too slow because of long time delays or too fast, too large, or too small to be studied in depth in the real world. In formalizing social systems like learning alliances, model runs provide the possibility to experiment with strategies that would lead to the alliance's failure on the basis of the managers' mental models. Managers have the possibility to challenge their mental models by experimenting in the virtual world.

---

[94] See Sterman (1991), p. 210.

[95] See Forrester (1975b), p. 213.

[96] See Sterman (2000), p. 27.

[97] See Meadows (1980), p. 27. For supplementary definitions of the term mental model, refer to Forrester (1961), pp. 49-50, Morecroft (1994), p. 7, Senge (1990), pp. 8-9, Lane (1999), pp. 187, 199, or Sterman (2000), p. 16.

[98] Sterman (1991), p. 210. The characteristics of mental models are a hint for irrational decision making that we discuss in Section 3.4.4.3.

[99] See Sterman (2000), p. 29. Sterman refers to first-order linear positive feedback loops with the simplest possible feedback structure.

[100] Policy resistance is the tendency for interventions to be delayed, diluted, or defeated by the response of the system to the intervention itself. See Meadows (1982), pp. 103-104, Sterman (2000), pp. 5, 9, and Sterman (2002), p. 504. Sterman presents examples of policy resistance: road-building programs designed to reduce congestion that have increased traffic, delays, and pollution or antibiotics that have stimulated the evolution of resistant weeds and pests, killed off natural predators, and accumulated up the food chain to poison fish, birds, and possibly humans.

[101] See Doyle and Ford (1998), p. 10. For designing formal models, mental models must be verbalized first. To model a system, the decision makers need to externalize the implicit knowledge about, for instance, policies, system borders, and variables, thus forming a verbal model. See Senge (1990), p. 174 or Morecroft (1994), p. 9.

[102] See Forrester (1972), p. 77.

The virtues and shortcomings of formal models could be seen as a mirror image of mental models. Formal models are explicit, precise and present a clear picture of the phenomenon. The mathematical language used for building them is standardized and unambiguous. Their notation is clear and therefore easier to understand than mental models. Underlying model assumptions are, or should be, stated. Consequently, individuals of different educational backgrounds are able to comprehend formal models.[103]

Oftentimes, however, formal models are complex and poorly documented. High model complexity prevents model users from developing confidence in the consistency or correctness of the model. This makes it hard for users to comprehend and accept the underlying assumptions. Moreover, formal models might not be capable of capturing relationships and factors that are either challenging to quantify, or for which numerical data do not exist, or that lie beyond the expertise of the modeler.[104]

To conclude, insight from models of all types can be transferred to the real world. Model builders or users may gain a good knowledge of the structure of the original.[105] However, as stated above, the human intellect is only limitedly capable of simulating mentally. Therefore, formulization seems to be necessary for people to fully understand the underlying system structure and its implications for system behavior.[106] In the following, we present different techniques to analyze models and discuss their characteristics.

2.3 Computer Simulation

2.3.1 Optimization and Simulation

Techniques like optimization or simulation can be used to analyze models. Yet, the techniques are suited for different circumstances.[107] Optimization models are prescriptive. This means that they provide hints regarding how to use an opportunity as successfully as possible. They offer a good tool in situations where people optimize choices. They have some limitations. First, one of the problems is the specification of the objective function that indicates the goal or objective. Second, the majority of optimization models assume linear relationships – nonlinearities, being one of the main characteristics of social systems, are not captured. Third, many optimization models ignore feedback effects that the real world consists of. Finally, many optimization models are static and only provide the optimal solution for a particular point in time. They therefore ignore the dynamics of the system and its environment. Even though optimization models might be well suited for some problem sets, due to the limitations

[103] See Forrester (1972), p. 77, Forrester (1975b), p. 214, and Sterman (1991), p. 211.
[104] See Sterman (1991), p. 211.
[105] See Stachowiak (1973), p. 140.
[106] See Sterman (2000), p. 38.
[107] For the following statements see Forrester (1994c), p. 249 and Sterman (1991), pp. 211-215. What Sterman refers to are models that Forrester categorizes into hard Operations Research methods like linear programming or queuing theory. See Forrester (1994c), p. 249.

presented, they are not appropriate for gaining insight into the development of learning alliances. They do not illustrate how people actually behave.

Simulation models make up for the limitations of optimization models. Generally speaking, simulations illustrate the models' behavior over time.[108] The term simulation is used differently depending on the field of research. In addition to experimental simulations which are carried out in laboratories, theoretical simulations also exist.[109] Simulations are called theoretical if a system is being simulated mathematically. Theoretical simulations are based on symbolic models and can be deterministic, probabilistic, stochastic, continuous, or discrete.[110] If theoretical simulations are done with a computer, they are called computer simulations. They are used for analyzing behavior over time. This is of special interest if the systems are too complex for mental simulations and exact mathematical-analytical methods.[111] The characteristic of high complexity holds for complex natural systems like analyzing climate as well as for complex social systems like managing alliances. In the meantime, computer simulations have become increasingly important for heuristics and they replace real experiments to a greater extent.[112] Concluding, a simulation model mimics[113] the real system. It is descriptive which means that it shows what would happen in a given situation. This characteristic leads to a wide range of applications. Simulation models can be used for forecasting, optimizing, theory testing, illustrating relations, training, or learning.[114]

STERMAN identifies several virtues of simulation models.[115] Simulations provide inexpensive learning laboratories in which time can be dilated or compressed. Actions that are irreversible in the real world can be repeated under various conditions. Also, simulation runs can be stopped at random or at certain points in time to reflect upon what has happened so far and for what reasons. Generally, simulations are useful in situations that are too dangerous or unethical to experiment with in reality, too slow because of long time delays or too fast, too large, or too small to be studied in depth in the real world.[116] In simulating social systems like learning alliances, simulations provide the possibility to experiment with strategies that would lead to the alliance's

---

[108] See Weber (2004), p. 172 and Engel and Möhring (1995), p. 47. With simulating models analysts can study models with respect to their static characteristics as to their dynamic behavior.

[109] In experimental simulations a process which does not necessarily consist of materials is reproduced in a material process. For example, a car dummy being tested in a wind channel is considered to be an experimental simulation as the surface material of the dummy and the original car might be different. See Schleichert (1995), p. 807.

[110] See Gramelsberger (2001), p. 11 and Schleichert (1995), p. 807.

[111] See Schleichert (1995), p. 808. Computer simulations are numerical simulations. The dominant method here is scientific computing. See Gramelsberger (2001), p. 12. From an epistemological point of view, numerical simulation can be interpreted as being positioned between theory and experiment. See Gramelsberger (2001), p. 15 and the cited literature.

[112] Simulations in combination with heuristics can be seen as theory guided deduction. See Gramelsberger (2001), p. 11.

[113] simulate, Latin: simulare = imitate, mimic. See Sterman (1991), p. 215.

[114] See Gramelsberger (2001), p. 12 and Sterman (2000), 37.

[115] See Sterman (2000), pp. 34-35.

[116] For example, studying an airplane crash into a nuclear power plant, effect of emissions of greenhouse gas on the atmosphere, nuclear chain reaction, collision of two galaxies, or quarks.

failure on the basis of the managers' mental models. Managers have the possibility to challenge their mental models by experimenting in the virtual world.

Findings or learnings from running simulation models can be transferred to the real world. Figure 2-2 depicts the relationship between learning from the real world and formal models, referred to as virtual worlds here.[117] Virtual worlds are part of a feedback loop in between the decision making feedback loop illustrated in Figure 2-1. Information feedback gained from virtual worlds can accelerate the reorganization of the structures underlying mental models. Changes in the structure of mental models change the structure of the system, creating different decision rules, and new strategies.[118] This is when learning takes place; in particular double-loop learning.[119]

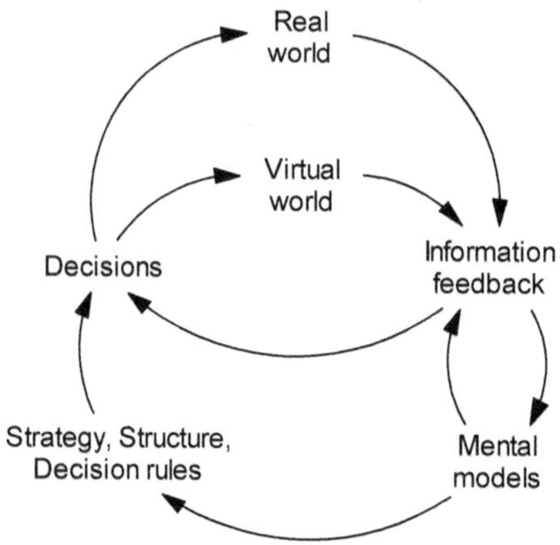

Figure 2-2: Formal models as virtual worlds as part of the learning feedback loop.[120]

Simulations, however, also have pitfalls. STERMAN identifies them in the accuracy of the decision rules, the choice of model boundary, and the quantification of soft variables.[121] The latter is of special interest for the purpose of this study as alliances in general often rely on soft variables like trust or knowledge and learning.[122] The majority of variables influencing decision making have not been measured and are therefore soft data. However, according to STERMAN they should be included if they are important for the purpose of the model.[123] FORRESTER states that "[t]o omit such variables is equivalent to saying they have zero effect – probably the only value that is

---

[117] Virtual worlds are formal models. The term includes simulations and microworlds. See Sterman (2000), p. 34. See Morecroft (1988), for a discussion of microworlds for policymakers. See also Rouwette et al. (2004), for a recent review of studies on decision making using simulators in the System Dynamics field.

[118] See Sterman (2000), p. 18.

[119] See Argyris and Schön (1978), pp. 20-26 and Section 4.2.

[120] Source: Sterman (2000), p. 34 and Sterman (1994), p. 318.

[121] See Sterman (1991), pp. 217-218.

[122] See Sections 4.6 and 4.6.4 for more insight into learning and trust.

[123] See Sterman (2002), p. 523.

known to be wrong!"[124] Soft variables are critical for understanding the structure of alliances. Therefore, instead of only working with hard variables that can be quantified, we also include soft variables in the model. However, when running a computer simulation, the computer calculates with finite and rounded numbers. Even with the smallest mistakes in the numbers, real systems work quite differently. Therefore, predictions from computer simulations have to be viewed with caution.[125] The purpose of simulation models should therefore lie rather in the development of the policy makers' intuition and judgment, which may be of bounded rationality.[126] Under these circumstances, simulation models make explicit the assumptions made and show the consequences of these assumptions.[127]

Despite these shortcomings, simulating formal models can overcome the decision makers' erroneous mental models. Simulating mentally or building a qualitative model of the problem structure might already reveal interesting insight. People's mental models might indeed already change due to the outcomes. However, only formal models that are tested via computer simulation imply and show real world components like feedback or time delays. This might lead to radical changes of the user's mental model. This can be achieved via two different approaches.[128] Either the individual whose mental model should be changed joins the modeling processes or models herself, for example, going through the modeling process described in Section 2.3.4, or, the individual uses a pre-designed simulation model which is called a management flight simulator.[129] The user of a management flight simulator not necessarily needs to fully understand the underlying model structure for using it. More specifically, MEADOWS remarks that the user does not have to cope with the difficult and time consuming modeling process.[130] Concluding, simulation models of different kinds speed and strengthen learning feedbacks.[131]

---

[124] Forrester (1961), p. 57

[125] See Gramelsberger (1996), p. 17.

[126] For a discussion on rationality and bounded rationality see Section 3.4.4.4. For bounded rationality and System Dynamics models see, for example, Morecroft (1983), Morecroft (1985), Sterman (1987), and recently Größler (2004).

[127] See Forrester (1985), pp.133-134 and Sterman (1985), p. 133.

[128] The simulation models developed in these two approaches serve different purposes. When the model is developed by the target group itself, it can be understood as a boundary object (see Zagonel (2004), pp. 2-3). The process within which a group of individuals has to agree on the structure of a formal simulation model can be understood as negotiating shared understanding of the issue at hand (see Zagonel (2004), pp. 1-2). For further insight into group model building see the relevant literature on group model building including, for example, Morecroft (1994), Richardson and Andersen (1995), Richardson and Andersen (1995), Vennix (1998), Vennix (1999), or Rouwette (2003). In cases where the model is developed by experts and used for policy analysis and learning with the client, the model represents more of a boundary object.

[129] There are different types of System Dynamics-based management flight simulators, like the People Express, Boom and Bust, Food and Brands, Commercial Real Estate, International Oil Tanker, Beefeater Restaurant Management Flight Simulators, and the Beer Distribution board game. Some management flight simulators can be ordered from the office of Professor John Sterman at the Sloan School of Management, MIT, Cambridge, MA 02142, U.S. Others can be ordered from Professor Kim Warren at Global Strategy Dynamics Ltd., Princes Risborough, Bucks HP27 OXB, U.K.

[130] Yet, someone who uses management flight simulators will not get as deep an insight as if she had modeled the structure herself. The focus lies in training systems thinking skills for which briefing and debriefing play a very important role. See Meadows (1989), pp. 636-639.

[131] See Sterman (1994), p. 322, Sterman (2000), p. 37, and Sterman (2002), p. 524.

System Dynamics offers such a simulation method on the basis of feedback loops. In the following, we first provide an overview of various simulation techniques and their application in management sciences. Then we present the System Dynamics method in more detail.

2.3.2 Simulation Approaches

Social scientists have used simulations for analyzing system structure and behavior for five decades. The mathematician V. NEUMANN[132] and the management and social scientist SIMON[133] were the first scientists to use programs for computer simulation.[134] Until the 1960s computer power increased immensely and so did the field of simulation applications proliferate. The emergent simulation techniques can be classified into three categories: discrete event simulations, equation-based modeling, and agent-based modeling.[135]

Discrete event simulations and equation-based modeling both came up at approximately the same time in the 1960s. Examples of discrete event simulations include queuing models for workflow management. Such models include static and dynamic elements, sources and sinks, and an event list. An event list records all the predictable events that might occur and that have to happen in the given order. The system only changes if an event takes place. After the change the system is stable until the next event, which is why this simulation technique is called discrete. Due to its discreteness feature, discrete event simulation would not be an appropriate technique for analyzing the dynamics of interorganizational learning in alliances in which events happen continuously.

The second approach is called equation-based modeling and also emerged in the 1960s. FORRESTER used computer simulations for his publications on oscillations in the industry sector, the dynamics of urban growth and of growth in a finite world.[136] They were the focus of public attention and people became much more aware of computer simulations. The publications provide differential and difference equations and they led to the field of System Dynamics.[137] System Dynamics is based on feedback loops, it incorporates accumulations and flows, and it takes into account a continuous view of structure and dynamics. These characteristics make System Dynamics an appropriate method to analyze the dynamics of interorganizational learning in alliances.

---

[132] See von Neumann (1963).

[133] See, for example, Simon (1969).

[134] Hoßfeld states that von Neumann (1963) and Goldstine (1972) inaugurated the beginning of numerical simulation when writing together about the future and necessity of digital computing. See Hoßfeld (1993), p. 6 referring to Goldstine and von Neumann (1963), and Burks et al. (1963), and see Gramelsberger (2001), p. 13.

[135] See Troitzsch (2004), pp. 1256-1268 for an overview.

[136] See Forrester (1961), Forrester (1969), and Forrester (1971).

[137] See Troitzsch (2004), p. 1256.

Last, a more recent simulation technique is the agent-based simulation. Its virtue is the option of designing models of any given number of different objects – the agents – that are connected via different types of interrelation. Agent-based models are most suitable for application in situations where important emerging behavior stems from heterogeneity in the attributes of the agents and from the network structure of their interactions. Applications range from land use and land cover changes[138], spread of disease[139], and organizational learning[140], trust between market participants[141], to processes of organizational change[142] in the field of management. Agent-based models have also been designed to study the dilemma of competition and cooperation.[143] In general, agent-based models are able to cover more detail complexity than system dynamics models. However, agent-based models are also more difficult to communicate. As the purpose of the simulation model developed in this study is policy analysis and learning, a system dynamics approach seems more appropriate. In the following, we therefore discuss the application of the simulation method in management sciences first. Then we explain the features of System Dynamics modeling in more detail in the subsequent section.

2.3.3 Simulation in Management Sciences

While applying simulations in natural science has always been common – even before computers were invented – they have also become accepted and applied in social sciences. At the beginning of the 1970s, FORRESTER and MEADOWS, BEHRENS III, MEADOWS, NAILL, RANDERS, AND ZAHN published their study on the limits to growth.[144] The study of scenarios of the development of the world situation was based on a System Dynamics model. Its popular scientific edition by MEADOWS, MEADOWS, RANDERS, AND BEHRENS III was a huge success, being translated into 29 languages.[145] In the meantime, the simulation approach is widely acknowledged in social sciences[146] and has also become popular in supporting theory development in strategic management.[147]

---

138 See Parker et al. (2001).

139 See Rahmandad (2004). Rahmandad shows that System Dynamics models may, under a broad range of circumstances, lead to similar insight into the spread of the SARS-virus at the beginning of 2003 to those that can be derived from agent-based models.

140 See Carley (1992).

141 See Gorobets and Nooteboom (2004).

142 See Levinthal (1997).

143 See Axelrod (1997b).

144 See Forrester (1971), and Meadows et al. (1974).

145 See Meadows et al. (1972) and for the latest edition, the 30-year update, see Meadows et al. (2004). In Section 2.3.1 we elaborate on simulation methods and in Section 2.3.4 more about System Dynamics. For a critique on the limits to growth study from an epistemological point of view, see Weber (2004), pp. 182-183.

146 Issues range from management to dynamics of diabetes, to the arms race during the cold war, to the battle between HIV and the human immune system, to the welfare reform (see Sterman (2000), pp. 41-42), to the socio-economic development in lagging regions in Switzerland (see Kopainsky (2005)).

147 See Zott (2003), p. 109. For early examples of applications of simulations in management, see Barney et al. (1991).

Generally, the research process can be differentiated in inductive and deductive approaches. The deductive approach assumes a system of axioms from which scholars derive statements. In an inductive approach scholars first collect data concerning certain facts. Scholars then derive statements on this basis, mostly using statistical methods. Computer simulations stand between both approaches.[148] Here, as with the deductive approach, scholars define a set of assumptions. However, theorems are not developed. Yet computer simulations generate data on structures and relations that scholars analyze. As this is typical of an inductive approach, it can therefore be proposed that simulations can be understood as a mixed approach with the characteristics of thought experiments.[149]

Simulations can be applied to various steps of the research process. First, simulations can be used to describe observed dynamic phenomena, as illustrated above. Next, simulations may support scholars in developing theories. Here, with the descriptive form of simulation, scholars can learn how simple assumptions may lead to complex system behavior.[150] Moreover, simulations can be applied to confirm the explanatory value of existing theories that are based on empirical datasets.[151] While empirically observed phenomena may consist of many interrelated effects their interdependence may be so complex that verbal or mathematical representations may be too intricate. Also, there may be several theories for explaining cause and effect. With simulation, scholars apply a holistic view covering insight from multiple theories. This enables more comprehensive explanation of empirical analyses. Finally, simulations are used for policy design.[152] Once a phenomenon is explained, its underlying influence factors are identified. Thus, simulations can be used to adjust the system toward the policy-designer's goal.

For the purpose of this study, we apply simulations to the first step of the research process when transferring the above-mentioned phenomenon on interorganizational

---

[148] See Axelrod (1997a), p. 24 and Heine and Kunz (2003), p. 375.

[149] See Chmielewicz (1994), p. 148.

[150] See Axelrod (1997a), pp. 24-25 and Heine and Kunz (2003), p. 375. Osterloh and Grand point out five different levels of theory building: formal systems, models, frameworks, concepts, and ad-hoc declarations. Yet they indicate that the two most common levels of theory building in business administration are models and frameworks. See Osterloh and Grand (1995), p. 5-7. Their definition of models goes along with Porter's (see Porter (1991), p. 97), who characterizes them as abstractions to separate key variables whose relations are studied in depth. In this sense models refer to formal statements on conditions of empirical applications. Models are sensitive toward their underlying assumptions. This causes difficulties in integrating many models into a general framework for approaching various situations or in making the conclusions of the various models consistent. See Porter (1991), pp. 97-98. Porter claims that frameworks are necessary for providing more structured and accurate tools. A characteristic of frameworks is their robustness toward underlying assumptions. Therefore, frameworks can be applied more generally and hence to different situations. Yet, it is not possible to derive clear recommendations for action. However, frameworks offer a set of possible alternatives. The final decision for an alternative has to be made according to each particular case. Therefore, case studies are widely important for designing frameworks. However, Porter stresses that models and frameworks should create a constructive tension with each other for theory building. See Porter (1991).

[151] See Weber (2004), pp. 176-178.

[152] See, for instance, Chmielewicz (1994), pp. 146-148 where he describes the application of a simulation for policy testing with examples of cooperation in firms under worker participation and introduction of a law on property speculation.

learning into a formal model. Furthermore, we test existing theories on interorganizational learning. To design the simulation model we use findings from two types of different sources: on the one hand we use data from empirical analyses published in the literature which are presented in detail in Chapter 4. This original information is mostly derived inductively by the authors. We also use information obtained in interviews from our case study on interorganizational learning. The procedure of carrying out the case study is presented in Section 2.4. Last, we give hints on policy design for managing a learning alliance successfully.

2.3.4 System Dynamics Modeling

Even though the systems concept discussed above holds for applying System Dynamics to analyze systems, its methodological roots lie within servomechanisms engineering, not cybernetics. According to RICHARDSON, the difference between the two lies in dissimilar feedback points of view.[153] Whereas phenomena from a cybernetics perspective are illustrated in terms of events, decisions, and messages, from the servomechanisms perspective they are described through dynamic patterns of behavior and persistent policy structure.[154] In the following we present four underlying concepts of the System Dynamics method: feedback loop, stock and flow, loop dominance, and the endogenous point of view.

System Dynamics[155] picks up the closed feedback-loop idea mentioned in Section 2.2.1. The feedback loop concept is the nucleus of the System Dynamics method.[156] The two different kinds of feedback loop referred to above in Section 2.2.1 are indicated with an R for a reinforcing loop and a B for a balancing loop, both depicted in Figure 2-3 in a causal loop diagram.

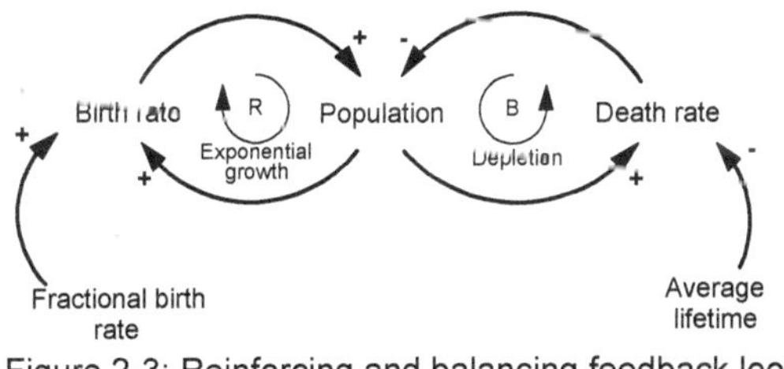

Figure 2-3: Reinforcing and balancing feedback loops in a causal loop diagram.[157]

The reinforcing loop on the left-hand side of Figure 2-3 reinforces what happens in the system. When describing what happens in a feedback loop one can start wherever it is convenient; for example, all else being equal, an increasing 'Birth rate' leads

[153] See Richardson (1991a), pp. 271-317, Richardson (1996), pp. 656-657, and Richardson (2001), p. 807.
[154] See Richardson (1991a), p. 341.
[155] See Sterman (2000), and Forrester (1961).
[156] See Richardson (1991b), pp. 146-147, Richardson (1996), p. 657, and Richardson (2001), p. 808.
[157] Source: Sterman (2000), p. 138.

to a higher 'Population'.[158] An increasing 'Population' leads to a higher 'Birth rate' than it would have been. Hence, the loop is closed and the initial system change – an increase in the birth rate – is reinforced. Moreover, the 'Birth rate' is positively influenced by the 'Fractional birth rate'. This relationship is accompanied with a higher average fertility. When looking at the behavior that is only generated by the reinforcing structure, population would increase exponentially.

However, as no real quantity can grow forever,[159] the increase in 'Population' must be slowed down by a balancing loop – one possible balancing loop is shown on the right-hand side of Figure 2-3. The 'Death rate' increases with an increasing 'Population'. All else being equal, the higher the 'Death rate', the smaller the 'Population'. The loop is closed and, as the B indicates, it is a balancing loop. It counteracts the initial change as the original change was an increasing 'Population'. Hence, the loop seeks balance and equilibrium. Apart from the loop, the 'Death rate' is influenced by the 'Average lifetime'. Here, the longer the 'Average lifetime', the lower is the 'Death rate'.

Such causal loop diagrams are helpful for presenting feedback loops and interdependencies. However, they imply some weaknesses that might mislead the analyst in interpreting possible dynamics that might evolve from the underlying structure.[160] This is because just showing variables, for example, does not capture inertia or time delays. Time delays arise as a consequence of accumulations, or stocks. Stocks and flows belong to the second central concept of System Dynamics.[161] Stocks "characterize the state of the system and generate the information upon which decisions and actions are based. ... [They] create delays by accumulating the difference between the inflow to a process and its outflow."[162] Flows either increase or decrease the stocks per unit of time. They are determined by the policies that describe how decisions result on the basis of the information feedback from the state of the system.[163]

Failure to understand the differentiation might lead to underestimation of time delays, to short-term focus, and to policy resistance – aspects that all seem relevant for the failure of many alliances. Even though stocks and flows are familiar to everybody in everyday life,[164] people have difficulty understanding the differences.[165] Therefore, stocks and flows are used unambiguously in System Dynamics. Stocks are indicated by rectangles and in- and outflows by pipes. Valves note how much quantity flows

---

158 We indicate variable names in inverted commas.

159 See Sterman (2000), p. 13.

160 See Richardson (1986), and Warren (2004), for an overview of problems with causal loop diagrams.

161 See Sterman (2000), pp. 191-192.

162 Sterman (2000), p. 192.

163 See Keough and Doman (1992), p. 16 and in more detail Forrester (1972), pp. 101-106.

164 Examples of stocks are inventory of a manufacturing firm, number of people employed, the balance on a checking account, water in a lake or in a bathtub, firm reputation, and trust within a group. Examples of relating flows that decrease the stocks are shipments, hiring, monetary spending, water flowing in a river or a drain, product quality, and opportunism. See Keough and Doman (1992), p. 16 and Sterman (2000), p. 192.

165 Analyzing the understanding of stocks and flows forms the focus of the bathtub dynamics tasks. See, for instance, Booth Sweeney and Sterman (2000), p. 249, Sterman (2002), p. 501, Atkins et al. (2001), Kainz (2002), Ossimitz (2002), or Kapmeier (2004).

per time in or out of a stock.[166] Clouds represent infinite sinks and sources for the flows. A cloud indicates the system boundary. Whatever lies outside the boundary is not of interest for the system behavior – according to the modeler or her clients. STERMAN draws attention to having a broader model boundary, not only in terms of whether a variable is endogenous or exogenous, but also of whether the modeler's or the clients' underlying implicit and unaware assumptions are taken into account.[167] Figure 2-4 illustrates the same feedback loops as Figure 2-3 only with stock and flow notations.

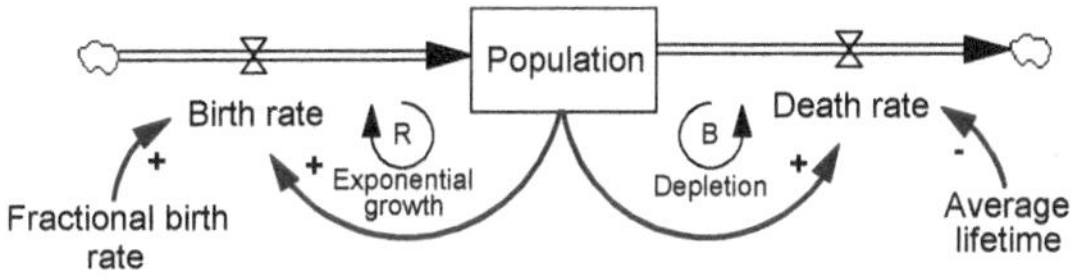

Figure 2-4: Reinforcing and balancing feedback loops in stock and flow diagram notation.[168]

To build a simulation model, the stock and flow structure needs to be translated into mathematical equations. Generally, the quantity of matter in a stock is the accumulation of the flows of matter in less the flows of matter out in a particular period. As opposed to what is shown in Figure 2-4, stocks do not have to be tangible. STERMAN notes that beliefs and memories can also be considered to be stocks.[169] This is of importance for the model developed in this study as many intangible variables such as knowledge or trust play an important role in learning alliances. The simple stock and flow structure from Figure 2-4 can be translated into the following integral equation:[170]

$$\text{Stock}(t) = \int_{t_0}^{t} [\text{Inflow}(s) - \text{Outflow}(s)]ds + \text{Stock}(t_0)$$

with the net rate of change as

$$d(\text{Stock})/dt = \text{NetChangeinStock} = \text{Inflow}(t) - \text{Outflow}(t)$$

As indicated in Section 2.2.1 intertwined nonlinear feedback loops form patterns of shifting loop dominance. In the example of population growth, the model structure can be enhanced with a 'Carrying capacity', shown in Figure 2-5. The ratio of 'Population' and 'Carrying capacity' indicates the population density. When the latter increases, the 'Fractional death rate' also increases: life expectancy diminishes because of less food per capita. Simultaneously, the 'Fractional birth rate' decreases.[171]

---

[166] The diagramming conventions are based on the hydraulic metaphor with water flowing in and out of water reservoirs. See Sterman (2000), p. 193.
[167] See Sterman (2002), pp. 512-513.
[168] Source: Sterman (2000), p. 285. Note that the balancing depletion loop does not seem as if it were closed in this stock and flow representation. Nevertheless, it is closed implicitly as the stock of population depletes with an increasing death rate (outflow).
[169] See Sterman (2000), p. 195.
[170] See Sterman (2000), p. 194.
[171] Refer to Sterman (2000), pp. 285-299 for an in-depth discussion on S-shaped growth.

The introduction of these variables closes two additional feedback loops, ‘Too many of us’ and ‘Enough food’.

If the initial population is small relative to its restrictions, the population first increases exponentially, but – as no real quantity can grow forever – the population sooner or later approaches the carrying capacity of its environment. Generally, the carrying capacity might be determined by the number of potential customers for a product or, to take the current example, the carrot supply for a rabbit population on an island. “As the system approaches its limits to growth, it goes through a nonlinear transition from a regime where positive feedback dominates to a regime where negative feedback dominates.”[172] This oftentimes results in S-shaped growth as a consequence of a smooth transition from exponential growth to equilibrium. This behavior implies no significant system delays (see the graph depicting the system behavior in Figure 2-5).

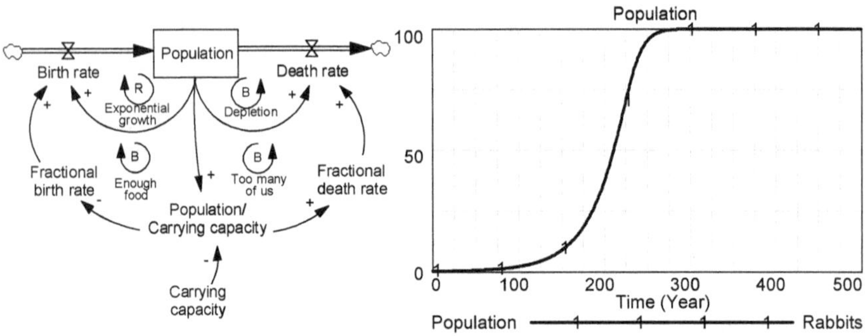

Figure 2-5: Stock and flow diagram for population growth in a fixed environment.[173]

Mathematically, the positive feedback dominates as long as the slope of the net rate of change[174] as a function of the stock is positive. The negative feedback dominates as long as the slope of the net rate is negative.[175] RICHARDSON emphasizes that only nonlinear models can endogenously alter their dominant structure and shift loop dominance.[176] Thus, System Dynamics models are able to imitate the nonlinearity that exists in the real world.

It is important to note that the shift in loop dominance from a positive to a negative loop in the above model is generated by the system structure itself. The concept of

[172] Sterman (2000), p. 285.
[173] Source: Sterman (2000), p. 285.
[174] If the net rate of change $\dot{S} = dS/dt$, where S represents the stock S, is larger than zero, positive feedback is dominant; if it equals zero, there is no net feedback from state to rate; if it is smaller than zero, the negative feedback is dominant. Other special growth models also exist, one of them being the logistic growth model, which is a special case of S-shaped growth. See Sterman (2000), pp. 296-347.
[175] See Sterman (2000), p. 289.
[176] See Richardson (1991b), pp. 147-148, Richardson (1996), p. 658, and Richardson (2001), p. 809. For a detailed formal loop dominance analysis see Richardson (1995), and Ford (1999). For the presentation of loop dominance analysis software based on the pathway participation metric, see Mojtahedzadeh et al. (2004).

endogenous change is the fourth fundamental concept of the System Dynamics modeling approach.[177] Causes of certain model behavior lie in the model structure and are not fed in from outside the system. For the analysis of interorganizational learning in alliances, this means that we are looking for reasons for failure that lie within the partnering companies' alliance structure and not in events outside their control.[178]

2.3.5 Validation of System Dynamics Models

As all models represent the real world in a limited and simplified way, they differ from reality. This means that models in general cannot be validated or verified.[179] However, humans use models all the time. It is therefore a question of how good the model in use is. So, to increase confidence in models, analysts can apply certain tests.[180] There is no single test that is sufficient as different tests focus on different aspects. STERMAN presents and discusses the tests developed for System Dynamics models over the last few decades in great detail.[181] He introduces twelve different tests.[182] Some tests focus more on analyzing model structure, others more on model behavior, and some test policy implications.[183] Here, we only focus on a few of them: boundary adequacy, dimensional consistency, extreme condition, and sensitivity analysis.[184] They give an overview of the different types of tests and are mostly applied.

First, boundary adequacy tests assess the appropriateness of the model boundary for the imminent modeling purpose. These tests focus on analyzing model structure. Model boundary charts determine the model boundary and clarify which variables are exogenous. In this way it is possible to examine whether a parameter that is set as exogenous really is exogenous or should rather be treated as an endogenous variable. Hence, the boundary adequacy test provides the opportunity to check if the important concepts for addressing the problem under study are endogenous to the model.[185]

Second, model builders check the model's internal consistency with the dimensional consistency test. This is also a structure validation test. Each variable needs to be specified with a unit of measure. Unit errors uncover mistakes in the model builder's

177 See Richardson (1991b), pp. 150-152, Richardson (1996), p. 658, and Richardson (2001), p. 809.

178 See Sterman (2002), pp. 504-505 for examples of corporate managers blaming outside events for company obstacles. See also Sterman (2000), p. 95.

179 See Sterman (2000), p. 846. Verify, Latin: verus = truth.

180 See Forrester and Senge (1980), pp. 210-211.

181 See Sterman (2000), pp. 845-891. See also Richardson and Pugh III (1981), pp. 267-320 or Barlas and Carpenter (1990), Peterson and Eberlein (1994), and Barlas (1996).

182 The tests presented are: boundary adequacy, structure assessment, dimensional consistency, parameter assessment, extreme condition, integration error, behavior reproduction, behavior anomaly, family member, surprise behavior, sensitivity analysis, and system improvement. See Sterman (2000), pp. 859-861 for an overview.

183 See Forrester and Senge (1980), pp. 211-226 and Barlas (1996), pp.188-195.

184 Unless otherwise indicated, the following statements refer to Sterman (2000), pp. 858-889.

185 See also the end of Section 2.3.4 for the importance of this statement.

understanding of the structure. However, the modeler needs to ensure that the variables she includes in the model have real world counterparts. Variables with pointless names or strange unit combinations need be excluded instantaneously.

Then, the purpose of the extreme condition test is to check each equation for whether the model output is still realistic if inputs or policies take on extreme values, such as zero or infinite. Extreme condition tests analyze model structure as well as model behavior. For example, if (raw) material supply drops to zero, no goods can be produced. On the one hand, the extreme condition test can be done by examining the equations directly. Here, the test asks whether the output of the policy is reasonable even if each input to the equation takes on its maximum and minimum values. On the other hand, the test can also be done in simulations. It is called reality check.[186]

Last, the sensitivity analysis tests the robustness of the conclusions derived on the basis of the model. There are three different kinds of test: numerical, behavior mode, and policy sensitivity. Numerical sensitivity is existent when a variation in assumptions changes the numerical values of the results. Behavioral mode sensitivity means that a variation in the assumptions goes along with a changing mode of model behavior: for instance, a smooth S-shaped growth changes into an oscillation. Policy sensitivity exists when a change alters or even reverses the suggested policy. Sensitivity analysis therefore focuses on both model behavior and policy implications.

As indicated above, there are more than the four tests presented in existence. It must be stressed that it is not sufficient to perform just one of the tests but to follow multiple of them to increase confidence in the model. Validation is a valuable and necessary step in the modeling process. It is done throughout the modeling process which is iterative itself.[187] In the following we present the modeling process in more detail.

2.3.6 Iterative System Dynamics Modeling Process

The System Dynamics modeling process is a feedback process itself and consists of five iterative steps – insight gained at any step can be of interest at other steps.[188] We briefly introduce the five steps in the following: problem articulation, dynamic hypothesis, formulation, testing, and policy formulation and evaluation.[189]

In the first step of the process, the modeler has to identify and articulate the problematic issue. Determining clearly what the problem is leads to the scope of the model and where to draw the model boundary. The modeler decides which variables are endogenous and create the perceived system behavior and which variables are ex-

---

186 See Peterson and Eberlein (1994).

187 See Sterman (2000), p. 87.

188 The classic system dynamics literature distinguishes between three and seven different steps. See Luna-Reyes and Andersen (2003), p. 275. However, the activities considered along the different stages remain similar.

189 The following statements in this section refer to Sterman (2000), pp. 87-105 if not otherwise indicated.

ogenous. As System Dynamics addresses dynamic problems, the key variables should show a certain behavior over time. When drawn, these graphs are called reference modes as the modeler turns toward them during the modeling process.[190] Choosing an appropriate time horizon to draw the reference mode is necessary as it may influence the evaluation of suggested policies.

When the problem has been identified, modelers develop a dynamic hypothesis. It is a working theory of how the problem under study developed. It includes subsystem diagrams for the overall model, providing an overview of the model. Among other things, it encompasses information about the model boundary, the level of aggregation, and not necessarily many variables. The latter are shown in detail in a causal loop diagram.[191] It represents the model structure showing the variables, the relationships, and the feedback loops. Causal loop diagrams are helpful for gaining first insight into the model structure, but, as explained in Section 2.3.4, also have some shortcomings. To quantify the diagram, it needs to be translated into a stock and flow diagram. It emphasizes the underlying physical structure, showing accumulations and in- and outflows.[192]

Afterward, the variables shown in the stock and flow diagram are fed with difference equations (formulation). When writing the equations, they should be assessed applying structural and behavioral tests.[193]

Finally, when the developed model invites confidence concerning its behavior and the underlying structure, it can be used for designing and evaluating policies for improvement. Insight from policy analysis might reveal worse-before-better or better-before-worse behavior, for example. According to RICHARDSON, complex systems may respond to policy changes in the long run rather than in the short-term and vice versa.[194] Or, a system might also be insensitive or resistant to parameter changes. According to STERMAN, policy design is more than just changing values of parameters. It may include the "creation of entirely new strategies, structures, and decision rules."[195] As structure drives behavior, looking for dominant feedback structures might lead to finding high leverage policies that might change the system behavior in a more favorable direction. Dominant feedback loops might be changed by redesigning the system structure, abolishing time delays, or even "fundamentally reinventing the decision processes of the actors in the system."[196] Model analysists should be aware of a possible behavior as a cause of the combination of various policies. Due to the nonlinearity of social systems, policies may not necessarily only add up their impacts but also reinforce each another.

---

[190] Sterman states that choosing an inappropriate time horizon may indicate no dynamics at all (if too short) or just a sudden peak (if too long) exemplified with the example of oil consumption. See Sterman (2000), pp. 91-93.
[191] See Figure 2-3. Designing causal loop diagrams can be related to qualitative System Dynamics.
[192] See Figure 2-4. Stock and flow diagrams are part of quantitative System Dynamics.
[193] See Section 2.3.5 for testing or validating the model.
[194] See Richardson (1991b), p. 165.
[195] Sterman (2000), p. 104.
[196] Sterman (2000), p. 104.

In the present context it means that the System Dynamics model supports decision makers in companies engaging in learning alliances to understand alliance dynamics and to learn to develop more robust policies for successfully managing such alliances. Managers should look for the possible reasons of alliance failure inside the parent companies' policies rather than in outside events.

2.3.7 Conclusion

Designing a simulation model seems to be an appropriate approach for analyzing the dynamics of interorganizational learning between two alliance partners. The underlying situation is of a complex structure with nonlinear relationships and time delays. LANT AND MEZIAS[197], CROSSAN AND BERDROW[198], and ZOTT[199] have used simulation models for studying various topics in organizational learning. To our knowledge, for the special case of dynamics of interorganizational learning this has only been done recently by KAPMEIER[200] and OTTO AND RICHARDSON[201] who used the System Dynamics methodology for their analyses inside the field of interorganizational learning with different foci.

As indicated in Section 2.3.3, we use System Dynamics modeling to describe the phenomenon of interorganizational learning, testing existing theory while consulting the literature and carrying out a related case study, which are leading to policy recommendations. Using modeling and simulations for these tasks in social sciences has become widely accepted. In particular, researchers and practitioners have applied System Dynamics to the field of management. Subjects cover, for instance, strategic management[202] in general, and in particular the learning curve[203], the analyses of industries like the credit-card business[204], origin of commodity cycles in aircraft[205], pulp and paper[206], plastics[207], or the real estate[208] industry, quality erosion in the service industry[209], capability traps and self-confirming attribution errors in the dynamics of process improvement[210], dynamics of project management[211], impact of leasing strategies on new car sales in the automobile industry[212], process and performance implication of firm diversification[213], competing for and through sophisti-

197 See Lant and Mezias (1990).
198 See Crossan and Berdrow (2003).
199 See Zott (2003).
200 See Kapmeier (2002), Kapmeier (2003), and Kapmeier (2005).
201 See Otto and Richardson (2004).
202 See, for example, Morecroft et al. (2002), and Warren (2002).
203 See Sterman et al. (1995), and Morrison (2005).
204 See Lyneis (1999), pp. 56-61.
205 See Lyneis (1999), pp. 61-66.
206 See Sterman (2000), pp. 824-841.
207 See Coleman-Kammula et al. (2005).
208 See Sterman (2000), pp. 698-707.
209 See Oliva and Sterman (2001).
210 See Repenning and Sterman (2002).
211 See Roberts (1999b), Ford (1995), and Taylor et al. (2005).
212 See Sterman (2000), pp. 42-56.
213 See Gary (2005).

cated customers[214], diffusion of new technologies[215], path dependence and positive feedback in the economy[216], or demand bubbles and phantom orders in supply chains[217]. System Dynamics has also been applied for confirming existing theories like punctuated change[218], fire fighting in new product development[219], or organizational collaboration[220]. In the meantime, business consultants also use simulation models for learning about their clients' industries and finding strategies.[221] As can be seen from the examples, it is widely accepted to apply System Dynamics models as decision-support in strategic management.[222]

As the case study provides additional insight into the underlying structure of the model, we explain qualitative research as another methodological basis in the following section.

2.4 Case Study Design

We decided to conduct a case study for a number of reasons. First, numerical data accessible in the literature only contain a small fraction of the information in the written database, which again is small compared to the information available in people's mental models.[223] FORRESTER identifies such qualitative data as a key source of information in the modeling process.[224] As with soft data, omitting "variables known to be important because numerical data are unavailable is ... less scientific and less accurate than using ... [the] best judgment to estimate their values."[225] Hence, qualitative information is crucial for understanding and modeling complex systems. Second, including companies' actual decision policies in realistic form in the System Dynamics model has been an important assumption in the field since its beginnings.[226] We receive this information from interviews and field observation – not necessarily from what is written in the literature. LUNA-REYES AND ANDERSEN note that the use of qualitative data is ever-present during all stages of System Dynamics modeling from problem articulation to policy formulation and evaluation presented in Section 2.3.6.[227]

---

214 See Rockart (2001).
215 See Sterman (2000), pp. 323-347, Struben (2004), Struben (2005), and related Größler and Thun (2004).
216 See Sterman (2000), pp. 349-406.
217 See Gonçalves (2003), and Gonçalves and Sterman (2005).
218 See Sastry (1997).
219 See Repenning (2001), Repenning (2002), and Rahmandad (2005).
220 See Black (2002), and Black et al. (2004).
221 The consulting company Booz Allen Hamilton calls these simulation games 'wargaming'. See Oriesek and Friedrich (2003), p. 65.
222 See Morecroft (1988), Morecroft (1994), Lyneis (1999), or Zahn (1999).
223 See Sterman (2000), p. 853 and also Luna-Reyes and Andersen (2003), p. 271.
224 See Forrester (1994b), p. 72.
225 See Sterman (2000), p. 854. In two chapters of his book, Sterman presents how scholars used detailed field studies to test their models and formulate decision policies. See Sterman (2000), pp. 536-537 and 569.
226 See Repenning (2003), p. 319.
227 See Luna-Reyes and Andersen (2003), p. 275. Conducting interviews is widely present in group model building interventions. See, for example, Vennix (1998), or Richardson and Andersen (1995).

There are various possibilities of data collection that give access to qualitative information.[228] We have decided to conduct a case study, as its essence lies in shedding light on decisions or sets of decisions. This includes background information on reasons why decisions were made, how policies were implemented, and which results were achieved.[229] The case study method is part of qualitative empirical social research, of which a high degree of openness regarding the outcomes is a major characteristic.[230] Therefore a qualitative approach is suitable for explorative questions. Its subtlety enables the researcher to grasp contexts that are either difficult or not possible to pick out as a central theme when using standardized questionnaires. This open and non-standardized survey method facilitates insight into otherwise concealed subjects. This is the kind of information we are looking for when designing the simulation model, as it enlarges the written database to be used in the modeling process.[231] Even though YIN points out that case study research is a way of investigating an empirical topic by following a set of prespecified procedures, an exact definition does not exist.[232] YIN suggests a definition stating that a case study is "an empirical inquiry that investigates a contemporary phenomenon within its real-life context, especially when the boundaries between phenomenon and context are not clearly evident."[233]

For the analysis of interorganizational learning in alliances we use a single-case study design to confirm, challenge, and broaden existing theory.[234] This way we contribute to research, whether the theory's suggestions are accurate or whether some alternative sets of explanations might be more appropriate.

Despite the virtues mentioned above, the literature on case study designs reveals some shortcomings.[235] The first complaint is that case studies usually take too long and produce too many unreadable documents. Nevertheless, the time needed to design the interview guides and conduct the interviews is not much different from the time needed to do other kinds of field study. Also, in this study we do not present everything said during the interviews. Yet, we present interviewees' statements at appropriate points to support or refute what is mentioned in the literature to support model building. Second, there is concern that case studies provide little basis for generalization. However, as with scientific experiments scholars can draw conclusions from single-case studies. Our focus lies in expanding and generalizing existing theories and not in enlarging incidences. Last, the greatest concern is the lack of rigor. Indeed, qualitative research may be designed in such a way that even some

---

228 Examples of qualitative data collections are interviews, oral history, focus groups, Delphi groups, observation, participant observation, or experimental approaches. See, for instance, Friedrichs (1990), pp. 192-375 or Luna-Reyes and Andersen (2003), pp. 9-13.

229 See Yin (1994), pp. 11-12 quoting Schramm (1971).

230 See Lamnek (1995), pp. 4-5. The quality of the information content can be used as the distinctive measure between quantitative (metric scales) and qualitative (nominative scales) research approaches. See Spöhring (1989), p. 15. For further reviews on qualitative empirical research see Schnell et al. (1999), p. 201 or Friedrichs (1990), p. 665, among others. Yin, however, points out that case studies can include and yet be restricted to quantitative evidence. See Yin (1994), p. 14.

231 See Luna-Reyes and Andersen (2003), p. 283.

232 See Yin (1994), p. 15 and Grunwald (2003), p. 80.

233 Yin (1994), p. 13.

234 For the following statements see Yin (1994), pp. 38-44 if not otherwise indicated.

235 For a comprehensive review of case study shortcomings see Yin (1994), pp. 9-11.

generalization is not possible. However, this criticism does not hold by and large. It is possible to meet this criticism by explaining the case study process and the results in enough detail that other scientists can easily comprehend it.[236] In the following we present the process of how we conducted the case study.

2.4.1 Case Study Modus Operandi

When looking for a case study we made sure certain criteria regarding a learning alliance were met. First, the present case study is a typical example of an alliance between two companies competing in the same market segment. The first company is based in Europe and the second is headquartered in North America. Also, the two parent companies are independent of each other. Additionally, they have agreed to cooperate for a set time period of three years in an alliance. Moreover, the two parent companies have agreed to work on certain alliance goals. Finally, both parent companies have knowledge that is of interest for joint research.

First discussion of the possibility of gaining the two companies for a case study took place in October 2003. In late summer of 2004 the non-disclosure agreement was signed. The actual period of the survey was from October until December 2004. To conduct initial research about the two participating companies we reviewed annual reports, newspaper reports, and publicly accessible industry analyses. We developed two different semi-structured interview guides[237] in fall 2003 and spring 2004 for both organizational levels in the alliance, here referred to as manager and scientist level.[238] The interview guides were tested in separate pretests on relevance and comprehensibility as a final test run.[239] The pretest on the manager level was done with a manager of a first-tier automobile supplier on October 24, 2004. His department does joint research with several original equipment manufacturers. The pretest on the scientist level was done with a scientist working for an original equipment manufacturer in the automobile industry on October 25, 2004. He has joined multiple collaborative research projects with partners. After the pretest we revised the interview guides with reference to the order of the questions or their wording.[240] The pretests were purposely not done with members of the actual case study companies in order to prevent bias at subsequent interviews.

After signing the non-disclosure agreement we were invited to join a 3-day exchange meeting of the alliance members. We were introduced to the team members by the American and European project leaders. They invited the members of both companies' teams to be available to participate in our interviews. During the meeting we had

[236] See Grunwald (2003), p. 82.
[237] For semi-structured interview guides see Vennix (1998), p. 116. For hints on designing questions see Vennix (1998), pp. 115-117.
[238] The necessity of designing different tests for the members of the two levels became clear because of indications from the literature: managers and scientists in an alliance deal with different tasks. Therefore they are interviewed accordingly.
[239] See Friedrichs (1990), pp. 221-222 and 234-235. According to Yin, a pretest is different from a pilot case study in that a pilot case study is used more formatively. See Yin (1994), p. 74.
[240] See Schnell et al. (1999), pp. 324-328.

the opportunity not only to observe the working atmosphere between the members of both teams,[241] but also to get to know the participants before running actual interviews. This had a positive influence on the creation of an atmosphere of trust later during the interviews. We made sure to establish contact with participants on the scientist and the manager level of both parent companies to guarantee balanced positions in the survey.

2.4.2 Case Study Data Collection and Analysis

All the desired interviews were able to be carried out from October 28 until December 22, 2004. We consulted the managers of both parent firms as well as one and two scientists, respectively. The interviews lasted between 90 and 120 minutes. With one scientist we met once more for a further 180 minutes. As we talked to each interviewee intensively, the interviews can be categorized under what is also called expert interviews in case study research. The participants allowed us to tape the conversations, which were then transcribed in their entirely.[242] They also allowed us to cite them under the premise of anonymity.[243] When doing so we refer to the interview passage in the footnote with a code that consists of two components: a document number and quote number.[244]

To accomplish the present study, we used different sources of confirmation. We conducted semi-structured, open-ended, and focused interviews with the participants. We also looked at archival records and documents. Among other things, the documents include parts of the alliance agreement. Finally, we were able to carry out direct observation when we joined the exchange meeting. The procedure of using multiple sources is called triangulation.[245] It enables the researcher to gain a broader scope of historical, attitudinal, and behavioral issues and hence balance the drawbacks of one method with the advantages of others.[246]

Focused interviews form the central point of this study.[247] The interviewee is asked for her assessment in a conversational manner while the interviewer follows a certain set of questions.[248] The interviews all began with general questions about the informants' roles and tasks in the alliance. Then the interviews proceeded with four sets of questions for the managers and five for the scientists on the subjects relating to interor-

---

[241] Joining such meetings is part of what is called direct observation in case study research. See Yin (1994), pp. 86-87 and Friedrichs (1990), pp. 288-290.

[242] For pros and cons of tape recording interviews see Yin (1994), p. 86, Friedrichs (1990), pp. 229-230, and Vennix (1998), pp. 122-123.

[243] For a discussion on the question of whether to disguise or accurately identify case study firms and the interview partners see Yin (1994), pp. 143-144.

[244] The software in use, ATLAS.ti, automatically assigns both consecutive document and quote numbers, separated by colons. Among other things, this makes it easy to find citations again. For example, a quote may be P3: 45 for quote 45 within document 3. For a review on software see also Miles and Huberman (1994), pp. 44 and 311-316.

[245] See Yin (1994), pp. 91-94 and Spöhring (1989), pp. 320-324.

[246] See Yin (1994), p. 92.

[247] Friedrichs indicates that different scholars use different terms for focused interviews, from open questioning to talks to qualitative interviews. See Friedrichs (1990), p. 224.

[248] The semi-structured interview is attached in Appendix 9.1.

ganizational learning. The set of questions was designed to gain deeper insight into different aspects of the factors determining the long-term success of research alliances.[249] Last, the interviewees were asked about their thoughts on what other topics we should have talked about to get a better understanding of the issue and who we should talk to in order to get a wider picture. The interviews ended with personal questions.

After the transcription we used different sets of analyses to examine the interviews. The textual information received can be used to support the assumptions of the System Dynamics model.[250] Quotations with main insight help to support model building. There are different types of designs for examining interviews.[251] The analysis tools used here mainly include grounded theory and content analysis.[252] Referring to grounded theory, GLASER AND STRAUSS stress that the researcher should approach the problem set principally with an open mind. This means that the scholar should conduct the analysis without any previous literature work. Instead, theory should emerge from the empirical data set.[253] Referring to System Dynamics modeling LUNA-REYES AND ANDERSEN point out that grounded theory can indeed be helpful. Identifying stocks and flows, or rating of particular soft variables can be quantified more easily through relating and linking themes or concepts across texts.[254] Content analysis is powerful for identifying reference modes and estimating model parameters.[255] To do so, we defined a set of codes. Codes can be understood as "efficient data-labeling and data-retrieval devices. They empower and speed up analysis."[256] We used to examine the interviews objectively and systematically.[257] Via the coding process we reduced the volume of data sets into analyzable units by generating categories on the basis of the current data.[258] This way we identified the interviewees' statements on certain topics. We were then able to link these to the theoretical concepts presented in the literature.
Findings from the case study analysis are cited throughout this work. In the following we present the alliance and the two parent companies involved in the case study.

2.4.3 Case Study Presentation

The case study focuses on a research alliance between two firms in the chemistry business. One of the partner firms is A, a large and diversified multinational Ameri-

---

249 For the factors determining the long-term success of a research alliance, see Chapter 4.
250 See Luna-Reyes and Andersen (2003), p. 283.
251 See Schnell et al. (1999), pp. 374-380.
252 See Luna-Reyes and Andersen (2003), pp. 284-286. For details on grounded theory see also Glaser and Strauss (1967), and on content analysis see Spöhring (1989), pp. 189-194.
253 See Glaser and Strauss (1967), pp. 45-49 and Glaser (1978), pp. 50-51.
254 See Luna-Reyes and Andersen (2003), pp. 284-285.
255 See Vennix (1998), p. 123 and Luna-Reyes and Andersen (2003), pp. 285-286.
256 Miles and Huberman (1994), p. 65. See Miles and Huberman (1994), pp.55-69 for a review on how to develop codes effectively.
257 Objectivity means that there are rules and procedures which serve as a basis for each step in the coding process. The rules are required to be as clear as possible, so that thirds can confirm on how a particular researcher came to certain conclusions or interpretations. Systematic implies that rules are consistently applied during the coding process. See Vennix (1998), p. 124.
258 See Miles and Huberman (1994), pp. 45 and 56-57 and Coffey and Atkinson (1996), p. 26.

can-based company. It collaborates on research in the polyolefins field with E, its European-based medium-sized competitor. Company E is specialized in polyolefins and its production capacity is about 1.2 times as large as its partner A's. The two legally independent firms have begun doing joint research on polyolefins within the research alliance C. The alliance started in 2001 and was scheduled to last for roughly three years. The two project managers of both parents see the outcome of the research alliance as critical for their parent companies' success.[259] The alliance's research content consists of three components: substance, process, and products.

A previous research alliance between A and one of E's predecessors was formed in the same research area in the 1990s. Scientists worked jointly and closely on the fundamental ideas of the substance which involved basic science for a period of seven years. After the alliance was dissolved, A and E's predecessor followed diverging paths on further research on the three components.

Besides E's predecessor, two other European players also conducted research in this field. A was interested in doing research with each of them and therefore started negotiations regarding a possible cooperation in the late 1990s. In the meantime E was formed through merging the three European players. Hence, A and E resumed talks about continued joint research on the three components. It took them roughly two years to agree on pursuing the research alliance C. The alliance's research content and goals were written down in a 174-page non-disclosure agreement. Every individual working in the alliance had to sign it to prove confidentiality.

As agreed on in the contract, both parent companies invest a minimum number of resources in the alliance (see Figure 2-6). If they do not meet this objective, they must pay a fine to the partner. E invests two-thirds of the alliance's resources, which roughly equals 30 scientists. Both research teams are guided by their project managers. Even though the scientists do not work in mixed teams, they come together twice a year for technical exchange meetings. They present and discuss the research they have done so far with respect to four major milestones agreed on in the contract. However, open exchange between the scientists only happens within the boundaries set by both partners' gatekeepers, who approve whatever is presented and talked about during the meetings. This guarantees that only knowledge that should be transferred from one partner to the alliance is actually being transferred. This is because E's corporate divisions are more intertwined than A's. E's scientists working for the alliance (could) also work for other divisions where the knowledge gained in the alliance could be useful and valuable. Therefore, gatekeepers make sure that there will be no unintended knowledge spillover[260] to other divisions. The divisions in A's organizational structure are more separated. Here, the chance for knowledge spillover is much smaller. Furthermore, both companies have obligations toward third parties that they have to fulfill. The gatekeepers pay attention to possible restrictions due to these obligations.

---

[259] See P3: 59 and P5: 6.
[260] Knowledge spillover is defined and discussed in Section 4.6.3.

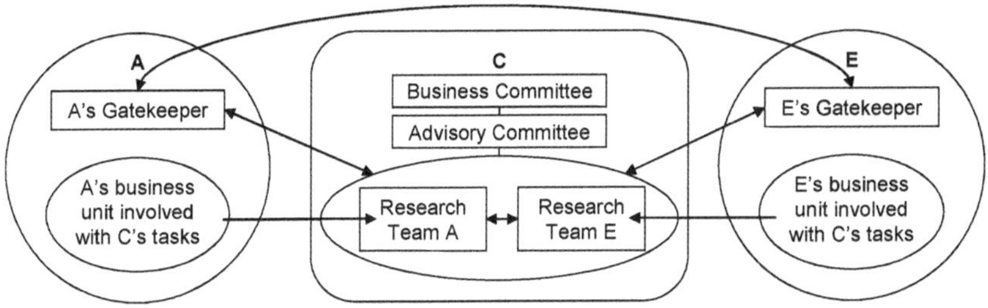

Figure 2-6: Relationships between companies A and E, and the research alliance C.

The agreement also includes establishing an Advisory Committee reviewing the research teams' activities, assessing progress against the alliance's objectives and milestones, and identifying potential activities needed to achieve the objectives. It consists of four people from each parent: project leaders, representatives of intellectual properties, business representatives and an eligible position. To protect themselves from being accused of price-rigging, the parents agreed on only one business representative from one party joining the committee. Furthermore a Business Committee is installed to provide senior management guidance to the Advisory Committee. It also has the power to decide on any changes regarding the alliance's funding as well as possible extensions of the alliance's duration.

The desired long-term outcome of the joint research is commercial success of the final products, which requires the design of a specific substance and a special working process. A and E will be licensing the process where E will be the only licensor. License-revenues will be split with A in a ration of 2(E) to 1(A). This split is proportional to the investment of each parent. However, as the alliance's research topic has to do with basic science, management is aware that there will be a time lag before the licensing can take place. Hence, it is estimated that the first monetary inflows will start after 2007.

We employ findings and comments from the interviews with alliance members later. For example, we refer to interviewees when presenting and discussing factors determining alliance dynamics in Chapter 4 and when describing the simulation model in Chapter 6.

To conclude the first chapter of this work, we first explained the problem statement in the introduction. Here, we showed that alliances become increasingly important for companies' long-term success, while a large percentage of them fail. We then presented the aim of the study, which is to gain deeper insight into the reasons for alliance failure, and explained the structure of the thesis. Further, we described our research approach. We laid out the state of the art of the research on interorganizational learning in alliances and explained in depth and put into scientific perspective the simulation modeling process that we use to analyze the behavior of alliance development. Finally we described the case study method, followed by an introduction of the case study itself. In the following chapter we define frequently used terms like alliances and the special case of learning alliances. We discuss several theoretical approaches for explaining sustainable competitive advantage with alliances.

3. Background and Literature Review

3.1 Overview

Theoretical background and a literature review of different aspects are the focus of the second chapter. We first discuss the concept of competitive advantage and shed light on how interorganizational cooperations, or alliances, can support their parent companies to achieve competitive advantage. Further, we define the term interorganizational cooperation and present different motivations for cooperating and different types of alliances. Afterward, we present the learning alliance as a special type of alliance in a separate section. Finally, we discuss different theoretical approaches for explaining sustainable competitive advantage with cooperations. The last aspect is the most comprehensive part of this chapter.

3.2 Competitive Advantage and Sustainable Competitive Advantage

One reason for corporations to enter alliances may be to gain competitive advantage over competitors.[261] Generating competitive advantage may be interpreted from different points of view. Competitive advantage can be described as a product or service superior to that of the competitors, for example.[262] To be superior, the product or service has to meet three criteria: first, it has to cover an important feature from the customers' point of view. In turn, this advantage also has to be perceived by the customers. Finally, competitors should not be able to catch up with the advantage immediately. BARNEY focuses on a more strategic point of view when stating that a "firm is said to have a *competitive advantage* when it is implementing a value creating strategy not simultaneously being implemented by any current or potential competitor."[263] In the field of strategic management scholars suggest that firms can get in such a position by using and developing their internal strengths, via replying to external opportunities, while avoiding firm-internal weaknesses, and neutralizing environmental threats.[264] They agree that competitive advantages are difficult to sustain.[265] This is because of the "progressive elimination from net effect of organizational factors that are clearly relevant to performance advantage"[266] as competition follows competitive imitation. Nevertheless, competitive advantage is important for companies' long-term success. PORTER identifies three types of strategy to achieve temporary competitive

[261] See Murray Jr. and Mahon (1993), p. 104. Powell and Durand discuss an epistemological approach to competitive advantage. Powell claims that firms can achieve superior performance without having competitive advantages. See Powell (2002) and Durand (2002) for a critique.
[262] See, for example, Simon (1988), p. 465.
[263] Barney (1991), p. 102. Italics in the original source.
[264] See Barney (1991), p. 99. This scheme refers to the strengths-weaknesses-opportunities-threats analysis. In Section 3.4.2 we will focus on the strategy-based approaches for explaining companies' motivation to enter cooperations.
[265] Barney offers an in-depth explanation about the problematic nature of sustained competitive advantage. See Barney (1991), pp. 102-103. See also Ghemawat (1986), pp. 53-54, March and Sutton (1997), p. 699, Eisenhardt and Martin (2000), p. 1106, Porter and Stern (2001), p. 28, Barney et al. (2001), p. 631, Nicolai and Kieser (2002), p. 585, and Peteraf and Bergen (2003), p. 1037. Berman, Down, and Hill, referring to data from the National Basketball Association, state that even the tacit resource implicit knowledge may only lead to competitive advantage, but not sustained competitive advantage. See Berman et al. (2002), p. 27.
[266] March and Sutton (1997), p. 699.

advantages: low cost, differentiation, and focused strategies.[267] Among other things, firms try to realize these strategies also by entering cooperations.

3.3 Interorganizational Cooperations to Achieve Competitive Advantage

Interorganizational collaborations provide an opportunity for firms to overcome competitive disadvantages. Yet, before studying contributions from several theoretical approaches on interfirm cooperation, we discuss the terms interorganizational cooperation and alliance in the following in order to ensure a common understanding of this type of organizational arrangement. We lay out how cooperations are situated between market and hierarchy, discuss the motives for firms to enter alliances, and present various types of interfirm collaboration. Subsequently, we discuss the learning alliance as a special type of interorganizational cooperation.

3.3.1 Definition of Terms and Contextual Delimitation of Different Types of Interorganizational Cooperations

The definition of interfirm collaboration is not coherent in the literature.[268] In general, an alliance or cooperation represents a form of coordination of economic activities. It is the generic term for varied forms of joint goal attainment.[269] Specifically, scholars use and interpret the term differently. Moreover, the phenomenon is referred to differently in the German and Anglo-Saxon literature.[270] Whereas in the German literature, scholars tend to write about cooperations (Kooperationen), [271] English-speaking academics prefer the term alliance or partnership.[272] However, despite the different interpretations and explanations the definitions of cooperations or alliances mostly have the following aspects in common.[273] First, two or more parent companies stay

[267] See Porter (1985), pp. 11-26. See also Hill (1988), pp. 404-411 and Veliyath and Fitzgerald (2000), p. 56.

[268] See, for example, the remarks by Rupprecht-Däullary (1994), pp. 5-18, Schwerk (2000), pp. 26-31, or Gebrekidan and Awuah (2002), pp. 679-680. Cooperate, Latin: cooperor = work with or together. See Lewis and Short (1966), p. 466.

[269] See Schwerk (2000), p. 26.

[270] See Rupprecht-Däullary (1994), pp. 5-15.

[271] See, for instance, Tröndle (1987), pp. 13-38 in particular, Rotering (1993), pp. 6-19, Prange (1996), pp. 172-174, Bachmann and Lane (1997), pp. 79-81, Pausenberger and Nöcker (2000), p. 396, Zahn and Foschiani (2000), pp. 494-495, Herbst (2002), pp. 9-86, and Rupprecht-Däullary (1994), pp. 5-11 and the references there.

[272] Referring to alliances, see, for instance, Teece (1992), p. 6, Mody (1993), p. 152, Gulati (1995b), pp. 620-621, Ariño and de la Torre (1998), pp. 323-324, Child (1998), p. 241, Anand and Khanna (2000), p. 295, Reid et al. (2001), p. 81, Contractor and Lorange (2002b), p. 4, Kale et al. (2002), p. 748, Tidd and Izumimoto (2002), p. 138, and Rupprecht-Däullary (1994), pp. 11-15 and the references there. She remarks that the term 'cooperation' is preferably used in economic publications. Referring to partnerships, see Hagedoorn et al. (2000), pp. 567-568, their definition of partnership encompasses cooperative arrangements between firms, universities, and government agencies. Again very differently, Zeng and Chen interpret the term 'cooperation' as the way the partner firms interact with each other in alliances. See Zeng and Chen (2003), p. 588.

[273] See, for example, Pausenberger (1989), p. 623, Büchs (1991), p. 3, Rupprecht-Däullary (1994), p. 16, Prange (1996), pp. 172-173, and Schwerk (2000), p. 28.

legally and partly economically independent when entering interfirm cooperations.[274] Second, they voluntarily restrict their decision autonomy in order to pursue common goals which they believe they are more likely to achieve in a joint effort than on their own. Last, the parents commit themselves to succeeding and coordinating tasks jointly, possibly on a long-term basis. Subsequently, however, we use the term alliance without making any differences to cooperation. This yields the following definition: we understand alliances as being all forms of interfirm collaboration between two or more legally and (partly) economically independent companies that voluntarily restrict their decision autonomy to pursue common interests and tasks, not only on a short-term basis.

Alliances between Market and Hierarchy

Alliances cover several modes of interfirm cooperation without ever involving the two extreme points identified from an industrial organization point of view, market and hierarchy.[275] At the one extreme, the market represents a form of economic activity in which market participants exchange specified goods more spontaneously and anonymously. Its coordination mechanism is the price. Further characteristics are that subjects have free market access based on the assumptions of bounded rationality and opportunism. Markets exhibit the lowest degree of mutual interdependence between participants. At the other extreme, hierarchy indicates that the coordination of economic activities is achieved via authority relations. A fully integrated firm is considered a hierarchy which takes advantage of economies of scale and scope, risk reduction and facilitates administrative coordination.[276]

As alliances incorporate both market and hierarchical elements they can also be labeled as hybrid organizations.[277] On the one hand, loose cooperation stands in the focus of the alliance the more an alliance's organizational design consists of market elements. On the other hand, the more an alliance's organizational design consists of hierarchical elements, the less important are mutual interdependence and cooperation between firms. Between market and hierarchy, the literature identifies different cooperative typologies.[278] The types of collaborative arrangements range from relational contracting to licensing and mid-term and long-term supply chain relationships

[274] For a discussion on economic independence see Rupprecht-Däullary (1994), p. 6.

[275] See, for instance, Williamson (1975), p. 8, Contractor and Lorange (1988b), pp. 6-7, Sydow (1992), p. 104, and Contractor and Lorange (2002b), pp. 4-5. Conner and Prahalad and Foss discuss the advantages of firms over markets regarding the efficiency of the use of knowledge and other related resources. See Conner and Prahalad (1996), Foss (1996a), and Foss (1996b).

[276] See Sydow (1992), p. 98, and Child and Faulkner (1998), p. 122. Granovetter critically reviews the scheme of markets and hierarchies from a sociological point of view focusing on actual patterns of personal relations by which economic transactions are carried out. According to this standpoint alliances stand out due to the presence of organizational hierarchical structures of markets – and not the market-oriented features of organizations. See Sydow (1992), p. 99. "Intermediate forms of this kind are so intimately bound up with networks of personal relations that any perspective that considers these relations peripheral will fail to see clearly what 'organizational form' has been effected." Granovetter (1985), p. 504. For a discussion on firms and markets see also Conner and Prahalad (1996), pp. 480-484.

[277] See Powell (1987), p. 68.

[278] See, for example, Contractor and Lorange (1988b), p. 6, Child and Faulkner (1998), pp. 120-122, and Contractor and Lorange (2002b), pp. 4-5.

to non-equity and equity joint ventures[279]. Equity joint ventures entail the largest investment and hence the greatest commitment. Alternatively, CHILD AND FAULKNER see strategic alliances at the highest level of interdependence.[280] They subsume joint ventures in the category of strategic alliances. The latter is a common term in alliance research. Often, instead of calling the collaboration between firms simply an alliance, some authors specifically term it strategic alliance. Yet, they stress that this is an alliance between competitors with strategic intent being the most important aspect.[281] The objective of strategic alliances is often to balance the firm's own internal weaknesses with the partner's strengths in regard to sustaining or improving the competitive position.

Systemization of Alliances

To realize the above-mentioned joint competitive advantage, partnering firms combine their strengths to weigh up their respective weaknesses. On this basis PORTER AND FULLER distinguish two different kinds of alliance. In X-alliances, "firms divide the activities within an industry between themselves (for example, one partner manufactures while letting the other market). In Y-coalitions, the firms share the actual performance of one or more value activities."[282] An example of the latter would be a joint research and development agreement. An additional categorization differentiates between link and scale alliances.[283] In scale alliances the partners contribute similar resources related to the same stage(s) in the value chain. This type of alliance includes research and development alliances or joint production. In link alliances the partners contribute different but matching capabilities.[284] As it is also possible for the firms to appropriate capabilities from their respective partners, DUSSAUGE, GARRETTE, AND MITCHELL interpret link alliances as close to being Trojan Horses.[285] Scale alliances, in contrast, are closer to coalitions as the involved companies may be able to increase economies of scale or strengthen their relative market position. Referring to these categorizations, the alliance presented in the case study in Section 2.4.3 is a Y-

---

279 See Harrigan (1988), p. 205, Inkpen (1995), p. 1, Inkpen and Crossan (1995), p. 596, Zhang and Rajagopalan (2002), p. 457. Joint ventures often imply the formation of a separate corporation, whose stock is shared among the partnering firms. See Contractor and Lorange (1988b), p. 7. Mergers and acquisitions entail a change in ownership structure between firms. A specific difference between alliances and mergers and acquisitions lies in the indigestibility problem. See Inkpen and Beamish (1997). For recent publications on mergers and acquisitions in the context of interorganizational learning see Anand and Delios (2002), or Hayward (2002).

280 See Child and Faulkner (1998), p. 122.

281 See, among other things, Harrigan (1988), p. 205, Hamel et al. (1989), p. 133, Jorde and Teece (1989), pp. 29-30, Parkhe (1993), p. 794, Holmqvist (1999), p. 424, Dussauge et al. (2000), p. 99, Kale et al. (2000), p. 218, Gebrekidan and Awuah (2002), pp. 679-680, Ho Park et al. (2002), p. 527, Hungenberg et al. (2002), p. 264, Ariño (2003), p. 67, and McCutchen Jr. et al. (2004), p. 54. An additional term often referred to in the literature is the network. Networks entail a system of several collaborative relationships between organizations. See Thorelli (1986), p. 37 and Sydow (1992).

282 Porter and Fuller (1986), p. 336. X-coalitions are also called horizontal alliances and Y-coalitions are similar to vertical alliances.

283 See Dussauge et al. (2000), p. 102 and Dussauge et al. (2002), pp. 711-712. An example of a scale alliance is the Auto-Europa alliance between Volkswagen and Ford to jointly produce a minivan, Volkswagen Sharan and Ford Galaxy, for the European market. The NUMMI joint venture is an example of a link alliance. For the NUMMI joint venture, see also footnote 297.

284 See Hennart (1988), p. 362 and Dussauge et al. (2002), p. 712.

285 See Dussauge et al. (2002), p. 723.

alliance, or a scale alliance. The European and American partner companies bundle their strengths at the same stage of the value chain to realize or sustain competitive advantage.

Motives for Entering Alliances

By entering alliances, companies seek to achieve firm-individual and/or alliance-wide objectives.[286] The motives for companies to form or enter alliances have a wide spectrum, e.g., reducing risk in R&D, achieving economies of scale or scope, accessing technology or markets, concentrating market power, co-opting or blocking competition, bundling complementary competences with competitors, or joint learning from and with the partner.[287] The last motive is especially widely acknowledged as a motive for companies entering alliances.[288] As this type of motive is the focus of the present work, we concentrate on it further in the following section.

3.3.2 Learning Alliances as a Special Type of Interorganizational Cooperation

Especially in dynamic markets, innovations may well be one of the most important ways to achieve competitive advantage.[289] These days, sources of competitive advantage are more frequently breakthrough innovations that increasingly rely upon interdisciplinary and interindustry research and lie beyond the research capabilities of one single firm.[290] This is because firms often do not have the complete bundle of capabilities and resources needed.[291] One reason for this is that tacit and complex resources required for innovations are largely path-dependent, specialized and idiosyncratic to a particular firm.[292] Whereas markets are effective and efficient for exchanging substitutable goods, they are not capable of bundling together the tacit resources the firm requires. Alternatively, alliances are more able to offer the necessary tacit resources than markets. They provide the "flexible relationship and the qualitative coordinative mechanisms that facilitate the effective transmittal and coordination of tacit knowledge flows."[293] Hence, entering alliances to learn together and from each other, and also with and from competitors, is an attractive option for firms to exploit and to explore new opportunities, sustain competitiveness in the market and

---

286 Firm-individual objectives can be interpreted as private objectives and alliance-wide objectives as common objectives; according to Khanna (1998), pp. 340-342 and Khanna et al. (1998), pp. 194-208. Private and common goals are also discussed in Section 4.5.2.

287 See Contractor and Lorange (1988b), p. 9, Glaister and Buckley (1996), pp. 303-309, Child and Faulkner (1998), p. 67, Zahn (2001), p. 11, Oesterle (2003), p. 639, and Hansen and Nohria (2004), p. 23.

288 See, for instance, Inkpen and Crossan (1995), p. 596, Prange (1996), p. 175, Zahn (2001), p. 11.

289 See Zahra and George (2002), p. 195. This statement stresses the company's internal strengths. For further reading on innovations, see Nooteboom (2000), pp. 1-3 or Hullmann (2001), pp. 54-61. Benner and Tushman offer a classification of innovations. See Benner and Tushman (2003), pp. 242-243.

290 See Lubatkin et al. (2001), p. 1353.

291 See Hamel and Prahalad (1994), p. 187.

292 See Teece and Pisano (1994), pp. 542-548, Mowery et al. (1996), p. 79, Teece et al. (1997), pp. 518-524, Madhok and Tallman (1998), p. 329, and Contractor and Lorange (2002b), p. 13.

293 Madhok and Tallman (1998), p. 329.

achieve superior performance.[294] Especially in dynamic industries like biotechnology, chemistry, electronics, or pharmaceuticals, alliances are vehicles for "faster, less costly and more permanent skill-borrowing."[295]

LUBATKIN, FLORIN, AND LANE identify four different archetypes of alliance that are suitable for interorganizational learning.[296] First, there are vicarious learning alliances that focus on benchmark agreements or buyer-supplier relationships, for example. In such alliances the partners can easily recognize and articulate the knowledge that they are interested in.

Second, knowledge absorption alliances are based on a one-way transfer of knowledge and its application to products. Often these alliances are established by firms that are competing in similar or the same markets.[297] The type of knowledge to be transferred is more abstract than in the first alliance type. Path-dependence and social embeddedness of knowledge make the knowledge transfer more difficult.[298] Therefore, the collaborating firms first need to understand the basic knowledge about a knowledge domain. Then they are able to understand the more specialized knowledge structures required to transform the learned knowledge into the new capabilities desired. The skill required to understand, assimilate, and apply knowledge is called absorptive capacity[299] and is critical for internalizing knowledge. As the absorptive capacities of both partners might differ, one of them might learn faster from the other

---

[294] See Powell et al. (1996), p. 117, Child and Faulkner (1998), p. 65, Dyer and Singh (1998), p. 661, and Harrison et al. (2001), p. 680. Furthermore, see March (1991), p. 83, Lado et al. (1992), p. 87, Conner and Prahalad (1996), p. 477, Foss (1996a), p. 471, Inkpen (1996), p. 123, Powell et al. (1996), p. 118, Lado et al. (1997), pp. 110-111, Koza and Lewin (1998), p. 256, Madhok and Tallman (1998), p. 327, Argote et al. (2000), p. 2, Harrison et al. (2001), p. 680, Reid et al. (2001), p. 85, Carayannis and Alexander (2002), p. 628, Calantone et al. (2002), p. 517, Bhagat et al. (2002), p. 204, Ireland et al. (2002), p. 415, Reagans and McEvily (2003), p. 240, and Rothaermel and Deeds (2004), pp. 203-205.

[295] Contractor et al. (2002), p. 496. Powell's, Koput's, and Smith-Doerr's analysis of highly dynamic industries supports this insight as they found out that innovations are mostly found in networks of learning firms rather than in individual firms. See Powell et al. (1996), pp. 116, 118.

[296] Unless otherwise indicated, the following statements refer to Lubatkin et al. (2001), p. 1360. The types are determined by their difficulty of governance and the tacitness of knowledge involved in the learning process.

[297] Lubatkin, Florin, and Lane provide the NUMMI-joint venture between American auto manufacturer General Motors and their Japanese partner Toyota as an example of a knowledge absorption alliance. The link alliance was founded in 1983 and it is referred to as successful for both partners. General Motors learned how to manufacture smaller cars and Toyota learned about the American market. See Lubatkin et al. (2001), p. 1361 and also Inkpen and Crossan (1995), p. 614, Levinson and Asahi (1995), pp. 50-51, Prange et al. (1996), p. 11, Inkpen and Beamish (1997), p. 189, Doz and Hamel (1998), pp. 12, 53, 64, 82, Larsson et al. (1998), p. 293, Dussauge et al. (2000), p. 103, Kale et al. (2000), p. 219, Khanna et al. (2000), pp. 786-787, Dussauge et al. (2002), p. 712, Mowery et al. (2002), p. 294 or as two early citations for NUMMI see Hampton and Norman (1987), p. 49 and Nielsen (1988), p. 482. Another example of competitors collaborating in the manufacturing industry is CFM, the aircraft engine alliance between French aircraft engine manufacturer SNECMA and its American partner General Electric. See Perlmutter and Heenan (1986), p. 136, Moxon et al. (1988), pp. 259-261, 266, 270, 274-275, Gulati (1995a), pp. 88-89, Das and Rahman (2002), p. 105, Zeng and Hennart (2002), p. 197 and 203, or Zeng and Chen (2003), p. 594 who also provide more successful examples of alliances. General Electric also cooperates with its competitor Pratt & Whittney to design and manufacture the GP7000 engine for the Airbus A380, offering the only substitute engine to the Trent900 designed by Rolls-Royce.

[298] See Cohen and Levinthal (1990), p. 135 and Granovetter (1985), p. 486.

[299] See Cohen and Levinthal (1990), p. 128 and Section 4.6.1.

than the other way round. The partner who has finished learning might then behave opportunistically and end the alliance early leaving its partner unsatisfied.[300] Either in link, scale, Y- or X-alliances, oftentimes the collaborating partners are competitors at the same time. Hence, firms have to be aware of the tension between the cooperative and competitive aspects when entering an alliance.[301]

Third, knowledge grafting mergers and acquisitions[302] open up the alternative of acquiring socially embedded knowledge in the partner firm. The rationale behind this type of learning alliance is that the knowledge held by the other firm is of sufficient strategic value to buy the whole company.

Finally, in reciprocal learning alliances, the partners' intention is to co-experiment and leverage each other's unique but complementary knowledge structures. Knowledge tacitness is highest in this type of alliance. The partners' core knowledge is inherent in different knowledge domains. Also, their knowledge bases and their commercial ambitions differ. This also means that the partners have difficulty understanding each other immediately. The last type of knowledge alliance is not as common as the other three kinds. The partnering firms' businesses do not have great overlap.[303]

The alliance presented in the case study can be characterized as a knowledge absorption alliance. Even though the collaborating partners' knowledge domains might differ slightly, their know-how is similar and their respective business areas are very similar. Still, the knowledge involved might be of high tacitness and the firms are competitors toward the marketing of their products.

From the position of the learning alliance partners, learning can be observed on four levels.[304] Each level is driven by a different motivation. First, the managers of an alliance partner may seek to learn about the alliance itself. By entering alliances, firms may attain relational capital while building up knowledge about designing and managing alliances which might be useful in future interfirm collaborations.[305] When firms understand well how to manage their alliances and position themselves better in the market through their alliances, scholars call this the firms' collaborative advantage.[306]

---

[300] This phenomenon is called learning race. Its roots and features are discussed in Section 4.5.2. See Hamel (1991), p. 85 and 88 and Khanna et al. (1998). For opportunistic behavior in alliances see a later paragraph in this section and Section 3.4.3.

[301] See Perlmutter and Heenan (1986), p. 136 and Khanna et al. (1998), p. 194.

[302] Lubatkin, Florin, and Lane apply a different definition of alliance when subsuming mergers and acquisitions under knowledge grafting alliances.

[303] Lubatkin, Florin, and Lane provide the example of the alliance between Maytag and Microsoft from August 2000 for a reciprocal learning alliance.

[304] For the following statements in the paragraph see Inkpen and Dinur (1998), p. 455, Inkpen (2002), pp. 268-269, and Inkpen and Tsang (2005), pp. 149, 154 if not otherwise indicated. Although alliances may consist of multiple partners, in the following we only consider the special case of a two-party alliance.

[305] See, Lyles (1988), p. 301, Child and Faulkner (1998), pp. 289-290, Dyer and Singh (1998), pp. 669-671, Gulati (1999), pp. 402-403, Anand and Khanna (2000), pp. 297-299, and Inkpen (2002), p. 268 and Inkpen and Tsang (2005), p. 149. Kale, Singh, and Perlmutter discuss the concept of relational capital. See Kale et al. (2000), pp. 218, 220-222, and 232-234.

[306] See Hamel et al. (1989), p. 133, Kanter (1994), p. 96, Lado et al. (1997), p. 110, or Hansen and Nohria (2004), p. 22.

Second, a partner firm can learn about its alliance partner.[307] Oftentimes, firms are uncertain whether the collaborating partner will behave as expected in the alliance. This risk is reduced by learning about the partner via interaction. According to INKPEN this does not serve as a direct motivation for entering an alliance. But the knowledge may be crucial to alliance evolution and used as support for effective alliance management.[308] Also, knowledge about the partner may be spread through the network in which firms are embedded.[309] This also enables other firms in the network to evaluate the firm's commitment to and honesty in alliances. Third, a firm can mutually learn with its partner. Learning with the partner happens when the alliance partners jointly create new knowledge required for reaching the alliance objectives.[310] Finally, a firm can learn from its partner in two ways. On the one hand, a firm may want to understand the partner's knowledge better in order to combine it successfully with the own knowledge. On the other hand, a firm might be interested in learning from the partner to use the knowledge in operations outside the alliance business.[311] In this study, we focus on the last two learning levels: learning with the partner and learning from the partner. In Sections 4.5.3 and 4.5.4 we discuss these learning levels in more detail.

Besides possible benefits of collaboration, entering alliances also reveals some disadvantages for the firms involved. On top of the usual risk of managing a single firm, corporations have to cope with the uncertainty of the partner's behavior in alliances.[312] This means that besides the risk of disappointing business performance there is the "risk of the partner not cooperating in good faith."[313] Performance risk relates to the external factors that may hinder the achievement of alliance objectives. It includes changing government policies, lack of competence on the part of the partner firm, or intensified rivalry.[314] Relational risk is defined as the probability and consequences of a partner not committing appropriately to the alliance and causing disappointments by behaving differently from what was expected.[315] As mentioned above, to learn from and with the collaborating partner, firms often pursue both cooperative and competitive strategies concurrently. Frequently, the cooperating partner is a competitor in the respective market field.[316] So, besides the cooperating aspect of following a common interest, there is also the possibility of gaining private benefits from the alliance.[317] This situation may lead partners to resort to opportunistic behavior like cheating, shirking responsibility, holding back on appropriate resources, or distorting information.[318] This behavior may be due to lack of trust between the par-

---

[307] See Ariño and de la Torre (1998), p. 308, Doz (1996), pp. 64 and 67-68, and Inkpen and Currall (2004), pp. 593-595.

[308] See Inkpen (2002), p. 269.

[309] See Granovetter (1985), p. 490 and the discussion on observed behavior in networks in Section 3.4.3.

[310] Learning with the partner is done for generating common benefits. They are discussed in Section 4.5.2. See Khanna et al. (1998), pp. 194-195.

[311] These objectives are called private benefits and are discussed in depth in Section 4.5.2. See Khanna et al. (1998), pp. 194-195.

[312] See Das and Teng (2001), p. 253.

[313] Das and Teng (2001), p. 253.

[314] See Das and Teng (2001), p. 253 and Ireland et al. (2002), p. 434.

[315] See Das and Teng (1996), p. 831, Das and Teng (2001), p. 254 and Ireland et al. (2002), p. 434.

[316] See Jorde and Teece (1989), pp. 26-30 and Nalebuff and Brandenburger (1996), p. 28.

[317] See Khanna et al. (1998), pp. 194-208.

[318] See Lado et al. (1997), p. 111 and Das and Teng (2001), p. 253.

ticipants, difficulties in relinquishing control, inefficiencies in decision processes, differences in corporate cultures, the complexity of the joint task, differential learning abilities, or undesirable knowledge transfer or even outflow that may impede successful alliance development.[319] Opportunistic behavior is indicated as one of the major reasons for alliance failure. Therefore we discuss this aspect in more detail in Section 3.4.1 when presenting transaction cost economics, in Section 3.4.3 when we talk about game theoretic implications on alliances, and in Section 4.5.2, when discussing the existence of both private and common benefits that may lead to such opportunistic behavior. Trust is often presented as a means to promote cooperative behavior. This is discussed in Section 4.6.3.

To conclude, to decide whether or not to enter an alliance, managers need to weigh the motives and the positive aspects of the alliance against its risks and determine which alliance type would fit the requirements. In the following chapter we introduce a selection of underlying theoretical approaches to explain the existence of alliances. We do this on the basis of the elements of definition presented above.

3.4 Selection of Theoretical Approaches for Explaining Competitive Advantage with Alliances

There is not a single theory that succeeds in explaining collaborative partnerships and cooperative strategies completely. Nevertheless, different approaches deliver valuable extensive insight into this complex problem set.[320] Therefore, we present some of the underlying theoretical approaches for explaining competitive advantage with alliances in this chapter. The range of existing theories is wide, from organizational economics to the strategy-based approaches to other organizational concepts like population ecology[321] or social identity theory[322]. Nevertheless, to explain all theories in length would be too extensive and sometimes not necessarily effective as these approaches would provide little insight in regard to the dynamics of interorganizational learning in alliances. Therefore, we only concentrate on the insight they provide with respect to alliances and interorganizational learning when laying them out. We begin by describing insight from organizational economics, and here especially from transaction cost economics. We continue with strategy-based approaches. Here we focus on the two main views, namely the static market-based and resource-based theories. Then we describe their dynamic descendents, including the competence-based view and the knowledge-based view. We close this section with the relational

319 See Powell et al. (1996), pp. 117-118 and Zahn and Foschiani (2000), p. 511.

320 See Zahn and Foschiani (2000), p. 498.

321 The population ecology approach does not concentrate on individual's behavior but on the behavior of whole populations, meant here as interconnected organizations. The approach implies that the firm's survival depends on its external fit with its environment. Key words in this context are variation, selection, and retention. See Hannan and Freeman (1977). For an outline see also Tilebein (2005), pp. 156-157.

322 The social identity theory holds that participants in alliances have multiple sources of identity, and thus loyalties due to the interface between the partnering firms. It suggests that members of an organization have stronger psychological bonds to their own organization, which may be a reason for opportunistic behavior. See Tajfel (1982) and also Lubatkin et al. (2001), p. 1359 for a reference to learning alliances.

view. Then we introduce findings from the network perspective. Last, we discuss insight from game theory. We present insight from classic game theory as well as from the recently upcoming behavioral game theory. Classic game theory assumes decision-makers' rationality, which is abolished by behavioral game theory. We show that the behavioral game theory approach provides valuable insight for explaining the dynamics of interorganizational learning in alliances.

3.4.1 Organizational Economics

We stated above that alliances can be seen as intermediate governance structures between markets and hierarchy. This concept is based on transaction cost economics that is part of the organizational economics paradigm, as are agency theory and property rights theory. Organizational economics deals with "identifying actions that minimize the costs of governance, which, in turn, maximize profits."[323] In the following we discuss the three theories' implications on alliances and interorganizational learning in alliances. We start with transaction cost economics, proceed with agency theory and close this section with a brief introduction to property rights theory.

Transaction cost economics was originally founded by COASE[324] and was developed further by WILLIAMSON[325]. The theory's attempt is not only to provide an explanation for the emergence and existence of the firm[326] as such but also, as indicated above, for which institutional arrangement from market to hierarchy may be economically advantageous under specific conditions.[327] In other words, the theory is about "how a firm should organize its boundary activities with other firms."[328] The theory suggests that alliances are more efficient than other forms when they minimize the sum of production and transaction costs more than with alternative arrangements.[329] Production costs may differ from firm to firm depending on the firms' proprietary knowledge, their ability to learn, and their economies of scale and scope. Transaction costs depend on the specific transaction conditions. Specific assets are identified as considerable drivers of transaction costs. This is because with increasing specification, an asset's value decreases in alternative applications.[330] Generally, increasing asset specificity supports the extension of firm boundaries. In alliances, specific assets could lead to a

---

323 Combs and Ketchen (1999), p. 869.
324 See Coase (1937).
325 See Williamson (1975).
326 For a discussion of the theory of the organization see, for instance, Madhok (1996), who gives a critique of transaction cost economics as an all-encompassing theory of the firm. See also Conner (1991), Conner and Prahalad (1996), and Mahoney (2001), who discuss the differences between transaction cost economics and the resource-based view (see Section 3.4.2.3) as theories of the firm.
327 See Kogut (1988a), p. 320, Gulati (1995a), p. 87 and Zahn and Foschiani (2000), p. 502.
328 Kogut (1988a), p. 320.
329 An example of production costs are costs of the exchange of output. Transaction costs include search costs (costs referring to gathering information to identify possible partners), contracting costs (negotiating and writing an agreement), monitoring costs (monitoring the agreement that each partner fulfills the agreed obligations), and enforcement costs (ex post bargaining and sanctioning). See Williamson (1975), pp. 20-40 and also Kogut (1988a), p. 320, Dyer (1997), p. 536, Zahn and Foschiani (2000), p. 502 and Swoboda (2003), p. 48.
330 See Dyer (1997), pp. 536-537.

disadvantage for one alliance partner if the other behaves opportunistically, which could be interpreted as "self-interest seeking with guile."[331] Opportunism in learning alliances, in which the significant resource is knowledge,[332] translates into the partners being interested in misrepresenting the value of their knowledge when negotiating the initial agreement to enter an alliance. They may also misinterpret their actions after signing the contract. Hence, if uncertainties about the knowledge to be exchanged increase, the risk of opportunism would also increase.[333] As indicated in the problem statement, opportunistic behavior by one partner may result in short-term exploitation of the partner, possibly followed by early alliance dissolution.[334] On the other hand, generally speaking, asset specificity would encourage firms to enter alliances based on the assumption of reciprocal dependency of specific idiosyncratic assets.[335] Reciprocal dependency through resource or knowledge complementarity, for example, would reduce the partners' opportunistic behavior and hence reduce transaction costs.[336]

To protect themselves against the risks of opportunism, firms can employ control mechanisms of governance structures, such as safeguards. These mechanisms aim at creating a cooperation atmosphere of equity and fairness among the partners. This can either be done with legal contracts or informal self-enforcing agreements like relational or goodwill trust or reputation or formal self-enforcing agreements like financial or investment hostages.[337] We will discuss the effect of trust on the development of interfirm relationships and learning thoroughly in Section 4.6.4.

Although transaction cost economics provides valuable insight into the existence of cooperative arrangements, it has its drawbacks; especially when explaining the dynamics of interorganizational learning in alliances. The theory's fundamental shortcoming is that it is static.[338] It also focuses only on single-party cost minimization, not on interfirm cooperations.[339] Here, difficulties arise when assigning potential transaction cost reductions to the partners. Also, transaction cost economics only considers one-off transactions, not repeated and continuing transactions – of which alliances consist.[340] Furthermore, transaction cost economics neither interprets joint learning as

331 Williamson (1975), p. 255.
332 Concerning knowledge as a resource see Section 3.4.2.4 in which we discuss the knowledge-based view.
333 See Lubatkin et al. (2001), p. 1358.
334 See also Parkhe (1993), p. 802 and Zeng and Chen (2003), p. 588.
335 See Williamson (1983), p. 519.
336 See Kogut (1988a), p. 321 and Dyer (1997), p. 536. Dyer found confirmation when studying and comparing the Japanese and American automobile industry. Toyota, supporting a more specialized supplier group, had lower transaction costs than competitors with a less specialized supplier group.
337 Dyer discusses in depth and summarizes the different safeguards and their influence on transaction costs and value. See Dyer (1997), pp. 537-539 and the cited references there as well as Dyer and Singh (1998), pp. 669-671.
338 See Nooteboom (2000), p. 104, Zahn and Foschiani (2000), p. 503, Zahn (2001), p. 13. For a comprehensive critique on transaction cost theory in regard to its practical application, see Ghoshal and Moran (1996).
339 See Zajac and Olsen (1993), pp. 133-134, Gulati (1998), p. 304 and Zahn and Foschiani (2000), p. 503.
340 See Ring and van de Ven (1992), p. 484, Gulati (1995a), p. 91, Gulati (1998), pp. 304, 350-352, and Khanna (1998), p. 341.

a means of knowledge creation nor addresses the learning motive at all.[341] Finally, GULATI criticizes the fact that the theory focuses entirely on "appropriation concerns that originate from the presence of contracting hazards and behavioral uncertainty"[342], which is too restricted. Concluding, transaction cost economics only provides limited insight into the dynamics of interorganizational learning in alliances.

The second theory of organizational economics is positivist agency theory. Insight from this theory on the dynamics of alliances is limited. Nevertheless, it entails valuable insight into the liaison of the partnering firms as it concentrates on exchange relationships between a principal who delegates responsibility to an agent.[343] The theory assumes that agents act in their own interest and therefore follow their own objectives. Consequently, principals need to monitor their agents, which requires appropriate resource spending. As this approach considers incomplete information, asymmetric information distribution and uncertainty, it has significance for explaining alliances. The asymmetric distribution of information between principal and agent may be of various types: hidden characteristic, hidden information, and hidden intention.[344]

First, hidden characteristics are present when the principal is not aware of certain of her agent's characteristics. This may lead to an adverse agent selection. Referring to alliance partners, this means that one prospective alliance partner firm may disguise some of its characteristics. When entering an alliance, its partner may then choose an unfavorable partner. Screening, which involves additional transaction costs, may be helpful to avoid this risk. The cooperation contract may then provide information about the partners' characteristics. Second, after signing the contract and in the course of the relationship, hidden actions and hidden information may be uncovered. Typically, the principal cannot observe her agent's actions (hidden action). Even if the principal can observe an action, there is usually some information missing for a complete evaluation of the action (hidden information). Referring to alliances, one partner cannot evaluate how much of the partner's outcome, for example, R&D results, can be traced back to the other's own decisions and actions. Hence, there is the potential risk of the partners opportunistically taking advantage of each other and acting against the interest of the other or even against the common interest. This is called moral hazard. Third, hidden intentions conceal the agent's objectives. A problematic situation may arise if the principal first makes irreversible investments, for instance, in specific assets, and then becomes dependent on the agent. Referring to interfirm relationships, hidden intentions may be hidden agendas. A firm may not openly communicate all the objectives that it is pursuing by entering the alliance, for exam-

---

341 See Kogut (1988a), p. 323, Sakakibara (1997), p. 146, and Nooteboom (2000), p. 104.
342 See Gulati (1998), p. 304.
343 See Jensen and Meckling (1976). There are two branches of agency research: the normative principal agent and the positive agency stream. The former seeks to provide recommendations regarding the design of optimal employment contracts under different assumptions. It uses mathematical models and is relevant in the economics literature. The latter branch seeks to explain and to solve real world governance problems. See, for example, Eisenhardt (1989), pp. 59-63 and also Combs and Ketchen (1999), p. 870 and Herbst (2002), p. 43 and their cited literature.
344 See Picot et al. (1997), pp. 85-86 for the following points except for the reference to alliances. The reference to alliances is based on our reflections.

ple. Once the alliance is established and investments are made, one partner may deceive the partner firm and feather its nest at the other's expense.[345] Partnering firms may protect themselves against the three types of information asymmetry via contract design, which involves agency costs.

As the third theory of organizational economics, the property rights theory[346] provides the basis for analyzing consequences of participants' behavior. The theory focuses on the assignment of rights to specific resources. In an alliance context, it gives information about the assignment of task-specific knowledge and the protection of particularly valuable resources as well as about the transfer of property rights to a potential joint management team.[347]

Summarizing, the three theories of organizational economics do provide limited, albeit valuable insight into the dynamics of interorganizational learning in alliances. In the following we continue with our evaluation of strategy-based approaches.

3.4.2 Strategy-Based Approaches

Whereas transaction cost economics hypothesize that firms interact with each other so that the total of transaction and production costs are minimized, strategy-based approaches hypothesize that firms transact in such a way that their profits are maximimized by improving their competitive position in relation to their competitors.[348] Following a simultaneous strategy of cooperation and competition through entering alliances may not only lead to competitive advantage but may also generate economic rents. As strategies can be interpreted as the search for economic rent,[349] we lay out various types of rent in the following. Subsequently, we discuss how linkages between companies may be a source of rent generation.

3.4.2.1 Rent-Seeking Behavior

The concept of rents is ambiguous and difficult. PETERAF who presents in depth twelve kinds of rent[350] therefore emphasizes its careful application. Here, we do not present all types of rent but just those that are identified as significant for learning in alliances. Generally, economic rent can be understood as excess return on a resource over its opportunity cost.[351] By definition, the specific resource suffers from

345 We discuss the outlearning phenomenon in Section 4.5.1.
346 See Alchian (1965) and Demsetz (1967).
347 See Zahn and Foschiani (2000), p. 504.
348 See Kogut (1988a), p. 322.
349 See Bowman (1974), p. 47 and also Lado et al. (1997), p. 117.
350 See Peteraf (1993), and Peteraf (1994).
351 See Peteraf (1994), p. 154. Peteraf defines economic, pure economic, quasi, appropriable quasi, Ricardian, land, inframarginal, efficiency, differential, entrepreneurial, managerial, and monopoly rents. She talks about factors instead of resources, referring to the economic base of the rent concept. Yet, Lado, Boyd, and Hanlon speak of resources and capabilities. See Peteraf (1994), pp. 154-157 and Lado et al. (1997), p. 111. For managerial rents see also Castanias and Helfat (1991), pp. 161-162, Castanias and Helfat (2001), p. 662 and Barney et al. (2001), p. 626. For a historical

scarcity and its fixed supply in the short-term.[352] Despite the apparent similarity between profit and rent in their definition of excess over opportunity costs, some types of rent can be consistent with firm losses while the firm is still profitable.[353] Resources are indeed fixed in the short-term with quasi rents. However, the rent diminishes in the long run because the resource supply adjusts to the demand situation. Ricardian rents are returns that accrue because of differences in resource quality. It is assumed that the supply of the highest quality resources is not sufficient to meet demand. The pure existence of Ricardian rents, however, is not sufficient for earning above average returns. Owning the resource that the rent is based upon is important. Additionally, the resource has to have a higher service value in some use than other resources of the same type. Monopoly rents are persistent with profits. They can be interpreted as returns to the factor which forms the basis of the monopoly, e.g., a patent. In the context of the Schumpeterian[354] framework competitive advantage may be attained and, under certain assumptions also sustained, depending on the firm's ability to develop capabilities[355] for innovation. If firms also succeed in innovating while collaborating, they may generate entrepreneurial or Schumpeterian rents.[356]

Referring to alliances, DYER AND SINGH suggest a different type of rent called relational rents, that might evolve in collaborations. According to the authors relational rents are generated "in an exchange relationship that cannot be generated by either firm in isolation and can only be created through the joint idiosyncratic contributions of the specific alliance partners."[357] The authors use the term rent although they also remark that technically "trading partners generate quasi rents."[358] MADHOK AND TALLMAN identify three different types of quasi rents that are relevant for firms that enter alliances: in addition to firm-specific quasi rents, transaction-specific rents are important on the single-firm level. Whereas the former type refers to the value difference of the resource, the latter reflects the value difference between the application of the resource in a specific use compared with the second best one.[359] The third type is the collaboration-specific quasi rent that is particularly tied to the alliance. It is based on the combination of both companies' firm-specific and transaction-specific quasi rents.

---

outline on rents see Lippman and Rumelt (2003), pp. 904-908, who explain how rent can be realized growing sunflowers on a piece of land.

352 See Peteraf (1994), p. 155 and Lippman and Rumelt (2003), p. 904, who clarify the difference between rent and economic rent.

353 Consider a press operator who receives $4,000 of revenues. Fixed expenses add up to $4,000 and operating costs are $1,500. The salvage value (for instance, the opportunity cost) of the machine is $1,000. Then, the press still earns $1,500 of quasi rents while firm losses add up to -$1,500. See Klein et al. (1978), p. 298 and Peteraf (1994), p. 156.

354 See Schumpeter (1950), pp. 134-142, who confers about creative destruction of economic systems through entrepreneurial activity. See also Schumpeter (1949), pp. 128-156.

355 We discuss capabilities and the underlying strategic approach of dynamic capabilities in more detail in Section 3.4.2.4.

356 See Teece et al. (1997), p. 527 and Galunic and Rodan (1998), pp. 1193-1194, who call this particular rent Schumpeterian rent and Lado et al. (1997), p. 115 and 119, who name it entrepreneurial rent.

357 Dyer and Singh (1998), p. 662.

358 Dyer and Singh (1998), p. 662.

359 See Madhok and Tallman (1998), p. 329 and Klein et al. (1978), pp. 299-300. Madhok and Tallman point out that the collaboration-specific quasi rent can be related to Khanna's concept of common benefits. See Khanna (1998), pp. 340-342.

In the following we discuss how the two differing and prominent views in strategic management explain how firms can generate economic rents while seeking competitive advantage. We start with the market-based view. It explains that firm performance critically depends on industry characteristics. Then we continue with the resource-based view, which states that firm's performance relies on firm specific assets.

3.4.2.2 Market-Based View

The market-based view was the dominant strategy model of the 1980s.[360] The framework, presented by PORTER, derives in part from the traditional structure-conduct-performance paradigm of industrial organization theory.[361] According to the framework, industry structure strongly influences the competitive environment and hence determines firm performance. Industry structure itself is driven by its attractiveness. So, the market-based approach suggests that firms should carefully analyze the attractiveness of the market and their own relative position in it. The attractiveness is shaped by the market's structural parameters, namely the five competitive forces: potential market entrants, buyers, substitutes, suppliers, and the rivalry among industry competitors determine industry profitability.[362] Concluding, competitive advantage is industry-driven.

Referring to collaborations, classic industry organization interprets such behavior as harmful collision. However, the recent market-based view understands cooperating behavior as economic advantage.[363] Cooperating firms may coordinate or share their value chains[364] and benefit by broadening the scope of their activities. This way, they strengthen their power toward buyers or suppliers, may thwart potential entrants, and outposition competitors and consequently gain monopoly rents.[365] ZAHN AND FOSCHIANI note that the market-based view provides valuable insight into the conceptional and analytical level vis-à-vis alliances.[366] For instance, managers may receive indications to enter an alliance when they analyze their firm's value chain and consider alternative market strategies. However, these considerations may only be interesting for evaluating whether or not to enter an alliance at that moment. Because of this deterministic point of view, the market-based view does not provide managers with insight into how their competitors and the market may evolve over time. In other words, the framework does not capture changes in the business relationships or pos-

360 See Teece et al. (1997), p. 511.

361 See Porter (1985), and Porter (1991). Traditional industrial organization theory is based on Bain's and Mason's early work. See Bain (1956) and Mason (1939). For a discourse on the classical industrial organization theory and the modified framework moved forward by Porter see Spanos and Lioukas (2001), pp. 908-909 and Lado et al. (1992), pp. 78-79.

362 See Porter (1985), pp. 4-11.

363 See, for example, Porter and Fuller (1986), pp. 322-325 and Zahn and Foschiani (2000), p. 498.

364 For clarifications on the value chain see Porter (1985), pp. 33-61 and for the generic strategy options the market-based view provides, cost leadership, differentiation, or focus, see Porter (1985), pp. 11-26.

365 See Teece et al. (1997), p. 510 and Spanos and Lioukas (2001), p. 909.

366 See Zahn and Foschiani (2000), pp. 498-499 and also Hagedoorn et al. (2000), pp. 571-572.

sible strategic intents of other market players from the five competitive forces that determine industry structure.

3.4.2.3 Resource-Based Theory

Under resource-based theory we subsume various approaches like the static resource-based view and its dynamic descendents.[367] We first characterize and describe the resource-based view in the following and discuss the latter approaches in Section 3.4.2.4. The main assumption of the resource-based view is that, as opposed to the market-based view, firm performance is due to firm heterogeneity rather than industry structure.[368] Firms are heterogeneous in relation to the resources and capabilities. This means that firms' resources or competences are imperfect. Thus, a firm can be seen as a bundle of unique resources.[369] The resource-based view replaced the market-based view as the leading strategic management theory in the 1990s.[370] Although its assumption opposes that of the market-based view, the two approaches are meanwhile seen as complementary to each other: a sole market-oriented analysis is as insufficient for explaining competitive advantage as a sole resource-oriented analysis.[371]

The resource-based view is based on the resource-conduct-performance paradigm.[372] It puts resources at the center of competitive advantage. Accordingly, resources and capabilities are heterogeneously distributed and are not perfectly mobile among firms. This is why firms in the same industry are characterized as heterogeneous. Generally, resources are "anything which could be thought of as a strength or

---

367 In doing so we are in accordance with Conner (1991), p. 477 and Mahoney (2001), p. 656 who subsume under the resource-based view (see Wernerfelt (1984)) the capabilities-approach (see Teece and Pisano (1994) and Eisenhardt and Martin (2000)) and knowledge-based theory (see Madhok (1996) and Kogut and Zander (2003), p. 509). For discussions on the recognition of the resource-based view as a theory of the firm in general see Conner (1991), Peteraf (1994), Wernerfelt (1995), Barney (1996), Conner and Prahalad (1996), Foss (1996a), Foss (1996b), Barney (2001), Barney et al. (2001), Mahoney (2001), Priem and Butler (2001), Tallman (2003), and Kogut and Zander (2003). The 2003 Strategic Management Journal Special Issue discusses findings into the resource-based view.

368 See, for instance, Barney (1991), p. 101, Porter (1991), p. 108, and also Dyer and Singh (1998), p. 660.

369 See Penrose (1959), p. 23. Even though Penrose's valuable contributions to the resource-based view should not be diminished, Rugman and Verbeke carefully review her original publications on the limits to the growth of the firm and related texts and find indications that many scholars have misinterpreted her contributions to the resource-based view. See Rugman and Verbeke (2002).

370 For a historical outline of the acceptance and breakthrough of Wernerfelt's seminal work and award-winning Strategic Management Journal 1994 'best paper' on the resource-based view (see Wernerfelt (1984)) see Wernerfelt (1995). The publications by Barney (1991) and Peteraf (1994) were further breakthrough articles. Freiling provides an in-depth overview on the development periods of the resource-based view. See Freiling (2000), pp. 20-33, where he suggests and explains five phases from the beginning to the recent phase of competence-based strategic management.

371 See, for example, Lado et al. (1992), pp. 82-84, Hinterhuber and Friedrich (1999), pp. 1001-1003, Börner (2000), p. 820, Zahn et al. (2000), p. 51, Spanos and Lioukas (2001), pp. 911-912, and Zentes and Schramm-Klein (2003), p. 264.

372 See Zahn (1998), p. 396 or Zentes and Schramm-Klein (2003), p. 262.

weakness of a given firm."[373] Resource-based differences between firms can help explain performance differences that might result in competitive advantage. Sustainability of such differences might depend on the difficulties that might arise with competing companies trying to access comparable resources. In order for such resources to be the source of above-average performance they need to meet four criteria.[374] First, they must be strategically valuable. This means that they enable a firm to improve its effectiveness or efficiencies leading to competitive advantage. Second, they must be rare. In other words, resources that competitors can easily access cannot lead the firm to achieve competitive advantage. Third, they need to be imperfectly imitable. This characteristic is achieved by resources that are history- or path-dependent, causally ambiguous, and socially complex. Finally, they should not be substitutable through other resources.[375]

Resources that fulfill these requirements include both tangible and especially intangible resources. Examples of the former are land, machineries, or raw materials and of the latter patents, corporate image, and particularly knowledge. These resources can be understood as being strategically valuable. Resource heterogeneity hence reflects the presence of a superior resource in the factor market that may be limited in supply. Applying such resources as those described above may consequently lead to the generation of Ricardian rents.[376] Their characteristic of imperfect mobility guarantees that they are bound to the firm. Moreover, LADO, BOYD, AND WRIGHT point out that competences may also generate quasi rents if they meet the above-mentioned requirement of being causally ambiguous. Causally ambiguous resources are difficult for competitors to imitate as their relationship to and interactions toward other firm-specific resources are vague.[377]

As not all firms have all the resources necessary to create innovations, one could state that firms suffer from resource-based constraints or shortfalls. Alliances permit firms to overcome these by sharing their limited resource bases with one another.[378] Together, they can form new resources and create innovations. From a resource-based view, firms therefore may have access to either supplementary or complemen-

---

373 Wernerfelt (1984), p. 172. Some scholars distinguish between resources and capabilities by claiming that capabilities refer to the firm's capacity to deploy the respective resources. See Amit and Schoemaker (1993), p. 35, Grant (1991), p. 115, or Makadok (2001), p. 388. Yet resources can also be defined broadly in the sense that they refer to both resources in a narrower sense and capabilities. See Barney (1991), p. 101, Peteraf (1993), p. 179 and Combs and Ketchen (1999), p. 868. Also, we subsume core competences as a resource in this outline. Core competences define a firm's fundamental business as central. See Prahalad and Hamel (1990) and Teece et al. (1997), p. 516.

374 See Barney (1991), pp. 105-112.

375 For the influence of path dependence on the transfer of resources, and especially intangible resources, see also Cohen and Levinthal (1990), p. 135, Teece and Pisano (1994), pp. 546-547, and Lane and Lubatkin (1998), p. 462. For causal ambiguity see Szulanski (1996), pp. 28, 30, 31, 36 and King and Zeithaml (2001),

376 See Peteraf (1993), pp. 180-182, Bamberger and Wrona (1996), p. 134, Teece et al. (1997), pp. 513, 527, Galunic and Rodan (1998), p. 1193, Makadok (2001), p. 388, and Spanos and Lioukas (2001), p. 911.

377 See Lado et al. (1992), p. 84 and Bamberger and Wrona (1996), p. 134.

378 See Hamel (1991), p. 84, Combs and Ketchen (1999), p. 868, and Wernerfelt (1984), p. 175. The latter, however, refers to mergers and acquisitions in which otherwise non-marketable resources are bought and sold in whole bundles.

tary resources.[379] If firms are interested in the first option, the collaborating companies then obtain more of the resources they already have. In terms of the alliance typology introduced in Section 3.3.1, they would enter a scale alliance and possibly a Y-alliance. When they look for complementary resources, they would enter a link alliance. In either case, firms seek to bundle up their internal resources with their partner in anticipation of economies of scale or scope, or of product innovation in order to enhance their resource base and strengthen their strategic position.

Nevertheless, even if the resources meet all necessary criteria for being strategically valuable, simply owning, bundling, or defending them is not enough to be successful in the market over a longer period.[380] The two approaches presented, the classic market-based and resource-based views, do not provide sufficient explanation for competitive advantage in dynamic or turbulent environments in which several market participants act simultaneously.[381] Both the market-based view and resource-based view are static approaches. In the meantime, scholars have taken up this critique and developed dynamic approaches based on the two. We present the recent dynamic approaches in the following section.

3.4.2.4 Dynamic Approaches

With recent approaches scholars tried to explain a firm's competitive advantage within dynamic environments. They do not focus on current optimal competitive advantages themselves but on features and processes that drive future competitive advantages. Recent approaches share that they do not solely focus on static market structures or resource criteria or qualities. On the contrary, they concentrate on their respective change and their reciprocal interrelationships. They do so by combining the internal and external perspectives and making them dynamic. Yet, they can still be related to one or the other perspective.[382] In the following sections we first present a selection of resource-oriented dynamic approaches.

Resource-Oriented Dynamic Approaches

There are several dynamic approaches.[383] In a book edited by MORECROFT, SANCHEZ, AND HEENE, for example, the authors integrate pre-existing resource-based approaches with a holistic and dynamic perspective to explain resources, capabilities, and management processes from a systems perspective, applying the System Dynamics methodology. Here, however, we focus on new approaches. While they all surely contribute their share to the explanation of firms, we only concentrate on those that provide insight into the existence and dynamics of interorganizational learning in alliances. Therefore, in the following paragraphs, we focus on the two main developments of the resource-based view, the competence-based view and the knowledge-based view. Then we discuss insight of the dynamic capability approach into interor-

---

[379] See Wernerfelt (1984), p. 175, Teece (1992), pp. 8-9, and Ireland et al. (2002), p. 428.
[380] See Zahn et al. (2000), p. 51.
[381] See Tilebein (2005), p. 15.
[382] See Tilebein (2005), p. 16.
[383] See Morecroft et al. (2002).

ganizational learning. Finally, we confer about the relational view.[384] We mention the conclusions in regard to the dynamics of learning alliances in passing.

Competence-based View and Knowledge-based View

The competence-based view and the knowledge-based view can be interpreted as being developments of the resource-based view. At the same time both views combine the inside and outside perspectives of a firm.[385] According to the competence-based view, it is critical for firms' success that competences are not simply present but are properly employed to achieve and sustain competitive advantages. The employment may lead to performance differences between the firm and its competitors. Performance differences are explained by the existence of core competences.[386] The latter are protected from diffusion to competitors with isolation mechanisms.[387] This way competitive advantage might be sustained for a longer period. Unlike the resource-based view, that focuses on resources that a firm owns at a certain point in time, the competence-based view considers an integrated view of the time period from past to present to future. In other words, it recognizes path dependencies of competences as it considers firm history. Past actions may sometimes be crucial for today's decisions, as they shape the firm's future behavior.[388] From a competence-based perspective, firms may strengthen their competitive position and shape their markets while entering alliances.

Even though it is stated above that the knowledge-based view is a development of the resource-based view, this statement might hold for interpretations of the contents and range of applications of these views. KOGUT AND ZANDER, authors of the award-winning and core publication of the knowledge-based view, state that chronologically speaking, however, the knowledge-based view was originally developed parallel to the resource-based view.[389]

---

[384] We leave aside approaches like the flexible commitment approach. For flexible commitments see Ghemawat and del Sol (1998). For an overview of this topic see Tilebein (2005), p. 21.

[385] For the competence-based view, see Teece and Pisano (1994), p. 538, Teece et al. (1997), p. 515, Teece and Pisano (1998), p. 57, Freiling (2000), p. 28, and recently Freiling (2004), p. 7, who also provides an in-depth discussion on its contribution to the theory of the firm, and the existence, change, and decay of the firm. Lado, Boyd, and Wright offer a competency-based model of competitive advantage. See Lado et al. (1992). Lippman and Rumelt state that differences in competences could be sustained in equilibrium. In such a situation, firms cannot imitate each other or only with uncertainty. They call this uncertain imitability. See Lippman and Rumelt (1982), p. 421.

[386] See Prahalad and Hamel (1990) and Hamel and Prahalad (1994), pp. 197 and 202-211

[387] See Rumelt (1984), pp. 567-568.

[388] See Teece and Pisano (1994), pp. 546-547, Teece et al. (1997), pp. 522-523, and Teece and Pisano (1998), pp. 65-66. This way of considering links over time periods is equivalent and therefore comparable to the simple feedback loop structure of a decision making process depicted in Figure 2-1 of Section 2.2.1.

[389] Kogut and Zander point out in their 10-year retrospective of their article on the knowledge of the firm (see Kogut and Zander (1992) and Kogut and Zander (1993)), that the "knowledge-based view of the firm developed in parallel and largely independently of efforts in strategy" Kogut and Zander (2003), p. 510, and hence of the resource-based view. Their 1993 publication won the Journal of International Business Studies Decade Award. The authors state that their philosophical source is Ryle's publication on the concept of minds (see Ryle (1949)), not necessarily Polanyi (see Polanyi (1967)). For further discussion on the knowledge-based view as a theory of the firm see also Grant and Baden-Fuller (1995), Grant (1996), Conner and Prahalad (1996), Foss (1996b), and Foss (1996a). The 1996 Strategic Management Journal Winter Special Issue focuses on knowledge and

Knowledge can be conceived as a special resource or core-competence of firms. Firms create and transfer knowledge and build up knowledge stocks. According to the knowledge-based view, the individually and organizationally held knowledge of a firm acts as a basis for creating firm-level capabilities and innovations. They develop via the recombination and/or integration of knowledge inside the firm. The knowledge builds up through learning, while making associations between past actions, their effectiveness, and possible future actions (see Figure 3-1, which depicts this relationship in stock and flow representation).[390] That is why capabilities and consequently knowledge act as a source of competitive advantage.[391] Concluding, knowledge can be understood as the main driver for strategic renewal and therefore as a strategic asset.[392]

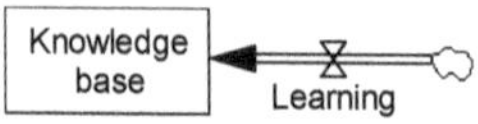

Figure 3-1: Knowledge base and learning in stock and flow representation.[393]

Along with the knowledge-based view, firms can be interpreted as organizations embodying different capabilities and skills.[394] Performance differences between firms thus result from those differences. For firms to overcome possible deficiencies they need to acquire knowledge. Yet, knowledge is an intangible resource that is path dependent and embedded in organizational routines[395], not easy to trade, and difficult to imitate. Therefore, transferring knowledge via the market may not be successful. If buying the whole firm that owns that embedded knowledge is not an option, alliances provide firms an opportunity to access the so far unavailable knowledge.[396] The motives that firms may follow in this situation are those described in Section 3.3.2. Moreover, we discuss further qualities and features of knowledge that may lead to various

the firm with contributions by Grant (1996), Liebeskind (1996), Mowery et al. (1996), Sanchez and Mahony (1996), Spender (1996), among others.
Some authors subsume insight from the knowledge-based view with insight from the learning theory under an approach of interorganizational learning (see Herbst (2002), pp. 24-33) or subsume insight from learning theory and interorganizational learning under one approach on its own (see Schwerk (2000), pp. 155-160). We do not follow either procedure here. We present the strategic perspective of the knowledge-based view here and learning and interorganizational learning in detail in Chapter 4.

390 See Fiol and Lyles (1985), p. 810, Nonaka (1994), p. 15, and Kale et al. (2002), p. 749.

391 See Kogut and Zander (1993), p. 631, Nonaka (1994), p. 33, and Kale et al. (2002), p. 749.

392 See Zahn (1998), p. 398.

393 Source: authors' representation following Brandt Husman, who states that the "knowledge stock is *the level of knowledge present in a firm at any point in time.*" Brandt Husman (2001), p. 4; italic representation in the original. Learning and unlearning represent knowledge flows into and out of knowledge, respectively. See Brandt Husman (2001), p. 4 quoting Dierickx and Cool (1989), p. 1506. Yet, the latter actually refer to the inflow into R&D-knowledge as R&D spending. See also Lyles (1988), p. 302, Bontis et al. (2002), p. 437, and Zahra and George (2002), p. 186.

394 See Kogut (1988b), p. 176.

395 Routines reflect the firm's consistency in behavior, patterns of interactions, and are embedded in the organization. See Nelson and Winter (1982), p. 14, Teece and Pisano (1994), p. 545, and Inkpen (1995), p. 51. Learning routines are thus regular patterns of interactions among people. The interactions permit the transfer, recombination, or creation of specialized knowledge. See Grant (1996), pp. 111-112 and Dyer and Nobeoka (2000), p. 347.

396 See, for instance, Kogut (1988b), p. 176 and Batt and Purchase (2004), p. 169.

firm behaviors in Chapter 4.6. In any case, owning and applying knowledge may lead to both monopoly and Ricardian rents.[397]

Dynamic Capabilities

The dynamic capability approach pays special attention to the mechanisms of acquiring and transferring knowledge. The approach is dynamic in the sense that it assumes that a firm can attain its competitive advantages in dynamic markets only because of its ability to continuously change.[398] Dynamic capabilities are the firm's idiosyncratic abilities and routines to accumulate, diffuse, and integrate internal and external capabilities, resources, and competences for continuous improvement of the firm's responsiveness toward the changing environment.[399] TEECE, PISANO, AND SHUEN emphasize that the heart of capabilities is embedded in organizational processes.[400] They are based on coordination, integration, reconfiguration, transformation, and learning.

Both specific processes of innovating and cooperating with a partner can be interpreted as a dynamic capability.[401] While they may increase the efficiency of current routines, they may also enable the firm to discover new process opportunities, hence facilitating organizational learning. Alliances can be understood as a means for organizational learning. Competences might be internalized from the partner and then developed to internal core competences, for example. Furthermore, firms may also develop an alliance capability. This particular process includes a formal system to capture experiences from each alliance. Experience enables the firm to manage multiple alliances, learn from past experiences and increase the efficiency of future collaboration processes.[402] Hence, learning as part of a coordinative management process also facilitates interorganizational learning.[403] In general, the outcomes of the processes are influenced by the current position of the firm in relation to its technological, reputational, and other assets as well as firm history with the paths the firm has taken and the experience it has gained so far.

---

397 See Liebeskind (1996), p. 94.

398 See Fiol (2001), pp. 693-694 and 695 and Barney et al. (2001), p. 630. Barney, Wright, and Ketchen emphasize that it is not possible for firms to sustain competitive advantages in dynamic markets. See also Section 3.2.

399 See Grant (1996), pp. 114-117 who talks about organizational capabilities, Teece et al. (1997), p. 516, Eisenhardt and Martin (2000), p. 1107, and to some extent Teece and Pisano (1994), p. 538 and Teece and Pisano (1998), p. 57. Kogut and Zander use the term combinative capabilities to explain a similar concept. See Kogut and Zander (1992), p. 384.

400 Unless otherwise indicated, for the following statement see Teece et al. (1997), pp. 518-524. For a thorough discussion of the determinants of dynamic capabilities and their dimensions see also Teece and Pisano (1994), pp. 541-549 and Teece and Pisano (1998), pp. 60-68. Zahra and George identify specific organizational capabilities influencing a firm's competitive position: acquisition, assimilation, transformation, and exploitation as determinants for a firm's absorptive capacity. According to the authors these capabilities are key dimensions of absorptive capacity which is needed for learning (see Zahra and George (2002), pp. 189-190). We discuss this in Section 4.6.

401 See Eisenhardt and Martin (2000), p. 1117.

402 See Khanna (1998), p. 351 and Anand and Khanna (2000), p. 298.

403 See Teece and Pisano (1994), p. 545, Teece et al. (1997), p. 520, Teece and Pisano (1998), p. 64 and Hagedoorn et al. (2000), p. 572. We discuss the aspects of organizational learning briefly in Section 4.2.

Dynamic capabilities might lead to new organizational and technical opportunities. Therefore, it can be stated that they create Schumpeterian or entrepreneurial rents.[404] However, although dynamic capabilities are rather idiosyncratic to a firm, they have considerable commonalities across firms. A lack of skill in adjusting the firm's dynamic capabilities to a rapidly changing environment may turn former core capabilities into core rigidities.[405] According to EISENHARDT AND MARTIN, dynamic capabilities violate the resource-based view postulation of lasting heterogeneity across firms in a rapidly changing environment.[406] To conclude, competitive advantage is not necessarily driven by dynamic capabilities but by resource-configuration.[407]

Relational View
The relational view refers to several aspects discussed above and integrates them with respect to interorganizational collaboration. While the unit of analysis of the resource-based view and its decedents is the individual firm, in the relational view it moves to the level of alliances. The relationship between firms is in the focus of this view. According to the relational view, competitive advantage may be achieved through idiosyncratic interfirm linkages. The assumption behind this view is "that a firm's critical resources may span firm boundaries and may be embedded in interfirm routines and processes."[408] Unless the relationship is idiosyncratic it can easily be imitated by competitors. In case of non-idiosyncratic relationships, the alliance would not be a vehicle for achieving competitive advantage. However, for the relationship to be idiosyncratic and a nucleus for competitive advantage, allied partners need to create resources that are particularly in conjunction with each other. DYER AND SINGH identify four potential sources. First, the partnering firms may combine, exchange, or invest in their relation-specific resources, capabilities, and knowledge. Also, they may install interfirm knowledge-sharing routines. Such regular patterns of interfirm interaction foster knowledge transfer, recombination, or creation of specific knowledge which may lead to innovations. Third, the partners may employ effective governance mechanisms to minimize transaction costs. This determinant, as indicated in Section 3.4.1 on transaction cost economics, is directed at the efficient design of third-party enforcements, for example, contracts, and self-enforcing informal safeguards like trust to overcome opportunism.[409] Again, as pointed out in Section 3.4.1, these means may also reduce opportunism.[410] Last, DYER AND SINGH point to an argument that we identify in Section 3.3 as one major motive for firms to enter alliances: the partners may combine their complementary partner-specific resources, knowledge, or capabilities. When firms consider these determinants and their mechanisms, they can

[404] See Teece et al. (1997), p. 527 and Lado et al. (1997), p. 119.
[405] See Leonard-Barton (1992), Teece and Pisano (1994), p. 547, Teece and Pisano (1998), p. 96, and also Benner and Tushman (2003), p. 242. See the first author for a comprehensive discussion on core capabilities and core rigidities.
[406] See Eisenhardt and Martin (2000), p. 1117.
[407] See Eisenhardt and Martin (2000), p. 1118.
[408] Dyer and Singh (1998), p. 661.
[409] Trust plays a key role in interfirm relationships. See Batt and Purchase (2004), p. 170. We discuss this topic in Sections 3.4.1 and 3.4.4.4, and in detail in Section 4.6.4.
[410] See Kogut (1988a), p. 321.

generate relational rents, understood as supernormal profits that cannot be generated by the partners alone, and achieve competitive advantage.[411]

Concluding, the relational view is insightful about the theoretical explanations for firms entering alliances. During the course of this work we will return to, reconsider, and re-examine DYER AND SINGH's propositions. Next we present the network approach that also deals with analyzing relationships between the partnering firms.

3.4.3 Network Approach

The network approach consists of various heterogeneous branches and is based on sociology and social psychology.[412] It incorporates aspects from transaction cost economics, systems theory, social exchange theory[413], and the resource dependence approach[414]. The network approach developed into a descriptive way of analyzing ties or relationships between actors, or from a business perspective, firms.[415] It builds "on the general notion that economic actions are influenced by the social context in which they are embedded and that actions can be influenced by the position of actors in social networks."[416] When applying the network approach to alliances, it explains the existence of alliances on the basis of partnering firms' positions within a network. It implies that a firm's strategic actions are influenced by the social context in which the actions and the organization are embedded.[417] Networks serve as information channels. They act as a two-way information source for the embedded companies.[418] First, relational embeddedness facilitates information from the firm's immediate connections with direct partners. Second, due to structural embeddedness – a firm's position in the network structure – the firm gains information about other network partners, the partners' partners. The information a firm can access is the network members' experiences about partnering with one or the other firm in the network and information about the quality of the collaboration skills of the members. This might be decisive for future partnerships, when the network can support a firm in identifying appropriate

[411] See Dyer and Singh (1998), pp. 662-663 and also our clarification in Section 3.4.2.1. Dyer and Sing explain each of the mentioned determinants in detail. See Dyer and Singh (1998), pp. 662-671.

[412] See Swoboda (2003), p. 55 and Granovetter (1992), pp. 28-29 for characteristics of sociology in economics. With reference to social psychology, we lay out insight from behavioral game theory in Section 3.4.4.4. It can be regarded as a branch of behavioral economics and extends homo-economicus based economics and includes considers insight from psychology. According to the social preference theory, social structures matter with their specific relations in which people are embedded when making decisions. See Camerer and Thaler (1995), p. 215.

[413] See Blau (1964) regarding social exchange theory. A social exchange is a situation in which the actions of one individual provide rewards or penalties for the actions of another individual and vice versa. Interaction might occur repeatedly. The other approaches the network approach incorporates are discussed thoroughly in this work.

[414] According to the resource dependence approach, firms enter interorganizational relationships to compensate dependence of external resources. Hence, one the one hand firms seek to keep their autonomy. On the other hand, they increase their influence on other organizations and their environment. See Sydow (1992), p. 197.

[415] See Schwerk (2000), p. 148 and Swoboda (2003), p. 55.

[416] Gulati (1998), p. 295.

[417] See Ireland et al. (2002), p. 427.

[418] See Granovetter (1985), p. 490, Granovetter (1992), pp. 34-37, and Gulati (1998), p. 296.

partners for collaborating.[419] Hence, network ties become very valuable resources for the firm.[420] Therefore, the theory stresses the importance of fostering existing and establishing new relationships between firms. It suggests that strong ties between firms would lead to increasing reciprocal trust and hence to efficient and successful partnerships.[421]

The next and last theoretical approach we present also concentrates on ties between the collaborating firms in which trust is not always ubiquitous. Game theory provides insight into how relationships may evolve over time, also considering trust and non-rational decision-makers.

3.4.4 Game Theory

As mentioned in the problem statement and continuously throughout the text, it is oftentimes competing firms who cooperate with each other.[422] The motivation is, among other things, pursuing joint research, as firms do not necessarily have access to the required resources on their own. In contrast to the above-mentioned approaches for explaining the evolvement of alliances, game theory analyzes and provides valuable insight into the competitive interactions between rival and simultaneously collaborating firms and how they find and pursue strategic actions that could be beneficial to them in interfirm alliances.[423] According to ZAHN AND FOSCHIANI, the approach can be categorized under the market-based view;[424] however, it considers a dynamic perspective as it examines actions and reactions of the partners involved. In the following we first describe the concept of coopetition. Then we present game characteristics and the Prisoner's Dilemma game that is often applied to a firm's decision about whether to cooperate. The Prisoner's Dilemma is based on analytical game theory, which assumes rational decision-making. Field studies have shown, however, that humans do not behave rationally: instead, they seek to behave fairly and altruistically. As this insight is of importance in the present research context, we discuss findings of behavioral game theory and apply these to interorganizational settings.

3.4.4.1 Coopetition

Cooperation between competing firms is called coopetition.[425] This term captures the dilemma in which firms are embedded: on the one hand they need to be more suc-

---

[419] See Gulati (1999), p. 400.
[420] See Håkansson (1987), p. 51.
[421] For comprehensive overviews on the network perspective see Gulati (1998), pp. 295-298, Håkansson et al. (1999), pp. 444-445, Schwerk (2000), pp. 148-155, Herbst (2002), pp. 55-57, and Swoboda (2003), pp. 55-56 and the literature cited there.
[422] See Hennart (1988), p. 361, Hamel et al. (1989), p. 133, Brandenburger and Nalebuff (1995), p. 58, and Nalebuff and Brandenburger (1997), p. 28.
[423] See, for instance, Lado et al. (1997), p. 115 and Teece et al. (1997), p. 511.
[424] See Zahn and Foschiani (2000), p. 499.
[425] See Nalebuff and Brandenburger (1997), p. 28.

cessful in the market than their competitors, pursuing promising strategies offering value-adding products and/or services created with superior resources. On the other hand, at the same time they might rely on their competitors as they share scarce resources which are crucial for market success. Referring to insight from game theory, BRANDENBURGER AND NALEBUFF illustrate the firm's position and its interrelations in the value net.[426] The value net depicts the market participants, such as customers, competitors, complementors, suppliers, the firm itself, and the intertwined linkages. The authors show that a single firm can take over more than one role in the value net simultaneously being another firm's substitutor, competitor, supplier and complementor on the same day, for example.[427]

LADO, BOYD, AND HANLON identify four different types of rent-seeking behavior that a firm may pursue in the tradeoff of cooperative and competitive firm behavior: competitive, monopolistic, collaborative, and syncretic rent-seeking behavior.[428] First, competitive rent-seeking behavior is characterized by high competition and low cooperation. It corresponds to the search for competitive advantage and superior performance on the basis of the two fundamental strategy perspectives discussed above, the market-based view and resource-based view.[429] The rents a firm may generate are therefore those described above, namely monopoly, Ricardian, quasi, or entrepreneurial rents – depending on the theoretical approach. The authors' criticism is that this perspective is too limited in three ways. First, it reduces firms' behavior to only counting on their gain being their competitor's loss, which is called a zero-sum game in game theory.[430] According to the authors, firms may not take into account that there are opportunities for positive-sum games in which both firms' benefits would increase while building barriers around their idiosyncratic resources or behaving opportunistically toward others.[431] Then, when pursuing competitive rent-seeking behavior, firms neglect their embeddedness in their social network, referring to the network approach discussed in Section 3.4.3. In addition, the rents generated may only be temporary if externalities exist. In this case, firms may tend to privatize possible benefits and communize costs incurred.

Second, when firms pursue monopolistic rent-seeking behavior, they follow a strategy that is characterized by both low competition and low cooperation. In this case, firms seek short-term monopoly rents. Nevertheless, this behavior is unfavorable for further corporate development as it may hinder innovativeness and generate core rigidi-

---

426 See Brandenburger and Nalebuff (1995), pp. 59-61, Brandenburger and Nalebuff (1996), pp. 16-19, Nalebuff and Brandenburger (1996), pp. 28-31, and Nalebuff and Brandenburger (1997), pp. 30-32.

427 See, for example, Hamel and Prahalad (1994), pp. 187-194 and Brandenburger and Nalebuff (1995), p. 60. The latter present the example of competing airlines, being simultaneously substitutors with respect to their customers, and complementors concerning the design of new planes by their suppliers, namely aircraft manufacturers like Boeing, Airbus, Embrear, Canadair, etc. Furthermore, if the airlines join an alliance or a code-sharing agreement they might be regarded as suppliers as they make free seats available to their partner airlines.

428 The following explanations refer to Lado et al. (1997), pp. 118-124 and the literature cited, unless otherwise indicated. See also Zahn and Foschiani (2000), pp. 505-508.

429 See Sections 3.4.2.2 (on market-based view) and 3.4.2.3 (on resource-based theory).

430 We discuss the characteristics of a game later in Section 3.4.4.1.

431 See Lado et al. (1997), p. 119.

ties.[432] This may lead to the firm's decay, especially if it is engaged in dynamic markets.

Third, when firms pursue collaborative rent-seeking behavior they pool their complementary resources. As indicated above, pooling complementary resources is a very common motive for firms to enter link alliances.[433] This coopetitive behavior is characterized by high cooperation and low competition in which firms may generate composite quasi rents. The name indicates that this quasi rent is generated by the firms' own resources that may only gain in strength when they are linked to idiosyncratic resources from others.[434] According to LADO, BOYD, AND HANLON, this behavior requires and fosters common interest, altruism, and reciprocity. It builds trust and may generate collaborative advantage; in contrast to advancing self-interest.[435] Nevertheless, stressing cooperative behavior may also be dangerous for naïve firms surrounded by egoistic firms displaying opportunistic behavior and focusing on taking advantage of others' trust, altruism and reciprocity, thus outlearning the partner in a learning alliance. Furthermore, cooperative rent-seeking behavior may also lead to strategic inflexibility, as reciprocal commitments or investments may increase the chance of ongoing continuity of the alliance even when the environment has changed in a way that would actually require alliance dissolution.

As the fourth type of rent-seeking behavior, syncretic rent-seeking behavior is characterized by high cooperation and high competition. According to the authors, this coopetitive behavior may improve a firm's strategic position by reducing costs and risks, stimulating joint learning and reciprocal knowledge transfer which may lead to innovations and hence to endogenous growth of the alliance.[436] Contrary to competitive rent-seeking behavior where the firms play zero-sum games, syncretic rent-seeking behavior permits positive-sum games in which the pie to be divided between the partnering firms may grow.[437] Firms engaging in this kind of coopetitive behavior increase their strategic flexibility and achieve competitive advantage via "leveraging their rare, valuable, and imperfectly imitable resources in competitive contexts."[438] Furthermore, they may achieve cooperative advantage by finding trustworthy partners inside their network and by pursuing strategies that lead to the attainment of common alliance goals. Drawbacks to syncretic rent-seeking behavior may be the increasing cost of maintaining this coopetitive strategy surpassing the possible benefits of the partnership. Also, it may be a hindrance if potential partners follow divergent interests and objectives with the alliance and have different expectations from the joint effort. Due to the characteristics laid out above, the alliance presented in the case study in section 2.4.3 can be regarded as syncretic rent-seeking.

---

432 For core rigidities see also the paragraph on dynamic capabilities in Section 3.4.2.4.
433 See Section 3.3.1.
434 See also Hill (1990), p. 500.
435 We discuss the effects of trust, altruism, and reciprocity on people's cooperative behavior in Section 3.4.4.4.
436 See Lado et al. (1997), p. 122 quoting Grossman and Helpman (1994), pp. 32-34.
437 See, for instance, Nielsen (1988), p. 477 and Sally (2003), p. 584.
438 Lado et al. (1997), p. 123.

Concluding, firms that have only limited resource access should look for maximum long-term benefits, and to achieve or maintain competitive advantage should either follow cooperative rent-seeking behavior or syncretic rent-seeking behavior. Yet, firms need to pay attention because, generally, as indicated above, when firms cooperate with competitors, the incentive to cheat emerges. This is because each partner finds it beneficial to increase its own gains at the expense of the joint alliance because it is acting out of self-interest.[439] This may lead to high alliance instability. In general, the reason for this is often illustrated with the help of game theory, and in particular with the Prisoner's Dilemma.[440] Before we describe and explain insight from the Prisoner's Dilemma into the development of alliances, we first introduce the fundamentals of game theory.

The definition of a game is unambiguous. A "game is simply the totality of the rules which describe it."[441] The rules of a game contain the number of players, the strategy[442] options that each player has with clearly defined rules about the order in which the players choose strategies (the moves), the information the players have available at the moment they choose their strategies, and how they rate the utility of resulting outcomes.[443]

Game theory provides insight into the understanding of interactions between the players of games, their respective strategies, and their outputs at the end of the game, if there are any.[444] Referring to business-related questions, game theory can be applied to study the relationship between firms – the players – and their strategies in oligopoly market settings in which the number of firms is large enough for each firm to expect what its competitors do.[445] This is of relevance when studying the dynamics of learning alliances as game theory permits the analysis of how interdependencies may evolve over time when two competing firms cooperate.

---

[439] See Hennart (1991), p. 486 and Parkhe (1993), p. 796. Höfer published her dissertation on strategic alliances and game theory. See Höfer (1997). Nevertheless, in her work she disregards insight from behavioral game theory. For insight from behavioral game theory see, for example, Camerer (1997) and Section 3.4.4.4.

[440] See Parkhe (1993), p. 796.

[441] von Neumann and Morgenstern (1953), p. 49.

[442] In game theory a strategy is understood as "an action plan developed by a player that uses all the information available and that prescribes a move at each stage of the game." Sally (2003), p. 584. See also Davis (1993), p. 18.

[443] See Sally (2003), p. 584 and Camerer (2003a), p. 2.

[444] See Ho and Weigelt (1997), p. 127, Child and Faulkner (1998), p. 26, and Sally (2003), p. 538. The seminal book by von Neumann and Morgenstern has established game theory as a field of research. See von Neumann and Morgenstern (1953), whose first edition was published in 1944. The scientists Nash, Harsanyi and Selten received The Bank of Sweden Prize in Economic Sciences in Memory of Alfred Nobel 1994 for their game theoretical contributions, or more specifically for their analysis of equilibria in the theory of non-cooperative games. For a historical outline of game theory, see Berninghaus et al. (2002), pp. 1-8 or Arrow (2003) and for differences in the conceptual basics of game theory past and present, see Selten (2001).

[445] See Camerer (2003a), p. 2.

3.4.4.2 Game Characteristics and the Prisoner's Dilemma

In the following, we briefly describe game characteristics. Generally, games can be played with at least two persons. Those are called two-person games.[446] Depending on the number of players playing a game they may increase to three-person games or n-person games.[447] Players can either play zero-sum or non-zero-sum games like positive-sum or negative-sum games. A zero-sum game implicates that one player's loss is the other's gain. In a positive-sum game, value is created and reflected in a win-win situation. In contrast, in negative-sum games value is destroyed. Furthermore, games may be played only once – single- or one-shot game – or repeatedly.[448] In a repeated game, the moves can happen simultaneously or sequentially.[449] The alliance in our case study can be interpreted as a repeated two-person positive-sum game: two companies are collaborating and interacting repeatedly while creating value.[450]

Usually, games can be represented in two different forms, the normal form and the extensive form.[451] The former describes a game situation with a minimum of formal concepts. It depicts the game as a matrix. Explicit information about the order of the moves or the players' knowledge about previous actions is excluded. This information is implicit in the players' strategies and payoffs. This missing information is made explicit when games are represented in extensive form.[452] Depending on the amount of information that should be available to the players we can distinguish between the following information deficits.[453] First, players may only have access to imperfect information. This is the case if a player only has partial information on the previous actions of the other players, for instance, a player has no evidence about whether or not the others have already made their moves. However, if a player holds this information, she has perfect information. Second, a player has incomplete information if she has less information about the decision situation than other players. A player may not be sure how many other players are involved in the game or may have less information about effects of decision options on the payoff than others, for example. Consequently, another player may have an information advantage over the first

---

[446] A player does not necessarily have to be a single person. If all players in a group agree upon a strategy they can be regarded as one player. See Davis (1993), p. 18.

[447] See von Neumann and Morgenstern (1953), pp. 85, 220, 283, and 330.

[448] See, for instance, Sally (2003), p. 584.

[449] See Jost (1998), pp. 14-15.

[450] See Dyer (1997), p. 544, who suggests that Toyota's interactions with its suppliers can be interpreted as repeated games. Multiple interactions among the players within one project can be interpreted as a repeated game. In addition, after one joint project is finished, new objectives become part of the relationship and the relationship might move on. This can also be interpreted as a repeated game.

[451] See, for example, Berninghaus et al. (2002), pp. 11, 89, Selten (2001), p. 4, or Sally (2003), p. 584. Additionally, the representational form of the characteristic functions exists. It is applied in representing cooperative games, as it captures mathematically possible arrangements between the players. See von Neumann and Morgenstern (1953), pp. 238-245. See Selten (2001), pp. 8-9, for a discussion on how to represent cooperative games.

[452] Prior to Selten's work it was generally accepted that both forms of representation are equivalent regarding the information content. Selten has shown that the extensive form provides additional information in the nature of strategic problems. See Selten (1965), Selten (1975), and Selten (1978).

[453] For the following points see Jost (1998), pp. 17-18.

player. The player has full information if she is informed about all relevant information that determines the dynamics of the game as well as the payoff.

If such information asymmetries exist, the better informed player may use this information advantage to her own benefit in case of lacking trust. So, unfulfilled expectations of the other player – assuming a two-person game – may lead to moral hazard or adverse selection.[454] Moral hazard refers to the inability of players to behave responsibly and to take appropriate risk-mitigating actions.[455] Adverse selection refers to the failure of players to differentiate between risks and the unwillingness of high-risk players to frankly reveal their actual risk condition.[456]

The last fundamental to mention is the players' utilities and utility functions.[457] A utility function is the quantification of a person's preferences toward certain objects. The utility function assigns each object a number and describes which object is the most desired, indicated by the highest number. This procedure requires certain conditions that are not discussed further here.[458] Referring to utilities in alliances, a firm may have a higher utility from exploiting the alliance partner short-term than from long-term exploration with the partner. This dilemma is also highlighted by the Prisoner's Dilemma, that we discuss in the following paragraph.

The Prisoner's Dilemma has not only been widely discussed in the literature in general, but also in the field of alliances to explain alliance failure or partner opportunism in particular.[459] It shows how competitive rivalry emerges within an alliance originally designed for collaboration. In the Prisoner's Dilemma, players are not allowed to

---

454 See Williamson (1975), pp. 14-15, Parkhe (1993), p. 805, or Jost (1998), pp. 18-19.

455 One alliance partner cannot directly observe its partner, for instance. As the project results of the latter are also affected by general conditions, the incentive increases to reduce its efforts in regard to contributing to achieve joint objectives. The partner could explain the lower performance by referring to the 'unfavorable general conditions' while pretending to have worked hard.

456 A firm is interested in entering a strategic alliance with unlimited time horizon, for example. When scanning potential partners, it is not aware of these partners' intentions regarding whether they are only interested in short-term exploitation of the firm. As a result, it may happen that the firm may only choose partners whose interests are adverse to its own.

457 Von Neumann and Morgenstern show that utilities may not only be ordinal but also cardinal. See von Neumann and Morgenstern (1953), pp. 15-31 and also Davis (1993), pp. 66-74 and Selten (2001), pp. 2-3 for a discussion.

458 See Davis (1993), pp. 67-69 for further discussion.

459 The Prisoner's Dilemma was invented by Flood in 1950 and was further formalized by Tucker. Its cover story originally goes back to two criminals caught by police. The evidence is not enough to put them in prison. Nevertheless, the circumstantial evidence indicates that both were involved in the crime. If they both deny it (hence, cooperate), they cannot be blamed for the crime, hence are free or charged with a minor crime like illegal possession of weapons. If one turns State's evidence (defects), she will be free and the other sentenced to prison as she still denies it (cooperates). If they both confess (defect), they both go to prison. It is assumed that they are not allowed to communicate with each other. See, for instance, Axelrod (1984), pp. 7-9, Parkhe (1993), pp. 796-797, Simon (1994), pp. 33-34, Sally (1995), pp. 58-60, or Hofstadter (1998), p. 60 for introductions. For its application in alliance research, see Parkhe (1993), p. 796, Gulati et al. (1994), pp. 61-64, Ho and Weigelt (1997), pp. 129-131, Child and Faulkner (1998), pp. 26-31, Larsson et al. (1998), p. 286, Ho Park and Ungson (2001), pp. 42-43, Lubatkin et al. (2001), p. 1358, Zeng and Hennart (2002), pp. 198-205, Zhang and Rajagopalan (2002), pp. 460-464, or Arend and Seale (2005). Sen even states that the "particular game has certainly been overdiscussed". Sen (1985), p. 342 and see similarly Fang et al. (2002), p. 451.

communicate and have to choose their moves simultaneously.[460] Also, the players are knowledgeable about both players' goals, values, knowledge, and payoff structures.[461] This mutual knowledge requires that they also know that both have that knowledge about each other. This goes along with complete and perfect information. The payoff matrix is shown in Figure 3-2. The first number in each box is the payoff to firm i, the second to firm j. If firm i chooses to cooperate and j to defect, or, in other words, to take advantage of the situation and act opportunistically, and starts a learning race, for example, firm i gets a payoff of -$1 and firm j $101.

		Firm j	
		Cooperate	Defect
Firm i	Cooperate	$ 100, $ 100	- $ 1, $ 101
	Defect	$ 101, - $ 1	$ 0, $ 0*

Figure 3-2: Payoff matrix of the Prisoner's Dilemma.[462]

A rational player reaches her maximum utility level when following a non-cooperative strategy, hence defecting, no matter whether the other player chooses to cooperate or to defect. This leads to the defection of both players being the unique Nash equilibrium.[463] It is marked with an asterisk (*). Nevertheless, mutual cooperation – the Pareto-optimal solution – would make both better off.[464] Even finitely repeating the Prisoner's Dilemma would not change the situation: again, the only Nash equilibrium is to defect in each round. This is because in the last round (n) each firm, or player, has a dominant strategy, which is to defect. Though both firms might imagine a cooperative affiliation during the whole game, one firm would see the opportunity to increase its payoff in the last round n by defecting. Due to the rationality assumption of both firms, mutual defection happens in round n. Therefore, the firms also apply this strategy in round n-1, in which they consequently also defect. Mutual cooperation then only lasts until round n-2; this procedure continues until the first round.[465] This procedure is called backward induction and is defined as the "ability to analyze a strategic situation, anticipate where it is going, and then make decisions today that will favorably affect future payoffs."[466]

Even though it is just simple mathematics, backward induction is "unnatural and difficult"[467] in real life, where people do not act rationally. Experiments with participants in

[460] Fehr and Schmidt examine differences between a Prisoner's Dilemma played simultaneously and one played sequentially. See Fehr and Schmidt (1999), pp. 842-843.
[461] See Sen (1985), p. 343.
[462] Source: following Margolis (1982), p. 18.
[463] See Fehr and Schmidt (1999), p. 842. The Nash equilibrium is a stable combination of the players' strategies in which each player's strategy is the best choice to the other players' strategies. See Sally (2003), p. 584.
[464] See, for instance, Zeng and Chen (2003), p. 199, Camerer (2003c), p. 1673, Camerer (2003a), p. 45, or Langerfeldt (2003), p. 225.
[465] See Margolis (1982), p. 18, Sen (1985), p. 344, Colman (2003), p. 148, and Sally (2003), p. 585.
[466] Ho and Weigelt (1997), p. 135.
[467] Camerer (1997), p. 181.

games like sequential bargaining have shown that "people do not think as strategically as most game theory applications presume."[468] The result is similar when playing the Prisoner's Dilemma with people in experiments. Here, even in a one-shot game, about half the time people trust each other and follow the cooperation strategy – contradicting analytical game theoretic predictions.[469] Referring to alliances, both firms can make the most of the alliance when trusting each other and cooperating. AXELROD was interested in analyzing which policy is the most successful in terms of generating maximum payoff in a Prisoner's Dilemma repeatedly played. He invited scientists from all over the world to participate in his research. The tournament winning policy – after two rounds and publishing the results of the first round – was tit-for-tat, submitted by RAPOPORT.[470] It starts with a cooperative choice, and from then on just does what the counterpart did on the previous move. So, a trusting, cooperative, and forgiving policy is the most successful.[471]

Mutual trust is critical for a good relationship and the resulting alliance dynamics.[472] As experiments to capture trust are the focus of behavioral game theory, we discuss the aspects and implications of this approach in more detail in the following.

3.4.4.3 Analytical and Behavioral Game Theory

Analytical, or classical, game theory can be seen as an area of applied mathematics. It assumes that people have full knowledge about each other, have stable, well-defined preferences and make highly rational choices which maximize their own utility.[473] Nevertheless, when actually playing the game, people show different behavior

---

468 Johnson et al. (2002), p. 40. In the two-person sequential bargaining game, player 1 offers player 2 a share of a monetary pie of, e.g. $5. If player 2 accepts, the split is done and the game ends. If player 2 rejects, the pie shrinks in size to, e.g., $2.5 in the second period. Player 2 then offers a share of the shrunken pie to player 1. The game ends if player 1 accepts. If player 1 rejects, the game continues with a pie of $1.25 in the third round, in which player 1 again makes an offer. If player 1's offer is rejected, the game ends and none of the players receives anything. This game is used for analyzing people's capability to do backward induction as the optimal offer can be calculated by working back from the last period: Assuming rational players, in the last step, player 1 would only offer a small slice, epsilon, to player 2 who will accept, as epsilon is more than nothing. Knowing this, player 2 would already offer player 1 a slice equivalent to the smallest pie plus epsilon and keep the rest – or player 1 would reject. Player 1, being aware of that while splitting the first pie, offers player 2 a slice equal to the size of the second pie less the third plus epsilon. Rational player 2 accepts this offer, which would be equal to $1.26. Experiments show that participants offer between $1.25, which is the equilibrium, and $2.50 which is half the first pie with an average offer of $2.00. Offers around the equilibrium are frequently rejected. Hence, people have difficulty applying backward induction. Camerer points out that people do offer around $1.25 after having been briefly trained in backward induction. See Camerer (1997), p. 181 and Johnson et al. (2002), pp. 17-18. However, studies with autistic adults show that they "offer less and accept very little, which suggests, ironically, that rational game theory only works in ultimatum games when deficits in 'mind reading' ... lead to extremely uneven offers." See Camerer (2003c), p. 1674.

469 See Camerer (2003c), p. 1673 and Camerer (2003b), pp. 227-228.

470 See Axelrod (1984), p. 31. Fourteen submissions from five scientific disciplines joined the tournament.

471 See Axelrod (1984), p. 112.

472 See, for example, Batt and Purchase (2004), p. 170.

473 See Thaler (1988), p. 195, Camerer (1997), p. 167, Camerer (1999), p. 10575, Fang et al. (2002), p. 463, Camerer (2003c), p. 1673. These assumptions are also the reasons why analytical game theory is often applied for studies in economics – just as they are the reasons why analytical game

from what the theory suggests. It seems as if human "behavior is at least 'intendedly' rational,"[474] but only limitedly so which could be why "people ... are .. not smart enough to satisfy in everyday decisions."[475] Behavioral game theorists, by contrast, aim at describing people's actual behavior.[476] They capture people's actual beliefs, desires, intentions, and computational capabilities by adding "emotions, mistakes, limited foresight, doubts about how smart others are, and learning to analytical game theory."[477] They do so by learning from scholars conducting field studies or doing experiments in laboratory conditions.[478] This makes behavioral game theory a branch of behavioral economics. Behavioral economics is the generic term for various streams of research which questions homo economicus-based economics and include psychological insight. In other words, behavioral economics combines the mathematical structures of economics with insight from psychology to weaken rationality assumptions and to advance economic theory.[479] By including facets from behavioral game theory experiments into our System Dynamics model on interfirm collaboration, we model people's actual behavior in addition to designing a mathematically correct model.[480] Even though most experimental games are two-person games, we can transfer insight onto the level of interfirm alliances – as people interact in firms, too, only on a different level.

3.4.4.4 Aspects of Behavioral Game Theory

In this section, we discuss how observations on people's actual interaction in games address principles from analytical game theory. We restrict ourselves to rationality, utility, and self-interest, dealing with the last two items together.

Analytical game theory suggests rational players have mutual common knowledge of the game and of each other's rationality. This assumption makes the Nash equilibrium the only solution to a game; a solution which is known to be the "best action

theory is not often applied to fields outside economic theory. See Camerer (2003a), p. 3. For a recent summary and discussion of complaints about rational game theory see Colman (2003) and the proceeding comments by research fellows on the same issue.

474 Simon (1955), p. 114 and also Simon (1957), pp. 196, 203.

475 Camerer (1997), p. 167.

476 See Camerer (2003a), p. 3.

477 Camerer (2003a), p. 3.

478 An example of a field study is Camerer, Babcock, Loewenstein, and Thaler's study on New York City's cabdrivers' working behavior. The cabdrivers quit working early on good days with high earnings per hour and quit late on bad days – instead of working longer on good days and quitting early on days when earnings were low. This is an example of people's bounded mental accounting contradicting life-cycle models of labor supply, which assume a positive relationship between hours supplied and transitory wage changes. See Camerer et al. (1997) and Mullainathan and Thaler (2001), pp. 1094-1100. An example of a laboratory experiment is the bargaining game which we discuss in footnotes 468 and 493.

479 Camerer points out that this combination is similar to physics providing information to chemistry or archaeology informing anthropology. See Camerer (1999), p. 10575. First publications on behavioral economics were written by Simon, later a Nobel laureate in economics. See Simon (1955) and Simon (1957). Behavioral economics is often applied in the settings of finance and savings. For recent summaries on behavioral economics see Camerer (1999) and Mullainathan and Thaler (2001).

480 See van Damme (1999), p. 204.

available to the player which is consistent with his or her knowledge that the other players are acting .. rational in the same knowledge that other players are .. rational."[481] As indicated in the previous section and as is widely acknowledged,[482] people are more bounded rational than rational. A good measure of the degree of a player's rationality is iterated dominance.[483] This can be illustrated with the beauty-contest game,[484] in which N players choose numbers between, e.g., 0 and 100. The prize goes to the player whose number is closest to, for example, 70% of the average. Rational game theory predicts that players will choose the Nash equilibrium of zero by continuing to iterate.[485] In experiments, however, numerous players choose 70% of 50 – which lies in the middle between 0 and 100 – so, 35. Then they have done one step of iterated thinking. Some players continue iterating another step and choose a number around 25, which is 70% of 35. Few think that the average will choose 35. Consequently, they iterate once more and choose 70% of 25, which is around 18. They would have done three steps of iteration. This requires people to believe that other players concentrate and the latter think that everybody also thinks hard. Experiments show that most players untrained in game theory do one or two steps of iterated dominance and choose numbers between 21 and 40. In other words, the majority guesses that other players will choose numbers around 50 and they then choose 35, or that others will choose 35 and so they choose 25. When playing the beauty contest game repeatedly, experienced players do better after the first rounds and approach equilibrium faster.[486] As from backward induction, scholars infer from the results on iterated dominance that people have limited cognition which can be manifested in people having difficulty with strategic reasoning and foresight. LEVINTHAL AND MARCH, linking it to knowledge management, stress that managers would prefer to focus on short-term exploitation such as opportunism because of limited foresight. The authors call this phenomenon temporal myopia.[487] Referring to learning alliances, this would explain why managers would prefer to exploit the partner if this benefits the firm in the short-term.

Moreover, CONNER AND PRAHALAD conclude from bounded rationality that two individuals cannot possess identical stocks of knowledge.[488] Hence, for designing our System Dynamics model of interorganizational learning and transferring insight to the interfirm level, we conclude that two firms' knowledge stocks can be drawn as two accumulations, as depicted in Figure 3-3. Finally, insight from behavioral game theory supports what was discussed in Section 2.2.2 in which we state that mental models are fuzzy, incomplete, and imprecisely designed. So, seen on a more abstract

---

481 Hagreaves Heap (1993), p. 76.
482 See Chiles and McMackin (1996), p. 89.
483 See Ho et al. (1998), p. 967 and Camerer (2003a), p. 16.
484 See, for example, Ho et al. (1998), pp. 947-948, Camerer (2003c), and Camerer (2003a), pp. 16, 200, and 209-218. The beauty contest game goes back to Keynes, who drew analogies between the stock market and a newspaper competition in which people estimate what faces other people will guess are most beautiful. See Keynes (1936), pp. 155-156. It is a one-shot game.
485 The unique Nash equilibrium is zero as rational players do not stop iterating until they reach a best-response point. This is zero as all players seek to choose 70% of the average.
486 See Ho et al. (1998), p. 959.
487 See Levinthal and March (1993), pp. 101-103. See Williamson (1975), pp. 254-255 and also Berninghaus et al. (2002), p. 271 and Miller (2002), p. 693.
488 See Conner and Prahalad (1996), p. 482.

level, from a psychological perspective limited cognition is the reason why people design models of reality.[489]

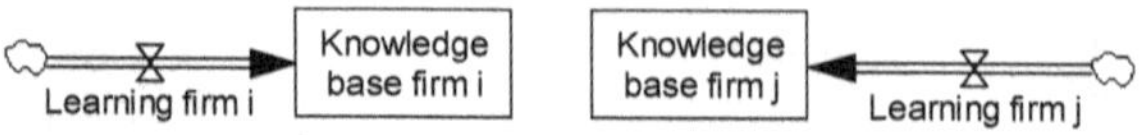

Figure 3-3: Knowledge stocks by firms i and j.[490]

Analytical game theory also assumes that players are self-interested and maximize their own payoffs, which is called utility maximization. Maximizing your own payoff in the Prisoner's Dilemma leads to mutual defection and to lower collective payoff than mutual cooperation. Experiments with playing the ultimatum game clearly falsify this assumption.[491] In this two-person game, a proposer makes a take-it-or-leave-it offer by offering an anonymous responder a certain amount of money x, for example $10. If the responder rejects the amount, nobody receives anything. If the responder accepts it, both receive the amount of money suggested by the proposer. Assuming rational behavior on the part of both players, the proposer should offer the smallest amount possible, such as $0.25, for example. This subgame perfect equilibrium leaves him $10 - $0.25 = $9.75 which the responder should accept as $0.25 is more than nothing. Theoretically, the proposer has all the bargaining power and can exploit the responder. Practically, this rational distribution of the amount is considered unfair. Players express their concern for fairness by offering a costly average between 40% and 50% with a means of 30-40%. More rational offers of 20% or less are rejected by the responders about half the time. They feel that less than half is unfair, although they end up having nothing.[492] Proposers actually act as profit maximizers when offering around half of the initial amount as they understand that unfair offers are rejected by the responders.[493]

---

489 See Amann (1999), p. 32 and Simon (1957), p. 199.

490 Source: authors' representation.

491 See Camerer (2003a), p. 43. For explanations and results of the ultimatum game in experimental settings see, for instance, Güth et al. (1982), Thaler (1988), Camerer and Thaler (1995), Johnson et al. (2002), Camerer (2003a), pp. 8-12 and 43-83, Carpenter (2003), and Gintis et al. (2003), pp. 157-159.

492 Offers of hyper-fair 50-100% are rare, as are offers of 0-10%. See Camerer (2003a), pp. 9, 49.

493 See Camerer and Thaler (1995), p. 214. Camerer provides a summary of recent results from ultimatum games in which scholars analyzed the influence of demographic variables on accepted and rejected offers. Generally, demographic variables like race, gender, academic background, testosterone, and beauty have mixed or mild effects. Yet, the effect of age is present: young children tend to be more self-interested and become fair-minded when growing older. This is critical in so far as it suggests that fairness is not innate but develops over time. See Camerer (2003a), p. 68. Also, results are independent of stake size in different countries. The ultimatum game has been played in Indonesia, the Slovak Republic, and Florida with amounts ranging from $10 to $400 to the equivalent of one month's wages. See Camerer (2003a), pp. 60-62. The ultimatum game has also been played with foraging groups, slash-and-burn horticulturists, nomadic herding groups, and sedentary, small-scale agricultural societies in Africa, South-America, and Asia. For those results see Henrich et al. (2001), pp. 74-76. Camerer reports on a discussion at a conference with fellow game theorists about a yet likely half split of a hypothetical stake of $1 million. See Camerer (2003a), p. 61.

Scholars interpret ultimatum game results as people having a feel for fairness – understood as an approximately divided surplus.[494] On the one hand, proposers think strategically when doing one step of backward induction. This means that they are aware of the fact that responders may sacrifice a certain amount of money to punish proposers if they make an unfair offer.[495] On the other hand, proposers also care about the well-being of others, which can be interpreted as simple altruism:[496] experiments with the dictator game in which the first player dictates how much of the stake the second player has to take, show that the majority of players do have a feel for fairness as three-quarters choose equal splits.[497] Scholars employ the social preference theory to explain this behavior. It seems as if people are constrained in their decisions by their responsiveness or commitment to their fellow human beings. Offers fluctuate around a social equilibrium in which players make offers knowing that the responders would reject anything that appears unfair. So, people's social preferences determine their actions.[498] Social preference also shows when the Prisoner's Dilemma is played with people in experiments. CAMERER remarks that "players seem unexpectedly skillful at avoiding the dilemma and finding their way to cooperation."[499] When playing it with small stakes, cooperation is a fairness equilibrium. It includes sacrificing a certain amount to reward the other player for cooperating and helping her to gain more. The players also state that they expect the other player to reciprocate cooperation.[500] Reciprocity and underlying social preference are significant: when people play the dictator game anonymously, with double-blind procedures, or with computers, mean offers drop considerably.[501] This means that the social structure with its specific relations in which people are embedded matters when making decisions. Social embeddedness, trust, and altruism foster the development of social relations and underlying trust.[502] BERG, DICKHAUT, AND MCCABE argue that next to reciprocity, trust influences human decision-making.[503] This may also be a reason why players decide to cooperate in multiperiod Prisoner's Dilemma games in experiments.

---

494 For the definition of fairness see Frank (2002), p. 165. In an article published in The New Yorker the author states that experiments have shown that even brown capuchin monkeys seem to have a sense of fairness. In the experiment, monkeys exchange cucumber slices for pebbles. Other monkeys stopped trading 80% of the time if one monkey in the group was given a grape for nothing in exchange. The conclusion is that monkeys want things to be distributed fairly. See Surowiecki (2003), p. 50.

495 See Fehr and Schmidt (2001), p. 6, Camerer (2003a), p. 56, and Fichman (2003), p. 137. Using backward induction, proposers might increase their offer if they feel that their offer might be interpreted as unfair by the responders.

496 See Margolis (1982), pp. 11, 15, Rabin (1993), p. 1281, and Fichman (2003), p. 136.

497 See Thaler (1988), p. 198 and Camerer (2003a), p. 56.

498 See Mumby and Putnam (1992), p. 474, Johnson et al. (2002), p. 20, and Crawford (2002), p. 5. Social preference implies positive altruism and negative envy. See Camerer and Thaler (1995), p. 215. Camerer evaluates different theories on their appropriateness to enhance the current prevailing theory of homo economicus on utility functions like altruism theories, inequality-aversion theories, and reciprocal approaches. He comes to the conclusion that reciprocal theories in which "players make a judgment about whether another player's action is kind or mean ... and have a taste for reciprocating both kindness and meanness with the same" (Camerer (2003a), p. 113) mostly fit the data collected by studies on fairness.

499 Camerer (1997), p. 170. See also Camerer and Thaler (1995), p. 215.

500 See Camerer (2003b), p. 227.

501 See, for example, Berg et al. (1995), pp. 127-129, Camerer and Thaler (1995), pp. 213-214, Johnson et al. (2002), p. 40, or Camerer (2003a), pp. 62-63.

502 See Granovetter (1985), pp. 487, 491 and Fichman (2003), p. 136.

503 See Berg et al. (1995), p. 138.

Generally, trust emerges over time from social exchanges in which people receive benefits from others and then pay back the favor later.[504] When playing tit-for-tat, altruism and reciprocity allows people who behave fairly and cooperate also to punish the other player by defecting after the other has defected.

Referring to alliances, insight from behavioral game theory can be applied to the following elements. First, insight from the bargaining game can be of interest for analyzing the bargaining over alliance objectives. When bargaining sequentially, firms learn how to propose well-intended and fair offers that are a profound basis for continued collaboration.

Second, the quality of the interaction between the partners is characterized by the firms' social relations, in which trust, reciprocity, and altruism play a certain role. Rational behavior and pure self-interest is not ubiquitous. This would imply that trusting partners would make generous mutual expenditures, and would share or transfer resources like knowledge with the collaborating partner. This way they would demonstrate their commitment toward each other, which is likely to reinforce trust and reciprocity between them – securing a good reputation in the community or network in which the firm is embedded.[505] However, when trust emerges over time it also gives the opportunity for the trustee to take advantage of the trustor.[506] In the case of interorganizational learning, this may lead to outlearning the partner firm who openly shares its knowledge. Hence, the racing partner gives up the long-lasting and difficult investment of trust-building which might result in loss of its own reputation. This might lead to a reduced ability to find future partners within the network because other firms may try to avoid entering an alliance with a firm with a questionable or unreliable reputation.[507] We discuss implications of trust and trustworthiness for alliance members' learnings in detail in Section 4.6.4.

Summarizing, insight from behavioral game theory encompasses that a concern for both the payoff and the behavior of other people exists. System Dynamics models may capture self-interest and social behavior. According to MORECROFT, such bounded rationality is implicit in System Dynamics models:[508] the way policies are formulated depends on the policy-designer's rationality and perception of the real world.[509] If the perception is determined by bounded rationality, policies reflect it.

---

[504] See Das and Teng (2002), p. 449.

[505] See, for example, Grossman and Shapiro (1986), p. 581, Grossman and Shapiro (1987), p. 379, Gulati et al. (1994), p. 68, Khanna et al. (1998), p. 193, Lane and Lubatkin (1998), p. 470, Apelt (1999), p. 12, Ho Park and Ungson (2001), pp. 49-50, Ireland et al. (2002), p. 438. Nevertheless, due to bounded rationality, firms often do not know what level of investment will be optimal. See Dyer (1997), p. 549.

[506] See Fichman (2003), p. 140.

[507] See Parkhe (1993), p. 802, Nooteboom (1996), p. 989, Dyer (1997), p. 550, Child (1998), p. 250, and Zeng and Hennart (2002), pp. 194-195. Firms are interested in collaborating with a partner with a good reputation as this reduces the costs of finding an appropriate partner firm – hence, reducing transaction costs. See Chiles and McMackin (1996), p. 88.

[508] See Morecroft (1983), p. 140. In his analysis of a simple sales organization Morecroft shows how intendedly but boundedly rational subprocesses can yield dysfunctional outcomes at the macro system level. See Morecroft (1985).

[509] See Sterman (2000), p. 517 and Größler (2004), p. 322

Thus, the System Dynamics model designed in the following chapters includes components of both self-interest and social preference.

3.4.5 Summary of Theoretical Approaches to Explain Competitive Advantage with Alliances

As no single theory exists that entirely explains how to achieve competitive advantage with alliances, we introduced and discussed insight from a wide range of theoretical approaches to the existence and the development of alliances. In this section we briefly summarize the insight from the different approaches we introduced.

We started this section with understandings from organizational economics. First, we discussed the transaction cost economics in detail. Although it is one of the static approaches and only considers one-shot transactions, it delivers valuable insight regarding the risk of opportunistic behavior of one parent exploiting its alliance partner. Yet, the approach provides control mechanisms like safeguards to overcome the risk of being cheated on. We discuss these control mechanisms in more detail in Section 4.6.3.

From agency theory we learned that alliance partners may be confronted with asymmetric information distribution. A partner may enter an alliance with hidden characteristics, hidden information, or hidden intentions, for instance. A hidden intention would be a partner having actual alliance goals that are different from those that the partners agreed on in the alliance contract.

Subsequently, we showed that property rights theory focuses on analyzing consequences of partner behavior in alliances assigning rights to specific resources such as knowledge. This theory is of special interest during the alliance negotiation phase in which the partners design the alliance contract.

Next we introduced the strategy-based approaches. After first defining the concept of rent-seeking behavior we then presented the static market-based view. The insight behind this approach lies in the positioning of firms and their prospective alliance(s) in the market place. In other words, to achieve or maintain competitive advantage it may be useful if not necessary for a firm to enter alliances from this perspective.

Then we focused on the static resource-based theory and its dynamic descendents. From a resource-based perspective, resources might lead to competitive advantage if they meet four criteria for being strategically valuable. If firms have resource constraints, they might be able to overcome these by entering alliances. Nevertheless, keeping in mind findings from transaction cost economics, the partner firm may try to take advantage of this situation and behave opportunistically to strengthen its own resource position. Knowledge may be seen as a strategically valuable resource. This is stated explicitly in the knowledge-based view that we presented subsequently.

Furthermore, from a dynamic capability perspective, firms need to have dynamic capabilities in order to perform organizational or interorganizational learning and to manage alliances in rapidly changing environments successfully.

As the last approach from a strategy-base perspective, we introduced the relational view. It combines findings from the above-mentioned approaches. According to this approach, competitive advantage may be achieved via idiosyncratic interfirm linkages. This can be achieved by combining firms' relation-specific resources, which fosters learning and innovations. Furthermore, the partners learn about installing governance mechanisms like the safeguards discussed in transaction cost economics to reduce opportunism. Last, the firms may combine their resources to overcome resource constraints – as suggested by the resource-based view.

Next, we introduced the network approach. It suggests that firms are embedded in a network of firms. Their reputation within this network is determined by the firms' behavior in alliances. This might be decisive information for another firm to enter alliances with a particular firm. According to this approach, strong ties between firms might increase reciprocal trust and may lead to efficient and successful collaborations.

Last but not least, we presented insight into alliances from game theory. Here, we first discussed the common cooperation between competitors. From a game theoretical perspective, both cooperative and defective behaviors in coopetitive settings can be explained – as is shown by the Prisoner's Dilemma. The idea of the Prisoner's Dilemma is based on analytical game theory which assumes rational behavior according to the homo economicus. Experiments, however, have shown that people do not behave rationally but try to act fairly and reciprocate fair behavior. This is further illustrated with experiments with other games. Insight from these games established behavioral game theory. Behavioral game theory stresses people's concern for the payoff – which is the assumption of analytical game theory – and the behavior of other people. Perceived fairness and reciprocity are drivers for mutual trust, leading to a successful alliance.

These findings are the basis for further explanation and discussion of the dynamics of interorganizational learning in alliances. In the following chapter we confer about the factors determining long-term development of such alliances.

4. Factors Determining the Long-term Development of Interorganizational Learning in Learning Alliances

4.1 Overview

Factors influencing the long-term development of interorganizational learning in interfirm collaborations are the focus of this chapter. It is split up into two major segments. In the first part of this chapter we discuss knowledge and learning in more detail than in Section 3.4.2.4, where we introduced the knowledge-based view. We then concentrate on what scholars identify as causes of alliance failure in general and of learning alliances in particular. Frequently, scholars identify the coopetitive dilemma in which firms are embedded as a reason for failure. Closely linked to the coopetitive dilemma is the concept of relative scope with common and private benefits.[510] On the basis of the two types of benefits, we explain different windows of competitive and thus opportunistic behavior that open up for managers in cooperative settings. Depending on their prospective benefits, for example, firms may apply different ways of learning in alliances, like learning with the partner or from the partner. Learning with the partner indicates cooperative behavior, whereas learning from the partner may be a motivation for competitive behavior. Among other things, these opportunities serve as simulation inputs for the policies discussed in Chapter 6. Moreover, we show how the outcome of a learning or R&D alliance, e.g. measured in patents, may be distributed between the parent companies.

In the second segment we focus on factors influencing learning in such R&D alliances. However, we cannot include all variables identified in the literature which apparently determine alliance dynamics. As explained in Section 2.3, we have to make abstractions for building a simulation model to understand better the dynamics that may evolve in learning alliances. Abstractions include simplifications of the system structure. We have to draw a model boundary to ensure that the model is not as complex as reality. Only this way can we double-loop learn from the model and design effective policies for real world learning alliances.[511] To do so we build a consistent model based on findings from the literature and the case study. In the upcoming sections we present and explain key factors that influence alliance behavior such as common and private learning, scientist allocation, managers' and scientists' trust, or scientists' openness, for example. We argue both generally and specifically, where appropriate. We introduce parts of the simulation model when suitable. We lay the foundations for possible policies that provide us with learning about learning alliances on a meta-level. Throughout this chapter we refer to findings from our case study. We use this insight to support formulation of the model simulation.

4.2 Organizational and Interorganizational Learning

The field of research on interorganizational learning is fairly young compared to those of organizational and individual learning. As they are, however, closely linked, it is

---

[510] See Khanna (1998), p. 340 and Khanna et al. (1998), pp. 194-195.

[511] For double-loop learning see the discourse in Section 2.3.1 and for policy design for complex systems see Section 2.3.6.

helpful to discuss the characteristics of organizational and individual learning to explain interorganizational learning.[512] Although much has been written on organizational learning, no single definition exists.[513] Most scholars distinguish between organizational and individual learning, stating that organizational learning cannot take place without learning between the individuals which an organization consists of.[514] Organizations are not able to store knowledge in the same way as individuals. They store knowledge in organizational routines, practices, and cultures. HEDBERG points out that "[a]lthough organizational learning occurs through individuals, it would be a mistake to conclude that organizational learning is nothing but the cumulative result of their members' learning. Organizations do not have brains, but they have cognitive systems and memories. As individuals develop their personalities, personal habits, and beliefs over time, organizations develop world views and ideologies. Members come and go, and leadership changes, but organizations' memories preserve certain behaviors, mental maps, norms, and values over time."[515] Thus, learning allows an organization to build up a common understanding of the organization and its environment through its members developing and sharing cognitive systems and memories.[516]

Entering collaborations with other companies provides firms with the opportunity of learning with or from its alliance or its alliance partner. Analyzing learning flows between alliance partners requires a shift in the focus from a single learning-firm to learning of an interconnected organization.[517] Yet, to analyze the dynamics of learning among organizations, or, interorganizational learning, we still look at learning in the individual firm or the alliance.

As no single definition for interorganizational learning exists yet, GRUNWALD approaches a working definition by distinguishing between two interorganizational learning perspectives: a cognitive and a behavioral perspective.[518] The behavioral perspective considers cognitive limitations of the people involved in the learning process. This means that they cannot learn or do not need to learn everything from the partner in the partnering organization. GRANT AND BADEN-FULLER, for example, state that because of organizational members' cognitive and time limitations, they need to specialize in their learning, otherwise they risk decreasing the breadth of their knowledge when their depth of knowledge increases.[519] As laid out in depth in Section 3.4.4.4, we agree with the statement on the individual's limited rationality in general. However, in the case of pursuing joint R&D, scientists are already focused on learning specific knowledge. In this case, as we will see later in this section, knowl-

[512] See Grunwald (2003), p. 49 and the literature cited there.
[513] See Child and Faulkner (1998), p. 284.
[514] See Fiol and Lyles (1985), p. 804 and Kim (1993), p. 37.
[515] Hedberg (1981), p. 6. Nelson and Winter argue in the same direction. See Nelson and Winter (1982), p. 105. Kim remarks that although organizations can only learn through their members, individuals can learn without an organization. See Kim (1993), p. 43.
[516] Cognitive processes are frequently used to explain organizational learning. Moreover, organizational learning theories are often based on the stimulus-response behaviorism. See Hedberg (1981), p. 7 and Kim (1993), p. 37.
[517] See Levinson and Asahi (1995), p. 51 and Larsson et al. (1998), p. 286.
[518] See Grunwald (2003), pp. 49-67.
[519] See Grant and Baden-Fuller (1995), p. 18.

edge sharing and consecutive mutual learning is necessary to generate new knowledge. This is how the behavioral perspective defines interorganizational learning.[520] In the following we discuss the cognitive perspective.

Depending on the individual firm's goals or prospective benefits, learning may entail a cooperative or competitive bias. The former is most important for firms that need their employees to learn with the partner, the latter for firms that aim to use the alliance as a vehicle for their employees to learn from their partner's colleagues.[521] Employees of both firms contribute their respective experience and knowledge for knowledge integration – or, as CHILD states: "This process implies that mutual learning occurs through a constructive integration of the different inputs offered by the partners and their members."[522] Members of both organizations are used to employing their specific routines and using their specific language. Therefore, to integrate each other's knowledge effectively it is necessary for them to decode their specific knowledge first.[523] When interorganizational learning has occurred, it can be concluded, from the cognitive perspective that this learning would not have happened if the alliance had not been initiated.[524]

Yet, neither the behavioral nor the cognitive perspective considers that humans are socially embedded. Social learning theories do so. They include, for example, ROTTER's 'locus of control'[525], BREHM's reactance theory[526], and BANDURA's model learning[527]. The latter's concept states that learning may not only occur through own experience but also through observing others. While studying other people's behavior, an individual learns about the consequences of the behavior. In similar situations, the individual may ask herself how her role-model would have acted and adjust her own behavior accordingly.[528] Model learning may be of particular importance in case knowledge is highly tacit – like, for example, in research and development alliances like the present case study alliance.

Scholars differentiate between various levels on which learning may occur. ARGYRIS AND SCHÖN's concept of single-loop, double-loop and deutero learning, for instance, entails three levels which we discuss in the following.[529] All of them may take place on the individual, organizational, or interorganizational level. They differ by their cognitive standards. Single-loop learning on the lowest level represents incremental, conscious, and deductive learning. While it advances a deeper and broader understanding of existing cognitions, single-loop learning does not create new knowledge. It is

---

520 See, for example, Müller-Stewens and Osterloh (1996), pp. 19-20, Prange et al. (1996), pp. 12-13, and Child (2001a), p. 659.
521 See, for example, Khanna et al. (1998), pp. 194-195 and Section 4.5.1.
522 Child (2001a), p. 659.
523 See Child (2001a), p. 661.
524 See Larsson et al. (1998), p. 287.
525 See Rotter (1954).
526 See Brehm (1966).
527 See Bandura (1979).
528 See Bandura (1976), pp.589-591.
529 See Argyris and Schön (1978), pp. 18-28. Child and Faulkner distinguish between learning on a technical, systemic, and strategic level. See Child and Faulkner (1998), pp. 285-286. This classification corresponds to Argyris and Schön's.

learning to do existing things better or more efficiently. Referring to learning alliances, single-loop learning occurs when interorganizational learning is used for improvement without leaving the prevalent research or technology path.[530] The structures of mental models, as depicted in Figure 2-1, do not change, which is why the world view remains unchanged.[531]

When structures of mental models are being changed, the same information leads to a different decision.[532] This is what ARGYRIS AND SCHÖN call double-loop learning, HEDBERG refers to as metalevel learning, TUSHMAN AND ROMANELLI as reorientation, and CHILD AND FAULKNER call reframing.[533] Double-loop learning questions existing structures, routines, and rules. It is critical for firms acting in changing environments: incremental improvements do not guarantee competitive advantage in environments which are characterized by technological discontinuities.[534] As the path-dependency of knowledge corresponds to that of technological innovations, double-loop, or radical learning is required to jump from one technology path to the next. Referring to alliances, double-loop learning not only involves learning about the partner's knowledge but also "how to exploit this new knowledge that makes them interdependent."[535] Double-loop learning may occur in alliances when the alliance parents appreciate their partner's learning strategy and understand how it interrelates with their own over time.[536] This way, managers may realize that they should play fair or how to answer an unfair move by the partner firm. Finally, the highest level is deutero-learning, which is learning how to learn on the meta level through reflexive cognitive processes.

In Section 3.4.2.4 we put forward that knowledge and learning depend on each other in such a way that their relationship may be represented in stock and flow terms. In other words, learning can be interpreted as the acquisition of knowledge.[537] Knowledge in turn is often confused with information.[538] Pieces of the latter are the basis for the creation, restructuring, and changing of knowledge.[539] Depending on the individuals' mental models[540] knowledge is then transferred from one individual to the next. The receiver of the message then chooses whether she has received knowledge or just information.[541] Knowledge transfer also depends on its articulability, or, in other

---

530 See Teece and Pisano (1994), pp. 546-547. Relating to technological innovations, path dependency suggests that historical choices of a firm affect future choices. See also Dosi, who provides an example of technological trajectories in the aircraft industry. See Dosi (1988), pp. 1128-1129.
531 See Sterman (2000), p. 16.
532 See Sterman (2000), p. 18.
533 See Argyris and Schön (1978), p. 21, Hedberg (1981), p. 8, Tushman and Romanelli (1985), pp. 171, 202-208, and Child and Faulkner (1998), p. 285. See Fiol and Lyles (1985), p. 809 for an early review.
534 See Tushman and O'Reilly III (1996), pp. 12-13 and Zahn et al. (2000), p. 57.
535 Lubatkin et al. (2001), p. 1354.
536 See Larsson et al. (1998), p. 297.
537 See Kim (1993), p. 38.
538 See Nonaka (1994), p. 15.
539 See Bhagat et al. (2002), p. 206.
540 See Section 2.2.2.
541 See Nonaka and Takeuchi (1995), p. 58.

words, to what extent knowledge can be verbalized or written.[542] POLANYI remarks that due to the tacitness of knowledge, individuals know more than they might be able to articulate let alone communicate.[543]

Tacit knowledge is rooted in action, involvement, and commitment within a specific context. It may only be revealed through its application.[544] It is therefore understood as personal and intuitive. This is why its transferability between individuals is considered to be slow, costly, and uncertain. Examples of tacit knowledge are certain skills or routines. According to the resource-based view and its dynamic descendants, firms' capabilities that are rooted in tacit knowledge as well as them being rare and difficult to imitate are the basis for competitive advantage.[545] Along with other factors such as complexity and experience with this capability, tacitness may increase knowledge ambiguity.[546]

Knowledge in turn differs in the degree of tacitness.[547] The knowledge type with the lowest degree of tacitness is know-how. This represents basic practical knowledge of a system like a production system. For more demanding tasks that entail more than just know-how this type of knowledge becomes less interesting for the learning partner. At the next stage, know-why goes beyond just the plain description of systems. It articulates how the know-whats are causally linked. This knowledge may be transferred by observing what is referred to as vicarious learning.[548] The firm's core knowledge resides in its areas of expertise, which are called know-whats. Know-whats are highly tacit and represent the understanding of relationships that contain many unspecified constraints like, for instance, the anticipation of competitor responses to changes in the environment. Understanding the partner's know-whats is crucial for a firm's locating, understanding, transferring, and applying its own know-hows and know-whys to develop new competences.

Explicit knowledge, on the other hand, is codified and specified. Codification improves the transferability of knowledge because it is easier to store, reproduce, communicate, and trade. Examples of explicit knowledge are product specifications or methods. Therefore, if any transfer is desired, tacit knowledge, either on the individual, group, or organizational level should be codified. NONAKA assumes that knowledge is created through dynamic conversion processes between tacit and explicit knowledge and suggests four modes: combination (from individual explicit to organizational explicit knowledge), socialization (from individual tacit to organizational

542 Inkpen and Tsang explicitly differentiate between knowledge transfer and learning. The former term is rather used in social capital literature. Learning is referred to among network scholars. See Inkpen and Tsang (2005), p. 154.
543 See Polanyi (1983), p. 4 and Polanyi (1997), p. 136.
544 See Grant (1996), p. 111.
545 See Sections 3.4.2.3 and 3.4.2.4, where we discuss the resource-based view and its dynamic successors. See also Lane and Lubatkin (1998), p. 462.
546 See Simonin (1999), p. 598. Causal ambiguity indicates the "recipient's depth of knowledge or irreducible uncertainty about cause-effect relationships." Szulanski (1996), p. 36.
547 The differentiation of knowledge types is based on Sanchez (1997), pp. 174-180 and Zahn et al. (2000), pp. 54-55. Lubatkin, Florin, and Lane use the same terminology – extended – although with swapped meanings. See Lubatkin et al. (2001), pp. 1355-1363.
548 For vicarious learning in alliances see Section 3.3.2.

tacit), externalization (from individual tacit to organizational explicit) and internalization (from individual explicit to organizational tacit). The dynamic interaction between the four modes should be ensured through organizational management to form a continual knowledge creation spiral.[549] HOLMQVIST extends this model to include the creation of joint knowledge in alliances.[550] Each of NONAKA's four modes is enhanced by knowledge conversion modes on the interorganizational level. This results in eight conversion processes in total, leading to interorganizational knowledge. Four of them initiate explicit joint rules and the remaining four tacit joint routines. Examples of the former are written standard procedures or documents. Interaction routines or routine behavior are examples of joint routines.

Organizations tend to stick to certain behaviors and routines that contributed to past success. When technology paths change, however, it is necessary to unlearn this knowledge.[551] As with organizational learning, organizations also unlearn via their members.[552] This type of unlearning is what DE HOLAN, PHILLIPS, AND LAWRENCE call intentional forgetting. Sometimes it is necessary for firms entering alliances to intentionally forget their routines to effectively cooperate with the new partner. This would then increase competitiveness. Alternatively, organizations may also accidentally forget. Firms may lose valuable knowledge, thereby reducing their competitiveness. In this work we follow LYLES, who subsumes both dimensions under the term unlearning.[553] Unlearning depletes the knowledge stock. Assuming a stock for common alliance knowledge, Figure 4-1 summarizes the interrelationship of 'Alliance knowledge base', 'Alliance learning', and 'Alliance unlearning' in stock and flow terms.

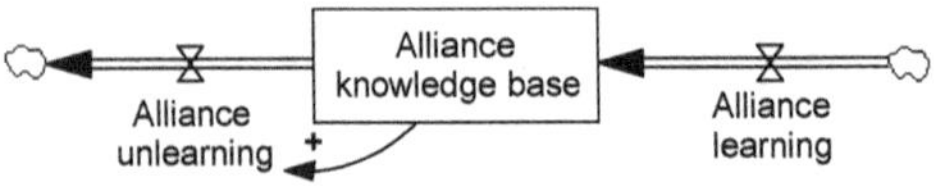

Figure 4-1: Alliance knowledge base, learning and unlearning in stock and flow terms.[554]

549 See Nonaka (1994), pp. 18-20.
550 See Holmqvist (1999), pp. 428-430. Carlile proposes an integrative framework for managing knowledge at organizational boundaries for creating innovation. Although his framework focuses on interorganizational boundaries, it could be adopted to interorganizational boundaries. The framework illustrates three increasingly complex boundaries – syntactic, semantic, and pragmatic – and three progressively complex processes – transfer, translation, and transformation. See Carlile (2004).
551 See, for example, Hedberg (1981), p. 18, Lyles (1988), p. 305, Hamel (1991), p. 97, and de Holan et al. (2004), p. 46.
552 Hedberg suggests an unlearning cycle of three modes: disconfirmation of mechanisms for selecting and identifying stimuli, disconfirmation of connections between stimuli and responses, and disconnection of connection between the responses. See Hedberg (1981), pp. 18-19.
553 See Lyles (1988), p. 305.
554 Source: authors' representation.

4.3 Interorganizational Learning and Alliance Performance

In this section we discuss whether interorganizational learning drives alliance performance. Research on performance drivers has been a relevant topic. However, in their article MARCH AND SUTTON claim that most studies on organizational performance define performance as a dependent variable. The authors of these studies seek to identify variables that produce variations in performance advantage. Yet, researchers often do not consider competitive advantage to be unstable.[555] Nevertheless, we do not seek to isolate key success factors with this study, which is what MARCH AND SUTTON accuse scholars of doing. We look for operational variables that managers can refer to when designing policy recommendations. Therefore, we first show that – considering MARCH AND SUTTON's remarks – according to studies, there might be an impact of alliances on firm performance. Then we identify tangible and operational measures for alliances' success that we will refer to in our simulation model.

DEERING AND MURPHY explain that alliances generally increase performance, stating that alliances accounted for 26% of the average Fortune 500 company's revenue and for 6% to 15% of their market value by 1999.[556] When focusing on the impact of learning on performance, learning in alliances increases firms' competitiveness from a theoretical viewpoint. Yet, the effect of learning on alliance performance remains indeterminate in the literature.[557] Also, scholars discuss aspects of performance measurement. Related studies focus on performance on both the alliance and parent firm level.[558] The former studies analyze how alliances perform, whereas the latter analyze whether parent firms profit from their alliances. Performance may entail multiple understandings. Once performance is studied, for example, it may focus on objective or subjective aspects.[559] Objective measures might include survival of the alliance, termination, duration, or facets. Still, an alliance may perform badly in financial terms but may gain a valuable strategic market position.[560] Also, even an unsuccessful alliance in financial or strategic terms may be continued by its parents due to high exit costs or inertia.[561] On the other hand, parent firms may terminate successful alliances because they had agreed on that in the alliance contract. In contrast to objective measures, subjective or process-oriented measures might include learning, competence-building, satisfaction, or goal attainment.[562] Knowledge-related alliance outcomes may be assessed by new products or technologies or patents.[563] Thus, goal attainment in learning alliances could be measured by reaching the number of patents that the parents sought for when entering the alliance, for example.

In the following, we discuss the link between learning and alliance performance. FIOL AND LYLES, for example, assume a relationship between learning and performance on

---

555 See March and Sutton (1997), p. 699 and Nicolai and Kieser (2002), pp. 579-580.
556 See Deering and Murphy (2003), p. 4.
557 See Robson et al. (2002), p. 404 and the references cited there.
558 See Ho Park and Ungson (2001), p. 38, Kim and Park (2002), p. 362, and Olk (2002), p. 119.
559 See Ho Park and Ungson (2001), p. 38.
560 See Nicolai and Kieser (2002), pp. 586-587.
561 See Gulati (1998), p. 307.
562 See Ho Park and Ungson (2001), p. 38.
563 See Reid et al. (2001), p. 93.

the organizational level.[564] Moreover, in their study on international joint ventures, LYLES AND SALK find that firms learning from their foreign partner perform significantly better than those in which only little learning takes place. Referring to measures, the authors study interfirm learning effects on both objective and subjective performance measures including financial criteria, knowledge and capabilities, and meeting of expectations.[565] This effect of learning on performance may not necessarily apply generally. Entities may learn incorrectly or they may correctly learn something which is incorrect, for example. Moreover, though learning might result in increased knowledge and capabilities, the opportunity to apply this knowledge and capability may not arise. In this case, performance is not increased.[566] On the other hand, INKPEN AND CROSSAN remark correctly that oftentimes it is difficult to observe a link between the two due to possible underlying time delays.[567] In such situations, people have difficulty relating cause and effect(s) to each other.[568] We side with MARCH's suggestion that learning strengthens organizational performance and competitive advantage in the sense that learning makes performance more reliable.[569]

We apply this understanding to interorganizational learning and performance in the following. Interorganizational learning leads to the creation of common benefits which may be operationalized through the number of patents that the alliance generates. The more 'Patents' the alliance scientists create, the closer they get to the alliance goal. The closer they get to the goal, the fewer additional 'Patents' they are able to create in this field of research. Hence, scientists' 'Group productivity' declines. This means that they are able to perform fewer 'Alliance research tasks'. Consequently, the 'Potential research output' declines and fewer additional patents can be generated. This is illustrated by the loop called 'Diminishing returns' in Figure 4-2. As it counteracts the initial change, it is a balancing feedback loop.

In this section we laid down the basic principles of interorganizational learning. We defined interorganizational learning and called attention to major characteristics of knowledge and learning. We have related those to interorganizational settings. As interorganizational learning sounds promising in regard to overcoming knowledge gaps and may entail many possible benefits managers who enter a learning alliance should be interested in pushing such an alliance to a successful outcome. However, they often fail to do so. In the following section we first describe how scholars analyze alliance dynamics and what they identified as the main reasons why alliances with a common learning intent often fail. Then we discuss the concept of private and common benefits. Afterwards we first provide an overview of factors influencing learning in alliances. Then we discuss some of them in more detail.

---

564 See Fiol and Lyles (1985), pp. 804-805.
565 See Lyles and Salk (1996), pp. 880, 885, and 897 and Lyles et al. (2003), p. 117.
566 See Huber (1991), p. 89.
567 See Inkpen and Crossan (1995), p. 603.
568 See Sterman (2000), pp. 695-698.
569 See March (1991), p. 83, Inkpen and Crossan (1995), p. 603, and Carayannis and Alexander (2002), p. 626.

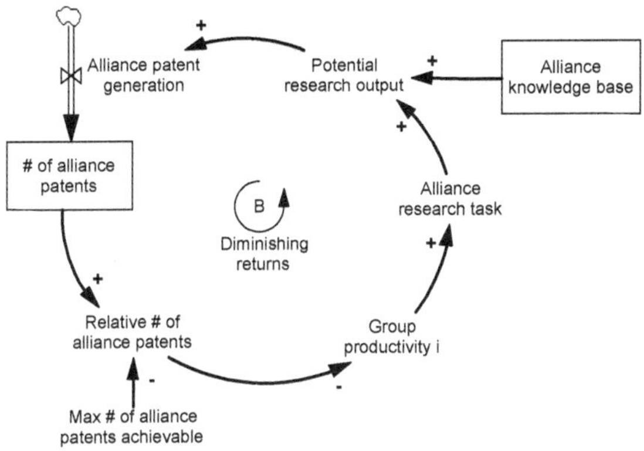

Figure 4-2: Stock and flow structure of 'Diminishing returns'.[570]

4.4 Development, Failure, and Success of Learning Alliances

Whereas the theories described in Section 3.4 explain the existence of alliances in general, scholars also deal with analyzing the issue of alliance dynamics after foundation. Just recently, INKPEN AND CURRALL emphasized once again that alliances may be understood as dynamic systems of adaptation and evolution.[571] Accordingly, VAN DE VEN AND POOLE present four different developmental theories which seek to clarify the dynamics of alliances: life-cycle, teleological, evolutionary, and dialectical theory.[572]

First, life-cycle theory explains alliance dynamics as a process of organic growth. Alliances undergo a set sequence of stages from foundation to dissolution. These stages are called, for example, emergence, transition, maturity, and critical crossroads,[573] or, referring to human relationships, partner selection and courtship, getting engaged, setting up house, learning to collaborate, and changing internally.[574] A shortcoming of the approach is its linear, irreversible, and predictable order of phases. Thus, accordingly, alliance termination is just a consistent and nothing but the logical consequence of smooth transitions from one stage to the next.

[570] Source: authors' representation. The index i represents the two different research groups involved in the alliance. We apply part of this feedback loop to explain the effects of openness in Section 4.6.2.

[571] See Inkpen and Currall (2004), p. 587, referring to Ariño and de la Torre (1998), Doz (1996), and Ring and van de Ven (1994).

[572] For the following statements see van de Ven and Poole (1995), pp. 512-519 unless otherwise indicated. The approaches were revisited by de Rond and Bouchikhi lately. See de Rond and Bouchikhi (2004), pp. 56-60 who are also referred to unless otherwise indicated.

[573] See D'Aunno and Zuckerman (1987), pp. 537-543.

[574] See Kanter (1994), pp. 98-108. Simonin introduces a similar terminology with honeymoon with initial euphoria and interest in partner's differences, stress and frustration, and pre-honeymoon with irreconcilable difference leading to alliance dissolution or readjustment. See Simonin (1999), p. 616.

Second, scholars following teleological theory emphasize that the "purpose or goal is the final cause for guiding movement of an entity."[575] In other words, organizations in general and alliances in particular are seen as goal-oriented while being able to learn and adapt to changing environments. RING AND VAN DE VEN suggest a recurring sequence of three repetitive stages, negotiation, commitment, and execution, that are mediated by efficiency and fairness.[576] Alternatively, DOZ presents learning, reevaluation, and readjustment as three repetitive stages driving alliance dynamics. He explicitly considers a learning dimension and defines the stages as being determined by initial conditions.[577] Successful learning about environment, tasks, processes, or goals may lead to successful alliance outcomes, whereas lack of learning may lead to inertia and (early) alliance dissolution. Unlike the life-cycle approach, teleological approaches consider unexpected events and outcomes. Managers may lead alliances to success when they succeed in increasing their efficiency. Or they dissolve the alliance "when rational calculations require it."[578]

Third, contrary to the theories mentioned above, evolutionary approaches underline that the environment is the driver for change. Approaches may only differ in the "rate of change and inheritability of the characteristics."[579] The insight from this theory is that, over time, organizations learn from their cooperating experiences and create ever fitter alliances. Managers' roles are limited to aligning alliances to the evolutionary environment.

Last, dialectical approaches assume that an organization is based "in a pluralistic world of colliding events, forces, or contradictory values that compete with each other for domination and control."[580] Those oppositions may be internal – for example, cooperation versus competition, rigidity versus flexibility, short-term versus long-term orientation, trust versus vigilance, or exploration versus exploitation[581] – or external – for instance, when firms' goals clash. Modification occurs when challenging events force a change in the status quo. Referring to alliances, this means that they may either be modified or terminated.

Indisputably, all theories provide valuable insight into the dynamics of alliances. In the present work we do not question the theories and their approaches to explain alliance dissolution. We examine the reason why alliances fail as a consequence of the interplay of variables in the underlying system structure. In the following we present different reasons for alliance failure. Most of them belong rather to the following two: either teleological (due to initial conditions of goal seeking) or dialectical approaches (because of too high tension levels due to competition and cooperation or vigilance and trust) might lead to a situation in which alliance dissolution seems to be the optimal solution from the managers' perspectives. However, it may well be that

---

575 Van de Ven and Poole (1995), pp. 515-516.
576 See Ring and van de Ven (1994), pp. 96-99 and also Ariño and de la Torre (1998), p. 308.
577 See Doz (1996), p. 64.
578 De Rond and Bouchikhi (2004), p. 58.
579 De Rond and Bouchikhi (2004), p. 58.
580 Van de Ven and Poole (1995), p. 517.
581 See March (1991), pp. 72-74, Das and Teng (2000), pp. 85-90, and de Rond and Bouchikhi (2004), pp. 59 and 64-66.

the alliance dissolutions studied in the literature happen as the last stage of an alliance's life-cycle (referring to life-cycle theory) or when the alliance organization does not get any fitter (referring to evolutionary approaches). Yet, as mentioned above, classifying the features into categories of these theories is not our intention.

In empirical studies, scholars have found that failure rates of interorganizational cooperations range from 50% to 50-60% to even 70% and 80%.[582] More dramatically, when asking managers if their alliances were successful, only less than half answered in the affirmative.[583] Hence, as already pointed out in Section 1.1, alliance performance goals are often not being met, which results in a high alliance failure rate – too high for alliances' alleged contribution to firms' financial success and competitive advantage. In addition, not only do prematurely ended alliances destroy shareholder value, but because of poor experience with alliances the managers of parent firms might be hesitant to reenter alliances in the future. Negative alliance experiences prevent managers from taking potential opportunities to collaborate with partner firms that would possibly inspire collaborative confidence.[584]

Scholars identify various reasons for alliance failure. Depending on the surveys' foci for dissolution causes, the analyses might have different emphases. The struggle to counterbalance long-term benefits with short-term focus on cost reduction[585] or organizational barriers like culture[586] are identified as reasons for failure. Or, referring to collaborative settings between companies in developed and less developed countries, KOGUT finds conflicts between parent companies and the joint venture as well as the control of mechanisms to be reasons for dissolution.[587] More generally – and these rationales may also hold for learning alliances – other reasons for alliance failure confirmed in various studies are, for example, insufficient trust,[588] lack of commitment[589] or reciprocity,[590] free riding,[591] unequal sharing of risk and benefits,[592] or unmet alliance expectations.[593] In particular, when referring to alliances where learning is one of the main objectives, a major reason for failure includes the risk of sharing proprietary knowledge,[594] which might result in unsuccessful common learning and consequently unmet alliance goals. On the other hand, hesitant sharing of proprietary knowledge might prevent a firm from being outlearned by its partner. Out-

---

582 See (Ho Park and Ungson (2001), p. 38, Dyer et al. (2001), p. 37, and A.T.-Kearney (2003), p. 40), Büchel (2003), p. 91, (Deering and Murphy (2003), p. 5 and Whipple and Frankel (2000), p. 22), and Gulati et al. (1994), p. 61, respectively.
583 See Harrigan (1988), p. 207
584 See Reid et al. (2001), p. 93.
585 See, for example, Whipple and Frankel (2000), p. 22.
586 See Dyer and Singh (1998), p. 668, Duysters et al. (1999), pp. 349-350, Whipple and Frankel (2000), p. 22, or Tidd and Izumimoto (2002), p. 143.
587 See Kogut (1988a), pp. 328-329.
588 See Kogut (1989), p. 185, Duysters et al. (1999), pp. 348-349, and recently Büchel (2003), pp. 92-95.
589 See Kogut (1989), p. 185, Duysters et al. (1999), pp. 348-349, and Tidd and Izumimoto (2002), p. 143.
590 See Kogut (1989), p. 185.
591 See, for example, Dyer and Nobeoka (2000), p. 348, Oxley and Sampson (2004), p. 725, or Pfähler and Wiethaus (2004), p. 686.
592 See Büchel (2003), pp. 92-93.
593 See Hagedoorn et al. (2000), p. 569.
594 See Hagedoorn et al. (2000), p. 569.

learning may possibly lead to a learning race between the partnering firms, which is another reason mentioned in the literature for ending an alliance before alliance goals are met.[595] A learning race may evolve as a competitive incentive to take advantage of the partner. Yet, in such a situation, alliance performance might be perceived differently by the parents as one parent achieves its goals whereas the partner might fail to do so.[596] The incentive to race can be a result of the relation of common and private benefits, depending on the scope of the firms and their alliances.[597]

The dilemma of common and private benefits in learning alliances has been discussed widely in the literature[598] as a main cause for alliance dissolution while leaving at least one unsatisfied partner. Therefore, we go deeper into this topic in the following. However, when analyzing this issue we must also consider the other reasons for alliance termination mentioned above.

4.5 Learning Alliance Objectives

In the subsequent sections we focus on objectives for firms to enter a cooperative venture with a competitor. Entering a learning alliance with a competitor not only provides the opportunity to learn with each other jointly, but also to learn from each other. This is the concept of relative scope, which we discuss first. Then we focus on the underlying idea of common and private benefits that result from the scopes of the allying firms. Afterwards, we demonstrate implications of private and common benefits for the dynamics of learning alliances. We show where firms entering an alliance need to be aware of opportunistic behavior in regard to prospective private benefits and common benefits. Furthermore we discuss learning with the partner for joint knowledge creation and learning from the partner and from the alliance for private knowledge creation. We support and/or question literature findings with the insight from our case study.

4.5.1 Learning Alliance's Partners' Relative Scopes

The construct of firm's relative scope illustrates the simultaneous underlying coexistence of cooperation and competition in learning alliances. Its nucleus lies in the parent firms' choice of alliance scope. Moreover, it considerably affects the character of benefits that the parents may reap from the alliance.[599]

---

[595] See Reich and Mankin (1986), pp. 78-83 who give examples of American firms being outlearned by their Japanese partner firms. See also Hamel (1991), pp. 85, 88, Doz (1996), p. 69, Larsson et al. (1998), p. 286, Ho Park and Ungson (2001), p. 37, Reid et al. (2001), p. 90, and Inkpen and Tsang (2005), p. 157.

[596] See Gulati (1998), p. 307.

[597] See, for example, Hamel (1991), p. 92, Child and Faulkner (1998), p. 289, Khanna (1998), pp. 340-342,, Inkpen (2000b), pp. 775-776, Khanna et al. (2000), pp. 782, 784, and 786, Ireland et al. (2002), p. 428, and Inkpen and Tsang (2005), p. 149.

[598] See, for example, Gulati (1998), p. 305, Khanna et al. (1998), pp. 194-195, Khanna et al. (2000), pp. 782, 785, and 787, or Zhang and Rajagopalan (2002), p. 473.

[599] See Khanna (1998), p. 340.

Each parent firm focuses on a certain set of activities called the firm's scope. This represents the firm's competitive domains,[600] characterized by geographical and product markets, technologies, manufacturing processes, information management, or human resource practices, for example.[601] Hence, the firms' competitive domains represent the firm's understanding of products, markets, business processes and routines.[602] When entering an alliance, the parent firms come to an agreement about the objectives or goals, such as benefits like patents to be attained in learning alliances, for example.[603] These benefits determine the alliance scope. Generally speaking, the alliance scope typically refers to some subset of markets in which the partner firms are involved.

The overlap between the scope of the alliance and the total market scope of each partner is called the relative scope.[604] The overlap may be complete, symmetric partial, or asymmetric partial. In the end, there may also be no overlap at all.[605] Assuming that the alliance scope is covered by the parent firms' scopes, the overlap of the latter determines the learning alliance's potentials and benefits. The greater the parent scopes' overlap, the more similar are the partners' resources and knowledge bases.[606] Knowledge flows between scientists of each parent firm are simplified, as similarity promotes communication and "increases the perceived relatedness of knowledge."[607] Correspondingly, the lower the resource and knowledge similarity, the greater is their complementarity.[608] As indicated in Section 3.4.2.3, greater complementarity goes along with more different but valuable resources that the partners contribute to the alliance. They enable the partnering firms to learn from each other or the alliance, assumably leading to competitive advantage [609] Yet, some overlap is necessary to ensure a profound basis for learning.[610]

Nevertheless, even though "each needs the other[s] to advance .. individual interests"[611] and to achieve common goals and aspirations, there is a great opportunity to learn from the partner in areas of one's own organization which are unrelated to the alliance.[612] For the purposes of illustration, consider a situation in which the two firms have an asymmetric partial overlap when forming the alliance (see Figure 4-3).

---

600 See Oxley and Sampson (2004), p. 728.
601 See Khanna (1998), p. 344 and Inkpen (2000b), p. 776.
602 See Oxley and Sampson (2004), p. 728.
603 See Gebrekidan and Awuah (2002), p. 680. Griliches states that patents are an output of R&D activity. See Griliches (1990), p. 1663 and Penner-Hahn and Shaver (2005), p. 123. In their study on learning in strategic alliances, Mowery, Oxley, and Silverman also use patents as a measurement. See Mowery et al. (2002), p. 293.
604 See Khanna et al. (1998), p. 195.
605 See Khanna (1998), p. 344.
606 See Oxley and Sampson (2004), p. 728.
607 Feinberg and Gupta (2004), p. 826. See also Kale et al. (2000), p. 224.
608 See Section 3.4.2.3 and Wernerfelt (1984), p. 175.
609 See Mowery et al. (1996), p. 79, Kale et al. (2000), p. 224, and also Ireland et al. (2002), p. 431.
610 See Tidd and Izumimoto (2002), p. 138 and likewise Grant (1996), p. 116 and Simonin (1999), p. 601.
611 Gray (1989), p. 6.
612 See Oxley and Sampson (2004), p. 728.

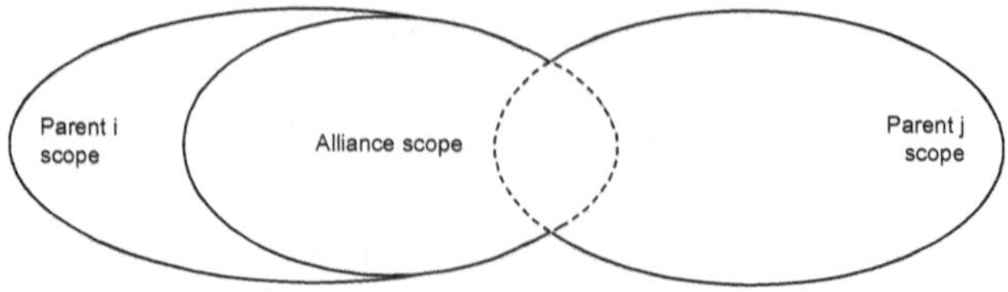

Figure 4-3: Relative scope, exemplified in an asymmetric partial overlap.[613]

The overlap between the alliance scope and Partner i's scope is significantly bigger than Partner j's overlap. Even though the two parent firms enter the alliance for mutual learning, the parents might evaluate the potential alliance benefits differently. For instance, the overlap of the alliance with Partner j's scope is relatively low. Consequently, from its perspective, the number of potential benefits for the overlap area might also be fairly low. However, there might be an incentive to enter the alliance because Partner j expects to generate benefits which may be useful in areas outside the alliance scope. On the other hand, as Partner i's relative overlap is relatively high, it might expect an appropriate amount of benefits valuable for the particular area. Briefly, in this example, one could assume that both parent firms might have different objectives for entering this particular alliance. This observation leads to the concept of private and common benefits.

4.5.2 Learning Alliance Objectives – Private and Common Benefits

The relative scope determines each parent's expected common and private benefits that they seek to generate in an alliance.[614] Common benefits represent the cooperative aspect of knowledge sharing and learning (see Figure 4-4).[615] They can be understood as those benefits that "accrue to the alliance parent from the collective application of the learning that both firms go through as a consequence of being part of the alliance; these are obtained from operations in areas of the firm that are related to the alliance."[616] In other words, once both parent companies have learned enough to be able to creatively integrate their knowledge bases, they may learn jointly to generate common benefits. HO PARK AND UNGSON observe that common benefits are usually future-oriented and ambiguous.[617]

---

[613] Source: following Khanna (1998), p. 345. The area bounded by the dotted line indicates the overlap of the alliance's and the parent companies' scopes.
[614] See Khanna et al. (1998), p. 195 and Khanna (1998), p. 341.
[615] See Tsai (2002), p. 180.
[616] Khanna et al. (1998), p. 195.
[617] See Ho Park and Ungson (2001), p. 42.

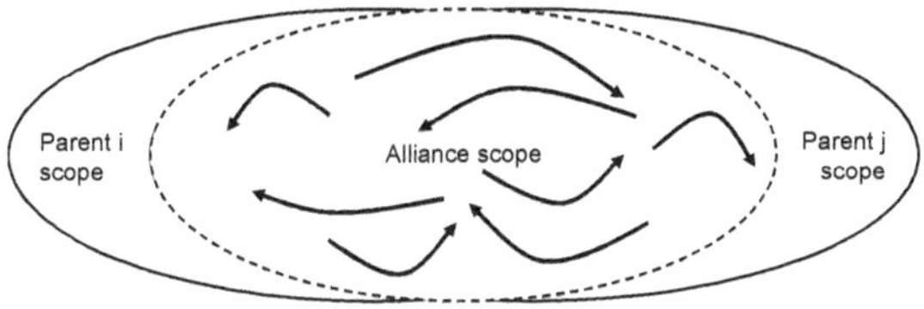

Figure 4-4: Common benefits in a learning alliance.[618]

Yet, private benefits often appear to be more immediate and tangible, intensifying opportunities for opportunistic behavior.[619] Conversely to common benefits, they represent the competitive aspect in learning alliances. KHANNA and KHANNA, GULATI, AND NOHRIA define them as those kinds of benefits that a parent firm can earn unilaterally by picking up complementary skills from its alliance partner and applying those to its own operations in fields unrelated to the alliance activities.[620] Subsequently, they do not reflect any common purpose to which the parent company expects – or wants – private knowledge to be applied (see Figure 4-5). Yet, this potentially useful knowledge is knowledge the parent would not have had access to without forming the alliance.

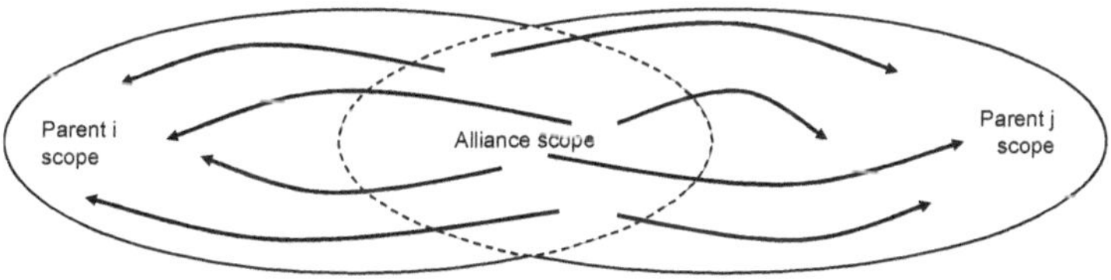

Figure 4-5: Private benefits in a learning alliance.[621]

KHANNA distinguishes between two types of private benefit; permanent and temporary private benefits. Permanent private benefits accrue to one parent company through the application of learning to markets that fall outside the alliance scope. In contrast, temporary private benefits refer to benefits that one parent company builds up through the application of learning to markets that fall within the scope of the alliance.[622] They are called temporary as the partner firm has not reached this learning level yet – but it may only be a matter of time. In the following we only consider permanent private benefits, which we simply call private benefits.

Implication of Private and Common Benefits for Alliance Dynamics

Introducing the relative scope with its underlying concepts of common and private benefits has implications for hypothetical dynamics of learning alliances. First, it pro-

[618] Source: authors' representation.

[619] See Ho Park and Ungson (2001), p. 42. Generating private benefits might be omitted by installating gatekeepers who control the knowledge flow. See Section 4.6.1.

[620] See Khanna (1998), pp. 341-342, Khanna et al. (1998), p. 195, and also Liebeskind (1996), pp. 96-97. Liebeskind exemplifies private learning on the level of individuals.

[621] Source: authors' representation.

[622] See Khanna (1998), p. 342.

vides the basis for understanding the parent companies' resource allocation patterns. Higher prospective benefits or payoffs increase the parents' resource allocations to the alliance. Correspondingly, with lower benefits, parent companies commit to fewer resources.[623] This effect still holds in situations in which potential aspirations may vary over time. When, over the course of an alliance, the parents realize that the alliance has the capability of generating further benefits, for example, they may vary their resources allocation accordingly. Referring to a learning alliance in which resource allocation may be measured by the number of scientists,[624] this positive relationship is as depicted in Figure 4-6.

Figure 4-6: Positive link between 'Prospective number of common patents' and 'Desired scientists'.[625]

Second, common and private benefits provide a basis for analyzing situations in which managers may observe opportunities and possibilities to take advantage of their partner and behave opportunistically. The intuitions for this behavior for common and private benefits differ. In the following, we lay them out consecutively considering extreme conditions.

In the hypothetical case of both firms only seeking private benefits, the parent firms expect no common purpose to which the commonly generated knowledge may be applied. Competitive intentions stand at the forefront of the relationship.[626] This means that both firms desire to access their partner's knowledge. At the same time, they would try to hide their own knowledge.[627] They wish to apply the new knowledge in areas fully unrelated to the alliance scope. In such an imaginary situation the firm would retreat from the relationship as soon as it has learned enough. There is no further incentive to stay in the alliance as the costs of continuing the relationship would exceed common benefits of zero. Moreover, none of the partners would like to be the laggard in this situation. As both firms are aware of this threat, they would race against each other to be the first to achieve their private goals, or, in other words, finish learning. As soon as the winning firm has learned enough, it would quit the alliance before the partner has finished its learning for private benefits.[628] This is what scholars call a learning race.[629] We discuss the learning race occurrence in more detail in Section 4.5.4 in which we focus on private learning in particular.

---

[623] See, for example, Gulati et al. (1994), p. 63, Khanna et al. (1998), p. 197, Kale et al. (2000), p. 219, Das and Rahman (2002), p. 105, Inkpen (2002), p. 272, or Zeng and Chen (2003), pp. 591-592.
[624] See Shan et al. (1994), p. 387, who state that R&D input may be measured in scientists and engineers.
[625] Source: authors' representation.
[626] See Larsson et al. (1998), p. 286. Yet, in their empirical study, Sukh Pak and Park could not find support for private benefits as a reason for tensions in alliances. According to their findings tensions are internal, like relationships, tasks, and process conflicts. See Sukh Pak and Park (2004), p. 429.
[627] See Zeng and Hennart (2002), p. 189.
[628] See Khanna et al. (1998), p.197.
[629] See, for example, Hamel et al. (1989), pp. 134-139, Hamel (1991), pp. 85, 88, Gulati (1998), p. 307, Khanna (1998), p. 343, Khanna et al. (1998), p. 198, Zahn and Foschiani (2000), p. 497,

To take the other extreme of only common benefits, the partnering firms collaborate to meet their common objectives and generate collaboration-specific quasi-rents.[630] RING AND VAN DE VEN and KHANNA, GULATI, AND NOHRIA state that 'Agreed upon number of patents in the contract' do not need to be equally divided between the parents for perceived fairness (see the upper part of Figure 4-7).[631] The partners' managers mutually negotiate, communicate their expectations, and agree on prospective common benefits during the phase of alliance formation. Consequently, they allocate their resource contribution to the alliance – or to their 'Scientists' – in accordance with prospective benefits – or, internally determined 'Aspiration levels' (see lower part of Figure 4-7). If they agree on an unequal number of common benefits for each they adjust their resource expenditures accordingly. The result is what the managers perceive as fair: the balance of their alliance contributions and benefits.

In a situation of pure common benefits, there is no incentive to race against the partner. However, there might be hidden agendas because of hidden partner characteristics that managers are confronted with.[632] We interpret goals that have not been shared openly between the partners as being part of such hidden agendas. Hidden agendas might lead to conflict among the partners. Incorporating the idea of hidden agendas into common benefits goes beyond KHANNA, GULATI, AND NOHRIA's original concept. The underlying idea is laid out in the following. Figure 4-7 depicts the example of an alliance of two partnering firms. It is assumed that they agree on a certain number of common benefits, here indicated as patents, in a contract.

The lower part of Figure 4-7 illustrates that the parent firms' actual, internally communicated benefits determine the resource allocation.

Mowery et al. (2002), p. 298, Zeng and Hennart (2002), pp. 189-207, Inkpen and Currall (2004), p. 594, and Inkpen and Tsang (2005), p. 157. Zeng and Hennart intensively discuss faulty assumptions in the learning race literature, explain motivations for learning races, and provide solutions to prevent them. See Zeng and Hennart (2002). In the economic literature, scholars discuss the patent-race which is comparable to the learning race. See, for instance, Grossman and Shapiro (1986), p. 593, Grossman and Shapiro (1987), p. 372, Malueg and Tsutsui (1997), p. 751, and Camerer (2003a), p. 208,.

630 See Madhok and Tallman (1998), p. 329.

631 See Ring and van de Ven (1994), pp. 93-94 and Khanna et al. (1998), p. 195.

632 See, for example, Inkpen and Tsang (2005), pp. 154, 157 and Section 3.4.1. Tidd and Izumimoto talk about implicit objectives. See Tidd and Izumimoto (2002), p. 143. For the underlying theoretical base to hidden agendas and hidden intentions, see the discussion on organizational economics in Section 3.4.1.

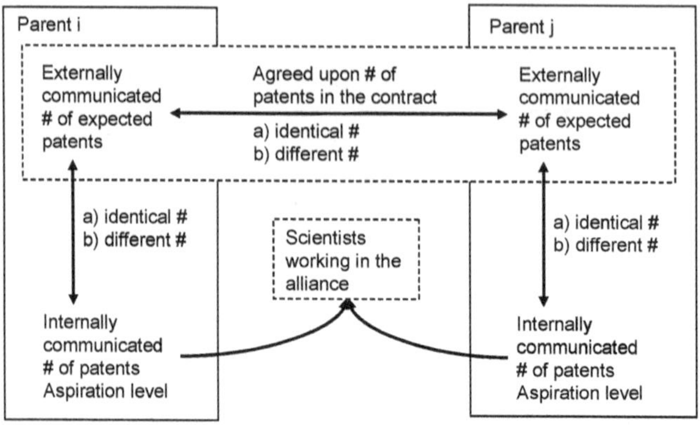

Figure 4-7: Possibilities for hidden agendas and scientist allocation in learning alliances[633]

Managers communicate to each other their intentions regarding benefits and scientist allocation. On this basis managers form expectations about the partner's scientist commitment (see Figure 4-8). The partner firm's managers compare the expected number of scientists with the actual number of scientists and may notice a deviation.

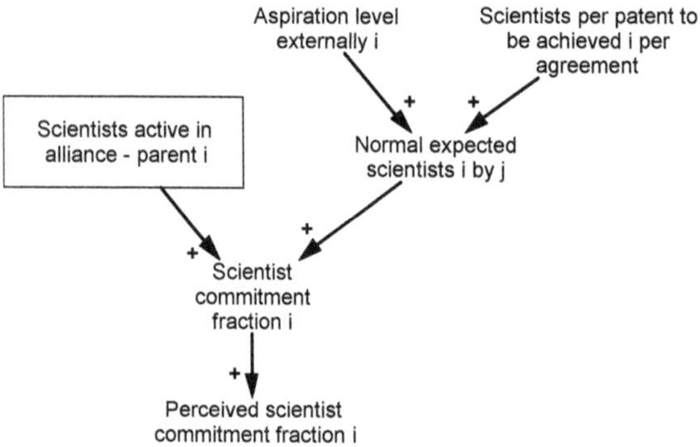

Figure 4-8: Simplified representation of 'Perceived scientist commitment fraction'.[634]

When the parents behave honestly, the number of scientists allocated to work in the alliance by one parent is exactly what the other expected. This is different when one parent cheats on the other. What the parents' managers agree upon might not reflect their actual respective 'Aspiration level' – or what they actually seek to achieve with the alliance (see lower part of Figure 4-7). Internally determined and communicated goals by the strategic management department, for example, might be higher or lower than those agreed on in the contract. Due to negotiation motives a partner may

[633] Source: authors' representation.
[634] Source: authors' representation.

just pretend to only be interested in an equal amount of patents, for instance. Yet, actually, its 'Aspiration level' might be higher or lower. It may then allocate a number of scientists to the alliance which deviates from the partner's expectations. There may be various reasons for this.

On the one hand, for example, we propose that a parent may have fewer actual prospective benefits than agreed on in the contract. As the actual potential benefits are lower and the firm is allocating its scientists accordingly, the number of scientists is lower than the partner expected. Its decision to fool its partner might be, for instance, because the other parent would not have agreed to enter the alliance had it openly shared that it seeks fewer goals. Or, at the same time it wanted to ensure that its partner spends more scientists on the alliance than itself to reach the goal sooner.

On the other hand, we propose that a parent firm wants to free ride. The free rider problem is discussed in collective action theory. This theory analyzes challenges related to realizing cooperation toward common benefits among self-interested individuals, groups, or organizations. When collaborating successfully, a common good, which would be common knowledge with respect to learning alliances, is accessible to the partners. However, one partner may enjoy the benefits of the collective good without contributing to its creation – hence, the partner may free ride.[635] Most likely, in the case of a two-parent learning alliance, a parent firm which seeks to behave opportunistically would not allocate anybody at all but would allocate fewer scientists. The parent would do so while maintaining a high level of desired benefits. Consequently, it expects the partner to do most of the research. If the partner accepts this behavior, the free rider receives its benefits with fewer investments.[636] We revisit both considerations regarding opportunistic behavior when we present our research propositions in Chapter 5.

Summarizing, both common and private benefits offer opportunities to behave opportunistically and betray each other. Most probably, however, alliances do not fall at either extreme of only private or only common benefits, but fall in between. While there may be hints for outlearning, we also propose the existing threat of being betrayed on common benefits. Considering both types of benefits, there would be a trade-off between cooperative learning together and competitive learning from each other.[637] Cooperative behavior to earn common benefits balances the incentive to race. So, the ratio of private to common benefits reflects a firm's incentive to engage in a learning race.[638]

---

[635] The free rider problem is also called the collective action problem. See, for example, Sandler (1992), pp. 17-18 and Dyer and Nobeoka (2000), p. 348. For collective action theory see, for example, Flam (1990) or Flam (2000). Free riding could also be interpreted as a firm having hidden intentions or characteristics, depending on the situation. See our discussion on hidden intentions and characteristics in Section 3.4.1.

[636] Concerning free riders see, for example, Dyer and Nobeoka (2000), p. 348, Oxley and Sampson (2004), p. 725, or Pfähler and Wiethaus (2004), p. 686.

[637] Learning with and from the partner in alliances is discussed in Sections 4.5.3 and 4.5.4, respectively.

[638] See Amburgey et al. (2000), p. 4 and Das and Rahman (2002), p. 105.

INKPEN emphasizes that the concept of relative scope is indeed insightful. But he criticizes that it conveys only a partial picture of interorganizational learning, while making a number of simplifying assumptions.[639] KHANNA, GULATI, AND NOHRIA reply to the criticism by explaining that they had to make simplifying assumptions when designing their model.[640] The critics do not put the construct of relative scope out of the question. KHANNA, quoting the Alliance Analyst from July 15th, 1997, states that a company's decision on a certain alliance scope is one of the most central tasks that the parent company carries out.[641] Hence, not only is the relative scope a present construct in real world alliances, it also provides theoretical insight into unveiling the dynamics of learning alliances. It covers the tension between competitive and cooperative behavior. So it features a dynamic perspective on alliance development.[642] In this work we analyze the learning alliance dynamics resulting from different arrangements of common and private benefits. We test the results with different assumptions of the partners' honesty and tendency to fairness. Therefore, we introduce the variables that we identified as decisive in alliance learning in the following. In the next section, for example, we study the influence of the partners' knowledge bases on the opportunities to learn either with or from the partner.

4.5.3 Learning with the Partner

In Section 3.3.2 we discussed the four learning levels on which a firm may learn in an alliance: learning about the alliance, learning about the alliance partner, learning mutually with the partner and learning from the partner. In the following, we focus on learning with the partner and from the partner in more detail. The former happens when both parent firms cooperatively create joint knowledge and common benefits. Learning from the alliance partner firms may create private benefits.[643]

According to LARSSON, BENGTSSON, HENRIKSSON, AND SPARKS, common or interorganizational learning can be "achieved by transferring existing knowledge from one organization to another organization, as well as by creating completely new knowledge through interaction among the organizations."[644] Interorganizational learning may sequentially focus on exploitation or exploration.[645] When organizations learn to refine their capabilities, they exploit their existing knowledge.[646] The benefit of exploitation is that firms create "reliability in experience."[647] This refers to improvement of productivity, routinization, or elaboration of existing technologies, for example. The

[639] Inkpen's remarks include concerns about Khanna, Gulati, and Nohria's model not considering the concept of knowledge relatedness, the order and the dynamics of learning, and different alliance forms. See Inkpen (2000b), pp. 775-779.
[640] See Khanna et al. (2000), p. 785.
[641] See Khanna (1998), p. 340.
[642] See Khanna et al. (1998), p. 193 and Inkpen (2000b), p. 775.
[643] See Inkpen and Currall (2004), p. 593.
[644] Larsson et al. (1998), p. 289.
[645] See, for example, Holmqvist (2003), pp. 108, 111. Holmqvist discusses the dynamic interactions of intra- and interorganzational learning processes. This goes beyond the scope of the present work.
[646] See March (1991), p. 72. According to March, the idea goes back to Schumpeter (1934), who called attention to the relation between exploring new possibilities and exploiting old certainties.
[647] Holmqvist (2003), p. 99.

drawback is that too strong a focus might lead to narrow-mindedness and dominant logic[648] hampering exploration activities. With explorative activities, firms experiment and innovate on the basis of existing knowledge.[649] A balance between long-term oriented exploration and short-term focused exploitation is necessary for a firm to stay competitive.[650] On this basis, KOZA AND LEWIN state that firms may enter an alliance just for one or the other purpose. In the same vein, ROTHAERMEL AND DEEDS propose that firms entering learning alliances which focus on research and development processes may follow a chronological order. First, firms enter exploration alliances with the motivation to discover new business opportunities – hence, they do joint research.[651] The authors provide the example of collaborating firms in the biotechnology industry desiring to acquire basic knowledge codified in patents.[652] These alliances are followed by focusing on exploitation. Here, firms focus on the development part of the R&D process. Their goal is to join existing knowledge across organizational boundaries in order to generate common benefits, which are then shared across the partners.[653] Firms maximize their assets in exploitation alliances. An example would be a biotechnology firm which cooperates with a competitor to commercialize an innovative product more efficiently. The case study we presented in Section 2.4.3 falls into the first category, which is why we focus in this work on the dynamics in exploration alliances.

It is argued that it is necessary for the partnering firms to understand their respective knowledge first. This allows them to sufficiently recognize and comprehend the partner's knowledge well enough before integrating both knowledge bases. Only then are they able to generate a common knowledge base with new learning content.[654] Yet, common learning between the partners is not always necessary for successfully working on alliance objectives.[655] In his study, GRUNWALD analyzes learning behaviors in four alliances of the software company SAP with other companies, for example. The requirement to meet the alliances' goals in each case study was to integrate existing technologies of both partners, for instance, to develop special software for an insurance company. SAP, contributing the software, had to cooperate with the insurance company, that understands underlying commission processes.[656] Even though the software designed was new, no new knowledge had to be generated, so that the standard software simply had to be adapted to the new customer needs.[657] The partners had to combine their project-relevant technologies, which required the understanding of how to use the partner's knowledge – not to learn from the partner.

---

648 For a discussion on dominant logic see Prahalad and Bettis (1986).
649 See March (1991), p. 72.
650 See March (1991), p. 71 and Holmqvist (2003), p. 99. See Garcia et al. (2003), for a feedback analysis of resource allocation to exploration versus exploitation in organizations.
651 See Rothaermel and Deeds (2004), pp. 202-205 and Koza and Lewin (1998). The latter authors state that often but not exclusively such learning alliances are joint equity relationships. As stressed above we analyze the dynamics of non-equity learning alliance.
652 See Rothaermel and Deeds (2004), p. 204.
653 See Rothaermel and Deeds (2004), p. 205 and Koza and Lewin (1998), p. 256.
654 See, for example, Grant (1996), pp. 115-116. In his argumentation, he refers to a common knowledge base inside one organization.
655 See Grunwald and Kieser (2003), p. 43 and Grunwald (2003), pp. 217-218.
656 See Grunwald and Kieser (2003), p. 37.
657 See Grunwald and Kieser (2003), p. 36.

Therefore, Grunwald argues, members of an alliance should learn as little as possible when the alliance's objective is the recombination of existing technologies.[658] According to his findings, only a low level of common knowledge is a necessary but not sufficient requirement for reaching common goals. Also, intensive common learning processes are not prerequisites for creating the required knowledge.[659] The example describes an alliance in which the partnering firms' scopes only overlap slightly or not at all. This is a different situation from the one in our case study. Here, the two firms form an alliance in final product markets in which they are direct competitors. They limit their joint activities to pure research and development in the area of application-oriented basic research. They create joint knowledge which requires more than the transfer of plain skills or techniques.[660]

Members of the parent firms' teams have a clear understanding of the existence and the development of common knowledge. When asked about the development of learning such project-relevant knowledge from the partner, for example, a scientist of our case study answered: *"Obviously it has gone through an evolution. When you first come together and both parties have gone through the exercise of documenting all of their knowledge in the joint research area and you exchange that knowledge initially, there is a large volume of information to absorb."*[661] Moreover, also referring to the early phase of the joint research alliance, one interviewee states that during this phase *"[c]ommon learning is not necessarily jointly created knowledge [yet]. Common knowledge has increased strongly because we exchanged much information between the teams."*[662] Until the early phase ran out, common knowledge only consisted of both parent firms' own knowledge, or of what the case study's agreement identifies as sole know-how.[663] The latter is the parent's confidential knowledge that has been developed or acquired independently of any contribution by the partner.

So, both parents' sole know-how provides the basic knowledge for the alliance's common knowledge base. A manager describes the common knowledge base at the early stage as a *"platform for joint discussions. We can take this knowledge for granted when we discuss things and talk with each other."*[664] In other words, it may be interpreted as the basis for future jointly created knowledge. The alliance contract agreed on by the firms in our case study is very precise and offers three alternatives

658 See Grunwald and Kieser (2003), p. 43. Grunwald calls this initial knowledge exchange cross-learning.
659 See Grunwald (2003), p. 218. Grant provides an example to support this argument: when he co-authors a paper he and his co-author do not need to completely learn from each other what the other knows. They need a mode of interaction to be efficient at co-authoring. See Grant (1996), p. 114.
660 See Inkpen (2000b), p. 776 and also according to Kogut and Zander (1992), p. 392. See also Sukh Pak and Park (2004), p. 429. The case study supports findings by Oxley and Sampson who empirically show that alliance partners limit their joint activities when being direct competitors. See Oxley and Sampson (2004), p. 724.
661 P5: 32.
662 P3: 140.
663 See P9:11.
664 P3: 142.

for a possible increase in the common knowledge base.[665] First, common knowledge may either be developed by both parents' scientists working directly with each other while integrating the sole know-how of either or both parents. Or it may be generated by one parent's scientists building upon preexisting joint know-how or the partner's sole know-how. Or, finally, it may be developed by both parents' scientists working together not including either's sole know-how.

An interviewee describes the development of the common knowledge base in retrospect as follows: *"So, [the common knowledge base] is a traditional kind of an S-curve, where it is slow at first, rapid increase and then it kind of flattens out."*[666] This behavior is represented in Figure 4-9. As can be seen from the figure, the maximum of these qualitative variables equals hundred percent.

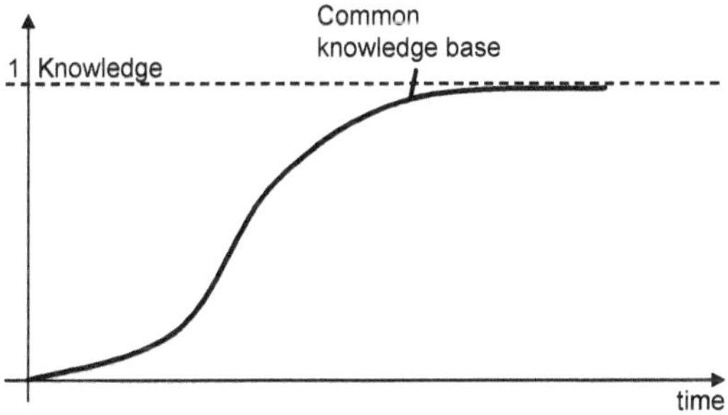

Figure 4-9: Reference mode: Development of the alliance knowledge base.[667]

4.5.4 Learning from the Partner and from the Alliance

Whereas learning with the partner focuses on the cooperative aspect in learning alliances, learning from the partner signifies this competitive characteristic.[668] Creating an alliance in which learning occurs is also an incentive to behave opportunistically – as indicated by transaction cost economics and game theory.[669] While acting opportunistically, parent firms undermine the alliance strategy.

Under the premise of prospective private benefits, firms are interested in accessing their partners' knowledge and applying it to areas outside the alliance scope. The reason for entering the alliance lies in the opportunity to access knowledge they

[665] See P9: 10. Common knowledge is what the contract specifies as joint know-how. Though there might be different interpretations of joint know-how in the case study contract and common knowledge in the literature, we identify the jointly developed knowledge in an alliance as common knowledge.
[666] P7: 51.
[667] Source: authors' representation.
[668] See Child and Faulkner (1998), p. 291.
[669] See Section 3.4.1 for details on transaction cost economics and Section 3.4.4 on game theory.

would not have had without forming the alliance.[670] Hence, they act selfishly. Referring to a cooperative relationship different from the case study alliance, one interviewee confirms the existence of such private learning by saying that "*[t]his technology spilled over to us – into a division that was not involved in any alliance activities. It was not developed in-house [by our firm]. It was invented by [our partner].*"[671]

HAMEL states that a parent firm with prospective private benefits would be interested in learning from its alliance partner as fast as possible to achieve these benefits. It may then have the opportunity to discontinue the alliance even if its partner has not finished learning enough to achieve its desired alliance benefits.[672] Alternatively, if both parents seek to learn from each other instead of with each other, they would race to learn.[673] The faster learner may increase its bargaining power over the partner and dominate the relationship – and again may end the alliance if the faster learning parent has finished its learning. Thus, cheating the alliance partner would result in a better and stronger competitive position.[674]

The partner who has been outlearned in such a situation perceives this as unfair behavior.[675] It feels betrayed and taken advantage of. If it has not attained its alliance goals or – if they exist – private goals, it is unsatisfied with the alliance and especially with the unfair partner. Consequently, because of the bad alliance experience with this particular partner firm, it no longer perceives the partner as an ally or a potential future partner for further common objectives. Furthermore, according to the network approach, it will most probably spread the word to damage the cheater's reputation.[676]

Scholars argue that the attractiveness of private learning lies in a more short-term oriented economic view of the managers. Common learning oftentimes takes longer; it is future-oriented and uncertain. In contrast, managers tend to think that the outcomes of private learning are more immediate.[677] Private benefits may begin to build up after having learned enough in the alliance to apply this learning to the partner's own operations in fields unrelated to alliance activities. In their model, KHANNA, GULATI, AND NOHRIA assume that private learning has finished before common learning may start when saying that "[p]rivate benefits are unrelated to this joint knowledge creation."[678] They state that some threshold level of learning has to be accomplished before either common or private learning can take place. KHANNA, GULATI, AND NOHRIA offer to soften their assumption by saying that the "sequence of private and common benefits can be altered."[679] We would like to qualify this by saying that "some threshold level of learning"[680] already represents common learning. The

[670] See Inkpen (2002), p. 269
[671] P11: 184.
[672] See Hamel (1991), p. 88 and Ireland et al. (2002), p. 431.
[673] See Hamel (1991), p. 85 and also Inkpen (2002), p. 272
[674] See, for example, Hamel (1991), p. 87 and Dussauge et al. (2000), p. 120.
[675] See Hamel (1991), p. 93.
[676] See Section 3.4.3 for explanations on the network approach.
[677] See Hamel (1991), p. 88 and Ho Park and Ungson (2001), p. 42.
[678] Khanna et al. (1998), p. 195.
[679] Khanna et al. (1998), p. 203.
[680] Khanna et al. (1998), p. 203.

threshold may, for example, represent the first exchange of information between the participating parties. Following LARSSON, BENGTSSON, HENRIKSSON, AND SPARKS, we identify this learning in Section 4.5.3 as interorganizational learning and consequently as the foundation of common knowledge. [681] This relationship is depicted in Figure 4-10.

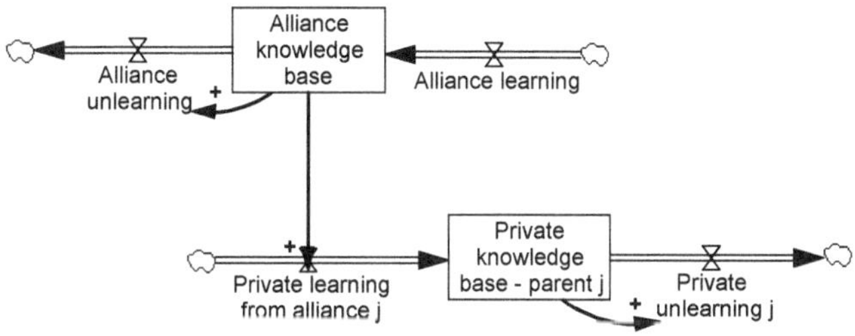

Figure 4-10: 'Alliance knowledge' feeding 'Private knowledge'.[682]

Alternatively, the threshold may be higher. In this case, the threshold would definitely be situated within newly and jointly created knowledge. Concluding, in view of the two alternatives, we argue that only common knowledge can be the basis for private learning. So, common learning has to take place before any private learning may occur. One interviewee indirectly supports our suggested sequence of common learning before private learning when stating: *"Of course there is know-how that we or our partner contribute to the alliance that could potentially flow in other divisions."*[683] On the basis of the above mentioned assumptions we infer a reference mode depicted in Figure 4-11 for the behavior of common and private knowledge presupposing a threshold for private learning. The behavior assumes further that private learning is permitted by contract. We discuss safeguards that might prohibit private learning in Section 4.6.1.

KHANNA, GULATI, AND NOHRIA state that a parent's ability to earn private benefits by applying what it has learned to a set of markets outside the alliance scope is influenced by two aspects: first, the extent to which the markets outside and within the alliance scope relate to each other, and second, the extent to which the parent company has the skills to accomplish the transfer of knowledge.[684] These two factors could also be interpreted as LANE AND LUBATKIN's concept of relative absorptive capacity that we discuss in the following section, besides other factors influencing interorganizational learning.[685]

---

[681] Larsson et al. (1998), p. 289.
[682] Source: authors' representation.
[683] P1: 58. The interviewee continues: *"But by contract I am not permitted to let it flow in other divisions."* P1: 73.
[684] See Khanna et al. (1998), p. 196.
[685] See Lane and Lubatkin (1998), p. 462.

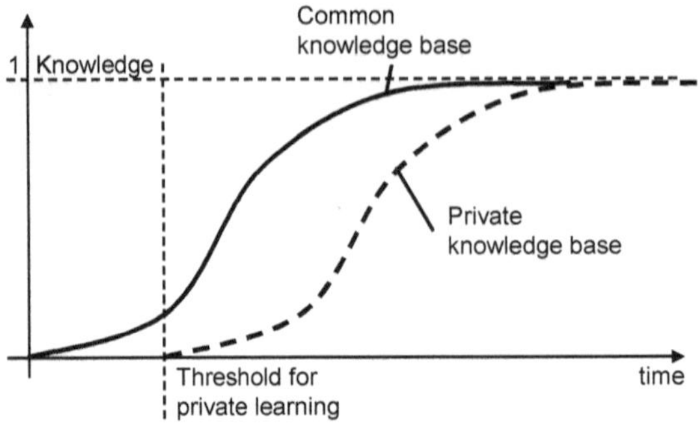

Figure 4-11: Reference mode: Common and private knowledge bases, assuming a threshold for private learning.[686]

4.6 Selected Factors Influencing Learning in Interorganizational Learning

Interorganizational learning is affected by several factors. While there are many potential benefits from learning in alliances, there are drivers and barriers for interorganizational learning. In the following we present an overview. Culture is an example of a learning barrier, for instance. If the cooperating firms' cultures are too distant, it might be difficult for the participants to learn from each other. LEVINSON AND ASAHI identify four types of culture affecting interorganizational learning: national, organizational, occupational, and small group culture. The authors state that each of these levels adds to the overall culture driving or hampering the learning process. Even when the national culture of the cooperating firms is similar, their organizational cultures might be different.[687] Second, alliance structure might also influence interorganizational learning processes: on the one hand, connections between the joining firms and other stakeholders determine knowledge flows. As mentioned earlier, they might either support or hinder learning. On the other hand, the number of participating firms in an alliance, then called a network, also influences the knowledge flows. According to LEVINSON AND ASAHI, the more firms participate in a network, the more they are able to identify new ideas. Then again, a firm's position in the network also contributes to learning. As we focus only on a two-party alliance, we do not go further into this detail.

Unlearning, as mentioned in Section 4.2, is also a learning barrier as sometimes it is necessary to unlearn outdated and past routines to open up for new learning opportunities.[688] Also, the more tacit knowledge is, the more difficult it is to transfer. Tacit knowledge needs to be encoded into explicit knowledge first.[689]

---

[686] Source: authors' representation.

[687] See Levinson and Asahi (1995), pp. 51, 54-56. See also Nahavandi and Malekzadeh (1988), p. 80 who study the effect of culture in mergers and acquisitions, Child (1998), p. 248 and Sukh Pak and Park (2004), p. 429.

[688] See Ireland et al. (2002), p. 411

[689] See also Section 4.2.

Moreover, knowledge might be sticky and therefore difficult to transfer from one organization to another. Stickiness describes the costs of acquiring, transferring, and using knowledge.[690] According to VON HIPPEL, knowledge stickiness grows with increasing costs and is increased by causal ambiguity.[691] This is because a completely successful appreciation and reproduction of knowledge is impossible because of uncertainty that prevents a full understanding of how path dependent knowledge features interact with each other.

Furthermore, the problem of knowledge stickiness encompasses not only the knowledge itself but also the sender's and receiver's characteristics, like, for example, their transparency or their absorptive capacity. For instance, lack of absorptive capacity may hamper the learning process while an increasing absorptive capacity may drive it. Whereas absorptive capacity determines the receiver's learning capability, organizational transparency or openness vis-à-vis its partner affects how much knowledge might be transferred from the sender to the receiver.[692] Additionally, knowledge transfer is determined by how much the partners trust each other. Trust is often interpreted as another strong influence of interorganizational learning or, as LANE, SALK, AND LYLES view it, of absorptive capacity.[693] For understanding and managing interorganizational learning and to understand the dynamics of interorganizational learning in alliances we focus on the roles of absorptive capacity, organizational openness, and trust.

4.6.1 Absorptive Capacity and Relative Absorptive Capacity

Firms that wish to learn with and from their partners in collaborative settings are generally able to acquire new knowledge better when they already have a knowledge base similar to the new knowledge that they seek to obtain.[694] This ability is determined by what HAMEL calls receptivity[695] and COHEN AND LEVINTHAL call absorptive capacity[696]. The latter is defined as a firm's ability to value, assimilate, and apply new knowledge in its own activities.[697]

As COHEN AND LEVINTHAL view absorptive capacity as a construct on the firm level, we need to apply it to the interfirm level. LANE AND LUBATKIN explicitly extend the construct to the need for interorganizational learning. They argue that "the ability of a firm

[690] See von Hippel (1994), p. 429 and Szulanski (1996), p. 28.
[691] See Lippman and Rumelt (1982), pp. 418, 420-421.
[692] See Hamel (1991), pp. 93-96 and likewise Holmqvist (2003), p. 111.
[693] See Lane et al. (2001), p. 1141.
[694] See Cohen and Levinthal (1990), p. 136 and Section 4.5.1.
[695] See Hamel (1991), p. 96.
[696] See Cohen and Levinthal (1990), p. 128. As indicated at the end of Section 4.5.4, Khanna, Gulati, and Nohria summarize the two aspects of absorptive capacity in a transferability factor. See Khanna et al. (1998), p. 196. Other terms for similar abilities are combinative capabilities. See Kogut and Zander (1992), pp. 391-392 and Kogut and Zander (1993), p. 640.
[697] See Cohen and Levinthal (1990), p. 128. According to Reid, Bussiere, and Greenaway, these facets qualify the absorptive capacity as being a capability in line with its resource-based view definition. See Reid et al. (2001), p. 88 and for the resources and capabilities Section 3.4.2.3.

to learn from another firm is jointly determined by the relative characteristics"[698] of the two firms. Besides the findings of their empirical study on the relevance of firms' structures and their compensation practices for interorganizational learning, the authors find that the knowledge bases of the partnering firms should overlap to some extent to ensure successful learning.[699] Then the firms share a common competence base and have similar experiences, as they may deal with similar – or even the same – customers or similar problems in new product development, for example. Thus, firms may understand and appropriate each other's knowledge better and are more likely to learn quickly and successfully with and from each other.[700] At the same time, however, as they have accumulated similar experiences, there might be only little need for joint research and development as they cannot learn that much from one another. Moreover, not only do they share similar challenges, but they may also have similar and overlapping dominant logics which might hamper joint learning.[701] Still, it might be desirable to have knowledge overlap. It creates redundancy, which encourages regular discussions, which in turn, is a significant element for joint learning.[702]

Nevertheless, if the parents' knowledge bases and their path dependent experiences are different, they might potentially be able to learn more from one another – however, as they have such different experiences, it might be challenging to learn collectively.[703] As stated above, for joint learning the collaborating firms need to appreciate the partner's specific language and routines.[704] This creates the potential of combining their complementary knowledge to generate a joint knowledge base. Furthermore, this leads to, as HOLMQVIST puts it, "an obvious paradox: the benefit of knowledge integration is in meshing the different specialized experience of different organizations – if two organizations have very similar experience there is no gain from integration – yet, if the organizations have entirely separate experience bases, then integration cannot occur beyond the most primitive level."[705] To differentiate more clearly how knowledge bases are positioned relative to each other, LANE AND LUBATKIN further distinguish between basic and specialized knowledge.[706] Basic knowledge implies general understanding of the field in which the firms operate. It is a prerequisite for the receiver to understand the sender's underlying assumptions and enables it to evaluate the received knowledge about its importance for possible applications in the own firm. To create new knowledge effectively, some knowledge must be quite different. This is what the authors define as specialized knowledge. Concluding, the partners only learn with and from one another if their basic knowledge bases are at least somewhat similar and their specialized knowledge bases are different.

[698] See Lane and Lubatkin (1998), p. 462. Originally, the authors refer to a student and a teacher firm.
[699] See the first hypothesis in Lane and Lubatkin (1998), pp. 464, 471.
[700] See Norman (2004), p. 612.
[701] See Lane and Lubatkin (1998), p. 466 and for dominant logic see Prahalad and Bettis (1986).
[702] See Senge (1990), pp. 240, 247, Inkpen (1996), p. 134, and Reid et al. (2001), pp. 91-92.
[703] See Dussauge et al. (2000), pp. 101-102, Dussauge et al. (2002), p. 710, and Holmqvist (2003), p. 111.
[704] See Section 4.2 in which we define interorganizational learning.
[705] Holmqvist (2003), p. 111.
[706] For the following statements refer to Lane and Lubatkin (1998), p. 464.

A second characteristic of absorptive capacity is its path-dependence, which means that it accumulates over time. In other words, once a firm has some absorptive capacity in a specific area, it may easily accumulate it in the next period to determine what additional knowledge might be relevant for exploiting any critical external knowledge.[707] To summarize, and applied to interorganizational learning, the higher the joint knowledge base, the better and faster the members of both firms learn with each other – in other words, the higher the 'Effect of knowledge on learning'. This makes further learning easier and leads to further build up of the 'Alliance knowledge base' (see Figure 4-12).

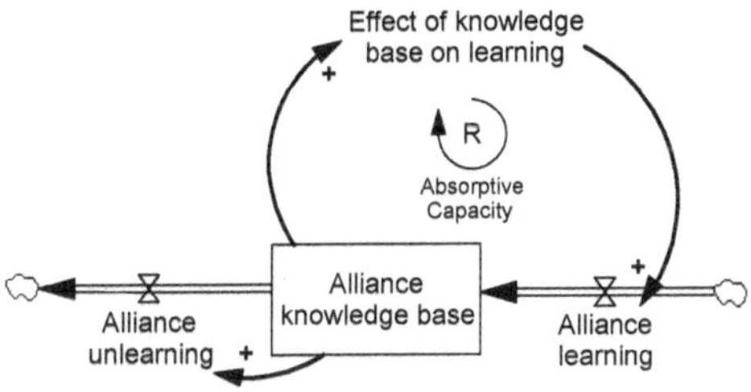

Figure 4-12: 'Alliance knowledge base' and absorptive capacity in stock and flow terms.[708]

4.6.2 Interorganizational Openness

Common learning is simplified when the cooperating parties understand each other's knowledge bases and the members of the alliance interact frequently with each other. Frequent interactions between scientists lead to knowledge flows between the firms which in turn is the basis for common learning. Nevertheless, not only do the scientists need to understand each other, they also must be open to sharing their knowledge with each other. HAMEL and INKPEN identify such organizational transparency or openness as critical for the knowledge flow.[709] Organizational openness can be understood as the willingness and ability of alliance partners to share knowledge and communicate openly with each other.[710] HAMEL defines transparency more broadly covering various determinants. According to findings from his explorative study, transparency is influenced by the social contexts of the partnering firms, like foreign languages or traditions. Moreover, knowledge tacitness and stickiness, absorptive capacity, and firm members' attitude toward group outsiders may restrict learning

[707] See Cohen and Levinthal (1990), p. 136. In spite of the increasing acceptance of the absorptive capacity concept, it is still difficult to empirically analyze its effect on outcomes. Zahra and George therefore extend the concept of absorptive capacity to potential capacity and realized capacity. The former entails knowledge acquisition and assimilation capabilities whereas the latter includes knowledge transfer and exploitation. The authors emphasize that these capabilities are distinct but complementary. See Zahra and George (2002), pp. 185, 189 for an overview.

[708] Source: authors' representation.

[709] See Hamel (1991), p. 93 and Inkpen (2000a), p. 1026.

[710] See Inkpen (2000a), p. 1026.

opportunities even if firms seek to be transparent.[711] In the following we use the term openness to be able to clearly distinguish between one partner's openness and the other's absorptivity skills.

In his knowledge acquisition framework, INKPEN proposes, among other things, that openness between the alliance partners determines the quality of knowledge exchange between the firms.[712] Firms might be reluctant to be open to a competitor with which they enter an alliance. When knowledge spills over they risk creating a stronger competitor. So, one option is to reduce its organizational openness while, for example, not sharing all the information necessary for building up a common knowledge base to work collectively on alliance tasks. This behavior is what HAMEL observes in his study on Japanese and American cooperative ventures. According to the members of the American partners, their Japanese partners were less open than themselves.[713] Therefore, they had the feeling of being in a weaker position in the relationship. Bargaining power clearly shifts to the advantage of one partner. This is perceived as unfair behavior. If one partner is less open, knowledge exchange is hampered. Referring to our learning alliance model, less 'Openness between the scientists' leads to decreasing 'Effective openness', which in turn reduces the scientists' effectiveness when doing their tasks (see the model structure in Figure 4-13). Consequently, joint interaction leading to common learning does not occur at its potential maximum. Long-term alliance success is jeopardized.

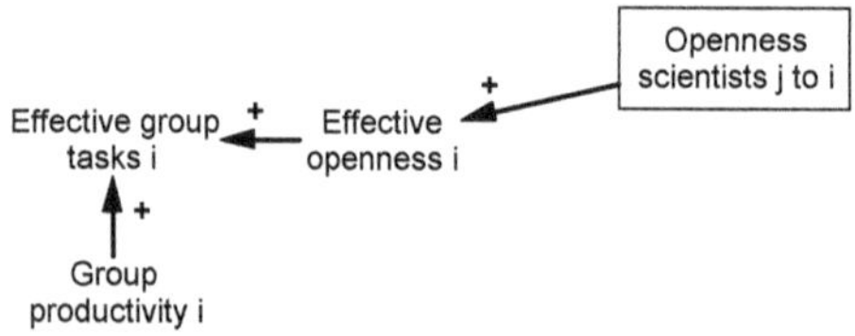

Figure 4-13: Organizational openness drives the scientists' effectiveness.[714]

Reciprocal organizational openness is essential because sharing knowledge is the main motivation for firms entering learning alliances.[715] Both parents need to have access to parts of both partners' knowledge bases to integrate them successfully. Though this holds for all organizational levels in firms, for learning alliances it is most important that the scientists are open with each other. Therefore, in the following we focus on organizational openness on the scientist level for our simulation model.

---

[711] Though Hamel does not use the terms absorptive capacity, knowledge tacitness and stickiness, he paraphrases them. See Hamel (1991), p. 94. We side with Larsson, Bengtsson, Henriksson, and Sparks who refer to these terms also. Moreover, they add communicative capacity as an extra factor limiting organizational transparency. See Larsson et al. (1998), p. 291. For knowledge tacitness and stickiness see Sections 4.2 and 4.6.

[712] See Inkpen (2000a), p. 1026.

[713] See Hamel (1991), p. 94.

[714] Source: authors' representation. The index i represents the two different research groups involved in the alliance. The variable 'Group productivity i' connects to the same variable depicted in Figure 4-2.

[715] See Ho Park et al. (2002), p. 542 and Norman (2004), p. 610.

Organizational openness does not exist per se. We identified two main features driving openness between the scientists: reciprocity and trust. First, as illustrated in Section 3.4.4.4, experiments in behavioral game theory demonstrate that people behave fairly in bargaining situations. Knowledge exchange and common learning can be interpreted as bargaining in the sense of "you may learn from me but I also learn from you."[716] So, when one scientist is open to her colleague from the partner firm, the colleague reciprocates this openness. More generally, members of one organization who receive knowledge from a member of the partner firm pay back this favor in a following period.[717] Consequently, when one parent is open to its partner, the partner tries to be similarly open to the other. This results in an ever increasing reciprocal openness between the collaborating partner firms (see the reinforcing loop in Figure 4-14), following tit-for-tat until a complete openness toward each other ensues. One scientist from one of the partners in the case study underlines that openness is especially present between scientists when stating that "*[i]n fact, we scientists like to talk to each other and exchange our knowledge with each other.*"[718]

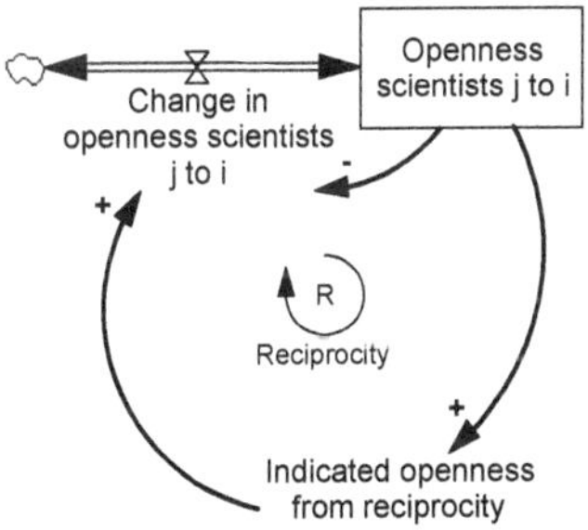

Figure 4-14: Reciprocal 'Openness between scientists'[719]

Second, trust contributes to the free exchange of information between committed partners.[720] When members on all organizational levels work in an atmosphere of trust with their partners, they do not feel as if they need to protect themselves from opportunistic behavior. Even if an alliance contract allows free flow of knowledge and spillover between the partners – without trust, knowledge exchange would be low in accuracy, comprehensiveness, and relevance.[721] One interviewee supports this observation that trust enhances openness between the scientists when saying that "*[t]he more you trust somebody, the more you discuss openly with them.*"[722] Both the literature and the members of both case study firms interviewed identify trust as a key determinant for learning alliance success. Therefore, we discuss the concept trust, its determinants and its effects in further detail in Section 4.6.4. Summarizing, openness

716 Inkpen (2000a), p. 1027.
717 See Das and Teng (2002), p. 449. See also Muthusamy and White (2005), p. 427, who explain reciprocal behavior applying social exchange theory.
718 P4: 70.
719 Source: authors' representation.
720 See Inkpen (1995), p. 67.
721 See Zand (1972), pp. 230-231 and Inkpen (1995), p. 67.
722 P6: 34.

between the scientists increases the quality of knowledge exchange, knowledge spillover, and interorganizational learning.

4.6.3 Preventing Unintended Knowledge Spillover

Possible spillover to the partner in terms of private learning is regarded as an inevitable consequence of interfirm collaboration despite efforts to protect knowledge.[723] Firms' managers should take this into consideration when entering learning alliances. Sometimes, however, firms do not want their knowledge to be spread to the partnering firm or to the alliance. As "knowledge is not a free-floating public good, but a controlled resource that moves between firms in a predictable fashion"[724], firms should select what knowledge they pass on to the alliance or to their partner. Contractual or non-contractual safeguards may be installed against unintentional and unofficial knowledge flows.[725] According to transaction cost economics, safeguards are installed to create an atmosphere of equity and fairness among the collaborating partners.[726] They may prevent the firms from being outlearned and to ensure perceived fairness among the participants. Hence, they protect the firms against opportunistic behavior.

Transaction cost economics[727] suggests contractual safeguards which are also called formal controls or third-party enforcements like, for example, legal contracts, to protect firms from partner opportunism.[728] According to INKPEN AND CURRALL, such contractual safeguards are "predictable, regular, and involve explicit information transfers, and are codified in rules, procedures, and regulations."[729] They may contain financial reporting guidelines, regular meetings between the managers, or explicit cooperative venture procedures. Such explicit alliance procedures may include the existence of technological gatekeepers. They are specialized personnel who are strongly connected to internal members and strongly linked to the external partner firm.[730] Their duty is to filter information access and disclosure between the parent firms and the alliance. Though scientists might be open toward each other and like to share their knowledge with each other, gatekeepers may restrict this openness. Gatekeepers play a major role in the governance structure of our case study.

---

723 See Inkpen (2000a), p. 1027 and Inkpen (2002), p. 276.

724 Tallman and Jenkins (2002), p. 168.

725 See Hamel et al. (1989), p. 136 and Dussauge et al. (2000), p. 102. More generally, Liebeskind discusses three broad classes of organizational mechanisms for protecting knowledge: rules, compensation schemes, and structural isolation. See Liebeskind (1997), pp. 629-653.

726 See the discussion on contributions of transaction cost economics to alliances in Section 3.4.1

727 See Section 3.4.1.

728 See Gulati (1995a), p. 87 or Dyer and Singh (1998), p. 669. Contracts of cooperative ventures provide "a legally bound, institutional framework in which each party's rights, duties, and responsibilities are codified and the goals, policies, and strategies underlying the anticipated [...] venture are specified. Every [...] contract has the purpose of facilitating exchange and preventing opportunism." Luo (2002), p. 904 and likewise Luo and Tan (2003), pp. 187-188.

729 Inkpen and Currall (2004), p. 590.

730 See Tushman and Katz (1980), p. 1071 and also Simonin (1999), p. 601 or Inkpen and Dinur (1998), p. 457.

In accordance with the alliance contract, both the American and the European parent nominate a designated gatekeeper to receive the partner's sole know-how. If the gatekeeper has decided that sole know-how may flow to the partner, this prior disclosed knowledge is no longer seen as confidential. It becomes common knowledge. So, the gatekeepers are responsible for determining what knowledge flows within and between their respective firms. By contract, they are instructed to maximize their own firm's knowledge flows to ensure a successful alliance.[731]

In the alliance in the study, gatekeeping is important because of two motives: first, both firms have third party obligations, and second, because of potential contamination of fields unrelated to the alliance scope with partner knowledge – in other words, potential private learning. Gatekeepers restrict scientists' openness in two ways. Not only do they decide which knowledge flows out of the firm but also which knowledge may flow into the firm. One manager comprehensively explains its necessity, referring to the first reason: *"Because of the other arrangements that we have and ventures in other parts of the company, [using knowledge from our partner in areas unrelated to the alliance scope] is something that we have to pay particular attention to. Being knowledgeable of other efforts within the company, we had to make sure that the technologies that we were applying were very specific to this particular field of study [...]. Clearly, there are learnings, sort of fundamental understandings [...], that are generally applicable and you would like to be able to leverage off those. But [...] we certainly couldn't take information from the [other] joint-venture [...], [and] apply that to this alliance. [...] We were restricted from doing that. When you are involved in these kinds of efforts, in particular when you are working for a company like [one of ours] where you have multiple business applications, [...] and you have set up these ventures or cooperations with other third parties in those particular areas, you've got to be very very clear as to what's in and out of the field. The whole issue of contamination is extremely important and something we take very seriously."*[732]

Another manager focuses on the second motivation, knowledge spillover to related research fields in the own firm but outside the alliance scope. *"We had to guarantee some way that no knowledge spills over from [our partner] to us so that our colleagues who work and do research in [a related field in our organization] at last are not contaminated and blocked in their research. If knowledge spilled over and spread to them and they can't prove that it was them who developed it we just couldn't use it. This means that everything we hear from [our partner] can potentially block [our own research] – even if we don't want to hear it. Therefore, the gatekeeper's tasks are to observe what we do in [our research field] and not to let through knowledge that he evaluates as dangerous for [the related research field in our firm] to know."*[733]

While gatekeepers may prevent partnering firms from being outlearned, their existence can be self-defeating at the same time. They may restrict the scientists to openly exchanging their knowledge with each other and cooperating closely and efficiently with the scientists from the partner firm. They may hinder collaborative learn-

[731] See P9: 9.
[732] P5: 13 - P5: 17.
[733] P3: 14.

ing if their policies are too tight.[734] In the case study alliance, gatekeeper restrictions were fairly strict, which can be inferred by one manager's statement: *"The necessity of gatekeeping actually prevents every spontaneous direct knowledge exchange."*[735] This means that gatekeeper restrictions that are too tight may hamper common learning and the development of common knowledge. However, this common knowledge is regarded as the basis for developing the agreed-upon alliance objectives, for example, patents.

Even though regarded as a hindrance to common learning, the installation of gatekeepers ensures that members of the participating organizations deal respectfully with the knowledge obtained from the partner. Moreover, regarding the difficulty of respecting gatekeeper restrictions, one manager affirms the following: "*I don't see that as a real downside, it is not a difficult thing to do. You have to work at it all the time, even at the back of your mind all the time: .. this is information that you have obtained from your cooperation partner and it's not yours to disseminate to other people."*[736] Also, it seems to be common for firm members who are often confronted with joint researching with alliance partners to consider gatekeeper restrictions: "*That's not an issue for us; we had to live with these kinds of agreements for years. [My firm] has a long history of engaging in joint-ventures and cooperations and I think they are good to do because there is a lot of learning out there that can help put technology forward quicker. But that is something we had to do. We had to put up some barriers within our organization to make sure that there was no confidential information leakage in other parts of the company."*[737]

Summarizing, gatekeepers restrict knowledge flows from the parent firms to the alliance as well as from the alliance to the parent firms. Therefore, from the abovementioned we can infer the following two stock and flow structures. Figure 4-15 represents the restrictions of knowledge flows from the parent companies to the shared knowledge in the alliance.

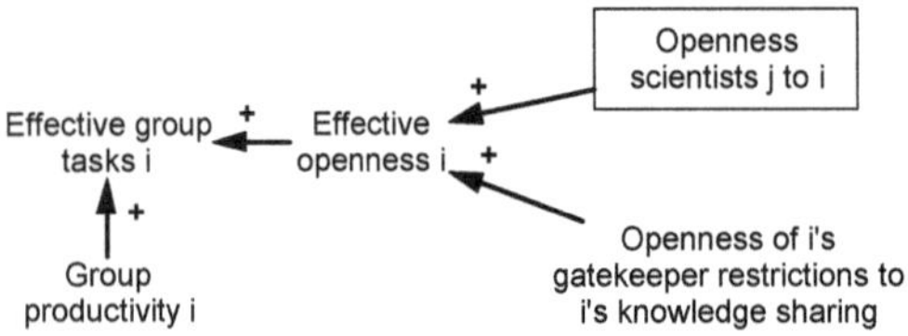

Figure 4-15: 'Openness of both parents' gatekeeper restrictions' on scientist productivity of the respective firm or group.[738]

Here, the openness of the parent firms' gatekeepers determines the scientists' productivity: the greater the openness, the more effectively they can perform their joint

[734] See Norman (2004), p. 613.
[735] P3: 28.
[736] P5: 19.
[737] P5: 19.
[738] Source: authors' representation. This figure enhances the model structure of Figure 4-13.

tasks. The structure distinguishes two scientist groups, indicated by the indices i and j.

Alternatively, knowledge may potentially flow from the alliance to the parent firms. This relationship can be transferred into stock and flow terms as indicated in Figure 4-16. How much is learned privately from the 'Alliance knowledge base' depends, among other things, on the 'Openness of gatekeeper restrictions to private learning'. In Figure 4-16 we explicitly distinguish the variables between parents i and j to emphasize that one parent's gatekeeper openness determines its partner's private learning opportunity.

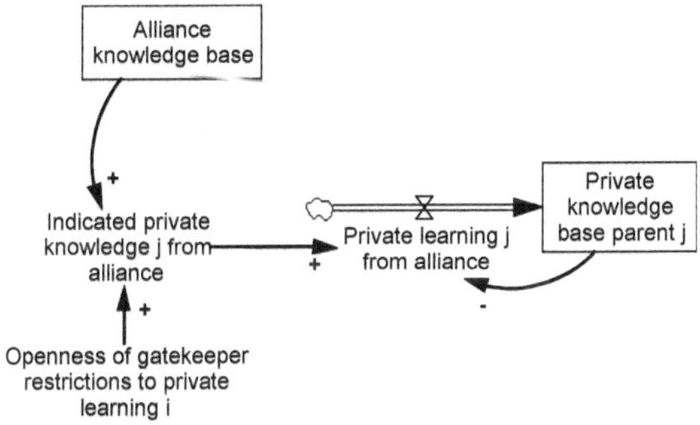

Figure 4-16: 'Openness of gatekeeper restrictions' by one parent influencing the partner's 'Private learning from alliance' opportunities[739]

Formal controls such as technology gatekeepers enable the partnering firms to have formalized, routine contractual structures in place, regardless of how well social controls operate on the interfirm level among managers and scientists. INKPEN AND CURRALL talk about a safety net that formal controls provide if social controls fail.[740] In contrast to such formal third-party enforcement, self-enforcing agreements are more uncertain, ambiguous, and organizationally embedded, and utilize "organizational values, norms, and cultures to encourage desirable behavior."[741] They involve safeguards that allow for self-enforcement over time. Within the group of self-enforcing agreements, DYER AND SINGH, following a slightly different definition of safeguards, distinguish between – again – formal safeguards and informal safeguards. Despite the wording we list formal safeguards under social controls, because – as opposed to formal third-party enforcements – no third party gets involved to decide whether a violation has taken place.[742] Formal safeguards in DYER AND SINGH's interpretation are economic hostages like financial and investment hostages that firms create to control opportunism by aligning the partnering firms' economic incentives. This may involve financial or symmetrical irreversible investments in specialized or cospecialized as-

[739] Source: authors' representation. The indices i and j represent the two different research groups involved in the alliance.
[740] See Inkpen and Currall (2004), p. 591.
[741] Das and Teng (1998), p. 501 and see also Inkpen and Currall (2004), p. 590.
[742] See Telser (1980), p. 27.

sets leading to a visible credible commitment to the partner firm.[743] The risk of potential opportunism is decreased by the fact that the value of the financial hostage would decrease if one partner behaved unfairly.[744] Moreover, the financial hostage may increase in value if both partners contribute fairly to the alliance.

DYER AND SINGH's informal safeguards depend on personal trust relations by direct contact or reputation, driven by indirect experience within the embedded network.[745] Social and non-contractual safeguards are more likely to develop, the higher the initial trust between the partnering firms. Scholars argue that social safeguards "supplement – and often supplant – formal controls."[746] In a situation of high trust between the partners, risk and fear of opportunism is low. An initial existence of such self-enforcing safeguards might lead to a less detailed written alliance agreement at the beginning of an alliance, when trust between the partners is usually low and governance costs are high due to more detailed contract writing and documentation, more frequently scheduled meetings, and frequent interactions with lawyers, more monitoring, and more intensive contract enforcement. This leads to the observation that informal self-enforcing social safeguards are more effective and less costly than formal third-party enforcements. Consequently, they reduce transaction costs.[747]

GULATI states that formal controls (like contracts) and social controls (like trust between the members of the partnering firms) may substitute each other.[748] Even though formal controls may be installed apart from social controls, the emergence of trust as a result of interpartner interaction may strengthen organizational ties between firms. According to INKPEN AND CURRALL, these intensified organizational ties may lead to greater weight of social controls. As the types of controls can be looked upon as substitutable, over time formal controls – even if in place – lose their importance for a successful continuance of the alliance with increasing trust between the partners.[749] This relationship is depicted in Figure 4-17.

As informal social controls like trust may replace formal controls, which are expensive and a driving force for increasing transaction costs in alliances, and because trust is identified as an important enabler for successful interfirm collaboration, as indicated above, it is worthwhile analyzing and discussing trust in more detail in the following.

---

[743] See Dyer and Singh (1998), p. 669 and also Williamson (1983), p. 519.
[744] Dyer reports of Japanese car manufacturers being more likely to use financial hostages like minority ownerships as a signal for long-term commitment than contracts, which their American competitors use. See Dyer (1997), p. 548.
[745] See Dyer and Singh (1998), p. 669.
[746] Dyer and Singh (1998), p. 669 and see also Granovetter (1985), p. 491.
[747] See Dyer and Singh (1998), p. 669 and Inkpen and Currall (2004), p. 590.
[748] See Gulati (1995a), p. 93.
[749] See Inkpen and Currall (2004), p. 591.

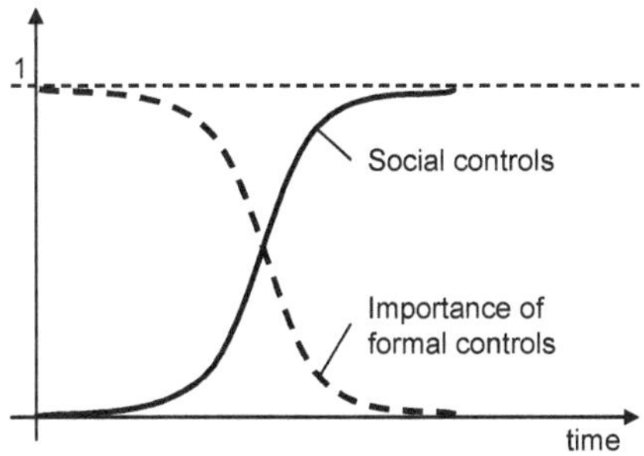

Figure 4-17: Social controls and formal controls are substitutable.[750]

4.6.4 Interpersonal and Interfirm Trust

Trust as a social control is regarded as a critical factor influencing interfirm knowledge transfer and common knowledge creation.[751] In an empirical study by the Association of Strategic Alliance Professionals on alliance capability, lack of trust between the cooperating firms alone contributes to alliance failure in 45% of the cases.[752] Despite its importance for cooperations – not only in the field of alliances – and because of its application in various research fields, scholars have not agreed on a single definition.[753] Sociologists, for example, pay attention to how social networks may influence trust and economists are interested in how trust may reduce transaction costs.[754] Hence, its concept is regarded as "subtle, diffuse, and elusive"[755], which causes CHILD to observe that it "remains an under-theorized, under-researched, and therefore, poorly understood phenomenon."[756] In the following we review some definitions and dimensions of trust.

4.6.4.1 Definition of Trust

Because lack of trust between the parties may lead to competitive confusion about whether or not the alliance partner is actually an ally, doubtful firms may prefer to end an alliance early.[757] With intermutual trust in place as a social control, trust is considered to be a type of expectation that alleviates the fear that the partner will act oppor-

[750] Source: authors' representation. In this illustration it is assumed that both controls add up to hundred percent.

[751] See, for example, Doz (1996), p. 69 referring to trust playing a major role in the civilian jet engine alliance CFM International between General Electric and SNECMA. See also Perlmutter and Heenan (1986), pp. 150-151, Inkpen (1995), p. 67, Inkpen (1996), p. 134, Lang (1997), p. 225, Whipple and Frankel (2000), p. 23, Zahn and Foschiani (2000), pp. 511-513, Das and Teng (2001), p. 255, Batt and Purchase (2004), p. 170, Norman (2004), p. 612, and Inkpen and Tsang (2005), p. 154.

[752] See de Man and Duysters (2002), p. 7.

[753] See Das and Teng (2001), p. 255.

[754] See Camerer (2003a), p. 83.

[755] Nooteboom (1996), p. 990.

[756] Child (2001b), p. 274.

[757] See Powell et al. (1996), p. 117.

tunistically.[758] Hence, firms do not need to protect themselves from possible opportunistic behavior by their partner any longer. Similarly, and putting more emphasis on risk of opportunism, DAS AND TENG explicitly referring to strategic alliances, suggest that "trust is about positive expectations regarding the other in a risky situation."[759] INKPEN underlines the expectations about partner behavior when saying that "trust reflects the belief that a partner's word or promise is reliable and that a partner will fulfill its obligations in the relationship."[760] Also stressing the importance of risk in the definition, ZAND views trust in an alliance as increasing one partner's vulnerability to the risk of opportunistic behavior by its partner. This is because the behavior of the latter is not under the control of the former in a situation where the costs of violating the trust are greater than the benefits of maintaining the relationship.[761] ANDERSON AND NARUS explicitly encompass the relationship's outcome that ZAND already mentions. They view trust as the belief that the partner firm will perform actions that result in positive outcomes and will not take unexpected action that may lead to negative outcomes.[762]

While the above definitions are based on expectations of the partner's behavior, CURRALL AND JUDGE, CURRALL AND INKPEN, and CURRALL AND EPSTEIN view trust as an action that puts one parent's fate in the hands of its partner. Referring to an alliance, this means that a partner's trust is indicated by a decision to engage in action that allows its fate to be determined by the partner.[763] It may also lead to a decision not to take action, for example, when a firm refrains from instaling formal safeguards or does not allocate resources.

Seen from a behavioral game theoretical perspective, MESSICK AND KRAMER see trust as a choice and trusting "as an altruistic act in that it is an act that increases the outcomes for the other while either increasing or risking a decreased outcome for the truster."[764] With this definition they go beyond the paradigm of the self-interest-seeking, utility-maximizing, and rational homo economicus that does net-present calculations of possible future actions. Only expectations about the "shadow of the future"[765] may hold back the partner from opportunistic behavior in the present. From this perspective, altruistic behavior can be excluded.[766] However, as stated in Section

---

758 See Bradach and Eccles (1989), p. 104. See also Gulati (1995a), p. 91 and Kale et al. (2000), p. 220. The English language offers a detailed differentiation of subtleties in meanings of terms. Therefore, Luhmann formulates differences of trust as familiarity and confidence. Familiarity being an inevitable fact of life eases the growth of both trust and confidence. Confidence is based on a belief in the continuance of experiences that people can extend to a wider set of to date unknown situations. Luhmann sees trust as a solution for specific problems of risk. But trust only develops in a world which is familiar. See Luhmann (1979), pp. 18-23 and Luhmann (1988), pp. 95-97.

759 Das and Teng (2001), p. 255, who quote Gambetta (1988a), pp. 217-218

760 Inkpen (1995), p. 67.

761 See Zand (1972), pp. 230-231 and also Chiles and McMackin (1996), p. 85. One case study manager supports this definition when saying that "[t]rust is how I make myself vulnerable to the partner firm." P3: 149.

762 See Anderson and Narus (1990), p. 45. Stein argues in the same vein. See Stein (2003), p. 176.

763 See Currall and Judge (1995), p. 153, Currall and Inkpen (2002), p. 484 and also Currall and Epstein (2003), p. 194.

764 Messick and Kramer (2001), p. 95. See also Fichman (2003), p. 134

765 Axelrod (1984), p. 126.

766 See Wurche (1994), p. 156.

3.4.4.3 in which we discuss findings from behavioral game theory, humans do not necessarily act rationally. Reciprocity and fairness, being connected with social utility, move to the foreground.[767] A parent becomes vulnerable to its partner if it trusts the latter. The partner's actions are then measured against certain expectations that can be characterized in terms of fairness. If the partner acts in accordance with the expectations the behavior is considered to be fair-dealing.[768] BROMILEY AND CUMMINGS argue in the same vein while focusing on trust in alliances. They define trust as the expectation that an individual or group fulfills obligations, behaves in a predictable manner, and negotiates honestly when the possibility for opportunism is present.[769] Mutual wellbeing of the partner firms is also part of MADHOK's definition. He views trust as the "perceived likelihood of the other not behaving in a self interested manner."[770]

Mistrust[771] or distrust[772] seem to be the opposite of trust, or just a lack of trust. It is, however, more than this, in that it encompasses negative expectations toward persons, objects, systems, and information.[773] It may lead to reserve, manipulability, stress, panic, or fear with regard to mistrusted people. KANTER underlines that the existence of mistrust between alliance partners may start a reinforcing feedback loop that might especially hinder alliance objectives.[774]

Despite some variations in the definitions explained above, in the context of learning alliances, we view trust as a partner firm having sufficient confidence in its partner to commit valuable resources including knowledge to perform joint transactions. It does so despite the risk of its partner taking advantage of this commitment.[775] Yet, according to KALE, SINGH, AND PERLMUTTER, there is an emerging consensus among scholars in alliance research that mutual trust creates the basis for a stable and successful relationship between cooperating firms.[776]

4.6.4.2 Sources and Objects of Trust

For a better understanding of the concept of trust, BACHMAN claims to differentiate between sources of trust and objects of trust – despite the fact that oftentimes terms are used in both ways.[777] Therefore, we discuss objects and sources of trust in the following. Afterwards we relate opinions of case study interviewees to the theoretical concepts.

---

767 See Camerer (2003a), p. 113.
768 See Fichman (2003), p. 136.
769 See Bromiley and Cummings (1995), pp. 223-224 and see also Lado et al. (1997), p. 129 and Zaheer et al. (2002), pp. 347-348.
770 Madhok (1995), p. 120.
771 See Kanter (1994), p. 105 and Büchel (2003), p. 93. The latter uses mistrust and distrust interchangeably.
772 See, for example, Luhmann (1979), p. 71 or Hamel et al. (1989), p. 135.
773 See Krystek (1997), p. 547.
774 See Kanter (1994), p. 105.
775 See Child and Faulkner (1998), p. 45.
776 Kale et al. (2000), p. 220.
777 See Bachmann (1998), p. 308.

Regarding the object of trust, LUHMANN distinguishes system trust and personal trust.[778] The former refers to trust in abstract social and technical systems, such as an organization like firms or systems for energy production. He claims that without minimum trust in systems, modern industrial societies would not operate. Personal trust, on the other hand, becomes more important in interorganizational settings.[779] Although trust in the partner's organization is necessary as such in interfirm collaborations, personal ties between the members of both alliance partners seem to grow in significance. They simply seem to make collaborative actions possible. Personal trust is based on reciprocal responding, positive experiences with people in exchange relations, and additionally may be based on emotional proximity. Furthermore, personal trust may manifest itself in trust either in a person's technical competence or goodwill. In interorganizational collaborations, interpersonal trust may exist on various organizational levels – on the scientist, manager, or executive level, for example. Over time, trust on one level may facilitate trust on another level and vice versa. "Trust is amplified as it travels across organizational levels."[780] One case study manager, even though referring to distrust, observes the connection between organizational layers: *"The [scientists] sitting in the room during exchange [meetings] easily sense if there is some sort of distrust or the managers are holding back from one another or the [scientists]. These are smart people. They would pick up on that real quickly. They follow suit. They would tend to hold back also."*[781] He continues and summarizes that *"if there is a level of distrust on the leadership level, there is going to be less trust on lower levels – maybe even more so, because [the scientists] are going to protect their individual company's position. If they sense that their managers are not cooperating with one another, they won't cooperate with one another on whatever level they are working at."*[782]

SYDOW puts sources of trust in relation with objects of trust to describe the object's conditions of constitutions.[783] Trust sources may influence both person and system trust. For his analysis, SYDOW employs three sources of trust identified by ZUCKER: process-based trust, characteristic-based trust, and institutional-based trust.[784] Institutional-based trust develops from formal societal structures like, for example, certifications, professions, traditions, or brand names. In interorganizational settings, institutional-based trust may include regulations either on interpersonal (personal trust) or interorganizational exchange (system trust) conditions. The latter may refer to, for instance, alliance contracts that determine knowledge exchange or common knowledge creation as well as contractual gatekeepers presented in Section 4.6.3. Regarding a strong emphasis of institutional-based system trust and personal trust, one case study interviewee expresses that *"[i]t is difficult to talk about [process-based and characteristic-based personal] trust when the alliance contract is 140 pages long."*[785]

---

[778] See Luhmann (1979), pp. 56-58 and also Krystek (1997), p. 547, Sydow (1998), pp. 42 and 44-45, Bachmann (1998), p. 308, or Apelt (1999), p. 12.
[779] See Krystek and Zur (1997).
[780] Inkpen and Currall (2004), p. 597.
[781] P8: 32.
[782] P8: 33.
[783] See Sydow (1998), p. 44.
[784] For the following explanation see Zucker (1986), p. 53 and also Sydow (1998), pp. 43-44.
[785] P4: 67.

In other words, institutional-based trust is definitely present on the personal and system level in our case study. Mutual knowledge exchange and creation is highly regulated.

Process-based trust depends on concrete past experience of exchange or exchange expected in the future. SYDOW points out that it is "deeply rooted within stable personal relationships and, hence, the social embeddedness of economic action."[786] Furthermore, he states that process-based trust may accumulate into reputation. In other words, fair and successful past interactions may generate such attributes of the person (personal trust) or organization (system trust) that help when entering into cooperations with this person or organization.[787] Finally, characteristic-based trust develops from concrete exchange experience. It is tied to a person's characteristics, such as family background or ethnicity (person trust), or properties of the social system that are relevant for the development of trust (system trust).

Other scholars use related but different trust concepts for illustrating various sources of trust. ZUCKER, INKPEN AND TSANG, for example, also identify institutional-based and process-based trust as trust sources though they do not explicitly refer to ZUCKER's statements.[788] First, referring to structural embeddedness, they explain the existence of institutional-based trust because of a firm's position in networks in which reputations about trustworthiness of a potential partner are embedded.[789] Second, referring to alliances, they interpret process-based trust similarly to ZUCKER when they state that it means that firms "regularly test each other's integrity, moving from small, discrete exchanges of limited risk to more open-ended deals that subject the parties to substantial risk."[790] Third, according to the authors, behavioral-based trust plays an important role in interfirm settings. Behavioral-based trust develops because of the behavior that people or firms reveal in relationships. This is the only time the authors clearly distinguish between trust objects – even though this would be appropriate for their first two sources of trust, too.

WHIPPLE AND FRANKEL also identify the two perspectives, character-based and competence-based trust in alliances. Though character-based trust could be interpreted similarly to ZUCKER's characteristic-based trust there are slight differences. WHIPPLE AND FRANKEL understand it as "qualitative characteristics of behavior inherent in partners' strategic philosophies and cultures."[791] Their definition of character-based trust includes partner integrity, behavioral consistency – which INKPEN AND TSANG both subsume under process-based trust – motive identification, openness, and discrete-

---

786 Sydow (1998), p. 43.
787 See Inkpen and Currall (2004), p. 593. According to the above explanation of reputation, it may be built up in a relationship from direct experience. Seen slightly differently, reputation may be interpreted as an indirect experience via the network a firm is embedded in, whereas trust results from direct experience of interaction. See Dyer and Singh (1998), p. 669.
788 See Inkpen and Tsang (2005), p. 154.
789 See also Lado et al. (1997), p. 129 and Currall and Epstein (2003), p. 194. For explanations of structural embeddedness see Section 3.4.3.
790 Inkpen and Tsang (2005), p. 154 referring to Lazerson and Lorenzoni (1999), p. 250.
791 See Whipple and Frankel (2000), p. 23.

ness. They see competence-based trust as driven by partner behavior and daily performance.

NOOTEBOOM and DAS AND TENG differentiate the same dimensions for sources of trust.[792] Similar to WHIPPLE AND FRANKEL, they understand competence-based trust as the "ability of a partner to perform according to the alliance contract."[793] In contrast, the other dimension is goodwill trust. It relates to the partner's "good faith, good intentions, and integrity."[794] This goes along with the partner's reputation in the network concerning its perception of fairness and therefore with ZUCKER's idea of process-based trust – regardless of the personal or the abstract system level. ZAHEER, LOFSTROM, AND GEORGE report a case in which a CEO of one alliance partner could be relied upon as fair and not opportunistic. This supported the building of goodwill trust and a further continuation of the alliance.[795]

Picking up the idea of emotional bonds between alliance partners, MCALLISTER also incorporates ZUCKER's idea of process-based trust, although he calls it affect-based trust.[796] According to his findings, affect-based trust on the one hand is driven by personal behavior, demonstrating interpersonal care and concern.[797] On the other hand, it is associated with the interaction frequency among the partners. Moreover, MCALLISTER, following LEWIS AND WEIGERT, identifies cognition-based trust, which describes whom people trust under which circumstances based on what are considered to be "'good reasons', constituting evidence of trustworthiness."[798]

CHILD considers MCALLISTER's categorization to be broad in comparison to his own.[799] He, along with LANE[800], defines cognitive trust as sharing of cognitions between the collaborating partners. This includes, for example, common ways of thinking, leading to mutual understanding of each other's past, present, and anticipation of future actions. Cognitive trust can only be increased by the partners getting to know each other better. Some cognitive sharing is necessary for calculative trust. It is based on expectations about one another, including calculations which weigh the cost and benefits of certain courses of action.[801] In other words, calculative trust builds upon the assurance that the partner will behave as it says. This makes an alliance parent dependent on the information attainable about its partner – leading to the problems of hidden information, hidden action, etc. identified in Section 3.4.1. Moreover, this approach involves ideas of relational embeddedness between the partners in which they develop shared understandings as a result of strong socializing relations.[802] There is a link between ZUCKER's definition of characteristic-based trust and CHILD's and LANE's explanation of normative trust. Normative trust develops as people share

---

792 See Nooteboom (1996), pp. 990-991 and Das and Teng (2001), p. 256.
793 Nooteboom (1996), p. 990.
794 Das and Teng (2001), p. 256.
795 See Zaheer et al. (2002), p. 356
796 See McAllister (1995), p. 29.
797 This perception sides with the idea of altruism. See Fichman (2003), p. 95.
798 Lewis and Weigert (1985), p. 970.
799 See Child (1998), p. 246.
800 See Lane (1998), p. 3.
801 See Lewicki and Bunker (1996), p. 120 and see also Child (1998), p. 244.
802 See Gulati (1998), p. 296 and see Section 3.4.3 for explanations of embeddedness.

common values and concepts of moral obligation. As CHILD points out, normative trust is more likely to evolve on the interpersonal level. This goes along with ZUCKER's definition of characteristic-based trust.[803]

During the case study interviews, scientists and managers made comments to the effect of emphasizing some drivers of trust. Yet, at times they cannot attach much importance to others for their particular alliance experience. Generally speaking, they frequently talk about personal trust between managers and between scientists. As one manager remarks, for example: *"[My contact person at our partner firm] and I talk on a regular basis. [...] So, face-to-face meetings happen at least 3-4 times per year between the parties. [He] and I talk, if not every week at least once a month, sometimes a lot more than that. There is a lot of keeping each other up-to-date with progress."*[804] He continues by observing that *"[p]ersonal relationships are so important in anything working, whether it's the customer, the supplier, or in our case, a competitor. Having a personal relationship makes so many things go easier. [...] We enjoy each other's company. We enjoy sitting around after dinner and having a beer in the lobby, if that's the situation. So, I think that helps. It facilitates a good working relationship. It would be difficult without some sort of a personal relationship to have the same level of trust that we do because we do that much."*[805] The manager clearly describes what MCALLISTER summarizes under affect-based trust. In other words, the frequent exchange between managers may lead to more knowledge about each other and a more personal relationship.

The manager explains that both partners purposely put strong emphasis on the development of mutual trust between them through mutual interaction: *"I think all of us have been in business long enough that we recognize the need for that. So we put some effort into it. We make sure that there are opportunities to share meals together, to have cocktails together, and have some social events as well as just the meetings. If there were no social interactions around the meetings they would not go as well. The more quickly you can develop personal relationships the better. That applies to the advisory committee members; it applies to the technical folks sitting around the table, also."*[806]

A scientist remarks, following this argument: *"We were doing team-building type of exercises and dinners, where we deliberately made sure people were not sitting together with someone from the same company. So you can at least engage in a conversation. And as we saw last night, we had a nice dinner at the museum and I know when they were [visiting us], we went to some sports events. It's little things like that, that may not seem that significant at the time but they do provide a mechanism for partners to build trust in a relationship. And once that took place then people tend to freely discuss things knowing that it's all in the common good for the cooperation."*[807]

[803] See Child (1998), p. 245 and Zucker (1986), p. 53.
[804] P8: 18.
[805] P8: 27.
[806] P8: 28.
[807] P5: 40.

Following CURRALL AND INKPEN's approach, who view trust as a decision to act,[808] we can translate the statements mentioned into the following stock and flow structures. The 'Number of interactions' between members of both partners drives the 'Trust' between them.[809] It is human nature for people who trust and feel close to each other to wish to meet and interact more frequently with each other. Hence, they make the decision to interact with the other. When they interact frequently, the members' mental models might adjust to each other, leading to a more common way of thinking (CHILD's and LANE's cognitive trust) and sharing of common values (CHILD's and LANE's normative trust). Summarizing, this results in a reinforcing loop which we label 'Let's meet!' (see upper feedback loop in Figure 4-18, in which we aggregate various trust objects into trust for reasons of simplicity).

We also found evidence for process-based trust in ZUCKER's and INKPEN AND TSANG's sense and for character-based trust in WHIPPLE AND FRANKEL's sense. For example, one manager states that, *"I believe that openness and integrity are prerequisites for trust."*[810] Or, put differently, because members of one parent were and are open and behave with integrity toward the members of the partner firm, they seek to seem trustworthy. One could also infer from this statement that they seek to behave "according to agreement"[811] – openly communicate and exchange and share knowledge – to achieve their common goals. As CURRALL AND INKPEN observe, openness is one form trust may take form of.[812] This behavior builds up goodwill trust according to NOOTEBOOM. Trust would result in a decision to be (more) open to the partner. Members of one parent expect their behavior to be reciprocated by the partner. Reciprocal behavior and fairness again influence trust,[813] resulting in a positive feedback loop which we label 'Fairness' (see lower feedback loop in Figure 4-18). Hence, we identify several sources of trust playing an important role in interfirm ventures. Yet, including all of them in the simulation model would increase model complexity considerably. Therefore, in the following, we do not differentiate between them. We simply subsume them under 'Trust', increasing model clarity.

808 See Currall and Inkpen (2002), p. 484.
809 See also Ring and van de Ven (1992), p. 489, Pless (1999), p. 167, and Inkpen and Currall (2004), p. 593.
810 P3: 159.
811 Nooteboom (1996), p. 990.
812 See Currall and Inkpen (2002), p. 486.
813 See Ring and van de Ven (1992), p. 488.

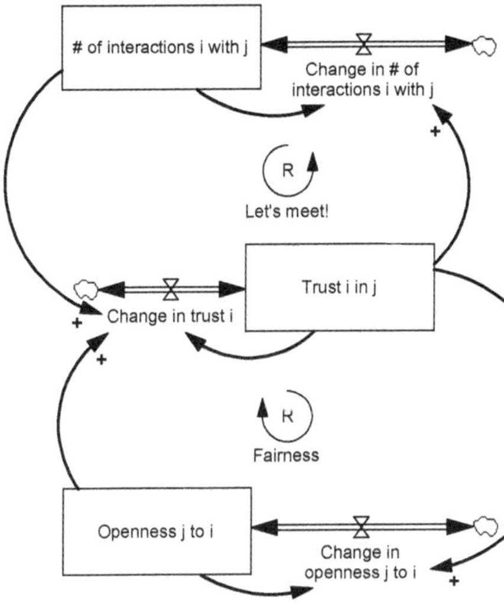

Figure 4-18: Stock and flow structure of 'Trust', 'Openness', and 'Number of interactions'.[814]

Above, we stated that trust exists on different organizational layers. Trust on the scientist level results in different actions from trust on the manager level. While it is open sharing of knowledge and open cooperation on the scientist level, trust as a decision to take action on the manager level might lead to showing credible commitment to the alliance. Such commitments may include, for example, financial hostages or resource commitments.[815] As indicated above, we analyze learning in alliances without any financial share, we focus on commitment of resources or, more operationally, scientists. Regarding scientist commitments, if trust between managers is high, managers are on the one hand convinced that the alliance is worth the investment and allocate their scientists according to the contract. On the other hand, they might be more willing to allocate the agreed number of scientists or even more. This leads to a 'Desired level of scientists' allocated by each parent firm that determines the 'Scientists active in alliance', as illustrated in Figure 4-19.

Yet, resource allocation does not necessarily need to be equal but it does need to be fair in relation to the prospective alliance outcome. GULATI, KHANNA, AND NOHRIA report from an alliance in which one parent did not send the number of employees to the alliance that was agreed on in the contract. The partner immediately adjusted its share according to the new situation and announced that the missing employees would only return if its partner fulfilled its obligations. In addition to the immediate ad-

[814] Source: authors' representation. The indices i and j represent the two different research groups involved in the alliance.

[815] See Dyer (1997), p. 548. For resource investment as senior management commitment see Hutt et al. (2000), p. 58. Other signals of commitment could be personnel assignments or direct hands-on involvement.

justment, manager trust suffered by the breaking of the agreement. Trust declined. The alliance was terminated shortly after.[816] Again, feelings of fairness and trust stand at the forefront of the policies. These relationships are illustrated in Figure 4-19.

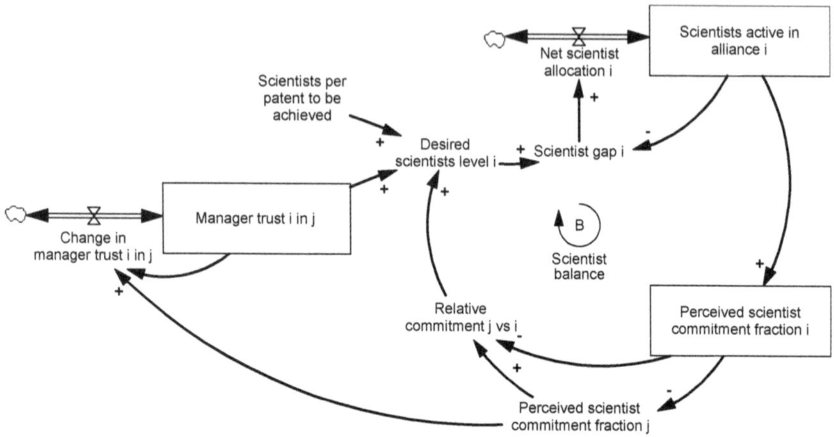

Figure 4-19: Stock and flow structure of 'Manager trust' and 'Scientists active in alliance'.

Credible commitments may again act as a signal of trustworthiness, which may increase the trust between the managers and strengthen the relationship.[817]

Moreover, interviewees clearly distinguish between trust objects as discussed above and competence-based trust.[818] Interviewees on both scientist and manager levels almost consistently remark that *"[t]rust to me is independent of the topic."*[819] One manager clearly and unmistakably states: *"I can surely respect somebody because of his or her skills and competences. I may think 'wow, I can really learn from that person'. But I can say that I don't trust him or her. [...] Those are two different things."*[820] Another scientist affirms that *"[c]ompetence is surely more important in the beginning of the alliance. I first have to see whether we play in the same division as the [scientists of our partner] and if we have similar basic expectations. [...] But this is simple exchange of matters."*[821] From our perspective, a partner's perception of a scientist's competence is determined by the latter's knowledge base. Seen from an organizational level, it means that the respective parents' knowledge bases determine the partner's perception of scientists' knowledge. This is determined by how much and what they are allowed to communicate due to potential gatekeeper restrictions.

[816] See Gulati et al. (1994), p. 63.
[817] See Sydow (1998), p. 39.
[818] See Nooteboom (1996), p. 990 and Das and Teng (2001), p. 256.
[819] P5: 48.
[820] P3: 150.
[821] P2: 70.

4.6.4.3 Interpersonal and Interorganizational Trust

Trust may develop on various levels between organizations. In their literature study, CURRALL AND INKPEN find that when studying trust scholars oftentimes do not properly align the levels of theory and the levels of measurement. The former refers to the unit the researcher seeks to examine, whereas the latter refers to the source of information. The authors identify three different levels on which they differentiate between who trusts – the trustor – and who is trusted – the trustee. Trust may develop on an interpersonal, an intergroup and an interfirm level. However, when researchers seek to analyze interfirm trust, they oftentimes measure trust between the firms' employees. Then the existence of interfirm trust is inferred from a survey of trust on an interpersonal level. According to the authors, this misspecification may lead to the reduced validity of the study.[822]

Usually, in cooperative settings trust develops between individuals. Trust may also evolve between groups. Then the focus needs to be shifted to the group level such as how decisions as results of trusting are made on the group level, for example.

When the level of trustor and trustee shifts from individuals to organizations, it is understood as interfirm or interorganizational trust.[823] It may involve firms themselves becoming objects of trust for members of other firms. Research in this field is only recent and studies show differing results.[824] CURRALL AND JUDGE, for example, imply that interorganizational trust is based on a generalized, trust evaluation of those individuals from the partner firm with whom they interact. Nevertheless, the partner firm consists of many more individuals than just those with whom they interact and to whom they do not build up trust.[825] Alternatively, ZAHEER, LOFSTROM, AND GEORGE find evidence that interfirm trust is more than aggregated interpersonal trust. According to their findings, interpersonal trust does not inevitably decline if a partner does not behave as expected – as opposed to interfirm trust.[826] From our understanding, and referring to LUHMANN's distinction between system and personal trust discussed at the beginning of Section 4.6.4.2, ZAHEER, LOFSTROM, AND GEORGE observe that personal trust is sustained while system trust declines. CURRALL AND INKPEN follow a different approach. According to their understanding, trust between firms can only be measured when analyzing the partners' policies containing information to engage in trusting actions toward the partner. Even though individuals make decisions, action takes place on the firm level, which reflects transactions between the partner firms.

As a last remark on trust, we would like to note that cooperation between organizations may occur without trust. Therefore, cooperation and trust should not be understood synonymously.[827] An example of an alliance which existed for nearly 15 years despite low interfirm trust is the airline alliance between KLM Royal Dutch Airline and Northwest Airlines. KUMAR AND NTI describe how both partners agree that trust was

822 See Currall and Inkpen (2002), p. 481.
823 See Zaheer et al. (2002), p. 348
824 See, for example, Currall and Judge (1995), Currall and Inkpen (2002), p. 480 for a review, and Zaheer et al. (2002).
825 See Currall and Judge (1995), pp. 151-152, who refer to boundary role persons.
826 See Zaheer et al. (2002), pp. 366-367
827 See Fichman (2003), p. 136.

non-existent. The partners only continued the relationship because the alliance generated a great deal of revenue.[828]

4.6.4.4 Dynamics of Trust

As stated above, trust evolves because of past interactions and experience.[829] It thus develops over the course of the alliance's existence. Moreover, it evolves slowly.[830] Therefore a longer time horizon provides more opportunities for the people in the alliance to develop mutual trust.[831]

Whereas CURRALL AND EPSTEIN state that trust starts around zero early in relationships, DAS AND TENG note that there is a minimum level of trust in any economic transaction.[832] As the focus of the present work lies in the dynamics of a learning alliance that has already been founded, we assume that there is at least some level of trust between the participating firms and their members. In any case, it takes constant effort to build up trust. It even takes constant effort to maintain the level of trust. It builds up like an S-shaped curve. This is also what the case-study interviewees observe in their alliance. As one manager states, *"during the project start trust has increased strongly. During the first half of the project it continued to increase that way. And at the end it increased only weakly."*[833] *"Again, it is very much an S-shaped curve type relationship"*[834], as another manager observes. This information provides the basis for the reference mode of trust over time depicted in Figure 4-20.

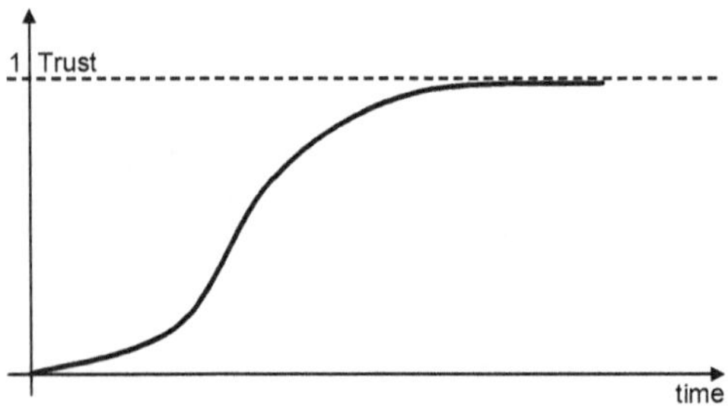

Figure 4-20: Reference mode: Trust.[835]

---

[828] See Kumar and Nti (1998), p. 363, referring to Tully (1996), pp. 44, 50. We speak of a limited time horizon from 1989 until 2004 because Air France merged with KLM Royal Dutch Airline in 2004.
[829] See also Kumar and Nti (1998), p. 361.
[830] See Glückler and Armbrüster (2003), p. 279 and Kühl (2003), p. 112.
[831] See Zeng and Chen (2003), p. 597.
[832] See Currall and Epstein (2003), p. 196 and Das and Teng (2001), p. 264.
[833] P3: 147.
[834] P8: 26.
[835] Source: authors' representation. The dynamics described are explained in depth in Section 7.2.3.

However, it may only take a minor sign of cheating or untrustworthiness to destroy an arduously built-up relationship. Trust disseminates quickly in a cycle of distrust, and distrust emerges.[836]

Summarizing the discussion on trust, trust is seen as an important, essential, and crucial feature for successful interfirm cooperation. At the same time it is a multifarious construct. Two objects like system and personal trust exist, for example, as do various trust sources. The discussion on trust sources is manifold. Authors from the same research field apply different terms to explain similar trust phenomena. Only for the relationship in alliances are trust sources like affect-based, character-based, normative, cognitive, and goodwill trust the focus of attention. Yet, we subsume and aggregate them under the term 'Trust' for clarity reasons. Further aggregation would not lead to additional insight on the dynamics of learning in learning alliances and, hence, does not stand in the focus of this work. Mutual trust is a crucial but fragile determinant in cooperative ventures. Therefore we explicitly study its influence on the dynamics in alliances in detail in Section 7.2.3.4.

4.7 Summary of Factors Determining the Long-Term Development of Interorganizational Learning

In Chapter 4 we presented some main factors determining the long-term development of interorganizational learning in alliances. We first discussed and defined the term interorganizational learning and we talked about what scholars identify as reasons for the success and failure of learning alliances. On the basis of these reasons, we identified those relevant for the aim of our study. We focus on those that determine cooperative and competitive behavior of parent firms in alliances. The parents' relative scopes decide on their prospective common or private benefits when entering alliances. We talked about the main learning modes, learning with and from the partner or the alliance. Furthermore, we presented the main factors influencing interorganizational learning, like, for example, absorptive capacity, interorganizational openness, and trust. In addition to discussing them, we also drew relationships between variables and drew feedback loops when appropriate. On this basis, we state our research propositions in the following. Afterwards, we describe the simulation model and present what we learn from it.

[836] See Sydow (1998), p. 38, Currall and Epstein (2003), p. 197, Kühl (2003), p. 112, and Inkpen and Currall (2004), p. 597.

5. Research Propositions

In this work we focus on the dynamics of two competing firms cooperating with each other in a learning alliance for developing patents. To do so, the firms rely on each other's knowledge bases as they do not have the required resources themselves.[837] Consequently, their intention is to learn with each other cooperatively despite being competitors in their markets. The dynamics we concentrate on emerge from two sources. First, we study the effects of opportunistic behavior in common learning from a feedback perspective.

Common Learning

On the basis of the context explained above, we postulate the following research propositions.

> *Proposition 1: Openness of the collaborating firms' gatekeepers fosters common learning in a learning alliance.*

The literature on interorganizational learning often states that organizational openness or transparency is, among other things, a driving factor for mutual knowledge exchange and new knowledge creation.[838]

> *Proposition 2.1: Opportunistic behavior in terms of free riding leads to loss of trust and early learning alliance dissolution.*

> *Proposition 2.1: Opportunistic behavior in terms of hidden goals leads to loss of trust and early learning alliance dissolution.*

As pointed out in Section 4.5.2, we suggest that two options for dishonest behavior exist when firms seek to learn together. The first relates to free riding when one firm allocates fewer resources than agreed while taking advantage of the partner firm, which then has a relatively higher share of investment. Second, a partner firm might have hidden intentions like hidden goals that it does not inform its partner about.[839] It may cover up being actually interested in fewer goals than agreed during alliance negotiations. The partner may choose this opportunistic option as it might be afraid that it would not reach an agreement to enter an alliance with the prospective partner if it had fewer common goals. Less potential alliance outcome corresponds with less investment. Consequently, the cheating partner allocates fewer scientists to the alliance. In both cases, the partner firm perceives the dishonest behavior and might, under some circumstances, dissolve the alliance.

> *Proposition 3: A trusting collaboration environment fosters common goal attainment in a learning alliance.*

---

[837] Firms seldom have all the required resources themselves for generating breakthrough innovations. See Lubatkin et al. (2001), p. 1353 and Sections 1.1 and 3.4.2.3.

[838] See, for example Hamel (1991), p. 85 and Section 4.6.2 on the need for organizational openness for successful joint knowledge creation.

[839] For hidden intentions see the explanations on organizational economics in Section 3.4.1.

The circumstances mentioned in the previous paragraph might include mutual trust between the alliance partners. As stated in Section 4.6.4.2, both opportunism and fairness determine trust. The underlying trust environment in which managers and scientists interact in a learning alliance affects the quality of mutual interactions; and hence the common knowledge creation and finally the goal attainment.

Private Learning
Second, we study effects of private goals on alliance dynamics. On the basis of the literature and case study analysis we postulate the following research propositions:

> *Proposition 4: Formal controls hinder private learning from a learning alliance.*

While formal controls, like gatekeepers, for example, control knowledge flows necessary for common knowledge creation, they also determine what knowledge may flow directly or indirectly to the partner firm. When they are restrictive, private learning is difficult to achieve.[840]

> *Proposition 5: Private learning from a learning alliance only occurs when common learning takes place.*

As indicated in Section 4.5.4, the current alliance literature states that firms first learn privately from each other before common knowledge occurs. Yet, we postulate that an alliance partner firm can only learn from an alliance after the scientists have exchanged their knowledge with each other and thus have created a common knowledge base.

> *Proposition 6: Private learning from a learning alliance may be concealed from the partner firm.*

Authors studying private learning in alliances suggest that if both firms learn privately from the alliance or each other, they enter a race to learn.[841] We question how firms would notice that they are being outlearned by their alliance partner. Since private learning is referred to as unfair,[842] firms would not openly communicate this to their partner. Therefore, there needs to be an indication in order for it to be noticed. We propose, however, that private learning does not necessarily need to be observed by the outlearned partner firm. It may be concealed from the partner.

Common and Private Learning
Third, we combine effects of common and private goals on alliance dynamics. Again, on the basis of the literature and case study analysis we postulate the following research propositions:

> *Proposition 7: Firms seeking private learning from a learning alliance make an effort to finish private learning before common learning is completed.*

[840] See the explanations in Section 4.6.3.
[841] See Hamel (1991), p. 85 and Inkpen (2002), p. 272.
[842] See Hamel (1991), p. 93.

With Proposition 7 we revise HAMEL's finding on learning from alliances. According to HAMEL, firms generally have the intention to accomplish their learnings as fast as possible.[843] We modify this observation by proposing that firms try to learn privately as fast as they can in order to be done with private learning before the alliance has attained its goals. If alliance partners behave opportunistically and have private goals they want to ensure that they at least have finished private learning if common learning fails.

Proposition 8: Detaching social controls from formal controls ensures a successful learning alliance.

In Section 4.6.3 we explained that over the course of a thus far successful alliance the partner firms' managers and scientists become more familiar with each other. This leads to, among other things, an increase in social controls like mutual trust. When social controls become more important in a cooperative venture, formal contractual controls may be pushed aside. The substitution of formal controls with social ones[844] opens up opportunities for opportunistic alliance partners to take advantage of their partner firm. We propose that maintaining formal controls while actively building up social controls is important for an upright cooperative relationship.

Proposition 9: Open alliance negotiations and clarity about goals and resource contributions lead to success of a learning alliance.

Both firms rely on each other to enhance their knowledge bases to pursue their goals. For the alliance to go smoothly, an open working atmosphere showing integrity is crucial. Frankness regarding joint goals and resource contributions are necessary before the start of an alliance to prevent antagonizing the alliance partner. A trustful relationship might stop partners from entering the alliance with hidden intentions: free riding and misleading agreements on goals do not then arise.

The research propositions presented enhance current research on interorganizational learning in alliances. Oftentimes alliance determinants are presented and analyzed independent from one another. Not only do we connect these components identified by alliance scholars and confirmed by interview partners from a real world alliance into one coherent and consistent model, but we also apply a dynamic point of view that enables policy-designers and decision-makers to perceive long-term effects of their decision-rules. In the following we present the simulation model that we apply to challenge the conjectures.

[843] See Hamel (1991), p. 88.
[844] See Gulati (1995a), p. 93.

6. Interorganizational Learning Model Description

6.1 Overview

In the following chapter we present the structure of the simulation model from which we seek to learn how to manage learning alliances successfully. Hence, the purpose of the model is to identify policy implications for managers who enter learning alliances with their firms to identify and prevent partner opportunism. The model allows policy-designers and decision-makers on the one hand to become aware of opportunities of how to protect themselves from their partner's potential opportunistic behavior, and how to design learning alliances for joint success. Here, opportunism may include risks of free riding, insincere statements regarding agreed common goals, and the threat of private learning.

As there are always two sides to a coin, the insight may also lead managers to look for how to take advantage of the partner firm: when managers are aware of how to protect themselves from opportunism, they may in turn use the insight presented here in order to behave unfairly toward the partner. So, the model may also deliver insight into where and how managers may cheat the alliance partner undetectably.

In the following we first talk about model boundary and model scope. Then we continue by providing reference modes that we refer to when presenting the model base run. The model presentation is separated into three parts. First, we present an aggregated feedback structure of the interorganizational learning model. Then, in Section 6.5.1 we present the detailed model structure of common learning only. Finally, we expand the model boundary and include the opportunity for private learning in section 6.5.2.

6.2 Model Scope

In this section we discuss model boundary and scope. To do so we present a model boundary chart. It "summarizes the scope of the model by listing which key variables are included endogenously, which are exogenous, and which are excluded from the model."[845] Listing variables that lie outside the model boundary is important for model users to decide whether the model is of interest for their purposes.[846] We extend the model boundary chart by noting which theoretical concepts some variable names refer to (see Table 6-1). It facilitates finding the information from the respective preceding chapters.

---

845 Sterman (2000), p. 97.

846 Using model boundary charts is an effective tool to illustrate that the important concepts for addressing the model purpose are endogenous to the model. This is why boundary charts are tools for assessing the boundary adequacy test. See Sterman (2000), p. 859 and Section 2.3.5.

Endogenous	Theoretical concept	Exogenous	Theoretical concept	Excluded
• Common benefits	• Common benefits	• Actual common goals	• Opportunism, Hidden information	• Financial aspects • Contracts negotiations • Alliance formation negotiations • Cultural aspects • Multiple sequential alliances between partners • Exploration and exploitation • Outside hiring • Trust between scientists • Three or more alliance partners • Bargaining power
• Alliance patents	• R&D output			
• Group productivity				
• Group research output per week				
• Commitment to learn and work on alliance tasks				
• Alliance knowledge base	• Interorganizational learning, Knowledge-based view			
• Absorptive capacity	• Organizational receptivity			
• Scientists active in alliance		• Scientist bonus	• Opportunism, Hidden information, Free riding	
• Perceived scientist commitment to alliance	• Reciprocity and fairness			
• Manager trust	• Informal safeguards	• Trust atmosphere between managers	• Informal safeguards	
• Number of manager interactions	• Reciprocity and fairness, Opportunism, Behavioral game theory	• Team storming phase interactions		
• Openness between scientists	• Organizational openness and transparency, Reciprocity and fairness	• Openness of gatekeeper restrictions	• Formal safeguards / Gatekeeper	
• Knowledge spillover	• Private learning, Knowledge spillover	• Communicated common goals	• Opportunism, Hidden information	
• Gatekeeper openness	• Formal safeguards	• Relevance of alliance knowledge for private needs	• Knowledge relatedness, Knowledge-based view	
• Private benefits	• Opportunism, Private benefits	• Actual private goals	• Opportunism, Hidden information	
• Private group productivity				
• Private group research output per week				

Table 6-1: Model boundary chart for interorganizational learning in alliances.[847]

As can be seen from Table 6-1 a large number of factors indicating long-term development of interorganizational learning in learning alliances are endogenous to the model. They are the principles of the model structure which drive model behavior. The model includes the idea of cooperative and competitive aspects through private and common benefits. Hence, we assume that the alliance partners know the number

[847] Source: authors' representation.

and type of goals they seek when entering the cooperative venture. The prospective common benefits, for example, are explicitly stated in the alliance contract of our case study research alliance. Closely coupled to prospective benefits are the allocated scientists provided by both parent firms to work on alliance tasks and how they jointly learn. Whereas KHANNA, GULATI, AND NOHRIA state that the allocation of resources is the main focus of their model to study alliance dynamics, they exclude both organizational receptivity and organizational openness.[848] As laid out in Section 4.6.1, receptivity, or (relative) absorptive capacity, is necessary for successful joint learning – or for private learning. Therefore, we include both concepts in our model and side with HAMEL's idea and INKPEN's remarks on their effect on alliance dynamics.[849] Openness in our model refers to openness between the scientists. It covers the idea of trust between scientists. This means that even though trust between scientists is not explicitly expressed as a variable, its consequence, openness, is included as an endogenous variable. Moreover, trust between the managers is included. Tightly tied to trust are manager interactions that are interpreted as trust building actions. We could have aggregated scientists' commitment to learn and work on alliance tasks in their productivity. Yet, one interviewee names scientist commitment to alliance tasks as being one of the main drivers for making progress in the alliance.[850] Therefore we include this variable explicitly. Private learning may be initiated when knowledge spills over from the alliance to the respective parent's knowledge base. It may be hampered by gatekeeper objections and lack of knowledge relatedness. Private benefits may be generated by the respective parents' group productivities and their output.

Exogenous parameters include those that encourage opportunistic behavior like common goals that differ from those that were agreed on in the contract. The same idea holds for the actual number of scientists allocated by the parents to the alliance: actual allocation may differ from prior contractual agreements. The model further allows gaining insight from parent firms seeking private benefits and consequently performing private learning. Moreover, the model allows us to change knowledge relatedness between the two firms, supporting or hindering joint learning. Also, as shown in Section 4.6.4, trust plays an important role for the alliance dynamics. Therefore, the trust atmosphere between the collaborating firms may be modified. This means we can distinguish between skeptical or trusting partner firms and analyze possible behavioral variations with different initial trust conditions.

A number of reasons mentioned for learning alliance success are omitted in the model. Though useful for explaining alliance failure in general, we decided to leave them outside the model boundary. We do not want to push the model boundaries too far, otherwise the model structure would become too complex for a useful analysis.[851] By presenting excluded factors we stress that the model might not be relevant for problem sets other than the model purpose indicated.[852]

[848] See Khanna et al. (1998), p. 194.
[849] See Hamel (1991), p. 85 and Inkpen (2000b), p. 777.
[850] See P2: 88 and the explanations in the subsequent section.
[851] See Sterman (2000), p. 90.
[852] See Sterman (2000), pp. 98-99.

Financial aspects might be important for some alliances – especially in areas where budget constraints play an important role.[853] This may indeed be the case in R&D alliances. Yet, alliance dynamics considering opportunism may also be explained without focusing on this aspect. It is therefore assumed that goal attainment forms the focus of the present analysis. Also, alliance scholars seldom refer to monetary constraints in their studies. Alternatively, one could argue that discounting prospective pay-offs is done during alliance negotiations. Nevertheless, formulation of alliance contracts and the period of alliance negotiations are not captured in the model.[854] Our analysis starts when the alliance teams begin to work jointly on alliance tasks. Moreover, cultural aspects are omitted as well. Opportunistic behavior may also occur between firms within the same cultural environment. Although we change the trusting atmosphere between the cooperating partners due to possible prior ties and although we draw conclusions from behavior in the alliance under study for possible future ties we do not look at multiple sequential alliance relationships between the same firms. Moreover, we do not differentiate between exploration or exploitation alliances. We focus on exploration alliances only.[855] It is further assumed that no outside-hiring is possible. This means that scientists may only be assigned to the alliance by the partnering firms. Further, we do not consider optimizing project size.[856] As indicated above, trust between the scientists is not explicitly referred to in the model. We aggregate scientist trust in openness between the scientists. In Section 4.6.4.2 we argued that trust is followed by action. Action on the scientist level is expressed by mutual openness. Including trust on the scientist level would extend the model boundary and increase model complexity, but would not imply further insight into the dynamics. Therefore we argue for omitting this variable for our modeling purposes.

In the following we present an aggregated view of the interrelations of endogenous and exogenous variables in a subsystem diagram. It illustrates the model's overall architecture and serves as an overview and does not contain much detail.[857] Each of the squares shown in Figure 6-1 represents a subsystem. When two squares are positioned behind one another, an identical subsystem exists for the second parent firm. Only one subsystem exists for the 'Alliance knowledge base', for example, but two exist for 'Scientists active in the alliance' – this makes sense insofar as both parent firms contribute their respective scientists to the alliance because of their policies. Therefore, both structures are modeled explicitly.

The overall structure can be divided into two major segments: common learning and private learning. The common learning segment consists of seven subsystems – considering only subsystems from one partner firm's view: 'Alliance knowledge base', 'Commitment to learn and work – scientists', 'Patent generation – alliance / Common

[853] Khanna, Gulati, and Nohria distinguish between R&D projects with and without budget constraints. See Khanna et al. (1998), p. 198.
[854] See Höfer (1997) for an in-depth discussion on the negotiation phase in strategic alliances.
[855] See Section 4.5.3, in which we give reasons for only analyzing exploration alliances.
[856] According to studies, an optimum team size exists in projects. Communication effort increases with an increasing number of team members. See, for example, Zielasek (1995), p. 53.
[857] See Sterman (2000), pp. 99, 102.

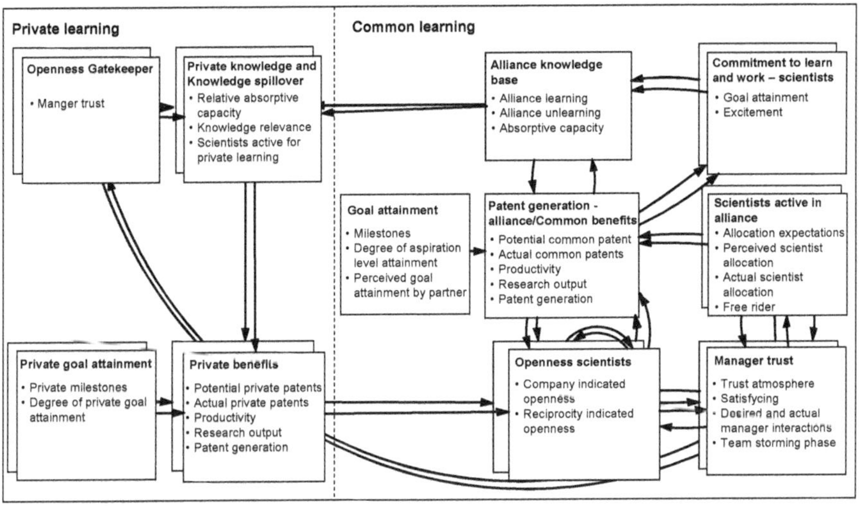

Figure 6-1: Scope and model structure.[858]

benefits', 'Scientists active in alliance', 'Manager trust', 'Openness scientists', and 'Goal attainment'. The private learning segment consists of four subsystems, 'Private knowledge and Knowledge spillover', 'Openness gatekeeper', 'Private benefits', and 'Private goal attainment'.

In the following sections we focus on describing the subsystems' underlying model structures. The model is quantified in equilibrium: the net rate of change of the stocks is zero. This may lead to either static equilibria or dynamic equilibria in which the outflows are just as high as the inflows to stocks. The latter are those in which all flows into and out of stocks are zero.[859] Applied to our model, it means that as long as the parent firms do not start to engage in the learning alliance, neither common nor private learning takes place and no patents are generated. The model is then shocked to start the alliance by allocating scientists to the learning alliance. Combined with different parameter settings, various behavioral patterns disclose the important relationships and feedback loops that are driving these patterns. On this basis we are able to draw conclusions for successful managing learning alliances.

6.3 Time Horizon and Reference Modes

According to STERMAN, setting a time horizon and establishing reference modes are some of the most useful processes in model building.[860] The time horizon we look at to study learning alliance dynamics is limited to 100 weeks. This equals roughly two

[858] Source: authors' representation. Squares indicate a subsystem structure. Squares positioned behind one another indicate identical model structures for a second parent firm.
[859] See Sterman (2000), p. 232.
[860] See Sterman (2000), p. 90.

years of working weeks. As we do not include alliance negotiations between high level managers in the model the time horizon is long enough to capture the entire pattern of behavior from the start of the alliance, when scientists first meet and get productive on alliance tasks, until they have reached the goals. It is assumed that alliance goals may be reached within roughly a year at best. Thus, a longer time horizon enables us to notice and analyze possible delays in policy runs. Critics may comment that this is fairly short for a learning alliance. Nevertheless, the case is intended as an example and policy-designers and decision-makers may customize the model to their specific alliance experience. Delays may then also be put in relation to their specific occurrences.

As stated in Section 2.4.2, content analysis in the case study helped us to identify important variables for alliance dynamics. We asked the interviewees to explain or draw how they perceived that the identified variables have developed over time. In Chapter 4 we presented some of these reference modes. In the following we present additional reference modes which we deduce from those presented above. Some of the variable names depicted in Figure 6-2 correspond to names of the subsystems in Figure 6-1 as these are the main variables of those subsystems. They capture how interorganizational learning develops as hoped for or how it is feared when the alliance is characterized by opportunism (see Figure 6-2).[861]

The reference modes of the hoped-for behaviors of 'Degree of common goal attainment' and 'Degree of private goal attainment' correspond with those of common (see Figure 4-9) and private knowledge (see Figure 4-11). This is because we assume that the 'Alliance knowledge base' development influences the degree of goal attainment with a delay. Regarding private goal attainment, alliance participants fear that knowledge might spill over to the partner firm to strengthen its private knowledge base. The reference mode for 'Manager trust' corresponds to the one identified by the interviewees and depicted in Figure 4-20. As trust between scientists is aggregated to 'Openness between scientists', the hoped-for behavior is similar to a hypothesized behavior of trust between scientists. The reference mode for 'Number of scientists – partner' in the alliance relates to the parent's expectation that the partner will fulfill its expectations and allocates the agreed number fast, and will not withdraw scientists until the alliance has reached its goals.

Whereas alliance managers and scientists hope that the 'Degree of common goal attainment' will reach smoothly its maximum, they fear that it will saturate on a lower level. The prospective maximum necessary for common goal attainment is not yet reached. This might have different reasons. First, the partner originally had fewer common goals and withdraws its scientists immediately after reaching its goal attainment, for example. As firms become competitors again right away, the firms' scientists do not share any knowledge with each other anymore. Consequently, 'Manager trust' would suffer. The firm would not have reached its goals and is dissatisfied with the alliance outcome.

---

[861] Hines suggests drawing hope and fear behaviors in reference modes. See Hines (2004), p. 3.

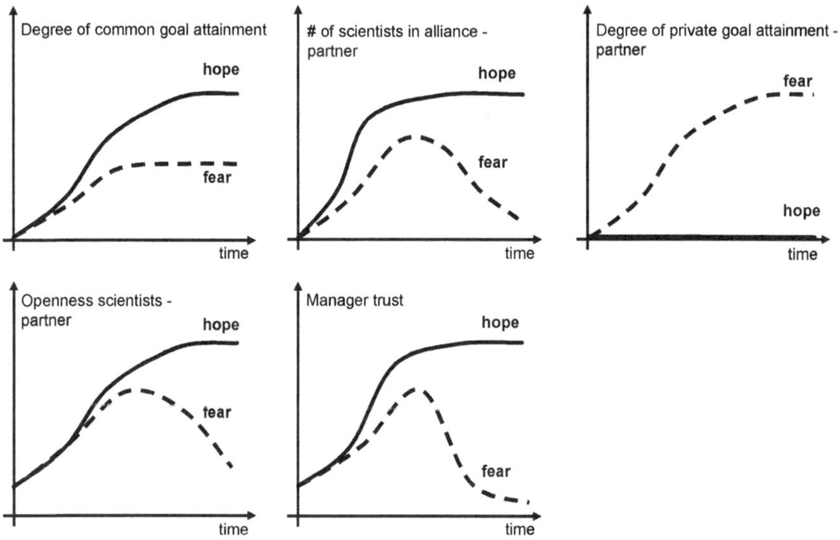

Figure 6-2: Reference modes: Hope and fear in interorganizational learning.[862]

Alternatively, the partner might have reached its private goals and withdraws its resources with the same consequences as mentioned above.

KHANNA, GULATI, AND NOHRIA are, to our knowledge, among the few authors in the alliance literature who present graphs over time that we could refer to as reference modes.[863] In their article, they draw behaviors for resource allocation for various learning race scenarios.

Their suitability for the present model, however, is limited due to a number of reasons. First, KHANNA, GULATI, AND NOHRIA's resource allocation patterns show abrupt changes. This would be an indication for discrete events. As stated in Section 2.3.2, discrete events are not appropriate for analyzing alliance dynamics. System Dynamics models represent time as continuous.[864] We could, however, overcome this shortcoming by smoothing the authors' illustrated behaviors.

Our second argument focuses on a different detail. For what the authors call an "optimal resource allocation pattern in a [learning] racing situation", they refer to GROSSMAN AND SHAPIRO's study on the patent race literature.[865] When presenting their view of resource allocation patterns, KHANNA, GULATI, AND NOHRIA assume a situation of pure private benefits in which both firms have to undergo a certain number of

[862] Source: authors' representation.
[863] See Khanna et al. (1998), pp. 199, 205.
[864] See Sterman (2000), p. 206.
[865] See Grossman and Shapiro (1987), p. 379.

learning stages to finish their private learning.[866] Furthermore, the authors suppose that a firm increases its resource expenditures when it has finished working on a learning stage, as it is closer to its goal. The partner firm would thus decrease its resource expenditures if it has not finished learning at this stage. We would like to add a few comments to this thought experiment.

First, the partnering firm would still be in a cooperative alliance – though in a hypothetical situation of only prospective private benefits. To enter an alliance the partners most probably need to sign a contract. The contract would also include regulations on resource expenditures. From our case study we learned that firms usually have to pay penalties if they do not meet minimum resource expenditure requirements.[867] Therefore, a firm cannot reduce its resource expenditures at will.

Second, GROSSMAN AND SHAPIRO, the authors cited by KHANNA, GULATI, AND NOHRIA, refer to a very different situation. In their model, GROSSMAN AND SHAPIRO clearly state that firms first do joint research. After having successfully completed the research, they see themselves as pure competitors again and continue working separately on further product or process development.[868] Thus, in this case, the firms are independent from each other again and no longer pursue joint work. In contrast, however, in KHANNA, GULATI, AND NOHRIA's case, the firms are still bound to each other. They need to respect the alliance contract. Therefore, from our understanding, to transfer the insight from resource expenditures in a patent race to a learning race within a learning alliance without critically modifying model assumptions is questionable indeed. Due to these reasons we disagree with KHANNA, GULATI, AND NOHRIA's suggestion about resource allocation in the special case of learning races in learning alliances.

After discussing the time horizon and presenting reference modes, we introduce the feedback loop structure of the simulation model

6.4 Feedback Structure of Interorganizational Learning

In the following we present the feedback structure of the interorganizational learning model. We bring together the structures discussed in Chapter 4 and close the feedback loops. We identified lack of feedback loops as one of the main issues in the current literature on learning alliances. In this section, we first introduce the feedback loop structure in a causal loop diagram. This causal loop diagram lacks mathematical rigor. However, its highly aggregated view enables us to gain a better understanding of the main feedback loops driving model behavior.[869] When presenting the feedback loops, we start explaining the major interorganizational learning structure that is in the focus of the model and then expand the model structure from common learning to private learning step by step. Newly added structure is highlighted with bold arrows.

---

[866] See Khanna et al. (1998), pp. 198-199.
[867] See P7: 28.
[868] See Grossman and Shapiro (1987), p. 383.
[869] See Coyle (1996), p. 40.

Variables surrounded by angle brackets, like <variable name>, represent shadow variables. These variables are defined elsewhere and are useful in helping to reduce clutter and increase the clarity of the picture. The structures and the formal model are designed and written using Vensim software.[870] Though we do not show a complete stock and flow structure, we indicate stocks as rectangles. During our explanation we might use variable names of the detailed quantified System Dynamics model that are not shown in this aggregated feedback loop view. We use the variable names for telling the underlying story. It also prepares the model user to understand the quantified model better which is described in the subsequent section, 6.5. The model refers to two companies, indicated by the indices i and j.

Learning with the Partner

Building up the 'Alliance knowledge base' stands at the center of the analysis – referring to the feedback structures presented in Figure 4-12 and Figure 4-2. In Figure 6-3 we show both 'Absorptive capacity' and 'Diminishing returns' in a single picture. The former loop shows that the more effectively the groups accomplish their tasks, the higher is 'Alliance learning'. The more joint learning takes place, the more the 'Alliance knowledge base' builds up. This has two effects. On the one hand, a higher knowledge base increases the scientists' 'Absorptive capacity' that fosters further learning. All else being equal, an increase in the 'Alliance knowledge base' leads to further 'Alliance learning', which again lets the 'Alliance knowledge base' increase. Accordingly, this structure represents a reinforcing feedback loop (see R1 – 'Absorptive capacity').[871]

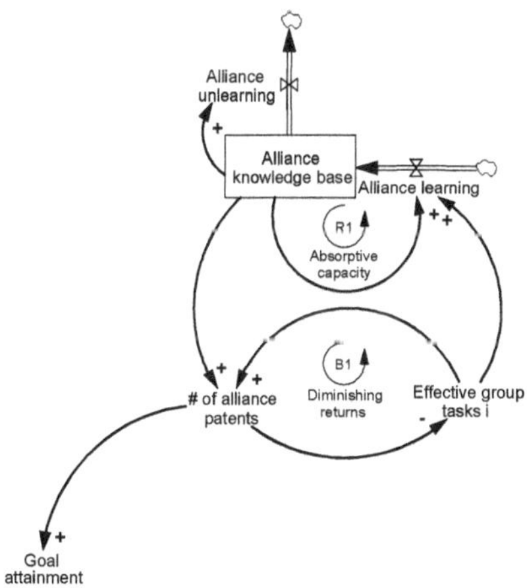

Figure 6-3: Feedback loops 'Absorptive capacity' and 'Diminishing returns'.[872]

[870] We built the formal model on interorganizational learning using the Vensim Simulation Environment DSS32 Version 5.0c1. See www.vensim.com for further details. The website offers a free download version of this software.

[871] See Lane et al. (2001), p. 1140 and Section 4.6.1.

[872] Source: authors' representation.

On the other hand, all else being equal, a greater common knowledge base enables the scientists to increase their research output. This is the basis for generating alliance patents. The more patents the scientists create, the closer they get to the alliance goal – which, as discussed in Section 4.3, may be measured in number of patents. Yet, while 'Goal attainment' increases, the 'Number of alliance patents' created by the scientists cannot rise to infinity. Thus, while the 'Number of alliance patents' increases and approaches a maximum, it becomes more difficult for the scientists to stay as productive, which is why their 'Effective group tasks i' decreases. When the scientists are less effective, they cannot learn as much anymore and they cannot create as many additional new patents as before. As it counteracts the initial change, this model structure represents a balancing feedback loop (see B1 – 'Diminishing returns').

Both groups' effectiveness is determined by a few variables which we explain in the following (see Figure 6-4). According to CALANTONE, CAVUSGIL, AND ZHAO, effectiveness is affected by the scientists' commitment to learn and work on alliance tasks.[873] Scientists become increasingly committed to the alliance the more they perceive progress, or, in other words, the more patents they generate (see R2 – 'Let's work – we're getting there!'). Even though scientists seem to have a high base motivation or commitment to their work, independent of the specific alliance,[874] commitment still can be increased. Referring to project milestones, one scientist states, *"If we reach a milestone within schedule, this is positive; this is great. And it increases our commitment as a direct consequence."*[875] However, it does not necessarily need to be reaching major milestones that strengthens commitment to work on alliance tasks. The scientist continues *"[a]lso small progress increases commitment."*[876] One scientist even quantifies a relationship by saying *"I think for the most part, maybe for 90% of the people, commitment is definitely correlated with goal attainment."*[877] We translate the statements into the following model structure. Ongoing progress, exemplified through generated patents, directly increases commitment. Furthermore, commitment is also increased by reaching the goals. When management defines stretch goals which are difficult to attain, commitment is not affected immediately as scientists still perceive some progress. This goes along with scientists perceiving that their role in the alliance makes sense on the way to achieving the goal.[878]

Nevertheless, scientists form expectations about effectiveness of their group tasks. They do so by considering the 'Expected time to reach goals', based on their 'Expected number of alliance patents' and the 'Expected research output'. They further put the actual 'Number of alliance patents' in relation to the expected 'Aspiration level'. This way they perceive progress and 'Commitment' increases when the actual goal attainment develops as expected.

---

873 See Calantone et al. (2002), p. 516 and also Finnie (1998), p. 18.
874 See P4: 64.
875 P2: 107 and similarly P4: 97 and P5: 67.
876 P2: 115.
877 P6: 42.
878 See, for example, Ring and van de Ven (1994), pp. 99-100. For stretch goals see Kerr and Landauer (2004).

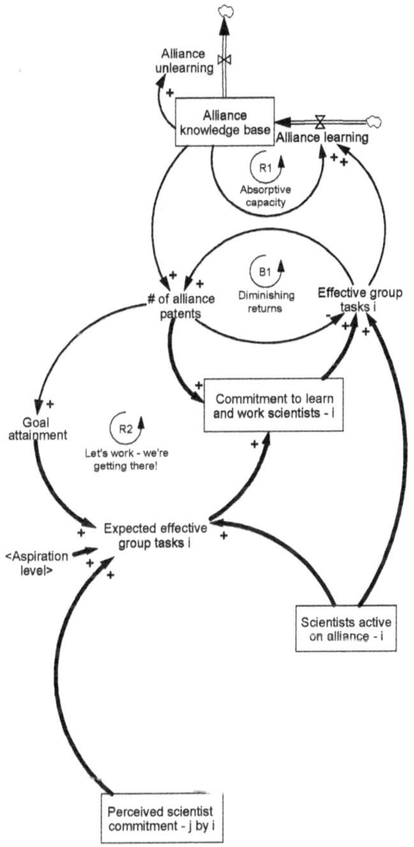

Figure 6-4: Feedback loop 'Let's work – we're getting there!'[879]

In addition to the scientists' commitment, also firm i's actual number of 'Scientists active in alliance' increase 'Effective group tasks i'. The more scientists the parent firms allocate to the alliance, the more creative people are when working on alliance tasks, increasing the effectiveness.[880]

As both firms allocate scientists and because the respective numbers influence each other we explicitly model both firms' scientist allocations independently. Generally, as stated in Section 4.5.2, 'Scientists active in alliance' are determined by the internally communicated 'Aspiration level' (see also Figure 6-5). Moreover, during the course of the alliance, each parent evaluates the partner's actual scientist allocation according to their expectations. Expectations are based on the 'Agreed upon number of pat-

[879] Source: authors' representation.

[880] As explained in Section 6.2 on model scope, we do not consider effectiveness restrictions because of too large team size.

ents' in the contract. Based on evaluations, the parents' managers perceive the partner's scientist commitment to the alliance. They put this number into relation with their own scientist commitment. As discussed in detail in Section 4.6.4.2, because of fairness and reciprocity tendencies in human interactions, the parent firms' managers adjust their scientist allocation accordingly. If, for example, the partner invests less, the firm also reduces its number of scientists (see B2 – 'Scientist balance').

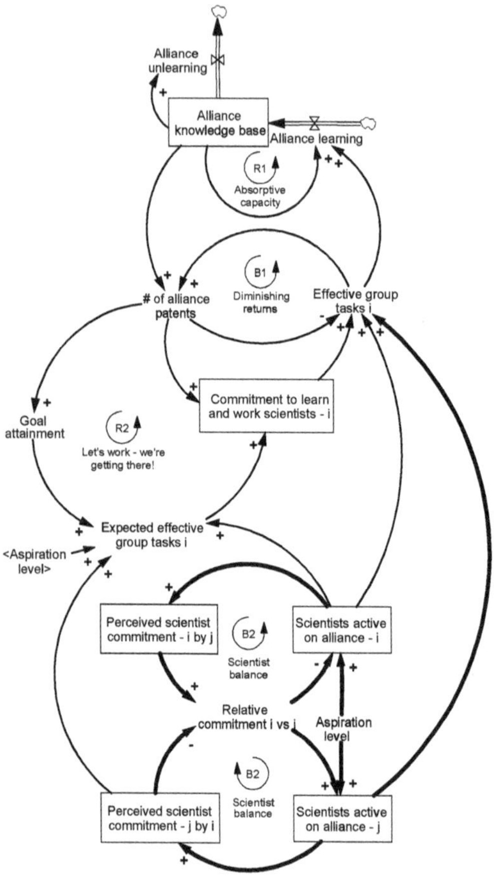

Figure 6-5: Feedback loops 'Scientist balance'.[881]

In Section 4.6.2 we discussed how 'Effective group tasks i' are also determined by the scientists' mutual openness to each other. Additionally, openness from one group of scientists to the other group reinforces 'Reciprocity' between them (see Figure 4-14 and see R3 in Figure 6-6). Openness between the scientists can be interpreted

[881] Source: authors' representation.

as a decision to action resulting in more openness.[882] So, in this work, mutual openness is understood as mutual trust.[883] Openness is maintained as long as the partner firms continue to collaborate. It is reduced as soon as one partner achieves its common goals. Then the former cooperating partners become pure competitors again. They have no interest in strengthening the partner more than necessary and do not continue to share any further knowledge – despite a successful cooperation.

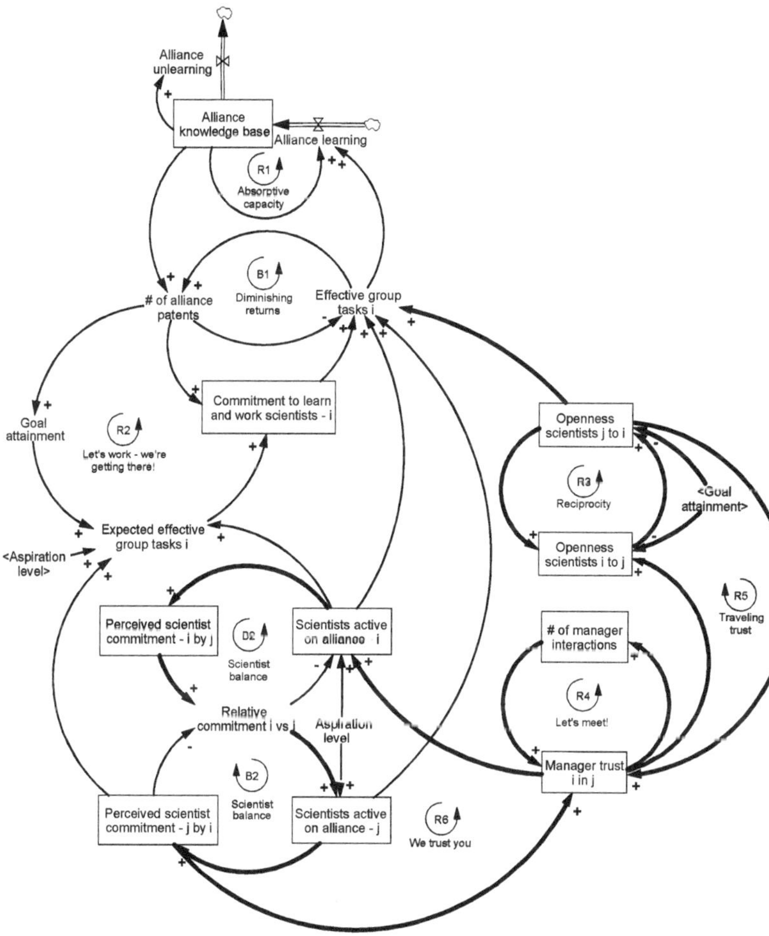

Figure 6-6: Feedback loops 'Reciprocity' and 'Let's meet!'[884]

[882] See Currall and Judge (1995), pp. 153-154, Currall and Inkpen (2002), p. 484, and Currall and Epstein (2003), p. 194.

[883] See our explanations in Section 4.6.2.

[884] Source: authors' representation.

As trust travels through organizational levels,[885] parent firm i's managers trust partner j's managers more if j's scientists are more open to their own group of scientists. Moreover, the more managers trust each other, the more openly the scientists in turn share their knowledge with their partner firm's colleagues, which again reinforces trust and openness between the groups (R5 – 'Traveling trust'). As pointed out in Section 4.6.4.2, trusting people seek to interact with each other, which in turn increases trust even further until a maximum level of trust is reached (R4 – 'Let's meet!').

Whereas openness is interpreted as a decision to act resulting from trust on the scientist level, the decision to act on the manager level roots in the willingness to allocate scientists. The more managers trust each other, the more they perceive the alliance as making sense. Hence, they are willing to actually allocate the number of scientists according to the contract, and perhaps even to overaccomplish this target by allocating slightly more. This action represents a signal to the partner's managers of the firm's commitment to the alliance and of being a trustworthy alliance partner. The partner's managers perceive the action and are interested in balanced scientist commitment and adjust their allocation accordingly (B2 – Scientist balance). Their goodwill in turn is perceived by the partner's managers, who trust them even more (R6 – 'We trust you').

All feedback loops presented in Figure 6-6 represent the structure of common learning in alliances. It allows us to capture and analyze possible policies from complete cooperative behavior to opportunistic cooperative intentions like, for example, a parent pursuing differing actual goals or differing scientist allocation from what was agreed in the alliance contract. Depending on which feedback loops dominate the structure, either cooperating or competitive behavior arises. Shifts in loop dominance may also shift the system from original cooperative to competitive behavior or vice versa. The present structure, though simplified from reality, is too complex to be mentally modeled. Therefore, formalization is necessary. We explain formal model structure in Section 6.5.1

Learning from the Alliance and the Partner

In the following we extend the model structure to include private learning. As can be seen in Figure 6-7, we add four more feedback loops, which we explain in the following. We begin by clarifying a possible increase of the 'Private knowledge base j'. In Section 4.6.3 we laid out that the more open parent i's gatekeeper is, the easier it is for the partner firm j to have knowledge spilled over from the alliance and to use it in areas unrelated to the alliance scope. So, alliance knowledge spills over from the 'Alliance knowledge base' to the partner firm's 'Private knowledge base j'. Further development of the private knowledge base depends on 'Relative absorptive capacity' (R7) and 'Diminishing returns' (B4). This learning and accumulation structure is similar to that determining 'Alliance knowledge base'.

[885] See Inkpen and Currall (2004), p. 597.

With this private knowledge, firm j may individually generate patents. Thus, depending on learning restrictions from B4 and R7, firm j might attain its private goals sooner or later. Then – in the case of private benefits – the previously cooperating partners become competitors again. Just like with reaching common goals, the partner j is then afraid of strengthening its competitor and consequently prohibits its scientists from openly exchange any further knowledge with firm i's colleagues. Declining openness decreases both groups' effectiveness in working on alliance tasks. Further 'Alliance learning' is made difficult, which in turn also means that additional knowledge spillover is reduced (B3 – 'We have successfully outleaned you'). As another effect, while parent j's scientists' openness declines, parent i's managers' trust declines, which leads to a withdrawal of scientists from the alliance and a possible alliance dissolution.

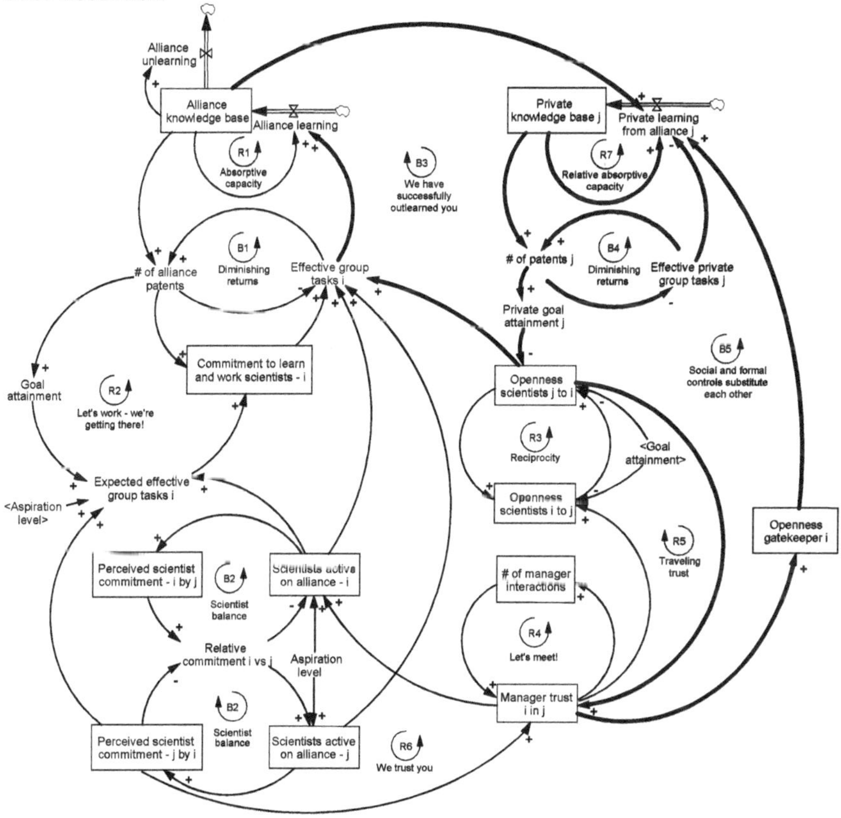

Figure 6-7: Private learning with feedback loops 'Relative absorptive capacity', 'Diminishing returns', 'We have successfully outlearned you', and 'Social and formal controls substitute each other'.[886]

[886] Source: authors' representation.

As a last point, we refer again to the gatekeepers' openness addressed above. This means of formal control is determined by the strength of social control in the alliance (see Section 4.6.4). The more parent firm i's manager trust the partner firm j's manager, for example, the less they might respect the contractual gatekeeper restrictions for knowledge exchange. This opens up the opportunity to firm j of facilitated knowledge spillover. When firm j reaches its private goals, it consequently gives its scientists the instruction to reduce openness. Firm i's managers notice this unexpected behavior, which is the reason why trust declines and the gatekeeper's role becomes increasingly important again (B5 – 'Social and formal controls substitute each other').

Learning with the Partner and from the Alliance
Summarizing, the combined model of cooperative and competitive interorganizational learning in alliances consists of thirteen major feedback loops, six of which are balancing and seven reinforcing loops. Due to mutual interdependence between the two collaborating firms i and j in B2 – 'Scientist balance, R3 – 'Reciprocity', R4 – 'Let's meet!', and B5 – 'Social and formal controls substitute each other', identical loops exist for both partner firms. For reasons of clarity we avoid showing more loops than those in Figure 6-7. They are detailed enough to understand the main interdependencies and feedback processes. In the following section we lay out the model's mathematical foundation. Corresponding to the clarification of the model structure in this section we begin with the subsystems of learning with the partner.

6.5 Structure of the Interorganizational Learning Model

In the following we present the intertwined model subsystems of the common learning segment (see Figure 6-1). Again, we point out that most of the variables are intangibles. As indicated in Section 2.3, building a model consisting of intangible variables might be confusing. Among other things, the choice of dimensions might not be immediately obvious. Nevertheless, we avoid using dimensionless units as this may open up opportunities to trick on internal unit consistency. Therefore, we use dimensions like 'knowledge points' or 'trust points'. We are aware of the fact that such units do not exist in the real world. However, we believe that the model is more consistent when clearly stating that 'knowledge points per week' increase a 'knowledge base' instead of 'dimensionless matters per week'. Finally, scholars would not be able to study the field of alliance research without using intangibles. Again, applying intangible or qualitative variables and data is better than omitting them.[887]

Next, we show the detailed and quantified stock and flow structure of the interorganizational learning model. Additionally we present the major equations, mainly those of flows that increase or decrease stocks. Nevertheless, we do not describe the subsections of 'Goal attainment' or 'Private goal attainment' as they only contain calculative structures. Their variables 'Degree of goal attainment i' and 'Degree of private goal attainment i' show when the scientists have generated enough patents so that the

---

[887] See Forrester (1994b), p. 72 or Sterman (2000), p. 195.

common – and/or private – goals are reached. Parameter names starting with a 'T' indicate the effect of a nonlinear function.

6.5.1 Model Subsystem: Learning with the Partner

In the following six sections we present the model structure for learning with the partner firm in the alliance. We first concentrate on the generation of joint knowledge. We continue with how common knowledge is used for generating joint patents. Patent generation depends, among other things, on the scientists' commitment, which is the structure we present afterwards. Then we continue with modeling scientist allocation to the alliance. We then focus on how we modeled the generation of trust between the alliance managers. We close this section by presenting the structure on scientists' openness toward each other.

6.5.1.1 Alliance Knowledge Base

The basic stock and flow structure of the knowledge base is known from Figure 4-12. Yet, in this paragraph we present the structure in more detail (see Figure 6-8).

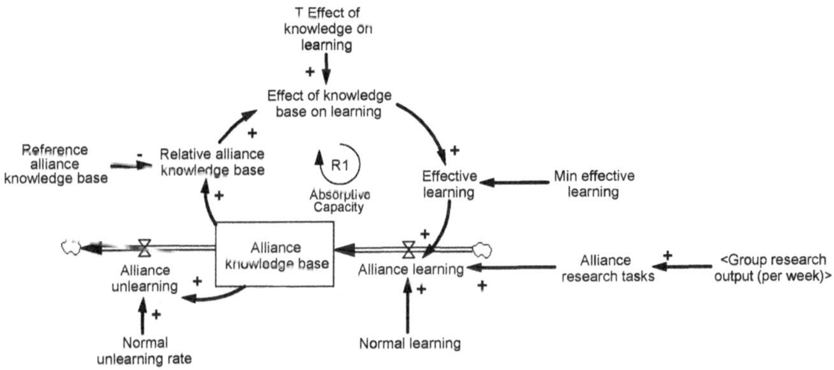

Figure 6-8: Stock and flow structure: Alliance knowledge base.[888]

'Alliance knowledge', like all stocks in the model, is initialized in equilibrium. It is increased by 'Alliance learning' and decreased by 'Alliance unlearning'. Unlearning assumes a constant 'Normal unlearning rate' which leads to first-order exponential decay.[889]

[888] Source: authors' representation.
[889] See Sterman (2000), p. 523.

$$AKB_t = AKB_0 + \int_0^t (AL_t - AU_t)dt \quad \text{(Eq. 6.1)}$$

where AKB Alliance knowledge base; AU Alliance unlearning; AL Alliance learning

'Alliance learning' equals scientists' 'Normal learning', multiplied by the 'Alliance research tasks' and the scientists' 'Effective learning' (see Eq. 6.2). 'Effective learning' (see Eq. 6.3) in turn is determined by a 'Minimum effective learning' that ensures that scientists jointly learn a minimum amount of knowledge even when the initial amount of common knowledge is zero. This variable is multiplied by the nonlinear, S-shaped 'Effect of knowledge base on learning', capturing the idea of absorptive capacity: if 'Minimum effective learning' is large, the effect is small. In other words, the more common knowledge the scientists already have, the better they understand each other's knowledge fields (R1 – 'Absorptive capacity'). But at the same time it is more difficult for them to learn more about their research topic. Consequently, if the 'Minimum effective learning' is small, the 'Effect of knowledge base on learning' is large. Scientists have the potential to jointly learn a lot. Over the course of the alliance the absorptive capacity effect becomes less influential when scientists have built up a considerable 'Alliance knowledge base'.

$$AL = NL * ART * EL \quad \text{(Eq. 6.2)}$$

where NL Normal learning; EL Effective learning; ART Alliance research tasks

$$EL = MEL + (1 - MEL) * EKBL \quad \text{(Eq. 6.3)}$$

where MEL Minimum effective learning; EKBL Effect of knowledge base on learning

6.5.1.2 Patent Generation

'Alliance research tasks' driving 'Alliance learning' are calculated in the 'Patent generation' subsystem. They are determined by both scientist 'Groups' research output', that are determined by the 'Effective group tasks i' (see Eq. 6.4). This is the central variable that we referred to in the feedback structure (see Figure 6-4). It is determined by many variables.

First, the groups' effectiveness on the research tasks depends on the 'Alliance research capacity', which translates into how many scientists each parent firm allocates to the alliance. Furthermore, we consider the tasks that scientists work on per week under normal conditions and multiply them by the groups' 'Relative commitment i' and their 'Effective openness i'. The latter variable subsumes the firm-specific scientists' openness and the openness of the gatekeeper who controls knowledge flows from her own firm to the alliance. Last, we consider the 'Effect of relative number of patents on research activity and capacity'. This effect includes what we described in Sections 4.3 and 6.4 under the term 'Diminishing returns' (B1). The closer the scientists get to the maximum number of patents achievable in their field, the more difficult it is for them to do further related research. As can be seen in Eq. 6.4, these are multiplicative effects. Multiplying effects with each other means that as one effect gets stronger, it dominates the other effects.[890]

$$EGT_i = RC_i * ERPA * NTSW * EO_i * ARC \qquad \text{(Eq. 6.4)}$$

where	EGT_i	Effective group tasks i	RC_i	Relative commitment i
	ERPA	Effect of relative # of patents on research activity and capacity		
	EO_i	Effective openness i	NTSW	Normal tasks per scientist per week
	ARC	Alliance research capacity		

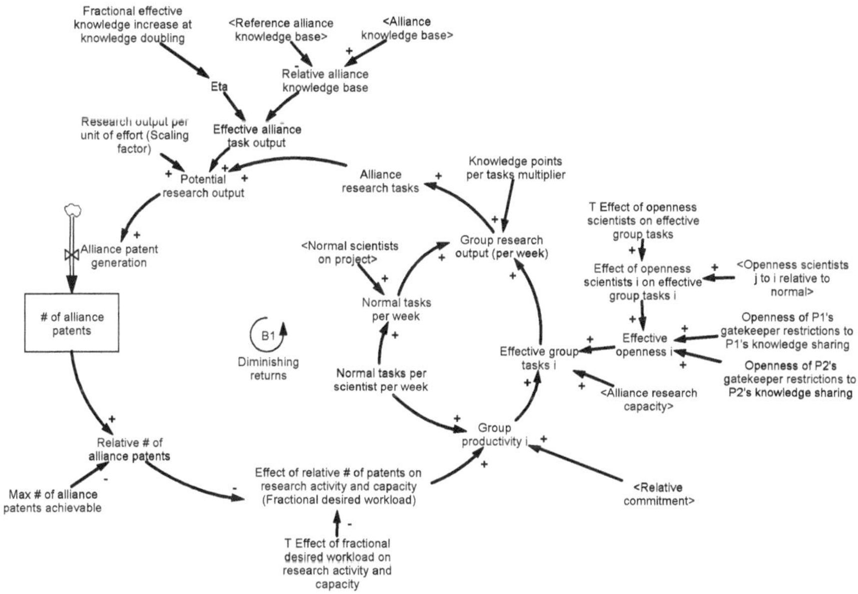

Figure 6-9: Stock and flow structure: Patent generation.[891]

How effectively both groups are working on their joint research tasks influences 'Alliance patent generation' (see Eq. 6.5). Both groups' joint research output represents how much new knowledge the scientists generate per week. New knowledge is then transferred into new patents. It is assumed that each new patent requires a certain amount of new knowledge. Furthermore, it is not the 'Alliance knowledge base' that directly determines patent generation. Yet, we put the 'Alliance knowledge base' in relation to the 'Reference alliance knowledge base'. The 'Reference alliance knowledge base' indicates how difficult it is for scientists in general to nest themselves in-

[890] For explanations of when to use multiplicative or additive effects, see Sterman (2000), pp. 525-529.

[891] Source: authors' representation. The model is able to simulate multiple milestones. The first milestone consists of 10 joint patents, for example, the second of 20 (cumulative) and the third of 30 (cumulative) patents. However, we only present simulations with one milestone throughout this work.

side a new matter of a particular research project. By dividing the 'Alliance knowledge base' by the 'Reference alliance knowledge base' we indicate how much of the maximum knowledge achievable in this research field the scientists have already learned. This term is taken to the power of η. η makes a statement about the effectiveness of the knowledge useful for the alliance research tasks when the 'Relative alliance knowledge base' doubles (see Eq. 6.6). If η is greater than one, effective knowledge increase is convex over knowledge doubling which means that 'Effective knowledge task output' increases at an increasing rate. If η is smaller than one, effective knowledge increase is concave over knowledge doubling. Or, in other words, 'Effective knowledge task output' increases at a high but decreasing slope.

$$APG = \sum_{i}^{j} GRO_i * (AKB/RAKB)^{\eta} * PKP \qquad \text{(Eq. 6.5)}$$

where				
	APG	Alliance patent generation	GRO_i	Group research output i
	RAKB	Reference alliance knowledge base		
	PKP	Patents per knowledge point	η	Sensitivity

and

$$\eta = \ln(FEKKD + 1) / \ln(2) \qquad \text{(Eq. 6.6)}$$

where FEKKD Fractional effective knowledge increase at knowledge doubling

6.5.1.3 Scientists' Commitment to Learn and Work

Next we discuss the scientists' commitment, which also influences 'Effective group tasks'. The stock 'Commitment to learn and work scientists i' is changed by the biflow 'Change in commitment scientists i' (see Eq. 6.7). A biflow is a two-way flow that could become positive or negative. If it becomes positive (negative), the biflow increases (decreases) the stock.

It is assumed that scientists who work and learn with each other in the alliance are to a certain extent committed to their tasks. At the same time, they form an indicated commitment. If a gap exists between their indicated and actual commitment, it takes some adjustment 'Time to change commitment'. This simple formulation describes negative feedback.[892]

$$ChCS_i = ((EAGAC_i + EDGAIE_i) * NC - C_i)/TC \qquad \text{(Eq. 6.7)}$$

where				
	$ChCS_i$	Change in commitment scientists i	$EAGAC_i$	Effect of alliance goal attainment on commitment i
	NC	Normal commitment	C_i	Commitment to learn and work i
	TC	Time to change commitment		
	$EDGAIE_i$	Effect of degree of goal attainment on initial excitement i		

'Indicated commitment i' consists of the additive connection of two effects (see Figure 6-10). The first is the 'Effect of degree of goal attainment on initial excitement'. In the beginning phase of a learning alliance, scientists are very excited about working on

[892] See Sterman (2000), p. 523.

alliance tasks – despite having accomplished only minor results as yet. Over the course of the alliance this effect decreases in strength and 'Indicated commitment i' is increasingly driven by perceived success. This is modeled by the nonlinear polynomial increasing 'Effect of alliance goal attainment on perceived alliance success'.

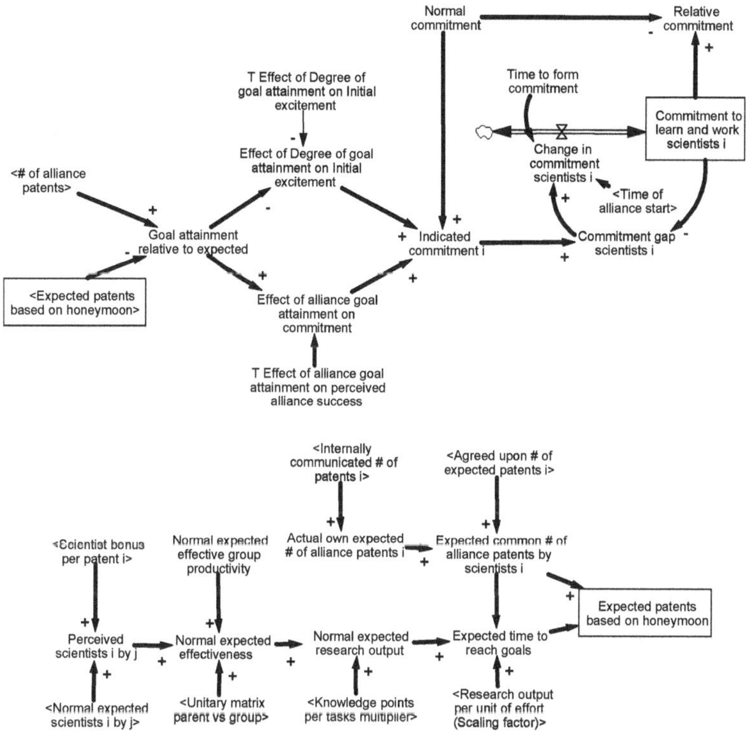

Figure 6-10: Stock and flow structure: Commitment to learn and work – scientists.[893]

6.5.1.4 Scientists Active in Alliance

Last, 'Effective group tasks i' (see Section 6.5.1.2) are determined by the number of scientists active on the alliance. They are changed by the biflow 'Net scientist allocation i'. Like the biflow structure in the preceding section, the underlying structure represents goal adjustment. Alliance managers compare the actual number of 'Scientists active in alliance – parent i' to the 'Desired scientists level i' of their respective firm in the alliance. The 'Desired scientist level i' is a product of the 'Indicated max scientist level i' and two effects. The 'Indicated max scientist level' is the maximum necessary number of scientists to accomplish either common or private goals (see Figure 6-11). In the contract, the parent firms have agreed on allocating a certain

[893] Source: authors' representation.

number of scientists to the alliance with the intention to work on common goals. Nevertheless, if a firm seeks to achieve private benefits in addition to common goals, it might decide to allocate more scientists. In the case of much more prospective private benefits than common benefits, for instance, the cheating firm might allocate additional scientists to the alliance to accomplish results fast and to ensure that all goals will be met. As discussed in depth in Section 4.6.4.2 the partner does not mind additional resource allocation to the one agreed on. It would not get suspicious. We herewith stress that this number of scientists does not represent the number of scientists working on accomplishing private goals in the parent company. These scientists work on creating common knowledge – which might be transferred to the parent firm. Private benefits may be generated. Alternatively, even in a situation of no private benefits, a firm might allocate more scientists than agreed on, if it so wishes. This number can be varied with the exogenous variable 'Scientist bonus per patent i'.

$$NetScA_i = ((IMaxSc_i * EIScR_i * ETSc_i) - ScA_i)/TAD \qquad \text{(Eq. 6.8)}$$

where	$NetScA_i$	Net scientist allocation i	$IMaxSc_i$	Indicated max scientist level i
	TAD	Time for allocation decision	ScA_i	Scientists active in alliance i
	$EIScR_i$	Effect of indicated scientists from reciprocity on scientist allocation i		
	$ETSc_i$	Effect of trust on scientist allocation i		

Next, we discuss the two effects influencing the 'Desired scientist level i'. First, one effect results from how managers perceive the partner's scientist allocation. Managers expect their partner firm to allocate a certain number of scientists, based on the communicated and agreed common 'Aspiration level' and the 'Scientists per patent to be achieved per agreement'. It takes managers some time to form those expectations. Managers compare their own and their partner's actual scientists allocations with the expected scientist allocations and then relates them to each other. Again, managers look for fair, not equal allocations. Fair allocation refers to the sharing of the prospective common benefits. As discussed in detail in Section 4.6.4.2 and Section 6.4, because of fair intentions managers seek to reciprocate and keep balance with 'Relative commitment j versus i' (B2 – 'Scientist balance'). The effect includes the following idea: it is a nonlinear slightly concave curve that indicates partner firm i's reaction to partner j's scientist allocation. If partner j's scientist allocation almost equals the number that it agreed on in the contract, firm i's managers do not worry about j's integrity. However, if the partner allocates less than a certain amount of the scientists indicated, the firm withdraws resources to achieve an equivalent contribution level – following tit-for-tat.[894] As stated above, neither firm worries about a partner deciding to spend more resources than agreed in the contract.

[894] See Section 3.4.4.4 and Axelrod (1984), pp. 20, 173.

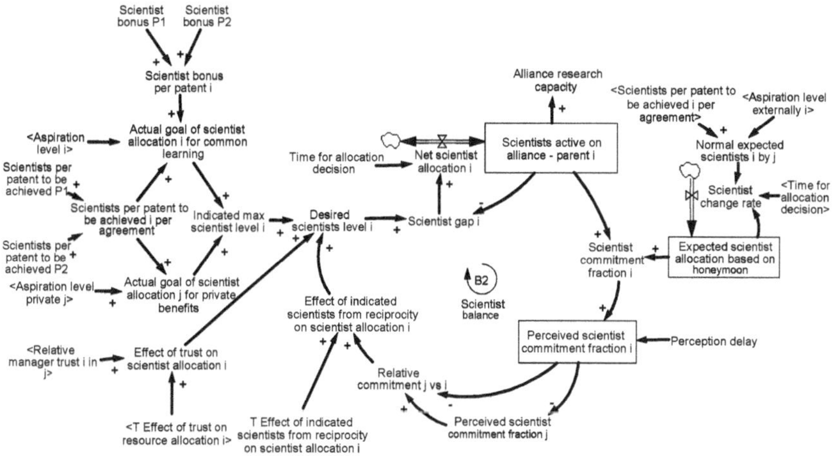

Figure 6-11: Stock and flow structure: Scientists active in alliance.[895]

Second, the other effect results from mutual manager trust. We also discussed this relationship thoroughly in Section 4.6.4.2. The nonlinear raising S-shaped relationship indicates that when parent i's managers evaluate their partner's managers as being trustworthy, they regard the alliance as a productive means to accomplish the goals. Consequently, they are willing to send scientists as agreed. They might even send a few scientists more to the alliance. On the other hand, the less the managers trust each other, the fewer scientists they are willing to send.

The effects to calculate the 'Desired scientists level i' are multiplicative as scientists allocation is so sensitive that it makes sense for one value to dominate the other in an extreme case.[896]

6.5.1.5 Trust on Parent Management Level

In the previous section we laid out how mutual manager trust influences scientist allocation. Next, we focus on the generation of manager trust in learning alliances. The state of 'Manager trust i in j' is fractionally changed, anchored to the actual state of 'Manager trust i in j'. It is therefore a hill-climbing process. The 'Normal fractional trust i in j change' is multiplied by two effects or external pressures to change, one of which consists of the sum of four additional external pressures (see Eq. 6.9 and Figure 6-13). We start with the multiplicative effect.

895 Source: authors' representation.
896 See Sterman (2000), p. 529 for multiplicative effects.

$$ChMT_i = EPGASA_i * (ESTC_i + EMIT_i + EOSMT_i + ERSMT_i) * NFrChMT * MT_i$$

(Eq. 6.9)

where				
	$ChMT_i$	Change in manager trust i	MT_i	Manager trust i in j – parent i
	$EPGASA_i$	Effect of perceived goal attainment i by j on sensitivity of i to j's actions – parent i		
	$ESTC_i$	Effect of satisfycing on manager trust change – parent i		
	$EMIT_i$	Effect of manager interactions on manager trust i in j – parent i		
	$EOSMT_i$	Effect of openness scientists j to i on fractional manager trust i in j change – parent i		
	$ERSMT_i$	Effect of j's relative scientists on i's manager's trust i		
	NFrChMT	Normal fractional change in trust		

The 'Effect of Perceived goal attainment i by j on sensitivity of i to j's actions – parent i' is a nonlinear relationship. It determines how sensitively firm i's managers' trust in j's managers changes with respect to their own goal attainment. In other words, managers become increasingly insensitive to any of the partner's actions the closer the firm approaches its goals. The relationship is multiplicative as it dominates all other pressures.

Next, we focus on the additive effects (see Eq. 6.9). The 'Net effect on trust i' sums up four effects on manager trust. They all consist of identical nonlinear relationships with a decreasing slope (see Figure 6-12 as an example). The effects can become negative and as they are additive, they might balance each other out in the 'Net effect on trust i'.

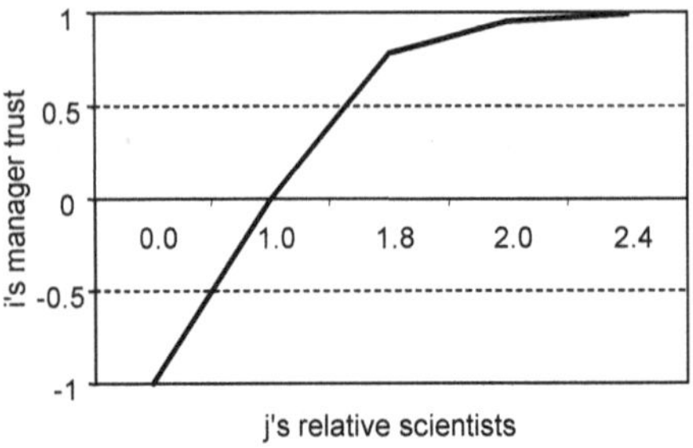

Figure 6-12: Nonlinear function, exemplified at parent firm j's relative scientist allocation on parent firm i's manager trust.[897]

The first effect, 'Effect of j's relative scientists on i's manager's trust – parent i', indicates that firm i's managers get suspicious when the partner j assigns fewer scientists to the alliance than agreed in the contract.[898] All else being equal, trust decreases. Yet, when the partner allocates more scientists to the alliance trust increases slightly to more than one. When allocated as arranged, trust does not change.

[897] Source: authors' representation.
[898] See the detailed discussion on this subject in Section 4.6.4.2.

Second, the nonlinear 'Effect of openness scientists j to i on manager trust i in j' indicates that firm i's managers trust their partner managers more the more open firm j's scientists are to firm i's scientists. Hence, this relationship includes the idea of reciprocity and fairness pointed out to in Section 3.4.4.4.

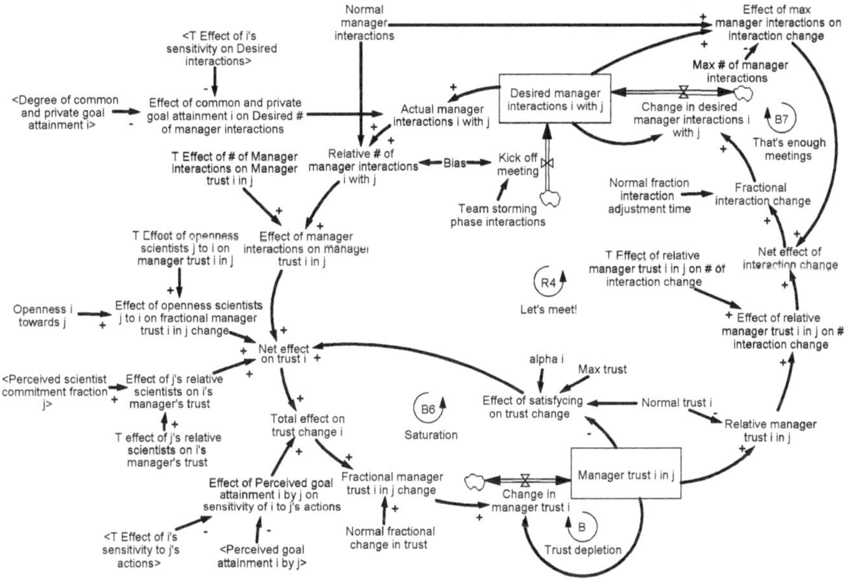

Figure 6-13: Stock and flow structure: Manager trust.[899]

As a third influence on 'Net effect on trust i', the balancing loop B6 – 'Satisfycing' indicates how fast or slowly trust between managers adjusts to 'Normal trust'. If 'Manager trust' is extremely high, for example, it gradually declines to 'Normal trust' considering no further trust-driving or trust-sustaining interactions between managers and all else being equal (see Figure 6-14). Usually, this holds for both directions, either from low trust to 'Normal trust' or from high trust to 'Normal trust'. Yet, we build in a minimum function for the parameter α, inverse of the adjustment time[900] (see Eq. 6.10).

$$ESTC_i = \alpha_i * \min(0, (MT_i - NMT)/(MT_i - MMT)) \qquad \text{(Eq. 6.10)}$$

where	$ESTC_i$	Effect of satisfycing on trust change i		
	MT_i	Manager trust i in j – parent i	NMT	Normal manager trust
	MMT	Maximum manager trust	α_i	Inverse adjustment time

Figure 6-14 gives a picture of the equation. 'Manager trust' is depicted on the x-axis. The vertical axis shows the 'Effect of manager trust on trust change'. Left of the

[899] Source: authors' representation.
[900] For time constants see Sterman (2000), pp. 276-279.

'Normal manager trust' the lines are dotted. Because of the minimum condition in Equation 6.10, this data is omitted. Therefore, the relevant data range is that between 'Normal manager trust' and 'Maximum manager trust'. In the following we focus on this range. We can see different structural behaviors given different values for α.

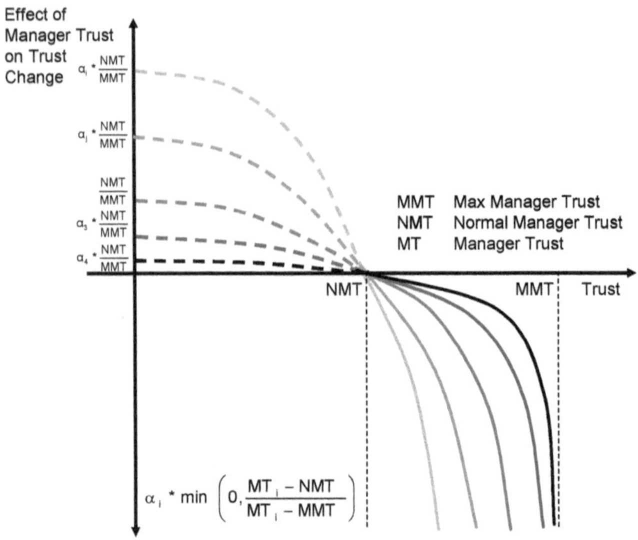

Figure 6-14: Effect of manager trust on trust change in varying trust atmospheres.[901]

The underlying idea is that α indicates how fast research partners can build up mutual trust starting at 'Normal trust'. Thus, in a trustworthy environment α_i is small, indicated by the dark line. It means that 'Manager trust' may build up easily. However, a research environment in which, for example, the parents do joint R&D for the first time, α_i would be large and 'Manager trust' would increase only slowly (light grey line). This is because a high number of interactions are necessary to sustain or even develop mutual trust. Nevertheless, this explanation is only applicable for the range defined above and not for the range between zero trust and 'Normal manager trust'.

The forth summand for calculating the 'Net effect on trust i' is the nonlinear 'Effect of interactions between managers' that considers that trust building means like mutual interactions increase trust. So, the more managers interact with each other, the more they trust each other. Trust declines if they do not interact regularly. There is no ef-

[901] Source: authors' representation. For the dotted lines left of 'Normal manager trust' α indicates the strength of self-correction or its volatility. It describes how fast 'Manager trust' recovers to 'Normal manager trust' after it has dropped. Referring to customer confidence in flying with a particular airline after a severe accident, for example, α describes how fast customer confidence recovers after the sudden drop in confidence.

fect on change in trust if the interactions are equal to the 'Normal number of interactions'.

How often managers interact with each other depends on the 'Desired number of manager interactions i with j'. This stock is changed by the flow 'Change in desired manager interactions i with j' (see Eq. 6.11).

$$ChDMIij_i = DMIij_i * (EMMIICh_i + ERMTijICh_i) * NFIAT \qquad \text{(Eq. 6.11)}$$

where	$ChDMIij_i$	Change in desired manager interactions i with j - i
	DMIiji	Desired manager interactions i with j -i
	EMMIIChi	Effect of max manager interactions on interaction change i
	ERMTijIChi	Effect of relative manager trust i in j on interaction change i
	NFIAT	Normal fraction interaction adjustment time

'Desired manager interactions i with j' are adjusted to a new state via multiplication by the 'Normal fraction interaction adjustment time' and the sum of two effects. As the effects are additive, neither of them becomes increasingly strong when growing.

The first effect on change is a restriction from the maximum number of possible interactions. An average working week only leaves time for a limited number of interactions, either personal interactions or conversations over the phone or by e-mail. The second effect depends on the actual 'Relative manager trust i in j'. This nonlinear relationship describes the following: when actual trust relative to normal trust is greater than one, managers seek to interact more frequently than required by the contract. If it is equal to one, they interact as frequently as required. If it is smaller than one, they do not wish to interact that frequently with each other. Mutual trust suffers.

Moreover, the 'Desired manager interactions i with j' can be increased once during the kick-off phase of the alliance by additional 'Team-building interactions' (see Figure 6-13). In the real world, team-building interactions could be required by alliance contract, for example.[902]

6.5.1.6 Scientist Openness

As indicated in the previous section, reciprocal openness between scientists influences trust between managers and vice versa. In the following we describe how openness between the scientists is determined (see Figure 6-15). It is the last subsystem structure of common learning.

[902] One case study interviewee describes what team-building interactions could entail. See Section 4.6.4.2.

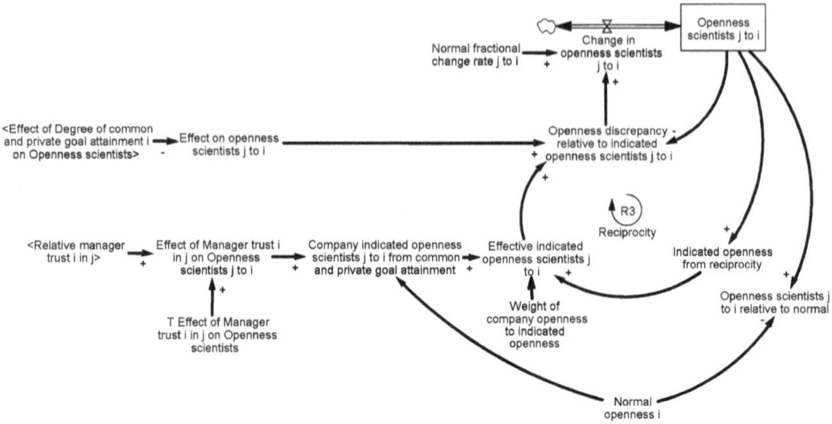

Figure 6-15: Stock and flow structure: Scientist openness.[903]

Like manager trust and desired interactions, openness between scientists is also hill-climbing (R3 – 'Reciprocity'). Its stock, 'Openness between scientists j to i – i' is changed via the 'Change in openness scientists j to i – i'. The flow consists of an actual state, the current 'Openness between scientists j to i – i' and the desired 'Effective indicated openness scientists j to i – i' (see Eq. 6.12). A possible discrepancy between the two states is closed via the 'Normal fractional change rate j to i'. The multiplicative 'Effect of goal attainment on openness j to i – i' requires a sudden reduction of openness between the scientist if the goals are met. As soon as goals are reached, the partnering firms become competitors again and any further knowledge exchange would unnecessarily strengthen the partner. Therefore, in this case, openness needs to be reduced.

$$ChOSji_i = ((WCI * (EMTijOji_i * NO_i) + (1 - WCI * IOR_i)) - OSji_i) * EGAOji_i * NFChROji_i \quad \text{(Eq. 6.12)}$$

where	$ChOSji_i$	Change in openness scientists j to i - i		
	WCI	Weight of company openness to indicated openness		
	$EMTijOji_i$	Effect manager trust i in j on Openness scientists j to i – i		
	NOi	Normal openness i – i	OSjii	Openness scientists j to i – i
	IOR_i	Indicated openness from reciprocity - i		
	$EGAOji_i$	Effect of goal attainment on openness scientists j to i - i		
	$NFChROji_i$	Normal fractional change rate j to i – i		

'Effective indicated openness scientists j to i – i' depends on the respective parent firm's policy whether the firm's managers can dictate to their scientists how reciprocatively they should behave. Over the course of the alliance, scientists gain experience about their partner firm's colleagues. If they behave fairly from the partner's point of view, scientists wish to reciprocate fair behavior because people seek fairness.[904]

[903] Source: authors' representation.
[904] See Section 3.4.4.4 on fairness in human interactions.

This 'Indicated openness from reciprocity' is one variable influencing the effective indicated openness. On a higher organizational level, managers also gain experience from interactions with the partner firm's managers. As explained in the preceding section, this results in mutual manager trust. Trust travels through the organization[905] and also influences scientists' openness toward each other. Depending on firm culture, it is either the manager's trust or the partner's scientists' openness that decides on how open the scientists are toward the partner firm's scientists. This is incorporated in the variable 'Weight of company openness to indicated openness'. If it is greater than 0.5, the 'Effect manager trust i in j' on Openness scientists j to i - i' is more relevant; if it is smaller than 0.5, it is the 'Indicated openness from reciprocity' that is more influential on the 'Effective indicated openness'.

The subsystem structures presented so-far are intertwined with each other. They represent the core structure of what we identify as responsible for common learning in learning alliances. Before we analyze the behavior that the structure produces, we extend the model boundary to include the structure for private learning. This way we create a complete model of interorganizational learning. The structure for private learning may be activated or deactivated.

6.5.2 Model Subsystem: Learning from the Partner

In the following three sections we present the extended model structure for learning privately from the alliance or the partner. We first concentrate on the generation of private benefits. We continue with how knowledge might spill over from the alliance. Finally, we close this section by modeling the gatekeeper's duty.

6.5.2.1 Private Benefits

The subsystem structure for the generation of private benefits, or, more operationally private patents[906], is largely similar to the alliance 'Patent generation' subsystem described in Section 6.5.1.2 (see Figure 6-9 and Figure 6-16). Therefore we do not present the model structure in depth but focus on a few modifications. Knowledge, for example, refers to private knowledge and not to alliance knowledge. Also, where it made sense we used the same constants as in the common learning structure. This way, we obtain comparability between the dynamics of the two structures. This is especially important for the base run. It ensures that both structures create similar behaviors. Yet, there are two structural differences. First, the number of scientists who work with the knowledge that spilled over from the alliance might be changed. So, the parent firm might add scientists to the private learning, which would then occur at a higher speed. Second, unlike in the alliance 'Patent generation' subsystem, the sci-

[905] See Inkpen and Currall (2004), p. 597.

[906] The term 'private patent' refers to benefits generated on the basis of private knowledge that spilled over from the alliance in combination with the firm's already existing organizational knowledge. We are aware of the fact that patents are known to the public and therefore cannot be understood as private.

entists' 'Relative commitment to learn and work privately j' is exogenous. We decided to do so to keep the structure simple. As we formulated the common learning substructures from parent i's viewpoint, we formulate the private learning substructures from parent j's viewpoint. This way it becomes obvious that parent j explicitly outlearns parent i via the alliance.

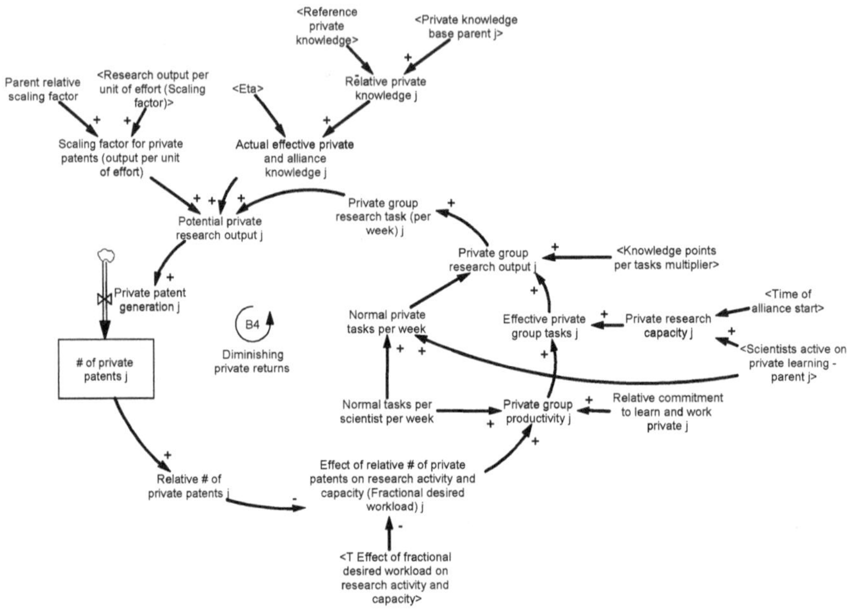

Figure 6-16: Stock and flow structure: Private benefits.[907]

6.5.2.2 Private Knowledge and Knowledge Spillover

For a firm to create private benefits it must generate private knowledge. It needs to spill over from the common 'Alliance knowledge base' that could only build up through the interaction of both parent firms' scientists (see Figure 6-17).

[907] Source: authors' representation.

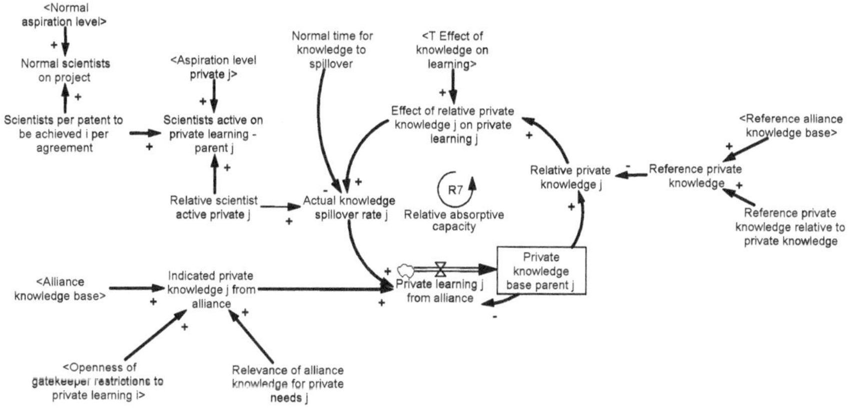

Figure 6-17: Stock and flow structure: Private knowledge base.[908]

The factors influencing the private learning of parent firm j are formulated in Equation 6.13. How much knowledge actually spills over from the alliance to parent j's knowledge base depends on the last term. The 'Effect of relative private knowledge j on private learning j' represents the idea of relative absorptive capacity (R7 – 'Relative absorptive capacity').[909] The fewer scientists who know about the topic to be learned, the lower is their ability to understand the incoming knowledge right away. Learning is accelerated when their actual knowledge base is already significant. As in the 'Alliance knowledge base' substructure, it is a nonlinear and S-shaped effect. How much is actually learned depends on the number of scientists working on generating private knowledge. We consider the time to learn privately with the 'Normal time for knowledge to spillover'. The resulting 'Actual knowledge spillover rate j' is the maximum possible private learning rate. It is multiplied by what can be learned from the alliance. This is specified in the 'Indicated private knowledge j from alliance'. The latter variable depends on the 'Relevance of alliance knowledge for private needs j', the 'Alliance knowledge base', and the partner firm i's gatekeeper's openness.[910] In each of the following three cases, parent firm j's scientists cannot learn anything from the common 'Alliance knowledge base' – independently of how many scientists are involved in private learning or how high their relative absorptive capacity is: first, alliance knowledge is not of relevance, second, scientists working on alliance tasks have not created any new common knowledge, or third, parent i's gatekeeper does not allow any knowledge flows.

$$PL_j = (AKB * RAKPN_j * AOG_i) - PKB_j * (ERPKPL_j * RS_j / NTKS_j) \qquad \text{(Eq. 6.13)}$$

where AKB Alliance knowledge base
RAKPNj Relevance of alliance knowledge for private needs j
AOGi Actual openness of gatekeeper restrictions to private learning i

[908] Source: authors' representation.
[909] For explanations on relative absorptive capacity see Lane and Lubatkin (1998), p. 462, Lubatkin et al. (2001), pp. 1353, 1361, 1365, and Section 4.6.1.
[910] For explanations on the gatekeeper's duty see Section 4.6.3.

PKBj	Private knowledge base parent j
ERPKPLj	Effect of relative private knowledge j on private learning j
RSj	Relative scientist active private j
NTKSj	Normal time for knowledge to spill over j

6.5.2.3 Openness Gatekeeper

The following substructure is the final substructure of private learning. As indicated in the previous section, the partner firm's gatekeeper decides on how much knowledge flows from the 'Alliance knowledge base' to the 'Private knowledge base'. If parent firm j learns from the joint 'Alliance knowledge base', parent firm i's gatekeeper does not have any objections to private learning. Whether the gatekeeper has such objections first depends on the contractual arrangements (see Figure 6-18).[911]

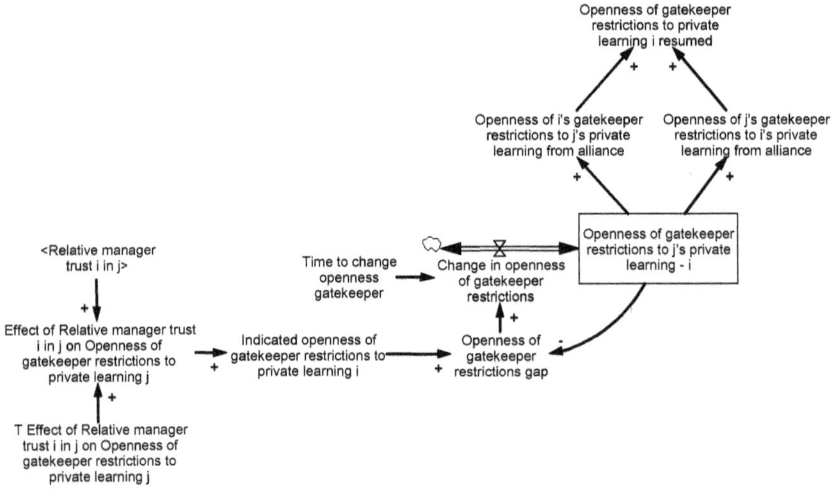

Figure 6-18: Stock and flow structure: Gatekeeper openness.[912]

How important the collaborating firms estimate formal controls for knowledge flows between the alliance and the parent firms to be is considered in the initialization of the stock 'Openness of gatekeeper restrictions to j's private learning – i'. If no private learning is allowed, the gatekeeper openness is at a minimum. This means that formal controls are fully implemented. The change of the stock is determined by the flow 'Change in openness of gatekeeper restrictions i' (see Eq. 6.14). It depends on the gap between the 'Indicated openness of gatekeeper restrictions to private learning i' and the actual state. The indicated openness relies on how trustworthy parent firm i's managers judge their colleagues from parent j to be. As laid out in detail in Section 4.6.3, the more important social controls in a partnership are, the less important be-

[911] For formal and social controls see Section 4.6.3.
[912] Source: authors' representation.

come formal controls like gatekeepers. If initial trust between the managers does not change, neither does the indicated openness. If trust increases, so does the gatekeeper's openness. Formal controls hence become less important. In the case of decreasing trust, gatekeeper's openness does not change at all. In summary, this substructure contains the substitution of formal controls by social ones.

$$ChGO_i = (ERMT_{ij}OGPL_j - OGPL_i)/TChGO \qquad \text{(Eq. 6.14)}$$

where	$ChGO_i$	Change in openness of gatekeeper restrictions i
	$ERMT_{ij}OGPL_j$	Effect of Relative manager trust i in j on Openness of gatekeeper restrictions to private learning j
	$OGPL_i$	Openness of gatekeeper restrictions to private learning i
	TChGO	Time to change openness gatekeeper

Gatekeeper's openness is the last substructure to be described. The combination of all substructures represents the full model of interorganizational learning in alliances. In the following we discuss model validation according to the iterative System Dynamics modeling process. Afterwards we present the behavior that the structure creates.

6.6 Model Validation

As indicated in Section 2.3.5, model validation is an important iterative ongoing part of the modeling process. In this section we focus on insight from model validation. We weigh model structure and behavior against real world structure and observation. We do so by analyzing the model a priori formally and evaluating it against descriptions from the relevant literature. We start with structure validation tests and continue with behavior validation tests that we explained in Section 2.3.5.

6.6.1 Structure Validation Tests

Model structure drives model behavior.[913] Therefore, structure analysis provides insight into sources for model behaviors. In the following we analyze model boundary, structure assessment, dimensional consistency, and parameter assessment.

Model Boundary Adequacy Tests

In Section 6.2 we laid out the scope of the interorganizational learning model. We used a model boundary chart and a subsystem diagram to assess the appropriateness of the model boundary for its purposes. By extensively reviewing the relevant literature on alliance research and from the insight revealed by our case study (see Chapter 4) we learned which variables are relevant for the model purpose, which are not, and which feedback structures they are part of. These variables are endogenous to the model structure (see Figure 6-1 and Table 6-1).

---

913 See Sterman (2000), p. 81.

Furthermore we examined whether we omitted important feedbacks from the model structure while exogenizing variables that should be endogenous to the model structure. Exogenous parameters can be interpreted as constants. They are not influenced by endogenous model variables over the chosen time horizon. If they are, these parameters should be endogenized.[914] All variables chosen to be exogenous determine the initial alliance conditions. This may encompass whether, for example, the alliance partners enter the cooperation with the intention of playing fairly or cheating. Motives for the latter may be the desire to achieve private goals or a different number of common goals than agreed. Furthermore, while defining the basic underlying trust atmosphere between the partners as an initial exogenous condition, trust between the managers may change endogenously over the course of the alliance. We laid out our intentions for exogenizing parameters when discussing the model scope in Section 6.2.

The boundary adequacy tests show that the model structure is based on profound literature and case study analysis. Given the model purpose, important variables are endogenized and feedbacks between the alliance and its environment are also considered.

Structure Assessment Tests

Structure assessment tests question whether the model structure is consistent with knowledge of the real system which is relevant to the purpose. This refers to the choice of an appropriate level of aggregation. In addition, we ask whether the model respects conservation laws and considers whether the decision rules are realistic.[915]

Analogous to the model boundary test, relevant model structure is determined by contributions from the relevant alliance and learning alliance literature and a specific case study on a learning alliance. After extensively reviewing model substructures, we do not find any violations of conservation laws. Real quantities, like 'Scientists active in alliance' or 'Number of alliance patents', for example, cannot become negative. Nevertheless, the variable 'Scientists active in alliance' is modeled as a rational number assuming the scientists' divisibility. This is realistic insofar as it could be interpreted as a proportionate yearly performance, considering participation in other projects, vacation, etc.

To gain information to formulate realistic decision rules we conducted interviews with scientists and managers engaged in a learning alliance.[916] We transferred insight into the mathematical formulation of flows. Also, we used the latest research findings from behavioral game theory to formulate policies:[917] when humans interact with humans, they do not necessarily follow rational decision-rules according to the homo economicus. A sense of fairness and reciprocity drives human behavior. We consider this insight in the two substructures in which scientists and managers interact with each other, 'Openness scientists' and 'Manager trust'.

---

[914] See Sterman (2000), p. 861.
[915] See Sterman (2000), p. 863.
[916] See Chapter 4.
[917] See Section 3.4.4.4.

Dimensional Consistency

We have applied the tests for dimensional consistency throughout model building. All variables are specified with units. As stated in Section 6.5.1 we decided to specify soft variables like trust, knowledge, or openness, for instance, with dimensions like 'trust points', 'knowledge points, or 'openness points' and not with dimensionless measures. Though the chosen dimensions do not exist in the real world, they enable us to avoid conceptional or structural flaws. Assigning 'dimensionless' measures would facilitate modeling as it would avoid the need for converting units from one substructure to the subsequent, e.g., from 'Manager trust' to 'Openness scientists' and vice versa. Both variables would have dimensionless units. Nevertheless, conversions are necessary for designing a coherent model structure and adding conceptual clarity. In addition, the model structure is more elegant when dimensions are converted into dimensionless units by normalizing the variables when entering robust nonlinear relationships. Normalizing means that input and output of nonlinear functions are dimensionless ratios of reference values.[918] If the input to a nonlinear function has dimensionless units, the need for conversion is not that obvious. Alternatively, the model builder might overlook or even ignore the necessity of normalizing as inputs and outputs have dimensionless units already. Considering dimensions, the interorganizational learning model passes the required units check.[919]

Parameter Assessment

Apart from parameters having real-life meanings their value needs to be estimated, too. STERMAN suggests two alternatives for such parameter assessment that can also be combined: formal statistical estimation and judgmental estimation.[920] We applied judgmental estimation by interviewing scientists and managers working in a learning alliance. To specify nonlinear relationships, for example, in interviews, the experts were asked about possible causes and/or effects of parameters identified by the literature as being important. They were also asked to estimate whether parameters increased or decreased over the course of their learning alliance.[921] Additionally they were asked how the effect of one variable on another varies if the first grows. This information then led to the estimation of nonlinear relationships applied in order to quantify the model structure.

With this approach we were able to ensure that the majority of variables used in the model derived from case study interviews and from reviewing the alliance research literature. As interviewees and the alliance literature seldom mention closed feedback loops, we occasionally had to fill in variables to close the loops. Nevertheless, these parameters also have real world counterparts. So, all parameters used in the model derive from real system elements and can unambiguously be reassigned back to them.

---

[918] See Sterman (2000), pp. 554-555.

[919] The System Dynamics modeling software Vensim successfully tests the unit check for the interorganizational learning model described in Sections 6.5 and 6.5.2.

[920] See Sterman (2000), pp. 868-869.

[921] See the semi-structured interview guide in the Appendix.

Conclusion Structure Validation Tests
In this section we analyzed the model structure. We showed that the interorganizational learning model is formally correct. The chosen model structure is based on recognized theoretical approaches and considers relevant real world parameters and their feedbacks. The model does not violate conservation laws and meets dimensional consistency requirements. We showed that every parameter has its real-life counterpart and meaning. Despite the high share of soft variables used in the model that are challenging to quantify we showed that the model is in close touch with reality. Summarizing, on the basis of the structure validation tests applied above, we conclude that the model structure is characterized by high validity. Apart from validating model structure, its behavior also needs to be analyzed. This is done in the following section.

6.6.2 Behavior Validation Tests

Behavior validation tests analyze to what extent model behavior corresponds with real system behavior. They also examine whether there are leverage parameters that may have a strong influence on the entire model behavior and how robust a model is in extreme conditions. We first show results of the extreme condition tests followed by those of sensitivity analysis and other behavior validation tests. The results of the behavior validation tests are depicted over an extended time horizon of 150 weeks to show that no unexpected behavior occurs after the originally explained time horizon of 100 weeks.

Extreme Conditions Tests
As laid out in Section 2.3.5, the purpose of extreme condition tests is to examine the model behavior's robustness with extreme inputs.[922] Reasonable model behavior increases the model user's confidence in the model structure. In the following we show that the model behaves robustly by simulating two extreme conditions by way of example. First we test model behavior under the premise that neither partner allocates any employees to the alliance. In the subsequent test we analyze model behavior under the condition that neither partner firms' gatekeeper allows any free knowledge flows from the parent firms to the alliance.

For the first test, we assume that neither parent firm assigns scientists or managers to the alliance despite having common goals. The expectation is as follows: when there are no scientists who can interact with each other, no knowledge can be exchanged, which means that no joint knowledge can be created and the goals are not attained. Also, as there is nobody interacting, trust between the partners' employees also does not change.

To simulate this extreme case situation, we need to change the parameter 'Scientists per patent to be achieved i per agreement'. This determines how many scientists

[922] See Sterman (2000), pp. 869-871.

each partner firm allocates to the alliance per prospective patent. In the Base run, it is assumed to be equal to one scientist allocated per patent. In this run it is set to zero.

Figure 6-19 depicts the model behavior over time. The model behaves as expected. The graph on the left shows that the 'Alliance knowledge base' remains zero (solid line marked 1). Both parents' 'Private knowledge bases' (lines marked 2 and 3) do not reveal any behavior and stay constant at zero. This is reasonable as the 'Private knowledge bases' are only determined by knowledge that spills over from the 'Alliance knowledge base'. The graph on the right-hand side of Figure 6-19 illustrates that 'Manager trust' stays constant at 1 'trust point'. This equals trust under normal conditions. This means that managers neither trust nor distrust each other particularly. They would be open to interacting with each other anytime.

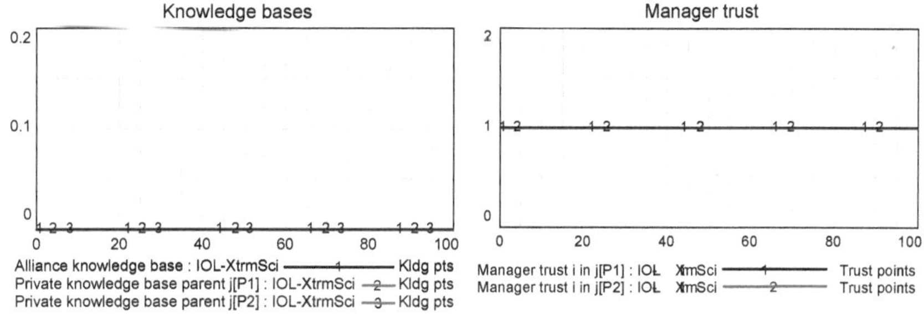

Figure 6-19: Dynamics under extreme condition of no scientists.[923]

For our second extreme condition test, we assume that the parent firms do allocate their employees to the alliance according to the alliance contract. Further, they should work on common tasks and create joint knowledge. Nevertheless, for some reason the lawyers of both parent firms designed a non-disclosure agreement that does not allow the scientists to exchange knowledge with each other. As laid out in Section 4.5.3, knowledge exchange is essential for creating joint knowledge. So, we expect that even though scientists are allocated to the alliance, they cannot generate common knowledge, which also means that they also do not attain common goals.

To simulate this extreme condition test, the 'Openness of i's gatekeeper restrictions to i's knowledge sharing' is set to zero. The parameter determines both firms' 'Effective openness i' and the 'Effective group tasks i' in the 'Patent generation' substructure. In the Base run, it is equal to one, which means that the scientist may openly communicate and exchange knowledge with each other.

It is assumed that the alliance is established in week five: parent firms assign their scientists to the alliance. It is further assumed that the parent firms seek ten patents each. Moreover, it is assumed that each parent allocates one scientist per patent to be achieved. Model behavior is as expected (see Figure 6-20). The upper right-hand

[923] All runs shown derive from the simulation model and hence are the authors' representations.

graph illustrates that trust between the managers builds up through mutual interaction. In Section 6.5.1.5 we explained that managers allocate slightly more to the alliance when they trust each other. Therefore, the 'Scientists allocated on alliance – parent i' are marginally higher than the ten scientists per parent (see upper left-hand graph).

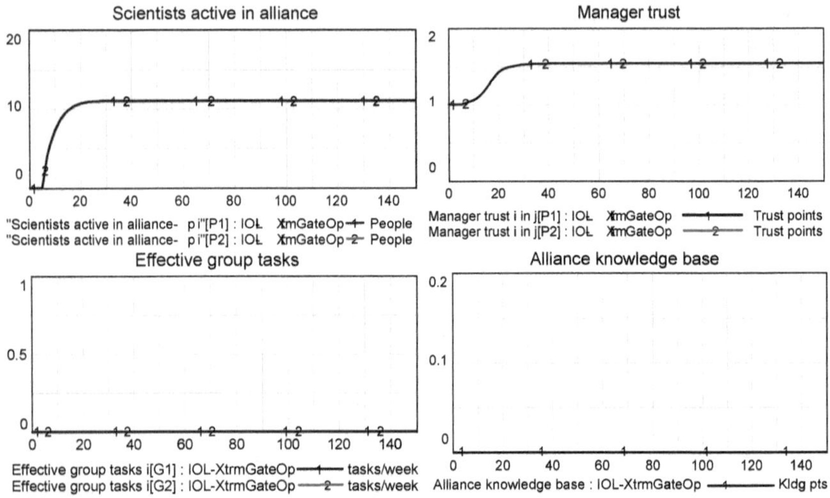

Figure 6-20: Dynamics under extreme condition of no open communication.

Yet, as both firms' gatekeepers do not allow any knowledge flows between the scientists, they cannot work effectively on their tasks (lower left-hand graph, one line for each parent) which is why they cannot create joint knowledge (lower right-hand graph). The 'Alliance knowledge base' stays constant at zero knowledge points.

Both specimen tests show that the model is robust in the face of extreme conditions. In both cases the model behaves as expected in a realistic fashion. Consequently, we can infer that the model meets the requirements of the extreme condition tests.

Sensitivity Analysis

In the following section we conduct sensitivity analysis to analyze the effects of external parameters on system behavior. By applying sensitivity analysis we seek to answer the question of whether a model is insensitive to numerical and behavioral changes in uncertain parameters. There are three types of sensitivity: numerical, behavior mode, and policy sensitivity.[924] According to STERMAN, numerical sensitivity exists in all models. It exists when a change in an input variable changes the model results. The model reveals behavior mode sensitivity when a small parameter change leads to a clear change of the model behavior pattern: for instance, if the behavior mode changes from S-shaped growth to overshoot and collapse. Finally, policy sen-

[924] See Sterman (2000), p. 883.

sitivity exists when a change in model assumptions reverses the effects of a suggested policy. Nevertheless, not all parameters are at the focus of sensitivity analysis. STERMAN stresses that sensitivity analysis needs to focus on parameters that are both highly uncertain and likely to be influential.[925]

The interorganizational learning model contains forty-two parameters. This includes parameters for both parents' model structures, indicated with i and j. We tested all parameters for their sensitivity. The great majority of them show insensitive behavior. Yet, four parameters, respectively two parameters of the two parents' identical structures, reveal sensitive behavior. In the following we illustrate both insensitive and sensitive behavior dynamics, testing two and one parameters respectively by way of example. We start with parameters that exhibit stable and robust behavior in sensitivity analysis.

Insensitive Behavior

The first example is a variation of 'Scientists per patent to be achieved P1'. Change in this parameter leads to differing scientist allocation by Partner firm 1. The original value for the base case is that firms assign one scientist per patent to be achieved. For the sensitivity run we increase the spectrum from 0.3 to 2 scientists per patent. Assigning less than 30% percent of the agreed number of scientists is not likely. Neither is allocating more than twice as many. It is assumed that Partner 1 and Partner 2 both agree on Partner 1 assigning fewer or more scientists to the alliance. Hence, as Partner 2 is aware of its partner allocating fewer or more scientists, the alliance is continued until all common goals are reached.

The graphs in Figure 6-21 show the dynamic confidence boundaries from univariate sensitivity analysis. The figures depict the 50%, 75%, 95%, and 100% confidence bounds for all the variables in a sample of 200 simulations. The left-hand graph in Figure 6-21 depicts the development of the 'Alliance knowledge base'. As intended, we see that scientists start to work on alliance tasks at the beginning of week 5. They slowly generate common knowledge which in the beginning consists of exchanged knowledge, on which newly created knowledge is built. Given these assumptions, there is a 50% chance that the 'Alliance knowledge base' will increase to between roughly 72 and 76 knowledge points, a 75% chance that it will increase to between 70 and slightly more than 76 knowledge points, a 95% chance that it will increase to between 68 and again slightly more than 76 knowledge points. Note that the confidence interval widens during the growth phase, then narrows and stays constant as the alliance is dissolved. The uncertainty in alliance knowledge is much greater during the growth phase because the number of Partner 1's scientists in the alliance dominates the learning opportunities. If Partner 1 only allocates only 30% of the scientists agreed, it takes longer to finally reach the goal.

We add that the 'Alliance knowledge base' declines after reaching a peak as no new knowledge is learned. The loops that are building up the knowledge base are inactive after reaching the goals, as the alliance is dissolved. Loop dominance shifts to the

[925] See Sterman (2000), p. 884.

first-order balancing loop, that gradually drains 'Alliance knowledge base' as scientists unlearn their knowledge.

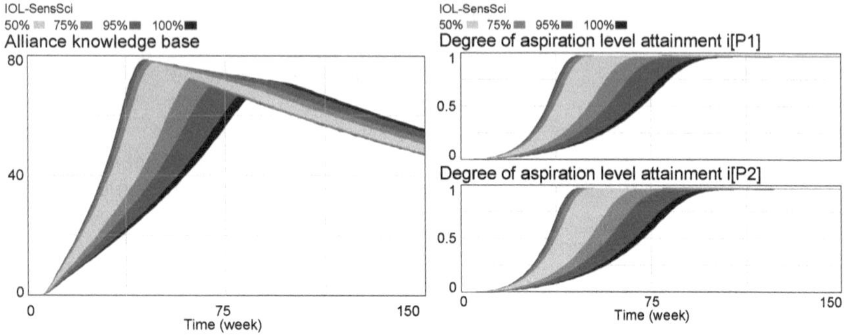

Figure 6-21: Sensitivity analysis: Partner 1's scientist allocation.[926]

The two graphs on the right in Figure 6-21 show both parents' 'Degree of aspiration level attainment' or, in other words, their goal attainments. As can be seen from the figure, the distribution of reaching the common goals is identical for both parent firms. Given Partner 2's differing scientist allocation, there is a 50% chance that the firms will attain their aspiration level between about weeks 42 and 60 and a 95% chance that they will reach their goals between weeks 40 and 90.

For the second sensitivity run, we vary the trust atmosphere in which both firms are embedded again with 200 simulation runs. This is indicated in the model structure with the parameter α,[927] for which the original value in the base case for both firms is 1. This value corresponds to both firms' 'Normal trust'. For the sensitivity run we increase the spectrum for α from 0.1 to 2. If α is less than 1, firms are in a trustworthy environment: it is relatively easy for them to increase mutual 'Manager trust' with trust-building actions. If it is higher than 1, the partnering firms are skeptical toward each other. Hence, it is increasingly difficult for them and it requires more effort to increase trust.

The upper three graphs in Figure 6-22 show the dynamic confidence boundaries from univariate sensitivity analysis of the same variables as in Figure 6-21. Compared to Figure 6-21, the confidence boundaries of 50%, 75%, 95%, and 100% are much tighter in Figure 6-22. Consequently, the model is quite insensitive toward changes in the parameter α.

[926] The asymmetric shape of the confidence bounds can be attributed to convex, concave, and S-shaped table functions in the model.
[927] See Section 6.5.1.5.

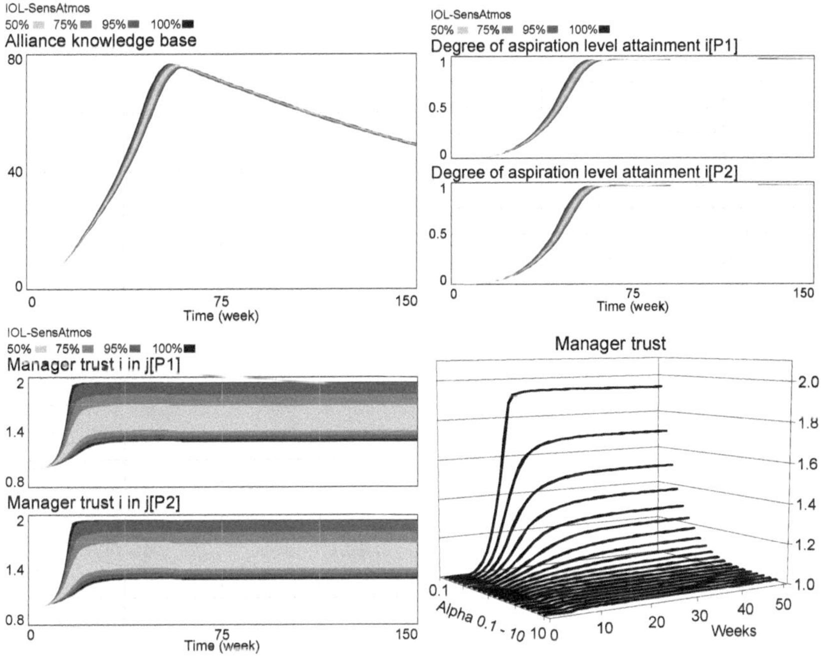

Figure 6-22: Sensitivity analysis: Variation in trust atmosphere.

Nevertheless, as the lower left chart in Figure 6-22 shows, the trust atmosphere does have an impact on the development of 'Manager trust'. In all runs, 'Manager trust' increases above 'Normal manager trust'. The reason for this is that both parent firms allocate their scientists to the alliance (see upper left-hand graph of Figure 6-22). Scientists do joint research together and common goals are attained (see upper right-hand figure of Figure 6-22) There is a 50% chance that 'Manager trust' will be between 40% and 70% higher than 'Normal trust', and a 95% chance that it will be between roughly 30% to 90% higher than 'Normal trust'.

The lower right-hand graph depicts the dynamics of 'Manager trust' with varying α in more detail. It seems as though we are observing behavior mode sensitivity. As can be seen, there is a smooth transition of the slope of increase with decreasing α. As expected, trust develops more highly in a trusting environment with the same number of trust-building means than in a skeptical environment. In the latter situation, it seems like trust barely changes. Yet, that is the case for the scale depicted in the graph. We observe that the equilibrium 'Manager trust' level increases exponentially with decreasing α. In any case, α determines the equilibrium value for 'Manager trust'. The model behaves as anticipated. Yet, considering the upper two graphs in Figure 6-22, though α is sensitive to 'Manager trust', the effect on variables in other substructures, like scientist allocation or goal attainment, for example, is low.

Concerning the two examples of sensitivity runs mentioned, to summarize the behavioral validity tests, the model can be interpreted as valid. In the following we present a sensitivity run of a sensitive parameter.

Sensitive Behavior
We identified four parameters as being sensitive to model behavior. Each partner's model structure entails the 'Fraction of actual internally communicated goals i' and 'Fractional scientist bonus i'.[928] As the parameters also exist for both partners, the total sensitive parameters add up to four. All of them show similar sensitivities, which is why we exemplify the runs showing only one parameter test.

In the first sensitivity run presented in the previous paragraph, Partner 2 was informed by Partner 1 that the latter had allocated more or fewer scientists than agreed on in the contract. In contrast, in the subsequent run Partner 1 does not inform its partner about deviations in scientist allocation. Varying the number of scientists in the alliance influences 'Total research capacity' and thus the weekly research output. Allocating more scientists increases research output, which means that alliance goals are met faster. Allocating fewer scientists reduces research output. Hence, alliance goals are met at a later point in time. Yet, as laid out in Section 6.5.1.5, scientist allocation not only has an impact on the 'Total research capacity', but also on trust between the firms' managers. Therefore, if Partner 1 allocates more scientists to the alliance, the trust Partner 2's managers have in Partner 1's managers slightly increases. On the other hand, if Partner 1 reduces its share of scientists – without informing Parent firm 2 –, Partner 2 is surprised and trust declines. Eventually, Partner 2 might also withdraw scientists from the alliance. In sum, we expect a change in Partner 2's behavior as a response to Partner 1's actions in this sensitivity run.

To run this sensitivity test we vary the parameter 'Fractional scientist bonus P1'. A change in this parameter leads to an increase or decrease in the 'Actual goal of scientist allocation i for common learning', given the 'Scientists per patent to be achieved i per agreement'.[929] 'Actual goal of scientist allocation i for common learning' determines the actual allocation of the respective parent's scientists. The original value for 'Fractional scientist bonus' is equal to 1. This means that there is no deviation from what the parents agreed should be allocated to the alliance (which is embedded in the parameter 'Scientists per patent to be achieved i per agreement'). For the sensitivity run we increase the spectrum from 10% to 200%. In other words, Partner 1 allocates between 10% and double the amount of scientists that it agreed on in the alliance contract.

As before, the two upper graphs in Figure 6-23 show the sensitivity analysis of the same variables as in Figure 6-21, 'Alliance knowledge base' and both parents' 'Degree of aspiration level attainment'. This time, however, they do not depict confidence bounds but individual traces of the different runs. We notice a change in behavior. In

[928] 'Fraction of actual internally communicated goals P1' is part of the 'Goal attainment' subsystem structure (see Figure 6-1) and 'Fractional scientist bonus P1' of the 'Scientist active in alliance' subsystem structure (see Figure 6-11).
[929] See Figure 6-11.

some runs, alliance knowledge reaches a high peak between around weeks 40 and 60; in other runs, it reaches a smooth maximum at a very low level between around weeks 10 and 25. Both parents' 'Degree of aspiration level attainment' go along with this dynamics. Both parents either reach their goals after week 40 or they do not even reach 10% of the agreed common goals. Goal attainment stays on a low level right until the end of the simulation.

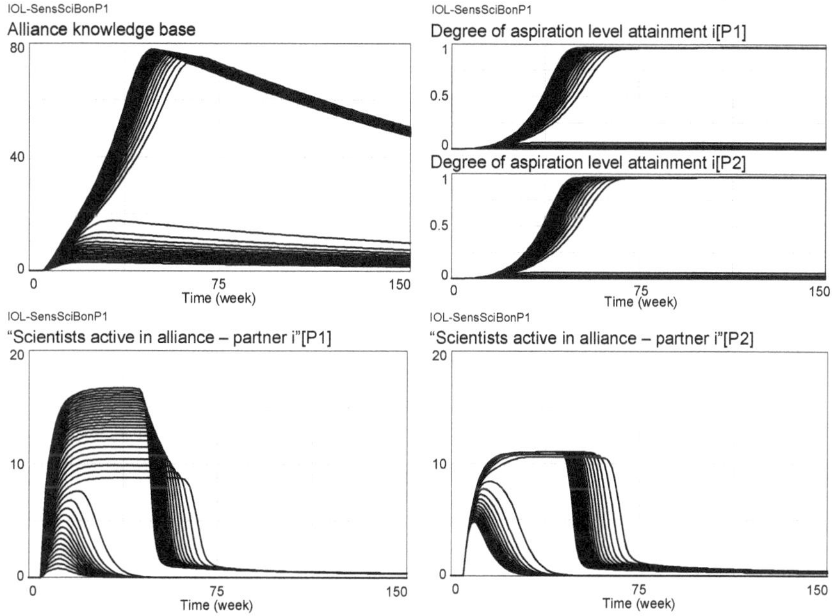

Figure 6-23: Sensitivity analysis: Unknown variation of Partner 1's scientist allocation.

The reason for this is the variation in Partner 1's scientist allocation (see lower left-hand graph in Figure 6-23). Partner 2 is surprised by a lower scientist allocation, for example. It accepts this behavior until a certain allocation threshold. Below this threshold, Partner 2 loses patience, trust declines and it consequently withdraws its scientists from the alliance – before reaching a reasonable fraction of goals. Partner 1's free rider ambitions overstepped the mark.

Nonetheless, as expected, Partner 2 does not have any objections to Partner 1 allocating more scientists than agreed in the contract. Neither does it reduce its own scientist share, nor increase it (see lower right-hand graph in Figure 6-23). Postponements in reaching the goals occur in situations where Partner 2 still accepts Partner 1 allocating fewer than the 10 scientists agreed on. Assigning fewer scientists reduces total 'Alliance research capacity' and consequently the weekly 'Group research output'.

Concluding, the sensitivity test shows that the model is not robust when faced with a variation in the parameter 'Scientist bonus P1'. Concerning the behavior of 'Degree of goal attainment', for example, behavior mode changes from an S-shaped growth to almost a steady plateau on a low level. As indicated above, this behavior is to be expected. This is the behavior that GULATI, KHANNA, AND NOHRIA observed in a field study they conducted: a U.S. alliance partner adjusted its scientist share after its Indian partner did not send its scientists to the alliance as expected. Shortly after, the alliance was dissolved as the Indian firm did not fulfill its resource obligation.[930]

As indicated at the beginning of this section, the parameter 'Fraction of actual internally communicated goals P1' reveals similar sensitivity.[931] This parameter determines the actual scientist allocation given a smaller actual internal 'Aspiration level'. This means that the parent firm entered the alliance to purposely fool its partner in terms of both goals to be attained and scientists to allocate. Up to a certain threshold, Partner 2 accepts this behavior. Then, at some point, trust is too low and Partner 2 withdraws its scientists and dissolves the alliance. We observe a shift in loop dominance that is further explained in the following sections and in detail in Section 7.2.3.4.

Further Behavior Validation Tests

Besides the tests mentioned above, we applied other behavior validation tests like the integration error, behavior anomaly, family member, or surprise behavior test.[932] The first examines whether the simulation interval, dt, yielding an approximation of the underlying continuous dynamics, is accurate enough for the model purpose. Testing various time steps we came to the conclusion that we would use dt=0.0625.[933] Considering the model's current time delays of adjustment times, the simulation interval is small enough to generate smooth transitions and similar model behavior as with smaller time steps.

Furthermore, the model does not show any surprise behavior that could indicate model flaws. The family member test asks whether the model generates behavior of instances in the same class as the system the model was built to mimic.[934] First, the model can be applied to every research alliance between companies in which the model assumptions presented in Section 6.2 hold. Furthermore, the model could be applied to another, more general level. The model could be applied to, in a qualified way, any situation in which interpersonal action and trust play an important role: people work on joint goals and share complementary knowledge, like architects working together on a particular project, students with different backgrounds learning together for a final exam, or scientists who come together for a limited time period, work on similar research tasks, and have complementary knowledge, for example. Hence, as

930 See Gulati et al. (1994), p. 63 and our relating discussion in Section 4.6.4.2.
931 The chosen parameters all refer to Partner 1. Yet, the same dynamics show when the parameters referring to Partner 2 are tested.
932 See Sterman (2000), pp. 874-889 for an in-depth explanation of the behavior validation tests.
933 Following, for example, Maani and Cavana (2002), pp. 75-76. See the authors for an explanation on determining simulation intervals.
934 See Sterman (2000), p. 881.

the model can be applied to a wide instance of systems, it represents a more general approach to interpersonal interaction and learning.

Behavior reproduction tests cannot be conducted as we do not have access to empirical data for our case study alliance. Nevertheless, in the following we compare the model base run with the reference modes identified by the members of the case study research alliance. The comparison allows us to instill further confidence in the model structure.

Conclusion Behavior Validation Tests

Summarizing this section on model behavior validation we conclude that the model can be interpreted as valid and robust. The extreme condition tests, for example, reveal plausible model behaviors supporting confidence in formal model correctness. Moreover, regarding findings from sensitivity analysis we conclude that, though the model is sensitive to variations in the four parameters 'Fractional scientist bonus i' or 'Fraction of actual internally communicated goals i', model behavior is still reasonable and robust. As both parameters determine the number of scientists from both parent firms allocated to the alliance, the behavior is reasonable. Alliance scholars point out research allocation as one main driver for alliance failure.[935] Therefore, we focus in more detail on this when analyzing model behavior in various policy runs supported by insight from case study interviews in the subsequent chapter.

[935] See, for example, Khanna et al. (1998) or Grossman and Shapiro (1987).

7. Model Behavior and Policy Analysis

7.1 Overview

In this chapter we analyze the model behavior in the base run and under different policies. We first present the base run behavior of pure common learning in Section 7.2.1. For our behavior analysis we continue with policy runs throughout Section 7.4. The policies applied refer to plausible control of the stakeholders.

We separate the behavior analysis into three parts following the subsystem structure presented in Figure 6-1. We first study cooperative and competitive learning with the partner (Section 7.2) and then competitive learning from the alliance (Section 7.3). In our analysis we identify trust as a crucial variable for alliance success. Therefore, we study the model structure of trust in depth in Section 7.2.3. We finally combine insight from the two preceding Sections 7.2 and 7.3 in the third segment in which we study cooperative and competitive behavior in situations of learning with the partner and from the alliance (Section 7.4). In each section we compare the policy runs to the base run behavior of the system.

7.2 Model Behavior Analysis: Learning with the Partner

When analyzing learning with the partner it is assumed that the parent firms only seek common goals. Either they are not interested in achieving private goals or the alliance contract is designed in such a way that knowledge transfer from the alliance to the parent firms is highly controlled and therefore limited by gatekeeper restrictions.[936] In the following we show a base run and four policy runs. In all runs it is assumed that the alliance starts in week five.

7.2.1 Base Run: Successful Interorganizational Learning in a Learning Alliance

The base run's assumption of only common benefits permits a comparison of the behavior to the hope-reference modes depicted in Figure 6-2. From the behavior comparison we can infer whether the model reproduces the behavior we expect from expert interviews in the case study and from the literature review. A correspondence between the two would allow us to gain more confidence in the model structure.

The base run represents a situation of successful interorganizational learning in a learning alliance. It is assumed that two partnering firms agree to share 20 patents evenly. This means 10 patents per parent firm, which equals the firms' 'Aspiration levels' in the model. The maximum possible level of patents is assumed to be 30. It is further assumed that the firms allocate one scientist per patent. Given the fact that the parent firms evenly split the patents – the learning alliance output – they also agree to assign the same number of scientists to the alliance – the learning alliance

[936] See Section 4.6.3.

input. So, none of the partner firms behaves opportunistically toward its alliance partner.

Figure 7-1 depicts the graphs over time for both partners' 'Scientists active in the alliance' and 'Manager trust' over a time period of two years. As can be seen in the graphs for the base run the lines for Partner 1 and Partner 2 lie on top of each other (lines 1 and 2). Therefore, even though there are two lines, we only perceive one. The left-hand graph of Figure 7-1 shows that both parent firms assign an identical number of scientists to the alliance at the beginning of week 5. The stock of scientists active in the alliance increases at a decreasing rate until the actual number of scientists corresponds to the respective parent's allocation goal. Scientists stay in the alliance until alliance dissolution and jointly create knowledge.

Trust between the managers is initially equal to 'Normal trust'. This is the trust level at which the partner firms enter the alliance. It is the initial expenditure of trust in the alliance partner that is necessary before joint learning occurs.[937] We assume for our model runs that managers only (re)enter a research alliance where at least some level of trust exists. If trust is lower than one, firms become hesitant, and if it is much lower than one, they become unwilling to enter an alliance with a competitor.

Meanwhile, in the base run, trust between the managers increases. From the beginning of the alliance, both managers and scientists participate in trust-building activities like team-building workshops, going to sports events, having dinner together, etc. Events like this bring people together, strengthen their interpersonal bonds and build trust.[938] Moreover, since the scientist allocation on both sides corresponds to their expectations, there is no reason to trust the partner firm less. Trust increases fast in the beginning because of the reinforcing loop R4 – 'Let's meet!' and then slows down, reaching maximum trust gradually.

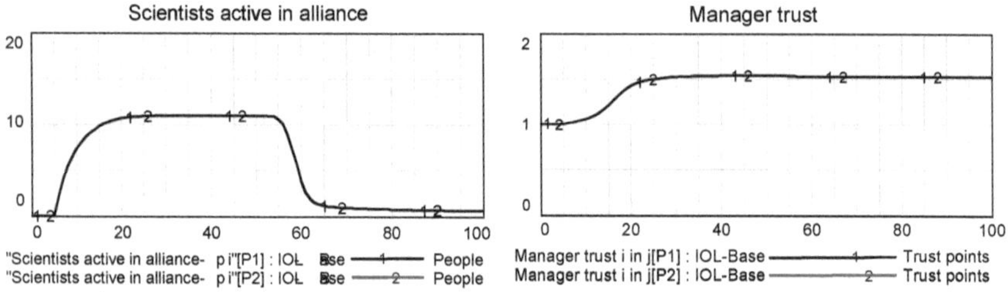

Figure 7-1: Base run: 'Scientists active' and 'Manager trust'.

As the parents' managers trust each other, they also allocate slightly more scientists to the alliance than previously agreed on as a sign of goodwill.[939] This goodwill is per-

[937] See Janowicz and Noorderhaven (2002), p. 11.
[938] This statement is based on insight from relational embeddedness in networks. See Section 3.4.3.
[939] Personal trust may be displayed in a person's goodwill. See the explanations on trust objects in Section 4.6.4.2.

ceived and reciprocated by the partner's managers. That is why the scientist allocation is balanced throughout alliance dissolution.

As explained in Section 4.6.4.2, trust travels through organizational levels. Therefore, and also because scientists begin to know each other better in real world alliances, mutual trust develops similarly on both the scientist and the manager level. As a consequence, scientists are open to one another and openly exchange knowledge and learn with each other. As scientists perceive their openness being reciprocated by the partner' scientists, openness increases further. Hence, mutual openness increases first at an increasing rate due to the reinforcing loop R3 – 'Reciprocity'. Then it increases at a decreasing rate until it reaches a plateau in about week 40 (see left-hand graph in Figure 7-1).

While openness increases, so does the scientists' commitment to learn and work in the alliance right after the start of the alliance (see right-hand chart in Figure 7-2). Technically, this can be attributed to the 'Effect of goal attainment on initial excitement'. One scientist explains the initial increase: *"In the beginning you have this show-off phase, the curiosity, the extreme expectation about this project that increases your excitement and commitment"*[940] Another scientist, referring to the behavior over time, adds: *"I think that the commitment level is very high initially. Then there is some sort of reality check that comes in. It's going to be a slam dunk. Then it is going to take time to foster. But then, I think you go through a little bit of a low and then it starts to pick up again. The reason that it picks up again is you are seeing success."*[941]

The base run mimics the commitment behavior that the scientist describes: commitment starts at 'Normal commitment', which describes commitment under normal conditions. For scientists, 'Normal commitment' can be considered high when the alliance research project deals with the research subject they are interested in.[942] It equals the value of one in the simulation model. Then it increases until it reaches a peak soon after the start of the alliance. The slope turns around and commitment decreases until it reaches a trough roughly in week 15. It recovers and increases smoothly with a slight S-shape until it reaches a plateau roughly at maximum commitment throughout the dissolution of the alliance and further. The fact that it stays on a higher level means that the scientists, though not working in the alliance anymore, would be committed to doing research again in this environment. They would be very open to engaging with the scientists from the partner firm again, as they have successfully completed the research project.

940 P2: 86.
941 P5: 61.
942 This statement is in line with the opinion of two scientists interviewed. See P2: 104 and P4: 64.

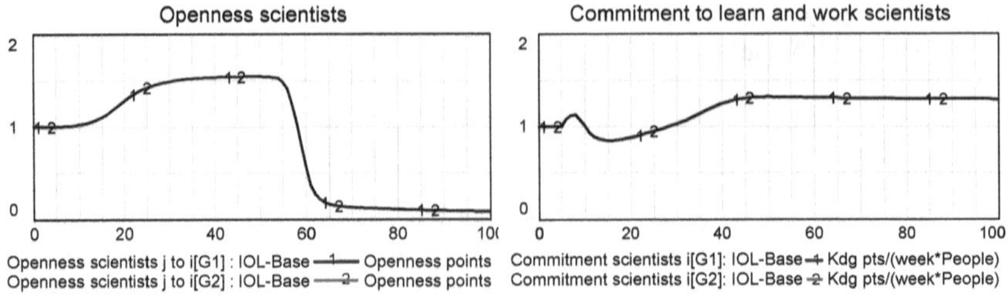

Figure 7-2: Base run: 'Openness scientists' and 'Commitment to learn and work scientists'.

As scientists openly share their complementary knowledge with each other and are committed to the research project, their productivity is high. They produce high weekly research output, which is illustrated by the 'Alliance knowledge base' graph in Figure 7-3. Alliance knowledge increases exponentially for two reasons. At the beginning of the alliance, the balancing loop B1 – 'Diminishing returns' is fairly weak. The 'Maximum number of alliance patents achievable' is almost out of reach. Therefore, it is easy to generate patents. During this phase, the reinforcing loop R1 – 'Absorptive capacity' is relatively strong and produces the exponential growth of the 'Alliance knowledge base'. Then, growth is slowed down by the balancing loop B1 – 'Diminishing returns'. The knowledge is used to create patents (see right-hand graph in Figure 7-3). Then, around week 60, ninety-five percent of the project has been completed, which means that the goals have been attained.

After reaching the goals, scientists are withdrawn from the alliance (see left-hand graph of Figure 7-1). In a real world alliance withdrawing scientists does not happen instantaneously but with a delay: scientists still have to complete their schedules and one or the other scientist is kept busy with alliance dissolution.

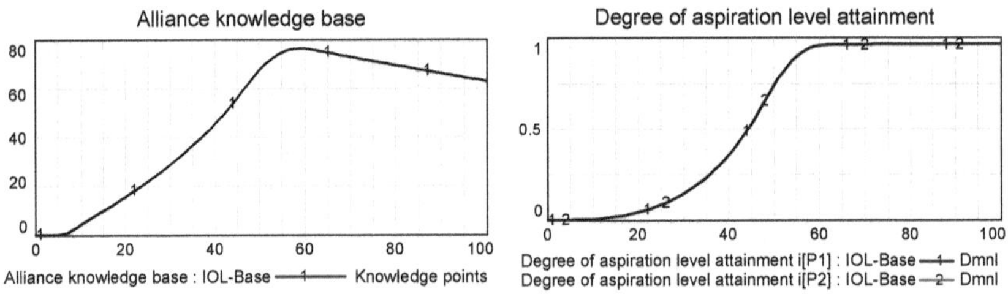

Figure 7-3: Base run: 'Alliance knowledge base' and 'Degree of aspiration level attainment'.

As the alliance is dissolved, the prior cooperating firms become competitors again. Therefore, even though the scientists shared their knowledge openly and cooperated successfully with each other in the alliance, they are no longer allowed to openly communicate with each other – even if they would like to (see left-hand graph in Figure 7-2). Any further communication might strengthen the other party's competitive position. Nevertheless, because both partners have cooperated successfully with each other and have reached their goals, trust between the managers stays on a higher level than prior to the start of the alliance. As 'Manager trust' is increased over the course of the alliance, the managers would not hesitate to reenter another learning alliance with each other. According to the network approach, in reality, managers will also spread the word about their experience with this particular research partner in their firms' networks.[943] Consequently, the firm's reputation of being a loyal and trustworthy alliance partner will increase.

The results from the base run and those of the hope-reference modes depicted in Figure 6-2 correspond highly to each other. In other words, the model structure reproduces the behavior observed and described by the case study interviewees and by alliance research scholars. This increases further model confidence.

On the basis of the base run we conduct policy runs which give us more insight into learning alliance dynamics.

7.2.2 Policy Analysis: Common Learning

In the following section we analyze model behavior by applying different policies.[944] As clarified in Section 2.3.1, policies are decision rules that are applied and installed by stakeholders that are part of the system under study.[945] By studying and analyzing model behavior using different policies, we gain insight into possible learning alliance developments. These findings are the basis for the managerial implications summarized in Sections 7.2.4, 7.3.3, and 7.4.4.

For our policy discussions, we focus on the behavior of the variables 'Scientists active in alliance', 'Manager trust', 'Openness scientists', and 'Degree of aspiration level attainment'. The graphs shown mostly depict the time horizon of 100 weeks, or roughly two years. For ease of comparison we show the base run dynamics in all graphs. Base run behaviors for Partner 1 and Partner 2 are indicated by lines 1 and 2, respectively. Policy runs are specified by line 3 for Partner 1 and line 4 for Partner 2, unless otherwise indicated.

For the different runs, we assume that Partner 2's goal is to create 10 patents in the alliance. It allocates 1 scientist per patent to be achieved. Partner 1's (hidden) intentions are mentioned when explaining the underlying policy situation. Again, we indicate if any of the parameter values or line numberings change.

---

[943] See Section 3.4.3.

[944] In System Dynamics analyses it is also common to do scenario analyses. Scenarios are systematic and comprehensible alternatives about the future, based on present conditions. See Geschka (1999), p. 521. They refer to changes in exogenous variables that stakeholders of the system cannot affect. Trajectories in the firms' environment, like, for example, competitors' actions, rise of a new technology, etc. are not of interest in our analysis. Hence, as we only test changes in variables that alliance stakeholders can affect we mainly apply policy analysis with the exception of run Private Learning Scenario PL2c in Section 7.3.2.

[945] See Kopainsky (2005), p. 149.

7.2.2.1 Common Learning Policy 1: Reduced Gatekeeper Openness

As an example of an extreme condition test we assumed that both parent firms' lawyers designed a non-disclosure agreement not allowing the scientists to exchange any knowledge with each other. A policy like that would question the alliance per se. Yet, in the present policy run we assume that, as in the case study, the two partnering firms are strong competitors not only in the market in which the learning alliance is positioned. As research relevant knowledge might also be of interest to other divisions in the firms, the research topic is highly sensitive. Firms are afraid of prospective private learning. Hence, knowledge exchange concerning common learning is highly restricted, too. In the case study alliance, gatekeepers control which knowledge may flow, what is said in presentations, and what is mentioned during meetings and phone or e-mail conversations. Interfirm scientist exchange between research sites is prohibited; any spontaneous interfirm conversation on the research topic, either by phone or by e-mail has to be approved by the gatekeepers. Presentations prepared for meetings need to be officially approved well in advance, too. Consequently, free knowledge exchange between the scientists is very difficult. Scientists tend to perceive this as a hindrance to sincere goal attainment.

As in the base run, the alliance goals cover 20 patents in total. They are shared equally between the cooperating firms. Gatekeeper openness for common learning is reduced by both parents to 30% of the base run's condition (see Table 7-1). The operational consequences of reduced gatekeeper openness are clarified above.

Parameter	Policy CL1
Openness of P1's gatekeeper restrictions to P1's knowledge sharing [G1]	0.3
Openness of P2's gatekeeper restrictions to P2's knowledge sharing [G2]	0.3

Table 7-1: Parameter changes for Common Learning Policy CL1.

Figure 7-4 highlights the difference in the behavior of the 'Degree of aspiration level attainment' with the policy run (IOL-CLPo1) to the base run. Overall, the general behavior is not much different. Both the base run and the policy run show S-shaped growth. Yet, for the policy run it is not that obvious as the chosen time horizon is not long enough. We observe slow exponential growth which, after the end of the time horizon depicted, changes into an S-shaped growth. Hence, we learn from the graph that it takes much longer for the scientists to reach the alliance goals. In fact they attain only about 25% after 100 weeks (see left-hand graph in Figure 7-4) and 65% of the common goals by the end of 150 weeks (see right-hand graph in Figure 7-4). After three years, the scientists are still working on their research tasks – which are accomplished after one year under the premise of complete openness.

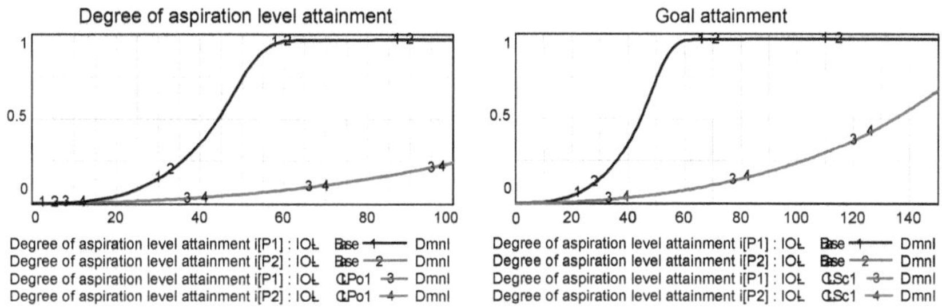

Figure 7-4: Common Learning Policy CL1: Reduced gatekeeper openness over a time horizon of 100 and 150 weeks.

We realize that even though gatekeeper restrictions are important for preventing out-learning by the partner, the restrictions may also hamper efficient collaboration between the scientists for common learning. Goal attainment is delayed. For the scientists it seems like the goals are even unattainable.[946]

7.2.2.2 Common Learning Policy 2: Free Riding

In the following policy run we assume that Parent firm 1 seeks to free ride. We already presented part of this policy in the sensitivity test. Here, we discuss the situation, the behavior, and its implications in more detail. In the previous runs, both parent firms are honest regarding communication of their common goals and scientist allocation. In this policy run, one partner firm behaves opportunistically and thus unfairly. In Sections 3.4.1 and 4.5.2 we discussed the underlying theoretical concept for this possible opportunistic behavior in common learning.

We assume that Partner 1's cheating managers enter the alliance with hidden intentions that remain undetected by Partner 2's managers. Hence, Partner 1 seeks to enjoy common benefits without fully contributing to their creation as agreed on in the contract. We present two different policies in this section. First, Partner 1 allocates a few scientists less than agreed beforehand. We change the value for the parameter 'Fractional scientist bonus P1' from 100% to 80% (see Table 7-2). Second, Partner 1 pushes the envelope and allocates even fewer (70%) – too few for Partner 2 to accept anymore. As in the first policy, the graphs show the policy runs in comparison to the base run (lines 1 and 2).

	Policy CL2	
Parameter	Policy CL2a	Policy CL2b
Fractional scientist bonus P1	0.8	0.7

Table 7-2: Parameter changes for Common Learning Policies CL2a and CL2b.

[946] Under these conditions, the common goals could be interpreted as stretch goals. See Section 6.4 in which we refer to commitment and stretch goals.

Common Learning Policy CL2a: Moderate Free Rider

Figure 7-5 depicts the model behavior in the case of Partner 1 being the moderate free rider. Although Partner 1 seeks the same number of common benefits as in the base run, it allocates only about 80% of the scientists (line 3 in the upper left-hand graph). After a perception delay, Partner 2 adjusts its resource contribution and does not allocate scientists as it would under normal conditions. Moreover, Partner 2's 'Manager trust' in Partner 1's managers suffers (line 4 in the upper right-hand graph). It does increase slightly at first because the managers assume that the alliance is developing as originally intended. Managers meet regularly and mutual trust increases. Nevertheless, after a while they realize that Partner 1 does not meet the required contribution. Consequently, trust decreases slightly and stabilizes at normal trust until week 20.

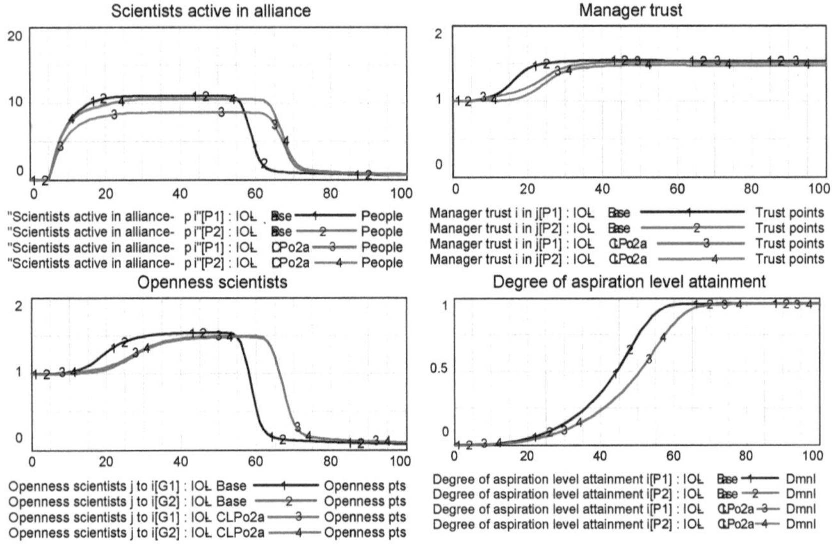

Figure 7-5: Common Learning Policy CL2a: Moderate free rider.[947]

Meanwhile, trust reveals inertia when traveling through the organization. Scientists' openness from Partner 2's research group first stays at the normal level. Frequent manager interactions and the greater openness of Partner 1's research group mean that the reduced scientist allocation becomes less important to Partner 2. Trust increases after week 15 in an S-shaped curve.

As a consequence, the difference between the two groups' reciprocal openness diminishes and openness slowly increases until it reaches a plateau after week 45. Yet, both openness and mutual 'Manager trust' increase to a lower maximum level than in

[947] G1 and G2 in the lower left-hand graph refer to both firms' groups of scientists, Group1 and Group2, respectively.

the base run. From Partner 2's point of view, this can be interpreted as remaining skepticism because of Partner 1's reduced scientist allocation.

Since the collaboration continues and scientists work on their research tasks, the two partners attain their common goals around week 70. This equals a 10 week delay compared to the base run. On reaching the goals, scientists are withdrawn from the alliance and their openness is reduced according to the firms' policies. Yet, mutual trust between the managers stays at a fairly high level. Even though Partner 1 has cheated on Partner 2, they both reach their common goals. In the end, both parents are satisfied with the alliance's outcome. They would reenter an alliance with the partner.

Common Learning Policy CL2b: Extreme Free Rider

Yet, the situation changes if Partner 1 assigns even fewer scientists to the alliance at Partner 2's expense. As can be seen in the upper left-hand graph of Figure 7-6, Partner 1 allocates fewer scientists than in Policy CL2a. Partner 2's managers are doubtful from the very beginning and trust remains nearly constant for about 3 weeks. Apparently, manager trust is sensitive to scientist allocation. Normal interactions between the managers or initial reciprocal openness between the scientists do not have enough effect on Partner 2's trust for it to increase. Partner 1's trust slowly increases at first: Partner 2 allocates its scientists according to expectations of Partner 1's managers. From Partner 1's point of view, there are enough interactions to get to know the partner's managers better and trust them more.

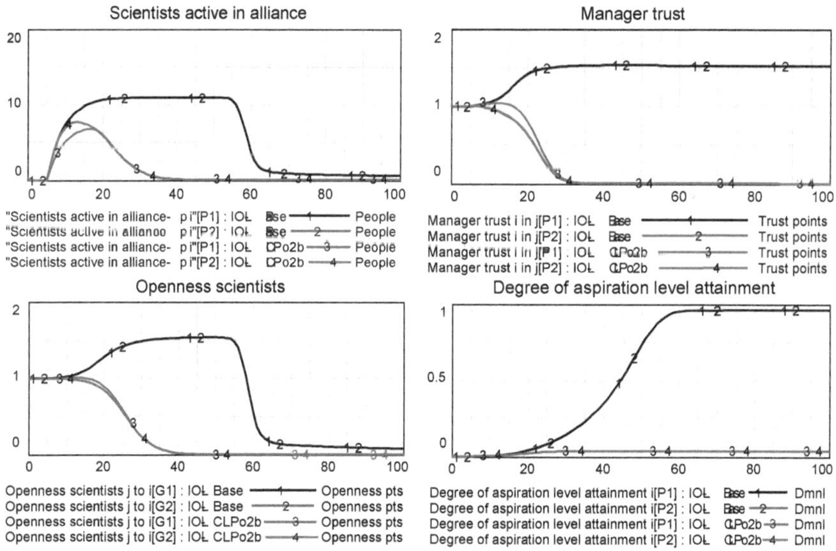

Figure 7-6: Common Learning Policy CL2b: Extreme free rider.

Because of Partner 1's low scientist allocation, Partner 2 feels betrayed. While the trust of Partner 2's managers starts to diminish after week 8, the openness of Partner 2' scientists reveals inertia and initially stays constant during the first weeks of the alliance until week 11. Then, after some time, manager skepticism moves to the scientist level. Consequently, Partner 2's scientists no longer share their knowledge as openly with Partner 1's scientists as they used to: openness starts to diminish. As an effect, Partner 1's scientists also reduce their openness because of reciprocity intentions (driven by the reinforcing feedback loop R3 – 'Reciprocity'). Partner 2's scientists are not as open as they used to be, Partner 1's managers' trust in Partner 2's managers declines. This is why Partner 1's scientists also reduce their openness further. Partner 2's scientists reciprocate this reduced openness leading to Partner 2's managers having less trust in Partner 1's managers et cetera. With decreasing trust, both firms' managers do not wish to interact with each other as often as they used to. This leads to less mutual trust. Managers withdraw their scientists from the alliance. This leads to the following final conditions: scientists neither work nor learn together. In total, they create only a small fraction of prospective common benefits. The 'Degree of aspiration level attainment' remains at a very low level. 'Manager trust' decreases to zero trust points. It means that the managers trust each other less than at the beginning of the relationship. Alliance participants are disappointed about the early dissolution. Because of the lost mutual trust, in the real world, it would be unlikely that the prior partners will reenter an alliance in the future. Partner 1 has gone too far with its objective to free ride. Not only does it not reach its goals; it also loses its reputation in the network in which it is embedded.

7.2.2.3 Common Learning Policy 3: Differing Aspirations

With the following policy we analyze the second option identified in Section 4.5.2 for hidden agendas. Whereas in the Common Learning Policy runs CL2a and CL2b[948] Partner 1's policy is to free ride, we now analyze the behavior if Partner 1 is not frank with communicating its common goals. A firm might be dishonest regarding the actual common goals it seeks when entering an alliance. As indicated in Section 4.5.2, one motive for such hidden agendas might be, for example, that Partner 1 is concerned that Partner 2 would not have agreed to enter the alliance had it openly shared that it was seeking fewer common goals.

Three different situations are subsumed under this policy. The first situation considers Partner 1 being honest to its partner about having fewer common goals than Partner 2. In the second and third situations Partner 1 seeks to cheat. In the second situation Partner 1 actually only has about 70% of the common goals that it pretends to have when entering the alliance. In the third situation its actual common goals are 80%. This leads to the following parameter values (see Table 7-3).

---

[948] See Section 7.2.2.2.

Parameter	Policy CL3 Policy CL3a	 PolicyCL3b	 Policy CL3c
ComAL1P1	7	10	10
Fraction of actual internally communicated goals P1	1	0.7	0.8

Table 7-3: Parameter changes for Common Learning Policies CL3a, CL3b, and CL3c.

First, Parent 1 reduces its 'Common attainment level 1' to 7 patents in the Common Learning Policy run CL3a. The 'Fraction of actual internally communicated goals P1' stays at 1. It means that what Partner 1's managers communicate to Partner 2 is equivalent to what is discussed internally between Partner 1's management only. For the runs CL3b and CL3c, Partner 1's policy is not to openly share its actual common goals with its alliance partner. Management evaluates fewer patents as reasonable alliance outcomes, for example. In order not to antagonize its alliance partner, Partner 1 does not communicate its actual goals honestly to Partner 2. So, for the Common Learning Policies CL3b and CL3c, there is a difference between what is externally communicated to Partner 2 and what are internally determined as common goals. Parent 1's 'Common attainment level 1' is equivalent to 10 patents – as in the base run. The 'Fraction of actual internally communicated goals P1' changes to 70% (Policy CL3b) and 80% (Policy CL3c) of the 'Common attainment level'. In other words, whereas Partner 1 agrees with Partner 2 on working on 10 patents each, Partner 1 actually seeks fewer patents.

Common Learning Policy CL3a: Fewer Common Goals and Honesty

For Policy CL3a it is assumed that Partner 1 has fewer common goals. It seeks only 7 patents whereas Partner 2 intends to work on 10 patents. It is further assumed that both partners honestly communicate their actual common 'Aspiration levels' to each other. As Partner 1 communicates that it has fewer common goals, both partners perceive it to be fair for Partner 1 to also invest fewer scientists in the alliance. Therefore, Partner 1's scientist allocation is lower.

As can be seen in the upper left-hand graph in Figure 7-7 Partner 1 allocates 70% (line 3) of the scientists it assigns to the alliance in the base run (line 1). Partner 2's scientist allocation is the same as in the base run (lines 4 and 2). As Partner 2 expects Partner 1's lower scientist allocation, Partner 2's 'Manager trust' in the partner's managers behaves exactly as in the base run (see upper right-hand graph). The same holds for the openness between the scientists (lower left-hand graph).

Yet, fewer scientists working on the alliance tasks reduces 'Effective group tasks' and 'Group research output'. Therefore, the scientists do not create joint knowledge as fast as in the base run. Allocating fewer scientists delays common goal attainment. The lower right-hand graph in Figure 7-7 illustrates this delay: lines 3 and 4, indicating Policy CL3a, lag about 5 weeks behind lines 1 and 2, which represent the base run. Patents are shared as agreed. This is also why both partners finish the alliance together after about 55 weeks. Then the partners withdraw their scientists from the alliance. This is also the time after which the scientists are not allowed to openly share their knowledge with each other anymore. Consequently, openness between the scientists decreases to zero. The upper right-hand graph shows that mutual manager trust stays high after alliance dissolution. This is because both parties are satisfied with the alliance outcome. Neither partner feels betrayed. Both have reached their goals, which is why they most probably would reenter an alliance with each other.

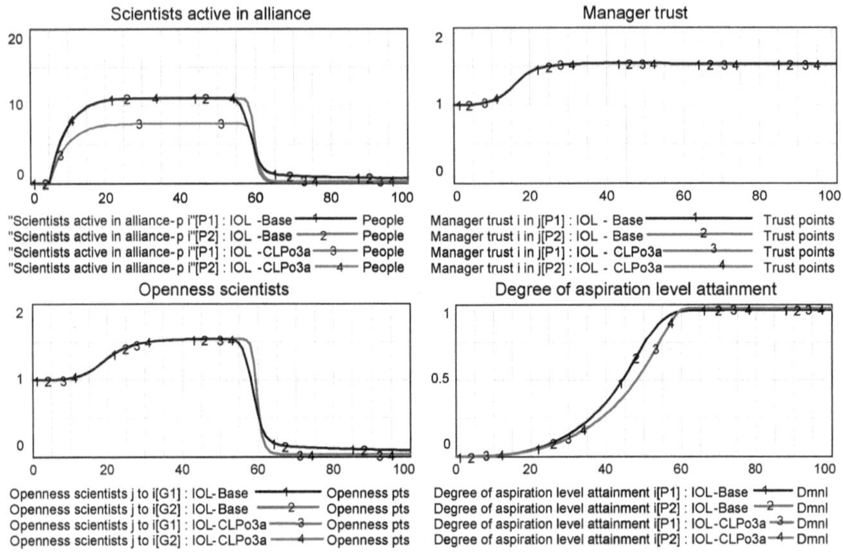

Figure 7-7: Common Learning Policy CL3a: Fewer common goals and honesty.

In our case study alliance, both partners mutually agreed that the American partner would allocate fewer scientists to the alliance. Hence, both are aware of the fact that the partners' scientist allocations are not equal to each other – but fair as they share the alliance outcome according to the inputs.

Common Learning Policy CL3b: Fewer Common Goals and Dishonesty

The situation is somewhat different with Policy CL3b. Here, Partner 1 has the same internal aspirations as with Policy CL3a. Yet, it does not communicate the lower 'Aspiration level' to its partner. During alliance negotiations it pretends that it is also wanting 10 patents. However, as the internal communicated goals are only 7 patents, it allocates fewer scientists to the alliance. On the alliance level, Partner 1 assumes that the two firms are working on generating 17 patents, while Partner 2 assumes they are working on 20 patents in total.

According to the upper left-hand graph in Figure 7-8 scientists are withdrawn from the alliance soon after the start. As with Policy CL2b, Partner 1's objective to cheat oversteps the mark. Overall, the dynamics are similar to those with Policy CL2b. This is because, as explained in Section 4.5.2, both the 'Fractional scientist bonus' and the common 'Aspiration level' determine the 'Indicated scientist level'. Either of the first two variables may influence the 'Aspiration level' in such a way that too few scientists are being allocated to the alliance. The effects are similar and therefore we only briefly describe the behavior.

Partner 2 does not accept Partner 1's low scientist allocation. Partner firm 2's manager trust stays almost constant for the first few weeks because it takes time to realize what the partner's actual scientist allocation is. Then trust decreases at an increasing rate (upper right-hand graph). Partner 2's scientists behave similarly and thus decrease their openness as they also do not trust their partner's scientists that much. Due to reasons of reciprocity, their counterparts also decrease their openness with a short delay (lower left-hand graph).

'Manager trust' decreases even further as the partner's scientists are no longer as open as they were at the beginning of the alliance. Decreasing trust leads to less desire to interact with the partner's managers. As Partner 1 still does not fulfill its scientist obligations, Partner 2 decides to withdraw its scientists from the alliance. In the end, the cheating Partner 1 achieves slightly higher total goal attainment than Partner 2 – which is so little that it is not even worth mentioning. Yet, the alliance is dissolved early with the result that not even 5% of the prospective common benefits are achieved. Moreover, neither partner's managers trust each other anymore. They most probably will not enter an alliance with each other in the future.

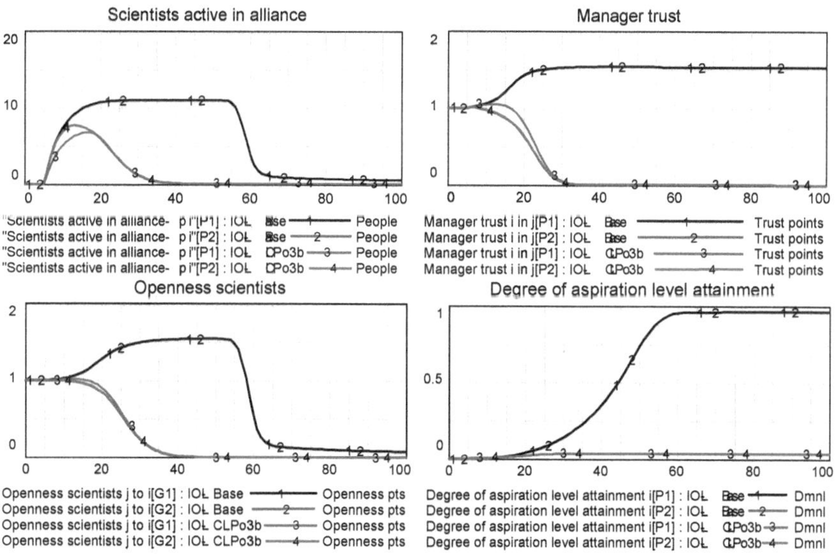

Figure 7-8: Common Learning Policy CL3b: Fewer common goals and dishonesty.

Compared to the Common Learning Policy CL3a in which Partner 1 honestly shared with its partner that it was interested in fewer common benefits, Policy CL3b does not add any value to Partner 1. It has neither reached its goals nor successfully presented itself as a dependable and trustworthy alliance partner.

Common Learning Policy CL3c: Not That Few Common Goals and Dishonesty
The situation is different as long as Partner 2 still accepts Partner 1's misbehavior. In the following example, Partner 1 is again interested in fewer common benefits than agreed on in the contract. Again, it does not inform its partner about this. In accordance with fewer common goals, it allocates fewer scientists to the alliance; yet not as few as in policy run CL3b (fewer common goals and dishonesty). Despite similarities between behaviors in the Policies CL2a (fewer common goals and honesty) and CL3c (not that few common goals and dishonesty) in the early phase of the alliance, the dynamics reveal significant differences at alliance termination.

As usual, the upper left-hand graph of Figure 7-9 depicts both partners' scientist allocation. We notice that Partner 1 assigns fewer scientists to the alliance (line 3). Partner 2 realizes this and adjusts its own assignment (line 4). Hence, it does not spend as much as in the base run (line 2). Because Partner 1 does not spend according to the contract, trust suffers and does not rise as fast as in the base run either (see upper right-hand graph). It grows slowly for two reasons: first, Partner 2 accepts Partner 1's lower allocation. Second, from the very beginning, Partner 2's scientists are open to Partner 1's scientists (see line 3 in the lower left-hand graph). Partner 2's managers acknowledge this openness. It gives Partner 2 the impression that Partner 1 is fully committed to the alliance despite the missing scientists. As the managers interact frequently, which increases mutual familiarity, Partner 2's manager trust increases smoothly – though at a much slower rate than in the base run. Partner 2's maximum manager trust is considerably lower than in the base run, reaching its maximum 15 weeks later. Partner 2 remains doubtful. Consequently, unlike in the base run, it does not allocate the additional scientists either (see lines 4 and 2 in the upper left-hand graph). Nevertheless, it continues the learning alliance with Partner 1 – also because first results are observable (see lower right-hand graph).

Meanwhile Partner 1's scientists are slightly more open to Partner 2's scientists than the other way round (lower left-hand graph). The motive for Partner 1's scientists' behavior is that they want to attain their goals. They understand that they need to be open in order to receive reciprocity: only when the partner's scientists openly communicate with each other can joint knowledge be created. As soon as the scientists reach the common goals in week 58, Partner 1 has no further incentive to stay in the alliance: any additional learning would not be beneficial to Partner 1 and would competitively strengthen Partner 2. Therefore, Partner 1's scientists are no longer allowed to continue researching with Partner 2's scientists. Additionally, all scientists are withdrawn from the alliance as fast as possible.

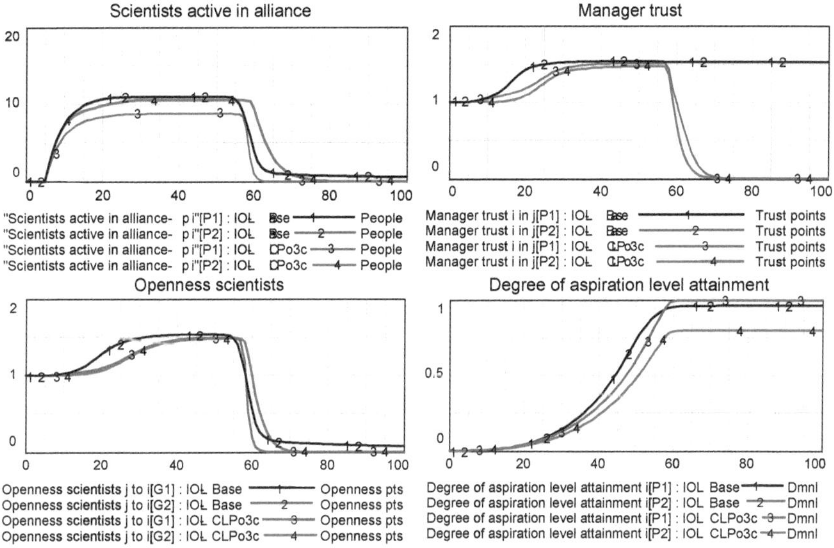

Figure 7-9: Common Learning Policy CL3c: Not that few common goals and dishonesty.

Similarly to Partner 1's moderate free riding in Common Learning Policy CL2a, Partner 2 also accepts a lower scientist allocation with Partner 1's present Policy CL3c. Nevertheless, by applying the first policy, both partners finish the alliance with satisfaction. With Policy CL3c, Partner 2 is completely surprised when Partner 1 withdraws its scientists. At that time (week 58) it assumes that the alliance is not yet done with its tasks: it has only completed roughly 75% – while Partner 1 has achieved all of its internal goals. Consequently, Partner 2's managers do not trust Partner 1's managers anymore. The alliance is dissolved and Partner 2 also withdraws its scientists from the alliance.

From Partner 1's point of view, the alliance is a success. Partner 2 does not become aware of Partner 1's hidden agenda until Partner 1 reaches its aspirations and withdraws its scientists. Nevertheless, we learn from the model that the cheating partner reaches its goals at around approximately the same time as it would have done if it had played fairly and communicated that it was interested in fewer common benefits (Policy CL3a). With Policy CL3a, trust stays high which is favorable for the alliance partners regarding possible future cooperative ventures. In contrast, with Policy CL3c the cheating partner antagonizes its trustworthy and trusting alliance partner. It loses Partner 2 as a potential future research partner.

Partner 2 is disappointed with the alliance's outcome. It only reaches slightly more than three-quarters of its goals. It knows that it has been cheated on by Partner 1. Trust is at a minimum. Partner 2 will not enter an alliance with Partner 1 anymore.

7.2.2.4 Common Learning Policy 4: Fewer Common Goals with Scientist Compensation

In the following we combine findings from the last two policies. From Policy CL3b we learn that Partner 2 feels betrayed and ends the alliance if it is not informed by Partner 1 about its having fewer common goals and allocating its scientists accordingly. Now we assume that Partner 1 again behaves dishonestly and, having fewer common goals, cheats on Partner 2; so few common goals with so few scientists that Partner 2 would certainly feel betrayed and dissolve the alliance soon after the start. It is assumed that Partner 1 is aware of these consequences. As Partner 2's manager trust depends on the scientist balance, among other things, Partner 1 therefore compensates its scientist allocation by assigning more researchers to the alliance. Table 7-4 subsumes the parameter changes for the policy run.

Parameter	Policy CL4
Fraction of actual internally communicated goals P1	0.5
Fractional scientist bonus P1	2

Table 7-4: Parameter changes for Common Learning Policy CL4.

As can be seen from Table 7-4, Partner 1 actually only seeks 50% of the patents that it agreed on in the contract. So, its actual aspirations equal 5 patents. Under the conditions described above it would also allocate only 50% of the resources (5 scientists). Yet, it counteracts this by allocating twice as much relative to the prospective output. Thus, net scientist allocation is 10 people, as in the base run.

As can be seen from the upper left-hand graph in Figure 7-10 Partner 1 allocates the same amount of scientists as Partner 2 (lines 3 and 4). So far the behavior matches that of the base run (lines 1 and 2). This is why manager trust (depicted in the upper right-hand graph) and openness between the scientists (see lower left-hand graph) develop similarly to the base run.

Yet, Partner 1 reaches its aspiration level sooner than in the base run. Line 3 in the lower right-hand graph increases at a steeper rate as the total number of patents to be achieved is lower. Note that the scale on the y-axis slightly differs from the graphs for goal attainment shown above. In week 44 Partner 1 reaches its goals. At that point Partner 2 has only attained almost 5 patents. That equals 50% of its aspirations. Partner 2 is surprised when Partner 1 withdraws its scientists from the alliance at such an early point. Partner 1's scientists no longer share any knowledge with their counterparts. No further common knowledge is created. Consequently, Partner 2's manager trust declines abruptly and fast. Partner 2's managers do not desire to meet with Partner 1's managers anymore. Trust declines further and all scientists are withdrawn from the alliance. The alliance is dissolved early.

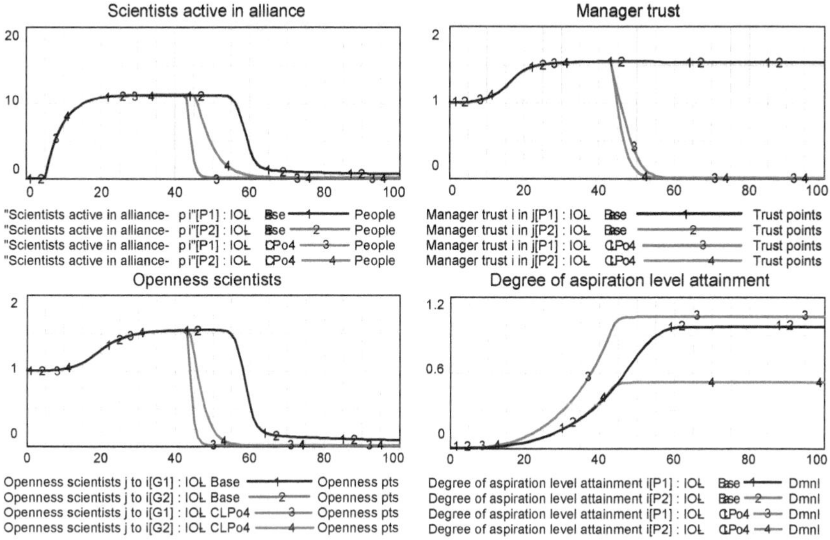

Figure 7-10: Common Learning Policy CL4: Fewer common goals with scientist compensation.[949]

From Partner 1's short-term oriented point of view, the alliance is successful: Partner 1 reaches its common goals and effectively cheats on Partner 2 by allocating more scientists so that the partner's managers do not get suspicious. Partner 2's trust increases and the alliance, from Partner 1's perspective, develops as intended. As opposed to Policy CL3b, the research alliance is not condemned to fail prematurely.

However, Partner 2 feels betrayed by Partner 1. It does not finish learning enough with the partner to create the intended patents. Trust is at a minimum level. In other words, Partner 2 would not reenter an alliance with Partner 1. So, in the long run Partner 1 may have lost a potential future research partner.

7.2.3 Critical Model Structure: Manager Trust – Model Analysis

From the policies described and interpreted above we learn that mutual manager trust determines whether an alliance is dissolved early or as intended. In the first case the alliance ends in a mutual success for both partners. Trust between the managers and the scientists increases during the relationship. In the second case, one partner firm is unsatisfied at the time of alliance dissolution as it does not meet its common aspirations. The cheating partner interprets the alliance as a success because it attains its goals at the partner's expense. Yet, mutual trust is gone. In the real world, the cheating partner's reputation as a loyal and reliable alliance partner is

[949] Note that the lower right-hand graph depicting the 'Degree of aspiration level attainment' is scaled from 0-1.2.

ruined. A network reputation for cheating may hinder the firm in the long run when looking for a research partner with complementary knowledge. Concluding, trust is obviously a critical variable in the alliance dynamics. This observation supports the findings, explanations, and interpretations identified by alliance scholars in the literature, which we laid out in depth in Section 4.6.4. As trust plays such a decisive role, we analyze the model structure determining 'Manager trust' in more detail in the following. We start with an analysis of the free rider situation and continue with a partner having fewer hidden aspirations in different trust environments. Then we go deeper into analyzing the model structure by separating the critical model structure from the rest of the model. We identify a tipping point which determines that trust either increases or decreases. We conclude this section with implications from the analysis for the full model.

7.2.3.1 Tipping Point Analysis Policy 1: Free Riding

For Common Learning Policy CL2 we analyzed two free rider situations: in Policy CL2a Partner 1 free rides moderately, which is accepted by Partner 2. In Policy CL2b Partner 2 no longer accepts a more extreme case of free riding and dissolves the alliance early. Figure 7-11 illustrates the behavior change from continuation to dissolution visibly. The two graphs highlight the effect of Partner 1's different 'Fraction of bonus scientists' on Partner 2's manager trust (left-hand graph) and on Partner 2's resulting scientist allocation (right-hand graph). Partner 2 accepts Partner 1's reduced scientist allocation until a certain threshold is reached. The threshold is at about 77% of the agreed scientist allocation. Just above the threshold trust develops slowly in S-shaped growth, which means that Partner 2 is more hesitant regarding its own scientist allocation (right-hand graph). Further above the threshold, trust develops faster in S-shaped growth (left-hand graph). The faster trust develops, the sooner Partner 2 fully allocates its scientists (right-hand graph). If the full number of scientists is allocated to the alliance sooner, they begin working on their tasks earlier, which also means that they reach the alliance's goals sooner. Therefore, both partners' withdrawal occurs 2 months earlier (week 56 with immediate complete scientist allocation compared to week 64 with hesitant scientist allocation).

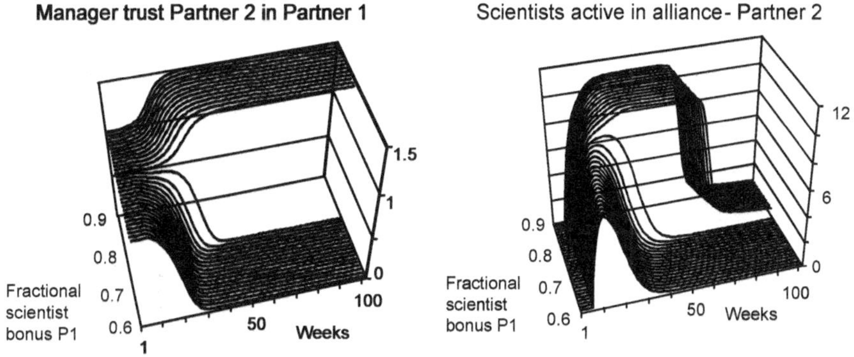

Figure 7-11: The effect of Partner 1's different scientist allocations ranging from 60% to 90%.

Below the threshold, if Partner 1 allocates fewer scientists, the situation tips. Partner 2 no longer accepts its partner's low scientist allocation. The 'Effect of j's relative scientists on i's manager trust' becomes negative and trust declines.

When relating the behavior to the underlying 'Manager trust' model structure in Section 6.5.1.5 we learn that under favorable conditions the reinforcing loop in the 'Manager trust' (R4 – 'Let's meet!') substructure causes trust to increase (as in Policy CL2a). The reinforcing loop works in an upward direction. It acts as a virtuous cycle. In Policy CL2b the situation deteriorates in a vicious cycle of declining trust and openness. In this case the reinforcing loop works in a downward direction. Partner 2's trust increasingly declines. The research alliance is condemned to fail prematurely. The threshold at which the behavior shifts from virtuous to vicious cycle is called the tipping point.[950] Generally, a tipping point analysis may highlight, for example, how new ideas or products diffuse in the market or a product becomes the standard.[951] In our analysis the tipping point is the threshold at which an originally successful alliance tips and fails.

[950] In epidemiology, the tipping point is the point at which a stable system transfers into a reinforced behavior in which the spread of a disease to the point where it becomes an epidemic or pandemic cannot be halted. For tipping point analyses in epidemiology, see Sterman (2000), pp. 305-321. It is common to transfer tipping point insight from epidemiology to other fields of study, including business administration. For examples see Sterman (2000), pp. 323-347 (innovation diffusion), Repenning et al. (2001) and Repenning (2001) (firefighting in project management), Rudolph and Repenning (2002) (stress management), Morrison (2005) (learning curve), Rahmandad (2005) and Taylor et al. (2005) (both project management). A popular recent book on the tipping point was written by Gladwell. See Gladwell (2000).

[951] An example of a related analysis is the VCR battle of the VHS and Betamax formats. VHS became the standard format after the VHS consortium of Matshushita, JVC, and RCA understood that they had to focus on the reinforcing loops that drove the growth of sales that increased the installed base. See Sterman (2000), pp. 359-364.

7.2.3.2 Tipping Point Analysis Policy 2: Differing Aspirations

Depending on the initialization of parameters, the position of the tipping point may vary. We analyze its movement with reference to Policy CL3. It is assumed that Partner 1 pretends to be interested in receiving 10 patents during the negotiation phase. This is what Partner 2 expects when entering the alliance. Nevertheless, Partner 1 has hidden common goals and actually seeks fewer patents. For a sensitivity analysis, we gradually change Partner 1's 'Fraction of actual internally communicated goals P1', thus its hidden common goals. We test the position of the tipping point in three different trust environments. As Partner 1 cheats on Partner 2, the latter either accepts or refuses further cooperation. This is determined by how fast Partner 2's managers build up trust, among other things. Technically, this refers to a change in the parameter α:[952] first we test the development of 'Manager trust' and the 'Degree of aspiration level attainment' in a skeptical environment, in which 'α P2' is equal to 10, then a normal trust environment ('α P2' is equal to 1), and finally a trustworthy environment with 'α P2' equal to 0.1.

To facilitate comparisons between the conditions, the following three figures are designed similarly. All graphs depict model behavior with a variation of Partner 1's actual common goals that it does not communicate to Partner 2. The sensitivity range varies from 70% to 84% of the 'Fraction of actually communicated goals P1' and is marked on the z-axis. The lower fraction is indicated in the foreground and the higher fraction in the background. An illustration like this gives an impression of the shift of the tipping point under different trust conditions. The left-hand graphs highlight the effect on Partner 2's manager trust. The right-hand graphs illustrate the effect on Partner 2's degree of common aspiration level attainment. All graphs are scaled on a time horizon from week 1 to week 100. The respective thresholds of Partner 2 still accepting Partner 1's cheating can be assigned to the change of the behavior mode. Regarding 'Degree of aspiration level attainment', for example, the dynamics change from almost constant behavior to S-shaped growth (see Figure 7-12). The latter can be assigned to Partner 2's acceptance of Partner 1 not behaving honestly.

Skeptical Environment

Figure 7-12 highlights model sensitivity to a variation in Partner 1's actual goals in an alliance with a skeptical Partner 2. As can be seen from the left-hand graph, Partner 2's managers are fairly sensitive toward Partner 1's actions. Trust does not increase much above 'Normal trust' even when Partner 2 still accepts Partner 1's actions. Yet, the tipping point when behavior changes is positioned at a high fraction (see left-hand graph): Partner 2 tolerates Partner 1 only assigning 80% of the agreed scientists. Just below the tip, Partner 2's managers' trust stays constant for a few periods and then suddenly drops. Even further below the tip, Partner 2's trust hardly develops. It decreases fast.

---

[952] See equation 5.10 in Section 6.5.1.5.

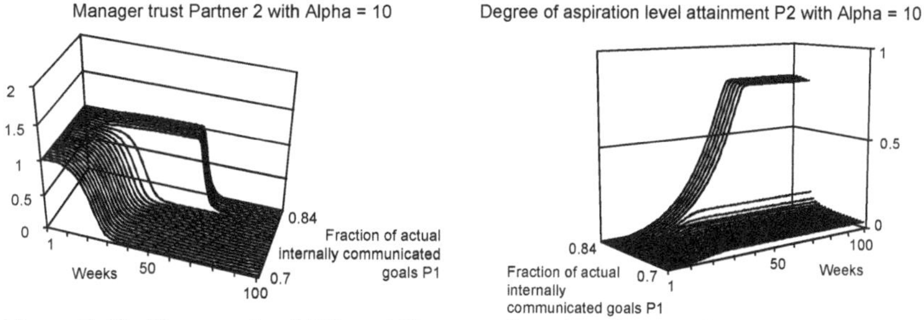

Figure 7-12: Manager trust P2' and 'Degree of goal attainment P2' in a skeptical environment.

When manager trust stays constant, the scientists from both partners keep on researching. They create a common knowledge base, which is the base for registering patents. Common goals are attained (see right-hand graph in Figure 7-12) – but only if mutual manager trust is sustained. As Partner 1 reaches its fewer common goals earlier than Partner 2, Partner 1 withdraws its scientists. This is the reason why Partner 2's trust drops after week 60. If mutual trust drops immediately after the start of the alliance, the 'Degree of aspiration level attainment' increases only slightly.

Normal Trust Environment

The behavior changes in a normal trust environment (see graphs in Figure 7-13). Trust builds up more easily. This is why 'Manager trust Partner 2' increases in an S-shaped behavior in the range in which Partner 2 accepts Partner 1's behavior (left-hand graph). Partner 2 is a very trusting partner.

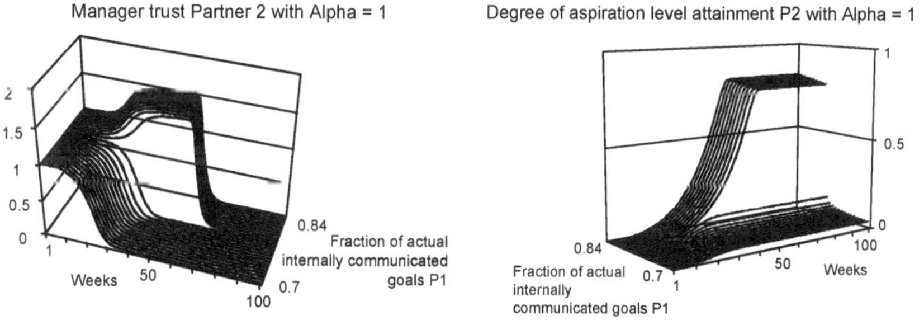

Figure 7-13: 'Manager trust P2' and 'Degree of goal attainment P2' in a normal trust environment.

From the left-hand graph we learn that the tipping point of not trusting Partner 1 comes to the fore. In other words, as Partner 2 is trustworthy, less effort to build up trust makes it easier for Partner 1 to cheat on its alliance partner. Partner 2 accepts the fact that Partner 1 allocates fewer scientists. In the end, when Partner 1 withdraws its scientists, Partner 2 even has a lower degree of goal attainment than in the situation above (right-hand graph).

High Trusting Environment
A scenario in which Partner 2's manager trust develops even faster and more highly (see left-hand graph in Figure 7-14) might be attributed to Partner 1's good reputation in the firms' network, for example. We learn from the graphs in Figure 7-14 that when Partner 2 is a highly trusting partner, Partner 1 may even enter the alliance with fewer intended (and non-communicated) common goals and scientists. The tipping point shifts even further to the fore. Partner 2 still accepts 75% of Partner 1's scientist allocation in the alliance. Yet, when Partner 1 dissolves the alliance, Partner 2 only achieves 75% of its goals (right-hand graph).

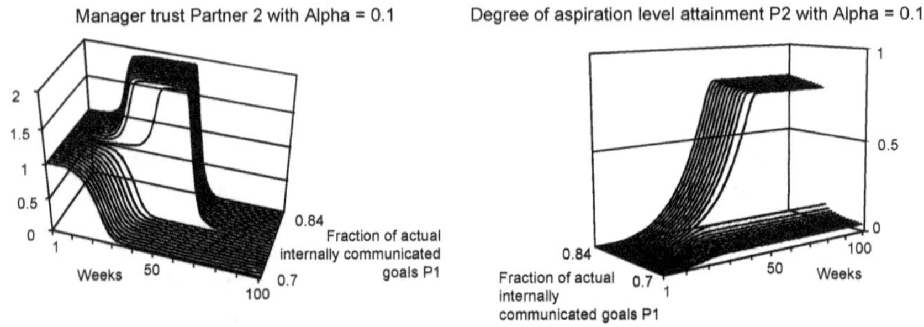

Figure 7-14: 'Manager trust P2' and 'Degree of goal attainment P2' in a trusting environment.

7.2.3.3 Perceived Fairness and Trust

In the sections above we highlighted the fact that the system exhibits a tipping point. It changes the behavior of 'Manager trust' from an upward direction to a downward direction. Furthermore, by changing model parameters, the position of the tipping point may move. Model behavior can be explained using insight from behavioral game theory (see the discussion in Section 3.4.4.4).

Put in game-specific terminology, when Partner 2's managers' trust decreases because Partner 1 allocates only 70% of the scientists agreed, Partner 2's managers perceive this as an unfair move in a collaborative two-person game. Though an ongoing alliance cannot be interpreted as an ultimatum game, we find hints concerning perceived fairness in this game: proposers playing the ultimatum game express their concern for fairness by offering a costly means of 30% to 40% of the take-it-or-leave-it offer to the responder.[953] They are afraid the responders might reject the offer because they feel it is unfair. Similar occurrences happen in the alliance: when Partner 1 allocates only between 70% and 80% of the scientists agreed, it corresponds to an overall share of 35% and 40% of the total number of scientists assigned. Only a small share of responders playing the ultimatum game would accept this offer. Yet, as both firms have agreed on investing a similar stake in the alliance, only investing between

[953] See Camerer (2003a), p. 49.

35% and 40% of the total sum is perceived as unfair by Partner 2. Summarizing, the declining trust of Partner 2's managers is understandable and corresponds to results from studies on fairness perception in behavioral game theory.

7.2.3.4 'Manager Trust' Structure Analysis

In the following paragraphs we analyze the tipping point that determines the shift from virtuous to vicious cycle. We do so by separating the critical structure in the model and use it for an in-depth analysis. This type of model analysis is called the partial model test.[954] The critical model structure is the 'Manager trust' subsystem structure. Initializing the subsystem in equilibrium and then exposing it to shocks enables us to analyze the generated behaviors. This way we are able to study the tipping point behavior generated by this structure only, neglecting any outside impacts.

Figure 6-13 in Section 6.5.1.5 illustrates the 'Manager trust' subsystem structure in an aggregated and simplified way. It contains variables with the indices i and j. The indices indicate that one variable actually represents two variables, i for one partner and j for the other. By using indices, the model structure is arranged more clearly. Yet, for a closer analysis we disaggregate the model structure and replace the indices with P1 and P2.

As can be seen in Figure 7-15 the structure consists of the following core loops. First, there are two second-order reinforcing loops (R4 – 'Let's meet!'). We exemplarily lay them out with Partner 1's structure:

'Desired manager interactions P1 with P2' -> 'Actual manager interactions P1 with P2' -> 'Manager trust P1 in P2' -> 'Desired manager interactions P1 with P2'

Second, there is a fourth-order feedback loop which is highly symmetrical. The reinforcing loops R4 – 'Let's meet!' exist for both parents. They are connected by the variable 'Actual manager interactions P1 with P2', which means that the fourth order loop exists by structural design. Hence, the reinforcing loops are intertwined (R8 – 'Interactions drive trust'):

'Desired manager interactions P1 with P2' -> 'Actual manager interactions P1 with P2' -> 'Manager trust P2 in P1' -> 'Desired manager interactions P2 with P1' -> 'Ac-

[954] See Morecroft (1985), p. 903. See Kopainsky (2005), pp. 119-127 as an example of partial model tests of a complete model. First, partial model tests are helpful for debugging subsystem structures. Second, they may also be applied to reveal intended rationality by organizational decision making. This means that "each organizational function or decision point is isolated from its environment until the environment is consistent with the mental model that underlies the decision rule. The subsystem can then be challenged by various exogenous patterns in its inputs." Sterman (2000), p. 605. Partial model testing shows that decisions may well be adapted to achieve local goals – however, these decisions may not lead to achieving whole system goals. Therefore, and as it is composed of many substructures, the whole model may exhibit different – and maybe counterintuitive – behaviors than its intendedly rational substructures. See Morecroft (1985), pp. 903-904. Regarding intended rationality see also the discussion in Sections 3.4.4.3 and 3.4.4.4.

tual manager interactions P2 with P1' -> 'Manager trust P1 in P2' -> 'Desired manager interactions P1 with P2'

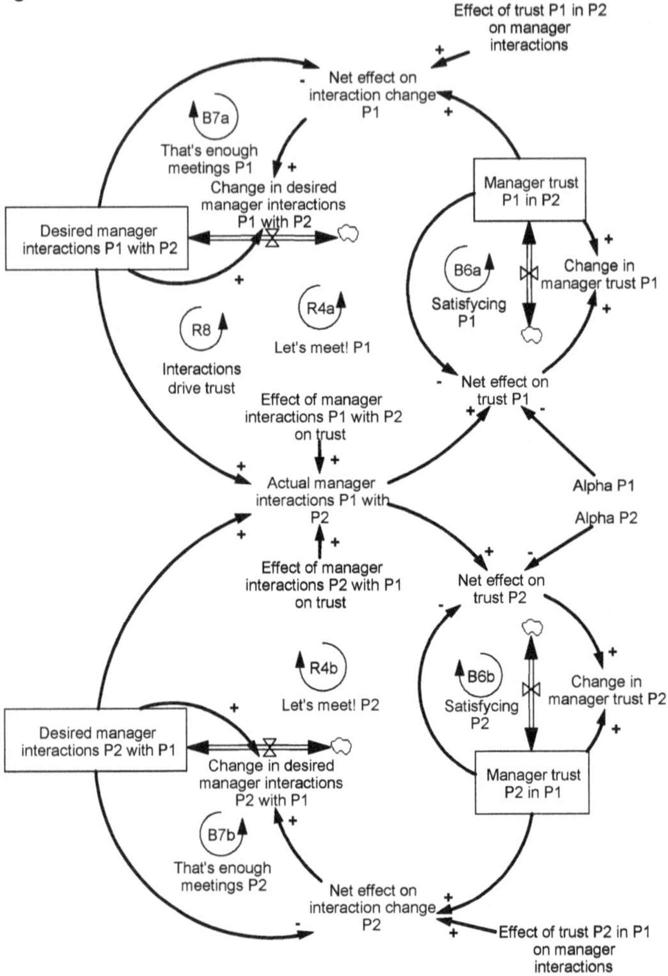

Figure 7-15: Illustration of intertwined feedback loops in the 'Manager trust' subsystem structure.[955]

Moreover, each R4 – 'Let's meet' feedback loop consists of another four first-order balancing loops, of which only two are pointed to expressively with a loop indicator (B6 – 'Satisfycing' and B7 – 'That's enough meetings). The remaining two loops,

[955] Source: authors' representation.

connecting stocks directly with their flows, are structurally intrinsic in hill-climbing ensuring state adjustment.[956]

Tipping point analysis of this fourth-order nonlinear system is more difficult than tipping point analyses by, i.e., RUDOLPH AND REPENNING[957], MORRISON[958], or RAHMANDAD[959], for example. Those models are characterized by a first-order nonlinear system with two feedback loops. A fourth-order nonlinear system creates behavior that is more complex. Hence, to make it easier to comprehend, we simplify the structure again and illustrate it in a phase plot. A phase plot depicts "how the net rate of change of a stock is related to the stock itself."[960] It is a graphical way to describe the structure of a system. Figure 7-16 illustrates how the rates of flow in the model depend on the stock of 'Manager trust'.[961] 'Manager trust', the stock in focus, is marked on the x-axis and its flow, the 'Change in manager trust' is noted on the y-axis.

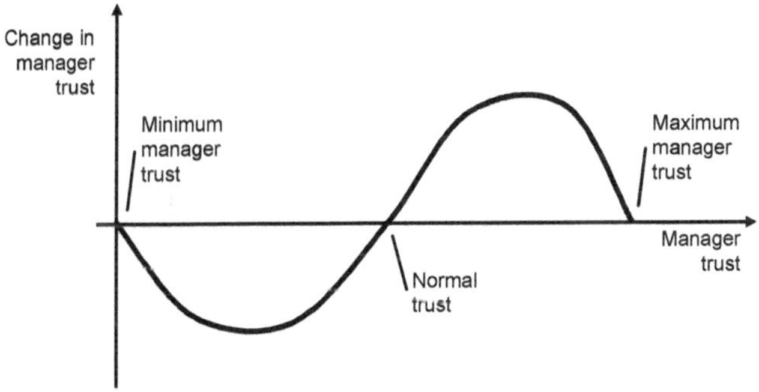

Figure 7-16: Simplified phase plot of 'Manager trust'.[962]

When actual 'Manager trust' is slightly smaller than 'Normal trust', its flows are negative, which means that trust depletes. It first decreases at an increasing rate and then at a decreasing rate until it reaches minimum trust. The reinforcing loop R4 – 'Let's meet!' works as a vicious cycle. In other words, the initial trust level was not high enough to remain at this state: if two managers do not know and trust each other they also do not have an incentive to meet and interact with each other. Only through interacting, exchanging opinions and views, talking, going to dinner together etc., and thus, participating in trust-building actions, can interest in one another increase, which leads to more mutual 'Manager trust'.

If 'Manager trust' is greater than 'Normal trust' the rates are positive. In other words, 'Manager trust' increases. It means that after reaching a certain threshold, managers

956 See Sterman (2000), p. 539.
957 See Rudolph and Repenning (2002).
958 See Morrison (2005).
959 See Rahmandad (2005).
960 Sterman (2000), p. 263.
961 See the explanation in Morrison (2005), p. 12 for a different tipping point analysis.
962 Source: authors' representation.

find each other trustworthy and pleasant. Trust first increases at an increasing rate because the interactions seem promising: managers get to know each other better and understand each other better. Then, with even more interactions, they do not necessarily become even better acquainted. While trust still grows, managers still seek to interact with each other more, which leads to slightly more trust. These activities are constrained by the managers' time. They can only meet and talk with each other as often as their schedules permit. Also, trust does not increase unlimitedly. Therefore, the rate at which 'Manager trust' grows increases at a decreasing rate until it reaches 'Maximum trust'. The reinforcing loop R4 – 'Let's meet!' works in a virtuous cycle.

Figure 7-17 shows the same model structure as Figure 7-16. Yet the figure reveals two important features of the system. First, it shows which of the feedback loops are dominant at what trust level. Second, it exposes the existence of three equilibria, of which two are stable and one is unstable.

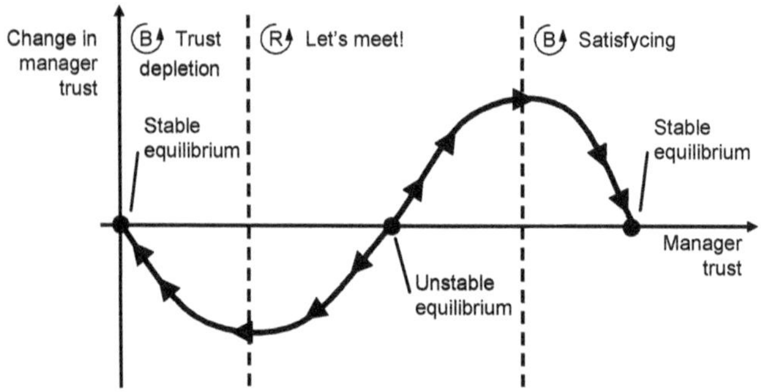

Figure 7-17: Tipping point in the phase plot of 'Manager trust'.[963]

If the system starts at 'Normal trust' and is slightly perturbed, small excursions are not counteracted. The system moves away from 'Normal trust'. As the policy runs above highlight this may lead to the two different situations. First, if trust is slightly increased by a kick-off meeting at which managers interact, for example, over time the system moves away from 'Normal trust' to 'Maximum manager trust'. Second, if trust slightly decreases due to not enough interactions, for instance, the system moves away from 'Normal trust' in the other direction. Therefore, 'Normal trust' is an unstable equilibrium. Though all loops are active, the reinforcing loop R4 – 'Let's meet!' is the dominant feedback loop. In Figure 7-17 this is indicated by arrows highlighting the trajectory of the system in disequilibrium conditions. Here, the arrows are heading away from the unstable equilibrium. Given the characteristics of an unstable equilibrium, it is highly unlikely that the system will stay at the equilibrium of 'Normal trust'. Instead, once the system moves away from this unstable equilibrium it does not return.[964]

---

[963] Source: authors' representation.
[964] Repenning (2001), p. 293.

Moreover, minimum manager trust and 'Maximum manager trust' are indicated as stable equilibria. This means that small excursions are counteracted. If the system starts with 'Manager trust' equal to minimum trust and managers interact a little bit with each other trust increases slightly but over time the system eventually returns to the point where it started. In the area of minimum equilibrium, the balancing loop B – 'Trust depletion' is the dominant loop, though all loops are active. Likewise the situation in the area around 'Maximum manager trust': if the system starts there and is slightly perturbed, over time 'Manager trust' returns to the point from where it started. The balancing loop B6 – 'Satisfycing' is the dominant force.

If the system starts at any point between the unstable and the stable equilibria, the positive loop may work in the following directions: if the system starts below the unstable equilibrium, the reinforcing loop R4 – 'Let's meet!' works in a vicious direction and moves the system toward minimum manager trust; if the system starts above the stable equilibrium, the reinforcing loop works in a virtuous direction and moves the system toward 'Maximum manager trust'. Therefore, the unstable equilibrium is interpreted as a tipping point.[965] The tipping point plays a critical role in determining system behavior as it is the point at which the reinforcing loop R4 – 'Let's meet!' changes direction.

In the base run and the policy runs shown above, initial manager trust was equal to 'Normal manager trust'. Given lower initial trust because of bad past alliance experiences, for example, 'Manager trust' would eventually decline until it reached minimum manager trust. Yet, if initial system shocks like kick-off interactions are large enough to push the system over the tipping point, it does not return to the lower stable equilibrium. Instead, the system follows a new upward trajectory and moves toward the upper stable equilibrium.

7.2.3.5 Pushing 'Manager Trust' Above the Tipping Point

In the following we highlight that interactions during the team-building phase may affect managers' initially reserved attitude toward their alliance partner. One alliance partner's participants may have had a direct bad experience with the partner firm, for example, or the partner's reputation concerning cooperation in alliances has recently suffered in the network. In any case, one partner's managers' trust in the other partner's managers is lower than normal. Figure 7-18 illustrates that 'Manager trust' initially (at t_0) is lower than 'Normal manager trust'. As indicated, under regular circumstances the reinforcing loop would work in a downward spiral and trust would decline to minimum trust, which is zero.

965 Repenning also calls an unstable equilibrium in these conditions a boundary. See Repenning (2001), p. 293.

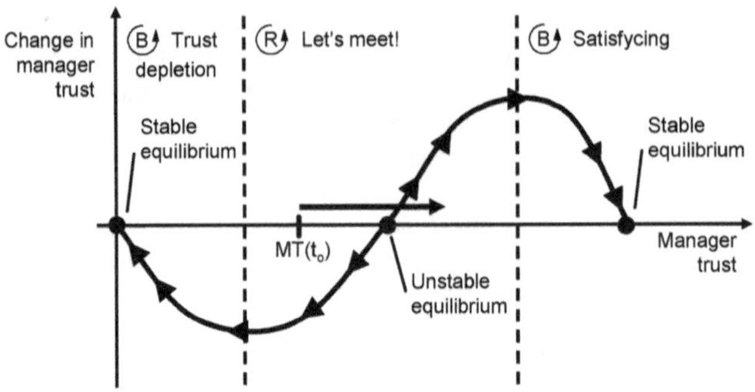

Figure 7-18: Pushing initial manager trust $MT(t_0)$ over the unstable equilibrium.[966]

Yet, we test whether manager interactions can push the system over the tipping point. When looking at model behaviors, note that the 'Manager trust' subsystem is isolated from the rest of the model. The left-hand graph of Figure 7-19 shows the behavior of both firms' 'Manager trust'. The behavior is S-shaped growth – as in the base run of the complete model (see right-hand graph in Figure 7-1). Note, however, that the maximum in the isolated model is slightly lower than in the full model (see right-hand graph in Figure 7-1). This can be attributed to additional additive effects influencing the 'Net effect on trust i' in the full model. Trust increases to a higher level.

For the second run, Partner 2's initial 'Manager trust' is reduced. Table 7-5 summarizes the parameter changes for the base run and the run with reduced trust applying the cut-off model. We assume that Partner 2's initial trust is reduced to 70% in the second run. The graphs in this section refer to a reduced time horizon of 50 weeks. A shortened horizon highlights differences in the start-up phase under various conditions.

Parameter	**Cut-off model** Base run	70% Manager trust
Initial trust P2	1	0.7
Team-building activities	0	0

Table 7-5: Parameter changes for the cut-off model: Base run and reduced manager trust.

As can be seen in the right-hand graph in Figure 7-19, Partner 2's initial trust is lower than in the base run. As expected, the reinforcing loop works in a downward spiral (line 2): mutual trust declines to the lower stable equilibrium, first at an increasing rate (because of the reinforcing loop) and then at a decreasing rate (because of the balancing loop). The reinforcing loop also works in the downward spiral with Partner 1's managers' trust (line 1). Because of so few manager interactions, Partner 1's man-

[966] Source: authors' representation.

agers' trust also diminishes, first driven by the reinforcing loop, then by the balancing loop.

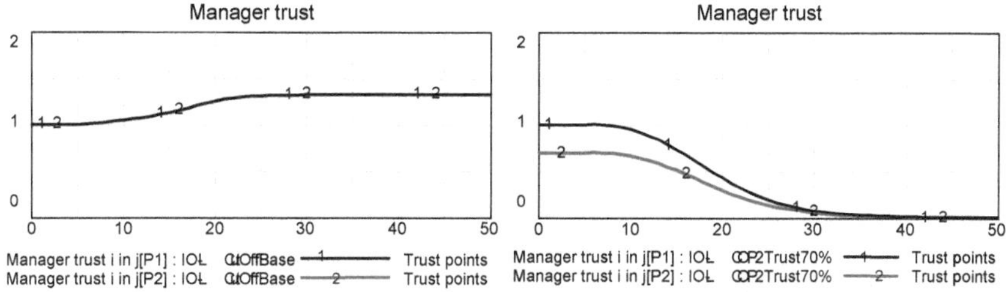

Figure 7-19: 'Manager trust' in the cut off model: Base run and 70% of 'Normal manager trust'.

In the following two runs, managers experience an extensive team-building phase. The team-building actions go beyond the alliance's research content, with the intention that the managers get to know each other better and hold each other in higher esteem. In the first case, the plan is to perform 25% more and in the second case 50% more mutual interactions than normal (see Table 7-6).

Parameter	70% Manager trust and 25% more team-building interactions	70% Manager trust and 50% more team-building interactions
Initial trust P2	0.7	0.7
Team-building interactions	0.25	0.5

Table 7-6: Parameter changes for the cut-off model: Reduced manager trust with team-building interactions.

Figure 7-20 illustrates the behavior of the two runs. Note that the runs are compared to Partner 2's managers having reduced initial trust (right-hand graph in Figure 7-19). As can be seen from the left-hand graph, the 25% increase in kick-off interactions is not enough to push the system over the tipping point. Though Partner 2's 'Manager trust' first slightly increases from 70%, the initial shock is counteracted and the system decreases to its lower stable equilibrium. Partner 1's 'Manager trust' first increases according to the structure presented in the phase plot. Yet, the two reinforcing loops are interconnected at the variable 'Actual manager interactions P1 with P2'. This is the average of the desired interactions of both firms' managers. As Partner 2's managers do not desire to meet more frequently, the interactions are also not enough for Partner 1's managers to trust Partner 2 more. Therefore, Partner 1's 'Manager trust' also decreases.

On the contrary, the 50% increase in interactions during the team-building phase is sufficient to push the system over the tipping point (see line 4 in the right-hand graph of Figure 7-20). The direction of the reinforcing loop is reversed, which causes the system to ascend in a virtuous cycle to the high stable equilibrium. Partner 1's 'Manager trust' reveals more complex dynamics (line 3). It increases in S-shaped steps.

This could relate to the combination of higher-order reinforcing feedback loops and the first-order balancing loops. Further in-depth analysis of this behavior would be subject to further research.

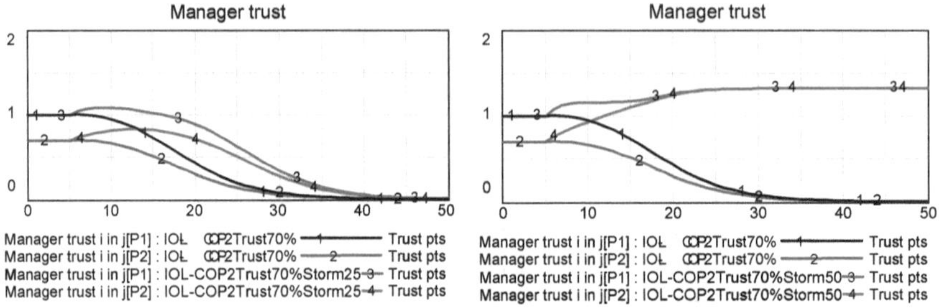

Figure 7-20: Twenty-five percent and 50% more kick-off meetings than normal to push 'Manager trust' over the tipping point.

As in the policy runs above, the behaviors depicted in Figure 7-20 reveal that the difference between decreasing and increasing trust is small. Figure 7-21 illustrates the results of a sensitivity run for a large number of shock sizes between 20% and 50% of initial 'Team-building interactions' on Partner 2's 'Manager trust' in its partner's managers. The graph highlights that up to a shock of about 35% the system first increases, then reverses, falling back to the initial trust level and then further to minimum trust. Yet, beyond this threshold the system increases to 'Maximum manager trust'.

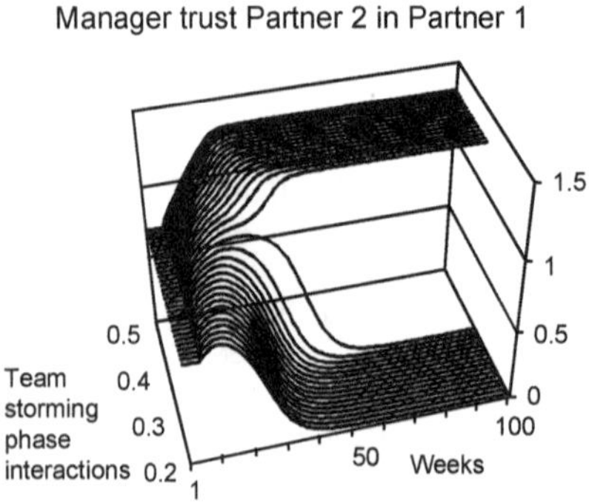

Figure 7-21: Response of cut-off model to kick-off meetings to push 'Manager trust' over the tipping point.

These dynamics lead to the following insight. First, the lower equilibrium suggests that too little initial trust may determine early alliance dissolution – even if, for example, Partner 2's managers' trust develops in a desirable way until the alliance has been working for 15 weeks and still subsequently collapses. In other words, if too little attention is paid to the alliance partners' participants in the early phase of the alliance, the system is bound to fall to the lower equilibrium.

Moreover, the existence of the tipping point implies that even when the system starts off in a favorable condition from the other partner's point of view as it trusts its partner (for example, if Partner 1's managers start with 'Normal manager trust'), the reinforcing loop R4 – 'Let's meet!' does not necessarily create a virtuous cycle. The loop might be affected in such a way by the partner's downward spiral that the system collapses. On the other hand, additional temporary shocks to the system, like extensive team-building phase activities, might be enough to push the system over the tipping point into an upward spiral of mutual manager trust – and lead the alliance to a success from a management standpoint.

Implications for the Full Model

These findings also have implications for the full model. First, as mentioned above, initial interactions between the participants strengthen the reinforcing loops R4 – 'Let's meet!' and thus support trust building in the early phase of an alliance. Pushing the system above the tipping point is necessary in cases where mutual trust is low and the alliance is at risk of failure. This is effective and beneficial for both partners behaving honestly in the cooperative venture.

Second, this insight is not only of interest for sincere partnering firms ensuring a successful partnership. Trying to push the system above the tipping point might also draw attention to firms seeking to cheat their alliance partners. If a firm free rides (applying Policy CL2) or has a hidden agenda (applying Policies CL3b and CL3c), it may employ additional interactions to turn a likely vicious downward cycle into a virtuous upward cycle. Therefore, the frequency of manager interactions could affect situations in which learning alliances fail in a sustainable way. A cheating partner might attach importance to manager interactions while the partner firm's managers are skeptical about partner integrity.[967] With many extensive manager interactions, the cheating firm's managers could, for example, build up a superficial façade of familiarity, honesty, and fairness that dominates possible violations of contractual resource requirements. While the honest partner firm engages in interactions in good faith, it is exposed to even more severe cheating.

7.2.4 Research Propositions Revisited: Managerial Implications for Learning with the Partner

Thus far we analyzed policy implications of common learning only. Before including private learning in the analysis, we discuss the managerial implications of the policy runs conducted above. Whereas alliance scholars mostly hold the dilemma of the co-existence of both common and private benefits responsible for alliance dynamics, we learned from the interorganizational learning model that dynamics may also occur in situations where only common learning is happening. The policy runs and model

[967] Firms test their alliance partner's integrity to sustain process-based trust. See the explanations in Section 4.6.4.2.

structure analyses carried out in previous sections lead to the following managerial insight for common learning. We first highlight the insight into successful collaboration between research partners in a learning alliance.

From the Common Learning Policy CL1, we learn that if firms require each other's compatible knowledge bases, both partners' researchers need to be open – or transparent – to each other for successful knowledge exchange and joint learning.[968] Researchers exchanging knowledge freely and openly, getting in touch with each other without any major restrictions, or visiting each other on their partner's research sites are important determinants of successful joint knowledge creation. Yet, mostly, a completely open knowledge exchange between researchers whose firms are direct competitors in the market place is unlikely. Therefore, contractual safeguards like gatekeepers are often installed to control the knowledge flows between the firms and their research alliance. Comparing the dynamics of the base run with those of Common Learning Policy CL1, we notice that joint knowledge creation is hindered and reaching of goals strongly delayed if the gatekeepers' duty is to severely restrict open knowledge exchange. Thus, the insight supports HAMEL's and INKPEN's observation and our Proposition 1.

> *Proposition 1: Openness of the collaborating firms' gatekeepers fosters common learning in a learning alliance.*

By Common Learning Policies CL2 and CL3 we refer to two modes of opportunistic behavior in the case of common learning: firms may have hidden agendas when entering alliances.[969] First, we tested the alliance dynamics if a firm free rides (Common Learning Policy CL2). Second, we analyzed alliance dynamics if a firm has lower actual goals than agreed during alliance negotiations (Common Learning Policy CL3). Policy CL2 consists of two situations: with Policy CL2a the free riding partner allocates a few scientists less. The partner's managers perceive the lower resource allocation and adjust their own scientist contribution. In the end, both firms reach their common goals – though at a later date since fewer scientists are working on the research tasks compared to the base run. Mutual 'Manager trust' stays high. This positive attitude toward each other increases both firms' reputation in the network as being trustworthy alliance partners – with slight reservations compared to the base run.[970] With Policy CL2b the free riding partner firm allocates even fewer scientists. It obviously oversteps the threshold of acceptance. The cheated firm feels betrayed, trust does not build up, and eventually the alliance is dissolved. The firms' reputations suffer in the network: cognition-based trust, being at a minimum, is significant for future cooperations.[971] The simulation leads to the following revisions to Proposition 2.1:

---

968 See Hamel (1991), p. 93 and Inkpen (2000a), p. 1026 and Section 4.6.2.

969 For hidden agendas see Section 4.5.1 and their underlying theoretical foundations of organizational economics in Section 3.4.1.

970 See Kleinaltenkamp and Wolters (1997), p. 66.

971 See McAllister (1995), p. 28.

Proposition 2.1a: Moderate perceived opportunistic behavior in terms of free riding leads to delayed goal attainment and success of a learning alliance.

Proposition 2.1b: Excessive perceived opportunistic behavior in terms of free riding leads to a failure of a learning alliance and its early dissolution.

Common Learning Policy CL3 consists of 3 situations. They all refer to a partner firm actually having fewer common goals. Coupled with fewer common goals is a reduced scientist allocation. With Policy CL3a, the firm communicates that it has fewer common goals than its partner and thus allocates fewer scientists. We learn from the simulation run that, because of the partner's frankness, the alliance is stable, trust develops as in the base run and the goals are reached only slightly later. As with Policy CL2a, the reason for this is the reduced workforce.

Likewise, with Common Learning Policy CL3b, Partner 1 also has fewer common goals and therefore allocates fewer scientists. Yet, it behaves dishonestly by not informing its alliance partner about its actual intentions. Partner 2 still assumes an equal resource allocation and is surprised by Partner 1 allocating less. Over the course of the alliance trust suffers and breaks down and the reputation is ruined. Partner 2 withdraws its scientists from the alliance. The alliance is dissolved.

The situation is defused with Policy CL3c. Partner 1 again has hidden intentions. Nevertheless, the hidden intentions are more moderate than with Policy CL3b. As with Policy CL2a, Partner 2 still accepts the lower scientist allocation. Trust only suffers slightly. Nevertheless, after Partner 1 attains its (relatively small number of) common goals, it withdraws its scientists from the alliance in order to avoid strengthening its competitor any further. The cheated partner firm does not reach its goals completely which is why it is dissatisfied with the alliance outcome. Consequently, unlike with Policy CL2a, Partner 2's trust declines and, according to the network approach, Partner 1's reputation in the network concerning any further research alliances in the near future is ruined.[972] This leads to the following revisions to Proposition 2.2.

Proposition 2.2a: Honesty regarding prospective common goals leads to the success of a learning alliance.

Proposition 2.2b: Perceived opportunistic behavior in terms of extreme hidden goals leads to a loss of trust, failure of a learning alliance and its early dissolution.

Proposition 2.2c: Perceived opportunistic behavior in terms of moderate hidden goals leads to a loss of trust and one dissatisfied partner firm in a learning alliance that does not reach its common goals.

[972] The network approach is discussed in Section 3.4.3.

Common Learning Policy CL4 underlines that the cheating partner firm can successfully hide its lower hidden goals while contributing the amount of scientists that its partner expects. Therefore we add:

> *Proposition 2.2d: Opportunistic behavior in terms of hidden goals can be disguised by allocating the amount of resources to the alliance that the partner firm expects. This leads to a loss of trust and one dissatisfied partner firm in a learning alliance.*

The analysis of the critical model structure in Section 7.2.3 highlights the importance of mutual 'Manager trust' in alliances. We learned from the analysis that a tipping point exists. Its implications are as mentioned above: its existence implies that even when the alliance starts in a favorable, trusting condition from one partner's point of view, it is not a given that trust will increase and create a virtuous cycle. If the other partner's trust is low, the bias may be so strong that its lower trust drags down the trust of the firm which shows goodwill. This might lead to alliance dissolution. Trust is a critical factor in determining alliance success: if the alliance starts out with a lack of trust or mutual trust suffers over the course of the alliance, the chance of alliance dissolution is high. This insight goes along with the empirical study mentioned in Section 4.6.4, stating that broken down mutual trust is a reason for failure in 45% of alliance dissolution cases. We find support for Proposition 3 and supplement it with more insight:

> *Proposition 3a: A trusting collaboration environment fosters common goal attainment in a learning alliance.*

> *Proposition 3b: One alliance partner trusting the other is not sufficient for sustaining and developing trust in the learning alliance in order to foster common goal attainment.*

> *Proposition 3c: Extensive trust-building activities support mutual trust building between the partners' managers and scientists and lead to the success of a learning alliance.*

In the following we enhance the model structure of the common learning segment with the private learning subsystem segment introduced in Sections 6.2 and 6.5.2.

7.3 Model Behavior Analysis: Learning from the Alliance

Thus far we analyzed and discussed managerial implications of firms' possible policies in pure common learning. In the following we extend the model boundary to include private learning. We analyze and discuss the policies of one partner seeking private benefits. In all runs, Partner 1 is the firm whose policies change. We examine how Partner 2 perceives the policies and how it reacts to them.

It is assumed that both partners have complementary knowledge. In order to stay competitive they need each other to develop joint knowledge that they cannot develop on their own to register new patents. Moreover, as the cooperating firms are competitors in the market, the respective partner's knowledge is also of high interest for businesses outside the alliance area. Hence, the partner firms are interested in jointly created knowledge spilling over to them but not to the respective partner.

To simplify and facilitate comparisons between the following runs and those depicted above we use the same time horizon. In the following we look at four different policy runs. For the first run (Private Learning Policy PL1) it is assumed that formal controls, like gatekeepers, prohibit any knowledge flow from the alliance to the partner firms. In the subsequent policy runs, we allow the formal controls to be substituted by social controls – in other words, trust. As discussed in Section 4.6.4.1, increasing trust provides an opportunity for the partner firm to take advantage of the trusting firm and learn privately. Technically, to activate the private learning model structure the following switch needs to be turned to 1 (see Eq. 6.15):

"Switch no PL=O and PL=1" = 1 (Eq. 7.1)

For the policy runs subsequent to Policy run PL1, the following switch endogenizes the gatekeeper's openness (Eq. 6.16) and activates the balancing loop B5 – 'Social and formal controls substitute each other (see Figure 6-7).

"Switch no Effect of manager trust on openness=0 and
Effect of manager trust on openness=1 P2" = 1 (Eq. 7.2)

In other words, when 'Manager trust' increases, 'Openness of gatekeeper restrictions to j's private learning – i' increases, too. Increasing gatekeeper openness means that the importance of formal control declines: as laid out in Section 6.5.2.3, trusting managers neglect installed contractual arrangements. This provides the partner firm with the opportunity to take advantage of the situation to learn privately.

For Private Learning Policies PL1 and PL2, Partner 1 seeks the same number of private goals as common goals, 10 patents. Yet, gatekeepers are installed in the first policy run to prevent private learning. Their restrictions on knowledge exchange are held constant throughout the simulation. For the second policy run, gatekeeper openness is endogenized, as explained above.

7.3.1 Private Learning Policy 1: Private Goals and Exogenous Gatekeeper Openness

In addition to the agreed common alliance goals of Partner 1 and Partner 2, the former also has prospective private benefits. It is assumed that it needs the alliance's knowledge base to generate 10 patents in an area unrelated to the alliance scope (see Table 7-7). Corresponding to the term private benefits, we label these patents private patents – though they are openly known to the public once they are approved.

Moreover, all values of the parameters in the private learning substructure correspond with those in the common learning substructure. The parameter 'Scientists per patent to be achieved P1', for example, not only determines the 'Scientists active in the alliance' but also the 'Scientists active on private learning - parent j [P1]'. The possible maximum number of private patents to be generated is set to 15 patents. As Partner 1 seeks 10 private patents, it is equivalent to a share of two-thirds of the possible maximum. It corresponds to the prospective common benefits that equal 30 patents of the maximum common benefits: each parent is interested in 10 common patents, i.e., 20 patents of 30 possible joint patents. Using the same values facilitates the comparison between the dynamics in the two substructures. It prevents distortion of the dynamics, which might lead to misinterpretations of the causes of evolving dynamics.

Private learning is made difficult as the alliance partners have agreed to install gatekeepers. Technically, the parameter 'Openness of P2's gatekeeper restrictions to P1's private learning' is set to zero (see Table 7-7). It means that gatekeepers intensively control the knowledge flows between the alliance and the partner firms. Any knowledge that can be of interest to areas outside the alliance scope either is not allowed to flow, or is marked confidential to the alliance. In other words, this particular knowledge has to be kept inside the alliance and must not be spread inside the partner firms. This policy prevents a firm being outlearned by the partner.

Parameter	Policy PL1
Openness of P2's gatekeeper restrictions to P1's private learning	0
PrivALP1	10

Table 7-7: Parameter changes for Private Learning Policy PL1.

Figure 7-22 highlights that the dynamics for this private learning policy are similar to those of the base run in Section 7.2.1. Both firms allocate their scientists to the alliance, as both have common goals (upper left-hand graph). As managers trust each other (upper right-hand graph) and scientists are open to each other (middle left-hand graph), they exchange their compatible knowledge with each other and create new, joint knowledge. Consequently, common goals are attained (lower left-hand graph). Yet, as gatekeeper restrictions are tight (middle right-hand graph),[973] alliance knowledge does not spill over to areas outside the alliance scope. Consequently, Partner 1 does not meet its private goals. Partner 1's goal attainment stays zero all the way through (lower right-hand graph). Understandably, Partner 1, though pursuing private benefits, does not withdraw from the alliance only because alliance knowledge does not spill over. If it withdrew, it would not reach its common goals, either.

[973] Note that the middle right-hand graph in Figure 7-22 only depicts Partner 2's openness of gatekeeper restrictions.

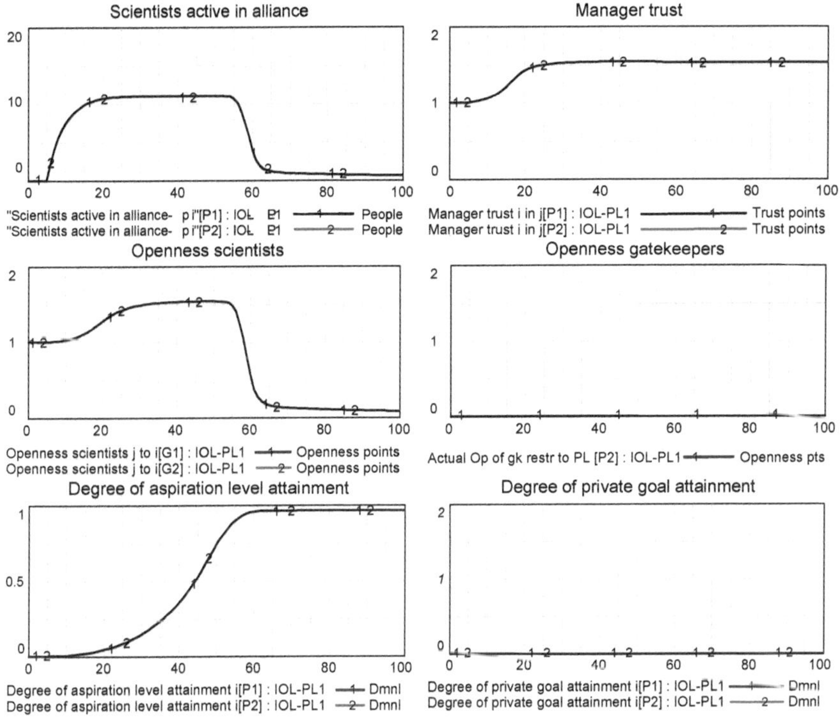

Figure 7-22: Private Learning Policy PL1: Exogenous formal controls – gatekeepers do not allow any knowledge flows from the alliance to other business areas in the partner firms.[974]

As in the base run, both alliance partners are satisfied with the alliance development. The mutual goals are met, and mutual trust is at its maximum – though Partner 1 had private goals and seeks to take advantage of its partner for alliance irrelevant purposes. The policy to install formal controls like gatekeepers successfully protects Partner 2 from being outlearned.

7.3.2 Private Learning Policy 2: Private Goals and Endogenous Gatekeeper Openness

Thus far, formal controls were exogenous which is why gatekeeper openness was not replaced by social control like mutual 'Manager trust'. Yet, according to Section 4.6.3, the more people trust each other in a relationship, the less important formal controls become. Therefore, in the following, the 'Openness of P2's gatekeeper re-

[974] Note that the lower right-hand graph depicting the 'Degree of private goal attainment' shows a different scale on the y-axis from zero to two. This is because the variable exhibits values above one in later policy runs.

strictions to P1's private learning' is endogenized (see Table 7-8) and effected by Partner 1's 'Manager trust' in Partner 2's managers.

Parameter	Policy PL2 Policy PL2a	 Policy PL2b	 Scenario PL2c
Openness of P2's gatekeeper restrictions to P1's private learning	endogenized	endogenized	endogenized
PrivALP1	10	10	10
Relative scientist active private j PL[P1]	1	3	3
Reference private knowledge relative to private knowledge PL [P1]	1	1	2

Table 7-8: Parameter changes for Private Learning Policies PL2.

In the following two runs, it is assumed that Partner 1's policy is that it has private goals of 10 patents. The difference between Private Learning Policies PL2a and PL2b lies in the allocation of scientists to private learning. The parameter 'Relative scientist active private', referring to Partner 1, is changed accordingly. In Scenario PL2c we analyze how a smaller overlap of the alliance and the private knowledge bases affect private learning.[975] By increasing the parameter 'Reference private knowledge relative to private knowledge PL [P1]' by the factor 2, Partner 1's scientists only have half the capability of understanding the alliance knowledge than in the previous runs. In other words, the alliance knowledge base and the partner's private knowledge base are further apart from each other. This reduces the scientists' relative absorptive capacity. It takes them longer to understand the knowledge components created in the alliance. Thus private learning must be slowed down.[976]

Private Learning Policy PL2a: Private Learning

The graphs in Figure 7-23 depict the dynamics of Policy PL2a. The graphs showing common learning do not differ from the graphs of Policy PL1 in Figure 7-22. We see that scientists are allocated, mutual trust between the managers and openness between the scientists increases and stays on a high level which supports knowledge exchange and joint learning for common benefits. Nevertheless, with increasing 'Manager trust' (upper right-hand graph), Partner 2's managers increasingly trust Partner 1's managers. According to INKPEN AND CURRALL, mutual trust leads to intensified organizational ties which diminish the weight of formal controls.[977] The upper right-hand and middle right-hand graphs highlight this substitution. The more Partner 2's managers trust Partner 1's managers between weeks 5 and 25, the more open the gatekeepers become. Yet, gatekeepers do not become increasingly open right away. As can be seen from the middle right-hand graph, openness increases after a delay. It takes managers time to perceive that they increasingly trust the partner. It then takes time to change the gatekeeper's openness incrementally, depending on whether the partner is perceived as being trustworthy and behaving fairly.

[975] This run is called a scenario as the future trajectory is changed. It is uncertain how the two knowledge bases (alliance knowledge base and private knowledge base) are related to each other. The parameter 'Reference private knowledge relative to private knowledge PL [P1]' is changed to analyze its impact on private learning.

[976] See Section 4.6.1 for explanations on relative absorptive capacity.

[977] See Inkpen and Currall (2004), p. 591 and Section 4.6.3.

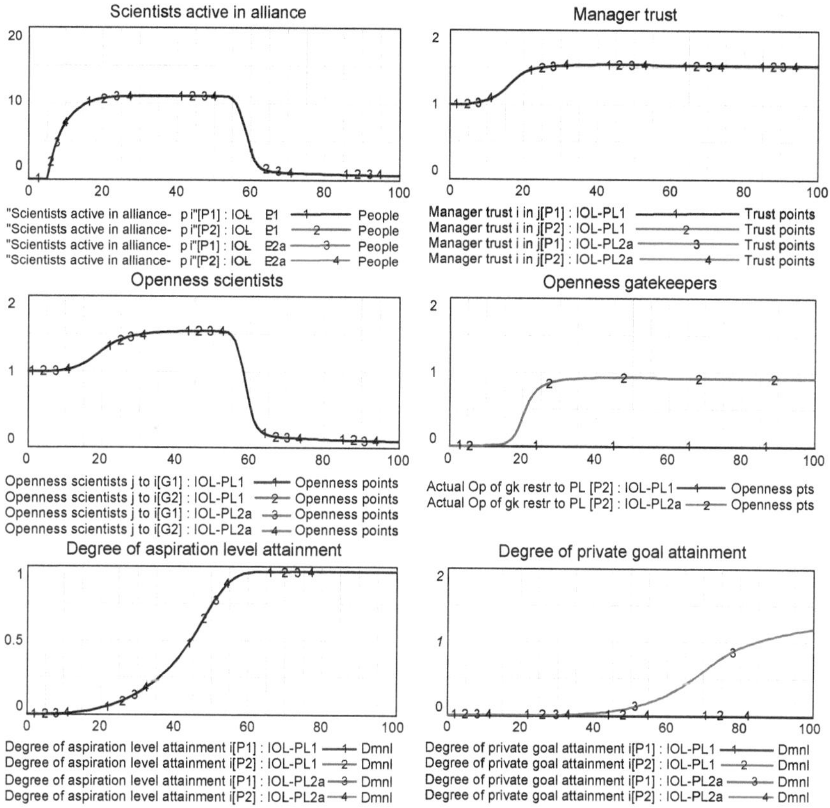

Figure 7-23: Private Learning Policy PL2a: Endogenized formal controls with high private goals.[978]

Thus, Partner 2 does not pay that much attention anymore to its gatekeepers fulfilling their duties. In a real world alliance, the partner would not, for example, declare documents as alliance confidential or would allow Partner 1's scientists to spend time in its research facilities as a sign of goodwill. This enables Partner 1 to learn privately from the alliance for areas outside the alliance scope. Knowledge spilled over from the alliance needs to be transferred to Partner 1's firm sites. Its scientists need to understand and apply it to the target areas – which requires time. Therefore, the private patent generation commences with a delay. First private patents are generated in about week 35. By that time the alliance has already generated 25% of its goals. The scientists are done with their joint tasks at around week 55, when not even 20% of the private goals have been attained. Nevertheless, Partner 1's scientists working on generating private patents continue researching with the alliance knowledge. As

[978] Note that the lower right-hand graph depicting the 'Degree of private goal attainment' shows a scale on the y-axis from zero to two.

alliance outcomes still exist after alliance dissolution, Partner 1's scientists may still use and apply alliance knowledge to private needs at a later point in time. They finally reach their private goals shortly after week 80 – when the alliance has already been dissolved for nearly half a year (see lower right-hand graph; note the different scale on the y-axis). Partner 1's 'Degree of private goal attainment' further increases and saturates at about 140% of the intended goals. It overshoots the goal, as it is assumed that the maximum number of private patents that the Partners may generate is 50% higher than the actual goals. At 10 private patents, it has not reached the possible maximum yet. Obviously, the generated 'Alliance knowledge base' that spills over to Partner 1 reveals more research potential than just the 10 patents.

Both partners are satisfied with the alliance outcome. Partner 1 and Partner 2 reach their common goals. Yet, Partner 2 does not know that its alliance ally is taking advantage of it and learning privately. Mutual 'Manager trust' stays high after alliance termination. That would enable Partner 1 to reenter an alliance with Partner 2 for doing common – and private – research (see upper right-hand and middle right-hand graph).

Private Learning Policy PL2b: More Scientists for Private Learning
Yet, Partner 1 does not know whether the knowledge that spills over from the alliance is sufficient to generate the private patents at the time the alliance is dissolved. Therefore, it might allocate more scientists to work on the private tasks to accelerate private learning. The scientists could work in several teams on specific tasks. For the following run it is assumed that Partner 1's policy is to assign three times as many scientists to learn privately than in the Private Learning Policy PL2a.

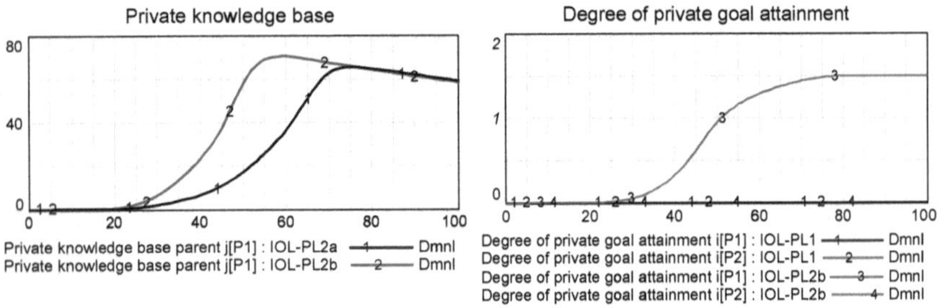

Figure 7-24: Private Learning Policy PL2b: More scientists for private learning.[979]

The variables in the common learning substructure behave identically to those depicted in Figure 7-23. Therefore, we only focus on the differences in the private learning substructure. As can be seen from the right-hand graph in Figure 7-24, Partner 1 reaches its private goals in week 52. This is about 30 weeks earlier than with Private Learning Policy PL2a. The policy to allocate a larger team of researchers to private learning obviously works supportively for the cheating partner. They generate more

[979] Note that the right-hand graph depicting the 'Degree of private goal attainment' shows a scale on the y-axis from zero to two.

knowledge earlier. The left-hand graph in Figure 7-24 highlights the difference in the developments of Partner 1's 'Private knowledge base'. The line marked with 1 (or 2, respectively) denotes the development of the knowledge base in the Private Learning Policy PL2a (PL2b) run. As can be seen, the stock increases at a higher rate and reaches its peak earlier. The scientists are able to generate more private knowledge faster from the spilled over alliance knowledge. After the peak the stock then decreases because the scientists forget and unlearn.

For the cheating Partner 1, Private Learning Policy PL2b is a better choice than the Private Learning Policy PL2a. Not only does it reach its common goals jointly with Partner 2 in a trustworthy working atmosphere, but it learns privately completely unbeknownst to its partner. It completely finishes its private learning before the alliance ends.

Private Learning Scenario PL2c: Less Relative Absorptive Capacity
In the following run it is assumed that it is twice as difficult for Partner 1's scientists to understand and apply the alliance knowledge created. The alliance knowledge base and the private knowledge base overlap less than in the previous run PL2b. Though the scientists require the knowledge generated by the alliance for their own needs, they do not understand the knowledge easily – they lack similar experiences, for instance, because they are applying a different research approach. Thus, the relative absorptive capacity is lower.[980] Also, they may not interact openly with the scientists working on alliance tasks. The partner's scientists could become aware of the intent for private learning.

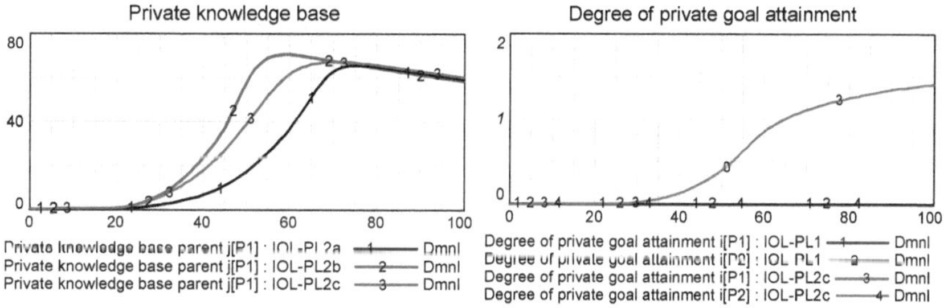

Figure 7-25: Private Learning Scenario PL2c: Less relative absorptive capacity.[981]

The right-hand graph in Figure 7-25 highlights that Partner 1's scientists reach their private goals in week 75. This is about a quarter of a year later than under normal conditions (see run PL2b). This suggests that it is more difficult for them to learn from the alliance. The left-hand graph in Figure 7-25 supports this suggestion. As above, the graph highlights the development of Partner 1's private knowledge base. Though it allocates more people to private learning, it is not evident that it reaches its private goals when the alliance is dissolved (line 2, compared to line 1). Therefore, policy-

980 See Section 4.6.1 for explanations on relative absorptive capacity.
981 Note that the right-hand graph depicting the 'Degree of private goal attainment' shows a scale on the y-axis from zero to two.

designers need to take into consideration that private learning may take longer than expected.

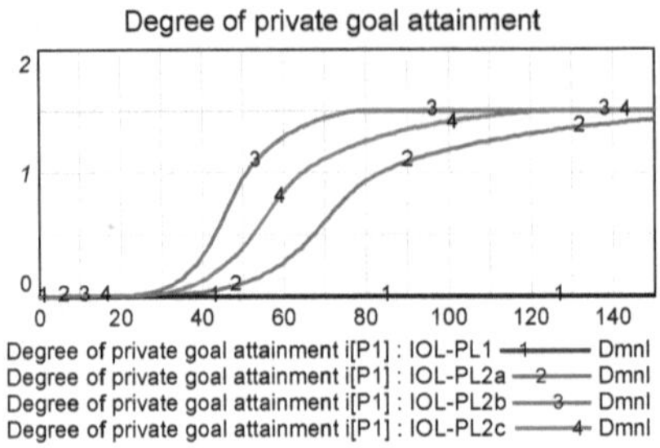

Figure 7-26: Partner 1's 'Degree of private goal attainment' in the various policy runs over a time horizon of 150 weeks.[982]

For reasons of clarity we summarize the developments of Partner 1's private goal agreements in Figure 7-26. As the dynamics are mostly cut off in the figures above, the time horizon is extended to 150 weeks. As can be seen, the general qualitative S-shape of the dynamics does not change in runs PL2a, PL2b, and PL2c. Only the moment at which the goals are reached varies. Policy-makers who seek to outlearn the alliance partner therefore need to consider the strategic importance of the private learning task, estimate the difficulty to learn, allocate appropriate resources to it, and ensure the possibility of outlearning in general. If formal controls are installed with the intent to restrict knowledge flows, it means that the managers need to take the trouble to gain the partner's trust. This is challenging for managers who need to perform the balancing act of combining cooperative (behaving honestly) and competitive (outlearning) behavior in the alliance. In Section 7.4 we analyze possible combinative policies for common and private learning.

7.3.3 Research Propositions Revisited: Managerial Implications for Learning from the Alliance

The preceding sections extended the common learning model structure with private learning and analyzed policy implications of private learning. Thus far, we did not yet combine policies for common and private learning. Therefore, the following discussion of policy implications only refers to private learning. If not permitted by the alliance partner firm, private learning reflects unfair behavior. Consequently, the policy runs and model structure analyses carried out in the sections above lead to the following managerial insight for competitive and unfair behavior in learning alliances.

First, the Private Learning Policy PL1 highlights that private learning does not occur if the alliance partners install restrictive contractual, formal controls. Formal controls

[982] Note that the graph depicting the 'Degree of private goal attainment' shows a scale on the y-axis from zero to two.

like gatekeepers, for example, monitor and organize knowledge flows between the alliance and the partner firms and vice versa. Their policies decide on which knowledge may flow to which business unit. If their policies are restrictive, private learning, as in our case study alliance, may be hindered. If their policies are loose or if formal controls do not exist per se, private learning occurs. Thus, we find support for Proposition 4.

Proposition 4: Formal controls hinder private learning from a learning alliance.

Second, as explained above, we learn from the behavior that it takes time to generate private benefits. Common knowledge first has to be created for private learning. It is the basis for knowledge spillover to the partner firms – if feasible at all. Or, put differently, only engaging in common tasks, exchanging knowledge, and learning together may initiate private learning. Engaging in common tasks, exchanging knowledge, and learning together builds up a common knowledge base. Consequently, only a common knowledge base – even if it is small – is the basis for private learning. Thus we find support for Proposition 5. Moreover, Private Learning Policy PL2a underlines that private learning may occur with a delay, well after the alliance is terminated. It requires time for the knowledge to spill over from the alliance. Scientists occupied with working with alliance knowledge content need to value the new alliance knowledge, and assimilate and apply it to their research needs outside the alliance scope.[983] If the alliance knowledge base and the private knowledge bases do not overlap significantly, private learning occurs with a further delay. Comparing Private Learning Policy PL2b and Scenario PL2c highlights this possible delay. In the latter run a reduced relative absorptive capacity hinders private learning progress. These findings question current learning alliance literature which suggests that private learning is finished before common learning occurs.[984] They lead to the following revisions of Proposition 5.

Proposition 5a: Private learning from a learning alliance only occurs when common learning takes place and only via the common knowledge base.

Proposition 5b: Private benefits from a learning alliance may occur with a time delay.

Third, we learn from the Private Learning Policies PL2a, b, and c that a partner does not even notice that its alliance partner is learning privately without its consent. During the collaboration in the alliance, Partner 1's managers and scientists behave cooperatively and fairly when in direct contact with the partner's managers and scientists. They participate in meetings and are interested in interacting with Partner 2's employees. They share their knowledge openly and are committed to working on the alliance tasks to move the alliance forward. Partner 1's managers and scientists do not behave any differently than in the base run for common learning. From Partner 2's point of view Partner 1 does not even provide the slightest indication that it is using its partner to strengthen its market position in areas outside the alliance scope.

983 According to the definition for absorptive capacity by Cohen and Levinthal (1990), p. 128.
984 See Khanna et al. (1998), p. 195 and our explanation in Section 4.5.4.

Yet, as the firms are competitors, it may well be that Partner 1 is even strengthening its position in an area which is in direct competition to the outlearned partner. Nonetheless, the outlearned firm does not notice that it is actually being outlearned. It is satisfied with the alliance outcome as it reaches its common goals. 'Manager trust' is high, which means that it would collaborate with Partner 1 again in the future – the partner that applied an unfair policy. For Partner 1 the alliance is a complete success: not only does it reach its common goals with Partner 2, it even successfully outlearns Partner 2 without Partner 2 noticing. Therefore, we find support for Proposition 6.

Proposition 6: Private learning from a learning alliance may be concealed from the partner firm.

This proposition stands in contrast to the outlearning literature.[985] It claims that partnering firms might enter learning races. Yet, this assumes that firms notice that they are in a learning race situation. We could not find indications of how firms realize that they are in such a position. If they do not realize that they are in the middle of a learning race, they cannot race. Consider, for example, a situation of knowledge exchange in which one partner's scientists are more reserved toward the other partner's scientists than the other way round. A race situation would assume that the first group of scientists seeks to learn privately without sharing their own knowledge. The other firm's scientists would also be interested in learning privately. Yet, they share their own knowledge more openly since they are aware that they need to move forward with joint knowledge first before private learning may begin. From the model we learn that because of reciprocal fairness, the second partner's scientist group would also reduce their openness. This would lead to a non-cooperative situation without any joint learning or knowledge exchange. Eventually the alliance would be dissolved early. We may assume that since the partners wanted to learn privately, the alliance was dissolved, but we do not find a direct indication of firms being aware of being in a learning race. They might be indirectly alerted because the partner does not openly share its knowledge.

In the preceding sections we analyzed cooperative and competitive aspects of common learning policies for learning in the alliance and competitive characteristics of private learning policies for learning from the alliance separately. In the subsequent section we combine learning with the partner and from the alliance.

7.4 Model Behavior Analysis: Learning with the Partner and from the Alliance

The following section completes the analysis of interorganizational learning in alliances. The managerial findings identified above lead to a wide range of possible combinative policies for common and private learning. Analyzing all combinations would not necessarily lead to more new insight. Therefore we highlight three situations of common and private learning policies that focus on the following aspects (see Table 7-9): first, Partner 1 makes Partner 2 erroneously believe that its behavior is

[985] See, for example, Hamel (1991), Khanna et al. (1998), Amburgey et al. (2000), Inkpen and Currall (2004), and Inkpen and Tsang (2005).

trustworthy. Second, Partner 2 doubts Partner 1's integrity while Partner 1 is indeed untrustworthy. Finally, both partners seek to take advantage of each other. We explain the policies in more detail in the following.

First, Partner 1 is dishonest toward its alliance partner regarding the agreed number of common goals. Under normal circumstances it would allocate fewer resources. Yet, applying Common Learning Policy CL4, it spends the amount of scientists that Partner 2 expects. Moreover, Partner 1 seeks a few private goals that are of high strategic value, which is why it allocates a large number of scientists to private learning. Partner 2 enters the alliance with honest intentions.

Partner 1	**Policy CLPL1**	**Policy CLPL2**	**Policy CLPL3**
Common learning	Fewer common goals than agreed upon, but compensates allocation	Fewer actual common goals than agreed upon	Free riding
Private learning	Few private goals	Few private goals	Few private goals
Partner 2			
Common learning	Common goals as agreed upon	Common goals as agreed upon	Fewer actual common goals than agreed upon
Trust	Normal trust	Low initial trust and reduced gatekeeper openness	Normal trust

Table 7-9: Partner behavior in the Common and Private Learning Policy runs.

Second, it is assumed that Partner 1's reputation in the network of being a trustworthy learning partner has suffered in the past. This is why Partner 2's managers are suspicious and do not fully trust Partner 1's managers at the start of the alliance. Their worries are not unfounded: Partner 1 does behave opportunistically. First, it seeks fewer common goals than agreed with Partner 2 in the contract. Moreover, it seeks private benefits that are of high strategic value for Partner 1. For this run it is assumed that gatekeepers extensively control the knowledge flows throughout the learning alliance.

Third, both partner firms behave unfairly. Partner 1 free rides and Partner 2 actually has fewer common goals than agreed on in the contract. In addition, Partner 1 has some prospective private goals. The dynamics of all runs are depicted in comparison to the base run, which is characterized by honest and fair learning behavior.

7.4.1 Common and Private Learning Policy 1: Unfair Partner 1 and Trustworthy Partner 2

In the first policy run, Partner 1 behaves unfairly regarding both common and private benefits. In contrast, Partner 2 behaves honestly and does not betray its alliance partner. Table 7-10 summarizes the parameter changes for the firms' policies. Partner 1 has prospective private benefits of 3 patents ('PrivAL1P1'). As they are of high strategic value, Partner 1 wants to ensure it attains them before alliance termination. Therefore, it allocates 10 times as many scientists to work on these private patents

('Relative scientists active private j PL') than under normal conditions. Furthermore, Partner 1 also did not discuss honestly the number of joint patents it wanted to work on with Partner 2 during alliance negotiations. It is actually only interested in half the number of patents agreed on ('Fraction of actual internally communicated goals L1P1'). It is afraid that Partner 2 would not enter the alliance if it were honest about its lower aspirations. In order not to raise Partner 2's suspicions it allocates the number of scientists Partner 2 expects ('Fractional scientist bonus P1'). As Partner 2 behaves honestly, there are no changes made to any of the policies in the base model.

	Parameter	Policy CLPL1
Partner 1	PrivAL1P1	*3*
	Relative scientist active private j PL	*10*
	Fraction of actual internally communicated goals L1P1	*0.5*
	Fractional team-building interactions	0
	Fractional scientist bonus P1	2
Partner 2	Initial trust P2	1
	Fractional team-building interactions	0
	Fraction of actual internally communicated goals L2P1	1

Table 7-10: Parameter changes for Common and Private Policies CLPL1.[986]

Figure 7-27 depicts the dynamics of this policy run in which Partner 1 cheats on Partner 2. The behavior for this policy run (lines 3 and 4) in the beginning phase from week 5 until week 45 for both parents' scientists allocation (upper left-hand graph), mutual 'Manager trust' (upper right-hand graph), and the scientists' openness (middle left-hand graph), is similar to the base run (lines 1 and 2). The scientists create joint knowledge and the partners begin to attain their goals. As Partner 1 has fewer common goals (which Partner 2 does not know about), its 'Degree of aspiration level attainment' increases at a faster rate. Over the course of the collaboration, the managers from both firms interact frequently with each other. Trust increases slowly and, as a social safeguard, becomes more important than formal safeguards. Consequently, because of the trustworthy working atmosphere, gatekeepers become more open (middle right-hand graph). Knowledge may now flow more openly from the alliance to the partner firms. This opens up the opportunity for Partner 1 to start outlearning the alliance (lower right-hand graph) after week 22. As stated above, this private learning is very important for Partner 1. Therefore, it allocates a large amount of scientists to private learning. This is why it already meets its (few) private goals in week 32. Additionally, the many scientists dealing with their research tasks for areas unrelated to the alliance scope put a great deal of effort into private learning. As they have not reached the possible maximum of private patents in week 32, they continue researching further. They overshoot their original target by four times as many, which equals the total maximum number of private patents, 15 patents. As Partner 2 does not show any reaction to the private learning, private learning again occurs in a dis-

[986] The numbers in *italics* mark the parameter changes for the policy run with respect to the base run.

guised way. So far, from Partner 2's perspective, Partner 1 behaves like an honest and frank learning partner.

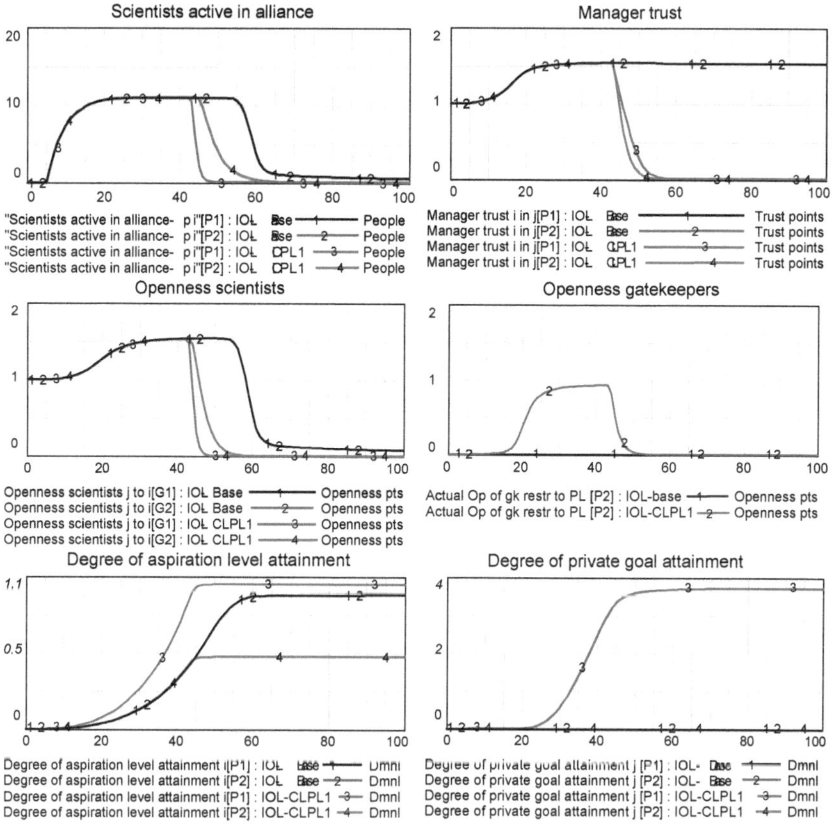

Figure 7-27: Common and Private Learning Policy CLPL1. Unfair Partner 1 and trustworthy Partner 2.[987]

However, in week 42 Partner 1 attains its common goals (line 3 in the lower left-hand graph). This has two effects. First, it withdraws its scientists from the alliance immediately (line 3 in the upper left-hand graph). As in the above policy runs on common learning, from Partner 1's point of view, Partner 2 becomes a competitor again. Second, as a result of this, management prohibits any further communication with the partner's scientists (line 3 in the middle left-hand graph). Reduced scientist communication also has two effects. First, the partner's scientists reciprocate this behavior and reduce their openness (line 4 in the middle left-hand graph). Second, Partner 2's

[987] Note that the lower right-hand graph depicting the 'Degree of private goal attainment' shows a scale on the y-axis from 0-4 and the lower left-hand graph depicting the 'Degree of aspiration level attainment' a scale on the y-axis from 0-1.1.

managers become skeptical. But as Partner 1's managers also do not wish to interact with Partner 2's managers, trust erodes. Partner 2 also withdraws its scientists. With decreasing trust, formal controls like gatekeepers again become more important (line 2 in the middle right-hand graph). Yet, it is too late to prevent Partner 2 from being outlearned.

From Partner 1's point of view the alliance is a complete success. First, it reaches its common goals. It successfully hides its lower actual aspiration level by allocating the number of scientists that its alliance partner expects. When reaching its goals, it ensures that it does not strengthen its former cooperative competitor any further by withdrawing the scientists immediately. Furthermore, it successfully learns privately for business outside the alliance scope. Without the alliance it would not have generated the knowledge required for reaching its private goals.

Partner 2 does not perceive the alliance as a success. It does not understand why Partner 1 withdraws its scientists at a point when the alliance, from its point of view, only has reached about 50% of its goals. In addition, Partner 1 behaved fairly from its point of view; managers and scientists were open and knowledge creation successfully moved forward. Partner 2 does not even know that Partner 1 also used the alliance to learn privately.

7.4.2 Common and Private Learning Policy 2: Unfair Partner 1 and Doubtful Partner 2

The situation is different in the following policy run. Again, Partner 1 behaves unfairly toward its alliance partner. Yet, the partner is doubtful about the partner's integrity. It balances cooperative and competitive aspects by entering the alliance, although it makes sure that the gatekeeper's duties do not dwindle.

More precisely (see Table 7-11), as in the Common and Private Learning Policy CLPL1, Partner 1 has private goals (3 patents). Yet, the managers do not value these as highly as in the previous situation. This is why Partner 1 allocates the normal amount of scientists to work on the private benefits ('Relative scientists active private j PL'). Moreover, as in the previous run, Partner 1's actual common goals correspond to 70% of the common goals agreed on with Partner 2. This time, however, Partner 1 does not allocate more scientists to the alliance.

	Parameter	Policy CLPL2
Partner 1	PrivAL1P1	*3*
	Relative scientist active private j PL	1
	Fraction of actual internally communicated goals L1P1	*0.7*
	Fractional team-building interactions	*0.4*
	Fractional scientist bonus P1	1
Partner 2	Initial trust P2	*0.8*
	Fractional team-building interactions	*0.4*
	Fraction of actual internally communicated goals L2P1	1
	Openness of P2's gatekeeper restrictions to P1's private learning	*0.1*

Table 7-11: Parameter changes for Common and Private Learning Policy CLPL2.[988]

It is assumed that Partner 1's reputation in the network has suffered because of alliances that have failed previously.[989] Partner 2 is aware of this information. Therefore its initial trust ('In trust P2') is lower than normal (80%). Moreover, its policy focuses on strict formal controls. The alliance installs gatekeepers that do not allow any knowledge to flow from the alliance to the partner firms. Yet, their effective openness is not zero but 10% ('Openness of P2's gatekeeper restrictions to P1's private learning'). This is an abstract way of describing that gatekeepers usually prevent any alliance confidential knowledge from flowing to the alliance partner. However, some documents or presentations containing confidential information flow to areas unrelated to the alliance scope where it is of great interest for further research. It is furthermore assumed that gatekeeper openness is not influenced by social controls. Trust does not have an effect on the formal controls.[990]

Figure 7-28 highlights that this learning alliance develops differently from that explained above. An intensive alliance kick-off event with many interactions at the beginning of the alliance increases the ties and intensifies the relationships[991] between alliance participants. Mutual trust immediately rises (see upper right-hand graph). The reinforcing loop R4 – 'Let's meet!' is activated in its upward direction. A high number of interactions enables the mutual trust of both partners' managers to increase further – despite the fact that Partner 1 allocates a considerably lower number of scientists to the alliance (see upper left-hand graph). According to its policy, it allo-

988 The numbers in *italics* mark the parameter changes for the policy run with respect to the base run.

989 This assumption is based on the insight from the network approach. The network in which firms are embedded provides firms with first- or second-hand information. See Section 3.4.3 on the network approach and embeddedness.

990 Technically, this is done by changing the nonlinear function 'T Effect of Relative manager trust i in j on Openness of gatekeeper restrictions to private learning j' to a linear constant function. Independent of the input, the output of this function is always 10% of the total openness. The feedback loop B5 – 'Social and formal controls substitute each other' is consequently deactivated (as in the common learning policy runs, although there it was 'switched off'). This corresponds to a situation in which gatekeeper restrictions are so strict that social controls do not have any effect on formal controls.

991 See Section 3.4.3 on the network approach.

cates only 70% of the agreed scientists. Yet, as managers trust each other, so do the scientists, with the consequence that they openly exchange knowledge with each other. Knowledge exchange drives joint knowledge creation and thus patent generation. Because Partner 1 allocates fewer scientists to the alliance, the groups do not work as efficiently as if it had allocated the appropriate number of scientists. Hence, patent generation is delayed compared to the base run (lower left-hand graph). But as Partner 1 has fewer common (non-communicated) goals than its partner, Partner 1's degree of goal attainment increases at a faster rate than its partner's (line 3 versus line 4).

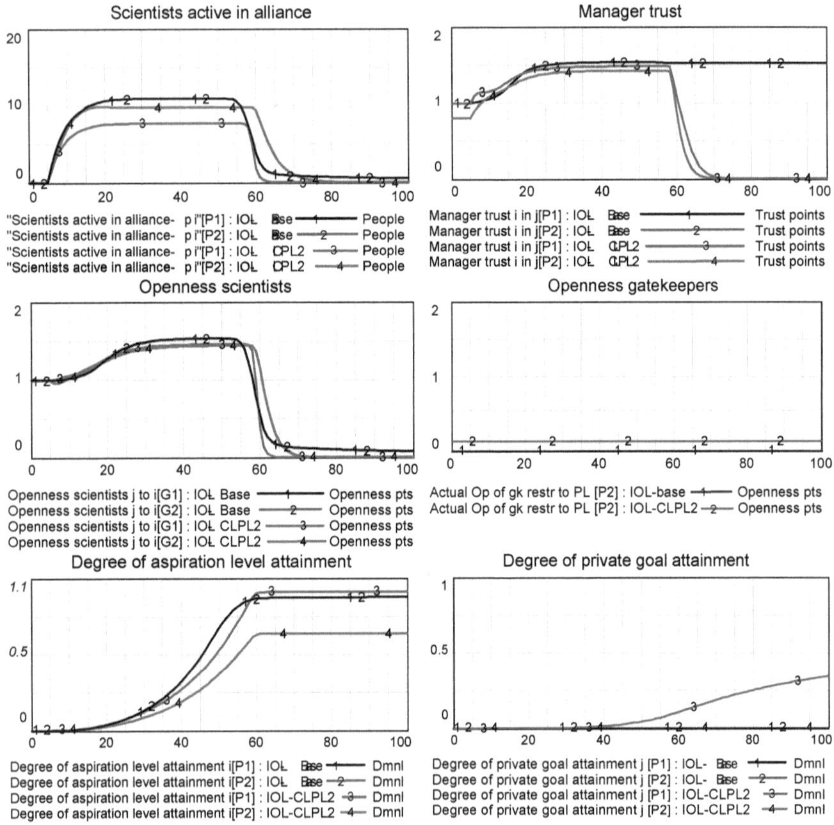

Figure 7-28: Common and Private Learning Policy CLPL2: Unfair Partner 1 and doubtful Partner 2.[992]

Throughout the collaboration, Partner 2's managers' trust in their partner is lower than in the base run. Under normal conditions, if Partner 1 had allocated the agreed

[992] Note that the lower left-hand graph depicting the 'Degree of aspiration level attainment' shows a scale on the y-axis from 0-1.1.

number of scientists, trust would rise to a high level – especially considering the extensive kick-off interactions. Trust suffers for two reasons. First, Partner 1 does not allocate the expected scientists. Second, because trust is lower, so is openness. 'Manager trust' and openness between the scientists affect each other in a reinforcing feedback loop (R5 – 'Traveling trust'). Yet, manager interactions keep trust from diminishing.

Partner 1 reaches its common goals in week 60. The two firms being competitors again from its point of view, it withdraws its scientists and both trust and openness decrease. The alliance is dissolved. Due to the tight gatekeeper restrictions (see middle right-hand graph), not much knowledge spills over to support private knowledge creation. At the time of alliance dissolution, only 10% of the private goals are met. Partner 1 still benefits from the alliance knowledge after alliance dissolution because of the scientists' time delay in understanding the knowledge.[993] Thus, the formal safeguard successfully prevents Partner 2 from being outlearned via the alliance. Insofar, Partner 2's doubt about its partner's integrity was justified. Installing the strict gatekeeper restrictions was the right policy to protect itself from opportunistic behavior. However, its managers were dazzled by the intensive mutual interactions in the beginning of the alliance. Its lower trust level and Partner 1's insufficient scientist allocation should have been a warning signal to it end the alliance. Nevertheless, Partner 2 reaches 70% of its prospective goals. It would not have reached these goals by doing the research on its own. It needed the partner's knowledge base to create these patents.

The dynamics of this policy run allow a deeper structural analysis. From a structural perspective, the loop that slows down private learning is the balancing feedback loop B5 – 'Social and formal controls substitute each other'. It is depicted in Figure 7-29 in a detailed view (see also Figure 6-7 for a feedback loop overview and Section 6.4 for a loop description). If partner j's scientists are open to partner i's scientists, partner i's managers' trust in j's managers increases (or the social control does). The increasing importance of social control reduces the importance of formal controls (like gatekeepers).[994] Weaker formal controls open up the opportunity for partner firm j to learn privately. The closer partner firm j gets to its private goals, the less open j's scientists become as they are no longer interested in sharing any further knowledge with partner i's scientists. Then, firm i's managers' trust declines and their gatekeepers' roles become more important. Yet, at this time, the alliance might be terminated already as firm j has attained its goals. It is too late for the formal controls to prevent any further learning as learning does no longer occurs.

---

993 This remark refers to scientists' relative absorptive capacity. See Section 4.6.1 for further explanations.

994 See Gulati (1995a), p. 93 and also Figure 4-17 which depicts the substitution of social and formal controls over time.

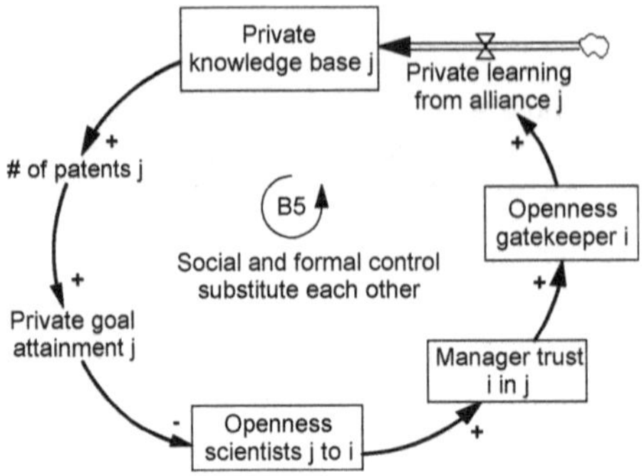

Figure 7-29: Separated feedback loop: B5 – 'Social and formal controls substitute each other'.[995]

Formal controls, if effectively installed in a learning alliance, protect a firm from being outlearned. Therefore, alliance managers should pay attention to installing formal controls and keeping to the contract – despite possible social controls that may arise, substituting formal controls. Considering the separated feedback loop in Figure 7-29, keeping to the contract could be done with two policies with similar results. One policy could be that managers work on weakening this loop. This policy means that trust in the partner's managers should not strongly affect installed formal controls.[996] The second policy option involves managers simply cutting the link between 'Manager trust' and 'Openness gatekeeper', as in this policy run.[997] In other words, a change in social control does not necessarily lead to a change in formal control. In this case the feedback loop B5 is not a closed feedback loop anymore. It is an open loop which no longer generates any feedback. This is why an increased openness between the scientists would increase 'Manager trust', which fosters joint learning (see Proposition 3a). Yet, at the same time it would no longer decrease 'Gatekeeper openness' which ensures that the knowledge flows keep being controlled by the gatekeepers.

7.4.3 Common and Private Learning Policy 3: Unfair Partner 1 and Unfair Partner 2

Both partner firms reveal opportunistic behavior in the Common and Private Learning Policy CLPL3. Both partners enter the cooperative venture for competitive reasons. Besides being interested in common goals, neither partner behaves honestly. As the policy run will show, Partner 1's managers reveal limited foresight[998] because they do not reach their goals: Partner 1 again has private goals ('PrivALP1') and doubles the amount of scientists working on the private goals ('Relative scientists active private j

[995] Source: authors' representation.
[996] Technically, this means that the nonlinear function between 'Manager trust i in j' effecting 'Openness gatekeeper i' is less sensitive to changes in trust.
[997] Technically, this means that the nonlinear function between 'Manager trust i in j' effecting 'Openness gatekeeper i' is transferred into a constant, linear function.
[998] See Section 3.4.4.4.

PL') compared with Common and Private Learning Policy CLPL2, for example (see Table 7-12). To work on the joint patents, Partner 1 only allocates 70% of the agreed scientists. Partner 2 also behaves unfairly, as it is actually only interested in 60% of the agreed goals ('Fraction of actual internally communicated goals L1P2'). Yet, both partners agree to perform 20% more team-building interactions than normal ('Fractional Team-building interactions').

	Parameter	Policy CLPL3
Partner 1	PrivAL1P1	*3*
	Relative scientist active private j PL	*2*
	Fraction of actual internally communicated goals L1P1	1
	Fractional team-building interactions	*0.2*
	Fractional scientist bonus P1	*0.7*
Partner 2	Initial trust P2	1
	Fractional team-building interactions	*0.2*
	Fraction of actual internally communicated goals L1P2	*0.6*

Table 7-12: Parameter changes for Common and Private Learning Policy CLPL3.[999]

The behavior the policy changes generate is depicted in Figure 7-30. As can be seen from the upper left-hand graph, both partners allocate fewer scientists to the alliance than in the cooperative base run. Partner 2 allocates even fewer (line 4) because its actual goals and consequently scientist allocations are, percentage wise, lower (60%) than Partner 1's free rider intentions (70%). Normally, neither partner would accept this low scientist contribution. Yet, extensive interactions at the beginning of the alliance increase the mutual understanding and strengthen the ties between the managers, which is why mutual 'Manager trust' increases (upper right-hand graph). Partner 1 trusts its partner a little bit less than the other way round. Its managers are less trusting because of Partner 2's lower resource contribution. As laid out in Section 4.6.4, trust travels through the organization, which is why scientists start to openly communicate, exchange knowledge, and learn from and with each other. Because of the immediate trust increase right after the start of the alliance, openness also increases faster than in the base run. Yet, neither trust nor openness increases to the base run level (lines 1 and 2). This has two implications. First, knowledge creation is hampered and the goals are met more slowly (lower left-hand graph). Second, being the social control of knowledge flows, trust only slightly replaces the formal control (middle right-hand graph). Gatekeepers' openness only increases slowly, which provides only reduced opportunity for private learning (lower right-hand graph). Partner 1 attains only 10% of its private goals after roughly one year and 30% when Partner 2 withdraws its scientists from the alliance.

[999] The numbers in *italics* mark the parameter changes for the policy run with respect to the base run.

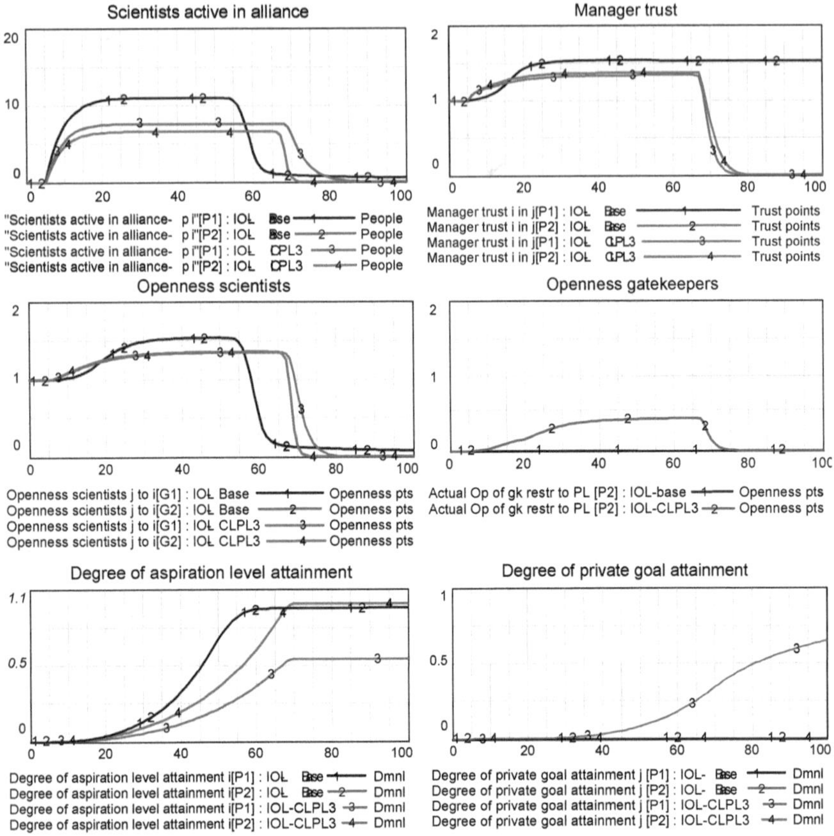

Figure 7-30: Common and Private Learning Policy CLPL3: Unfair Partner 1 and unfair Partner 2.[1000]

Partner 2, seeking only 60% of the goals agreed, reaches its goals in roughly week 70 and immediately withdraws its scientists. The alliance is terminated at a point where Partner 1 has only reached about 60% of its goals. Partner 1's scientists who do research with the alliance knowledge for areas lying outside the alliance scope, continue their work and finally reach 80% of the goals after about half a year after alliance dissolution.

From Partner 1's point of view, the alliance was half a success. Whereas it only reaches 60% of the common goals, it still achieves 80% of its private goals. Partner 1 cannot blame Partner 2 for cheating as it also behaves opportunistically itself. Partner 2 achieves all of its joint goals and prevents itself being outlearned too much. Its

[1000] Note that the lower left-hand graph depicting the 'Degree of aspiration level attainment' shows a scale on the y-axis from 0-1.1.

managers stay skeptical and the gatekeepers avoid too much outflow of knowledge to areas unrelated to the alliance scope.

7.4.4 Research Propositions Revisited: Managerial Implications for Learning with the Partner and from the Alliance

In Sections 7.2.4 and 7.3.3 we resumed policy implications regarding common and private learning separately. In the following we highlight insight from policies that concern both common and private learning. We thus look at the dilemma of cooperative and competitive behavior in learning alliances on two levels: the policy runs analyzed in the sections above lead to insight for opportunistic behavior concerning the subject of common learning and in regard to private learning in a collaboration between research partners.

First, since private learning may occur with a delay, private benefits may still be generated after alliance dissolution. Yet, uncertainty remains regarding two aspects: the first referring to the learning content, and the second referring to the time of alliance dissolution. First, the joint alliance knowledge might not be sufficient for generating private knowledge. When private learning occurs while the alliance is still active, scientists could slightly influence joint research in a promising direction for private learning. Second, the partner that privately learns might transfer its own behavior to the partner's prospective behavior: it may assume that the partner might behave opportunistically as well. Therefore, the cheating partner might be afraid that its partner could dissolve the alliance before reaching the agreed goals. Therefore, they could make an effort to speed up private learning. Common and Private Learning Policy CLPL1 highlights that it is a real incentive for the cheating partner to increase the number of scientists working on private learning. In a large and challenging research project, various steps in the research process may be distributed to more manpower. Under the assumption of doing parallel research, assigning more scientists could ensure that private learning is finished before the alliance meets its joint goals. Therefore, the simulation result from Common and Private Learning Policy CLPL1 supports Proposition 7.

> *Proposition 7: Firms seeking private learning from a learning alliance make an effort to finish private learning before common learning is completed.*

In Section 4.6.3 we stated that formal and social controls substitute each other. While the alliance is progressing, members of both cooperating firms get to know each other better and scientists jointly create new knowledge and apply it to generate patents. All this goes along with interactions between alliance participants; interactions which strengthen interpersonal bonds and thus increase mutual trust.[1001] People for whom social controls like trust become increasingly dominant in an interfirm cooperation pay less attention to formal controls like gatekeepers. We learn from Common and Private Learning Policy CLPL1 that firms cheat on a trustworthy partner with

---

[1001] Interactions can be interpreted as sources of process-based trust. See Zucker (1986), p. 53. See also the in-depth discussion in Section 4.6.4.2 about sources and objects of trust.

fewer formal controls in place. Yet, we learn from Common and Private Learning Policy CLPL2 that weakening or disconnecting the balancing loop B5 – 'Social and formal controls substitute each other' prevents a firm from being outlearned privately by its partner. While gatekeepers strictly control the knowledge flows between the alliance and the firms, trust between managers and scientists still develops. Strengthening social controls is important for the cooperative venture to be a mutual success. Nonetheless, formal controls are important to hamper undesired knowledge outflow. Strict formal controls could be interpreted as a sign of doubt about partner integrity and low trust levels. Managers need to find the right balance between attaching importance to formal controls while stressing the development of mutual trust. The balance depends on firm-specific and partner-specific characteristics, including culture, previous ties, etc.

Although formal controls must not hamper common learning, this would counteract Proposition 1.[1002] Still, we find support for Proposition 8.

> *Proposition 8: Detaching social controls from formal controls ensures a successful learning alliance.*

From Common and Private Learning Policy CLPL3 we learn that cheating is not worth it. In our runs, when both firms enter an alliance with an insincere attitude expressed by hidden intentions concerning scientist allocation or common goals, alliance success is questionable. A smaller number of scientists reduces research effectiveness, which delays research output and thus joint goal attainment. Specifically, as Partner 1 seeks to cheat its partner by doing free riding, Partner 2 unsuspectingly counteracts that plan by actually seeking fewer joint patents. Partner 2 should have stated that it has fewer joint intentions and Partner 1 should have mentioned that it might not have the required scientists at its disposal. Then, the firms could have agreed on a settlement that was favorable for both parties. The alliance could have evolved as with Common Learning Policies CL3a, in which Partner 1 openly communicates to Partner 2 that it is aiming for fewer joint goals and therefore allocates fewer scientists to the alliance. Partner 2 accepts this and the learning alliance becomes a success for both firms. Insight from Common and Private Learning Policy 3 and Common Learning Policy 3a leads to support for Proposition 9.

> *Proposition 9: Open alliance negotiations and clarity about goals and resource contributions lead to the success of a learning alliance.*

With these three research propositions on common and private learning we conclude the analysis of the dynamics of interorganizational learning in alliances. Altogether, we suggest a total of nine research propositions on the basis of our analysis of the dynamics of interorganizational learning. In the following chapter we summarize our results and present suggestions for further research.

[1002] Proposition 1 is explained in Section 7.2.4.

8. Discussion and Conclusion

8.1 Summary

In Section 4.2 we stated that alliance managers accomplish double-loop learning when they appreciate the partner's learning strategy and understand how it interrelates with their own. Managers realize how to play fairly or how to answer an unfair move by the partner firm. The present thesis provides managers whose firms enter learning alliances with insight into how to manage such cooperative ventures. In the following we summarize how we proceeded to contribute to alliance research.

In our introductory Chapter 1, we defined the research problem. Learning alliances become increasingly important for firms' success. Yet, a great majority of them fail. Though alliances, and especially learning alliances, have been subject to research, studies mostly focus on specific building blocks, neglecting a holistic and dynamic view. Therefore, we looked at the whole picture, formalized literature and case study findings, considered competitive and cooperative policies, and analyzed the dynamics of learning alliances over time. We provide a dynamic and consistent approach based on a feedback perspective to study the dilemma of simultaneous cooperative and competitive behavior in learning alliances. The policy analysis led to new insight into learning alliance management. Moreover, based on what we learned from the model, we are able to derive implications for further research. We would not have been able to formulate most of them without considering a feedback loop perspective and formalizing the model.

In Chapter 0 we focused on describing the research approach. It is challenging for managers to fully grasp the underlying complex structures of interfirm collaborations. Complex system structures result in behavior that is oftentimes difficult for decision-makers to understand. Studying current alliance research literature revealed that scholars mostly focus on examining certain aspects of interorganizational collaboration. Though the results provide valuable insight, the information more or less stands side by side. We integrated the findings into an internally consistent and comprehensive quantitative model. Before transferring the insight into the model, we first discussed various modeling approaches, including the System Dynamics modeling method that we applied to conduct our research. To quantify the model we applied insight from a specific learning alliance case study and from the literature on such alliances. We explained the case study approach and introduced the learning alliance case study that we referred to when describing the full model structure in Chapter 4.

In Chapter 3 we intensively reviewed the relevant learning alliance literature. The discussion included competitive advantage and laid out how entering alliances might support firms in achieving it. We then defined the terms interfirm alliances in general and learning alliances in particular, provided a systemization, and talked about motives for firms to enter alliances. Several theories can be applied to explain collaborative partnerships. Yet, as not all of them fully explain how to achieve competitive advantage with alliances, we focused on and clarified their respective insight. When reporting on them, we explicitly referred to their implications for alliances only.

We started with concepts based on the organizational economics paradigm. Transaction cost economics and agency theory provide valuable insight into learning alliance failure: transaction cost economics deals with opportunistic behavior of alliance partners. The possibility of taking advantage of the partner's knowledge might lead firms to opportunism and short-term exploitation of the alliance and then to early alliance dissolution. The theory also provides mechanisms to prevent opportunism, like formal (contractual agreements) and social controls (trust). It illustrates how firms in alliances are challenged to find the balance between cooperative and competitive behavior in alliances. Agency theory's contribution to alliance research is how firms may be motivated to behave opportunistically: alliance partners may have hidden characteristics, hidden information, and hidden intentions when entering the originally cooperative venture. Hidden intentions characterize the partner firms' actual objectives. A firm may seek to free ride, for instance, or it actually has fewer or more common goals than agreed on with the partner.

We then described the strategy-based approaches comprehensively, both from the outside-in (market-based view) and the inside-out perspective (resource-based view). The latter provides especially valuable insight as learning in alliances focuses on strengthening the firms' knowledge base, which can be interpreted as an intangible resource. Intangible resources may fulfill requirements to improve or temporarily sustain a firm's competitive advantage. Yet, the resource-based view is static, which is why we laid out its dynamic descendents. The competence-based view and the knowledge-based view focus on knowledge as being a driver for competitive advantage. Because of knowledge's characteristic of being path-dependent, each firm has its idiosyncratic knowledge base. Firms need the complementary knowledge of other firms to overcome knowledge deficiencies required for a breakthrough innovation.

Further, we looked at the network approach that highlights a firm's position in a network of firms. A firm's reputation within its network may determine whether another firm is interested in engaging in a collaborative venture. Strong ties between firms may increase reciprocal trust – which is considered a social control from the transaction cost economics point of view. Reciprocal trust may lead to an efficient and successful alliance.

As a last theory, we presented findings from game theory. The Prisoner's Dilemma highlights the cooperative and competitive dilemma in which firms find themselves in collaborative settings. Yet, the underlying analytical game theory assumes rational behavior according to homo economicus. Nevertheless, experiments have shown that people do not necessarily behave rationally. Therefore, we presented and discussed findings from behavioral game theory. The approach emphasizes that humans tend to behave fairly and reciprocate fair behavior. This insight is important for explaining that scientists openly share their knowledge with each other in alliances.

In Chapter 4 we discussed the factors that influence long-term development of interorganizational learning in alliances. Insight from the approaches presented in the preceding chapter into the firms' motivations to enter alliances laid the theoretical foundation for discussion on factors determining content and success of interorganizational learning. Not only did we present insight into these determinants based on the learning alliance literature, we also referred to findings from the case study presented in Chapter 0. Where appropriate we translated the results into System Dynamics terminology. Also, we presented the behavior of certain variables over time, according to either literature findings or statements by case study interviewees. After discussing the term interorganizational learning and its influence on organizational performance, we presented what alliance scholars identify as crucial for alliance success or failure. As the literature suggests a wide range of factors, we focused on those that determine firms' cooperative and competitive behavior in learning alliances.

According to the literature, one determining factor is the concept of firms' relative scopes. Firms' scopes determine whether cooperative (common benefits) or competitive (private benefits) objectives reflect the main reasons for firms to enter learning alliances. This may lead to alliance partners emphasizing learning with the partner and/or learning from the partner or the alliance. Yet, on the basis of the theoretical approaches presented in Chapter 2, we found out that common learning is not free of opportunistic behavior: common learning also provides an opportunity to take advantage of the partner firm in interorganizational learning ventures. We presented these options and referred to them in Chapter 7.

Factors influencing interorganizational learning were presented subsequently. These included absorptive capacity and relative absorptive capacity, interorganizational openness, and gatekeepers to support or hinder knowledge flows. We thus especially turned our attention to discussing mutual trust between the alliance participants. Scholars identify trust as a crucial variable in cooperative relationships between competitors. We first defined this intangible variable before discussing its sources and objects.

In Chapter 5 we presented our research propositions. These focused on three main domains: first, on learning with the partner, then on learning from the partner and the alliance, and finally on combining learning with the partner and from the partner and the alliance.

Chapter 6 focused on the simulation model. After discussing the model scope, the chosen time horizon and the reference modes, we presented an aggregated qualitative feedback structure of the model. Then we introduced the quantitative System Dynamics model. We first presented the model subsystem structure representing learning with the partner. We then continued with a description of the structure dealing with learning from the alliance and the partner. We conducted several tests for model validation.

After gaining confidence in the formal model, we simulated it in Chapter 7. We then analyzed implications from various policy runs. Policy analysis was divided into three sections. In each section we first presented the underlying circumstances of the policies, picking up the insight from the preceding chapters: whether the firms enter the alliance with honest or dishonest intentions, or whether they seek to learn jointly or privately. First, we focused on common learning only. Second, we continued with policy analysis, taking only private learning into account. Finally, we presented the results of combined common and private learning policies. Each section ended with an in-depth discussion of managerial insight from the policy runs. They either lead to confirmation of the research propositions presented in Chapter 5 or possibly to their revision.

In the following we summarize the insight we gained from running the formal model and from the policy implications we identified. Furthermore, we suggest further promising directions for future research which we derived from our study.

8.2 Findings and Insight from Model Behavior Concerning Interorganizational Learning Alliances

In this study we synthesized a theoretical framework describing the dynamics of interorganizational learning in alliances. On this basis, we developed an internally consistent formal simulation model applied to analyze the dynamics of firm behavior in collaborative ventures in detail. Here, the focus was laid on alliance partners' competitive and opportunistic actions in an alliance originally designed to collaborate cooperatively. We identified crucial factors influencing learning alliance dynamics, which we summarize in the following. First, we present the insight gained from the analysis of the private learning feedback loop structure. Then we summarize policy implications for preventing private learning. Subsequently, we recapitulate the insight from the model structure into common learning. After that, we present policy implications to prevent opportunism in common learning. The propositions are discussed in depth and refer to the Sections 7.2.4 (common learning), 7.3.3 (private learning), and 7.4.4 (common and private learning).

The insight presented in this study may also lead managers to consider taking advantage of the partner firm. When it is only the managers of one partner who are aware of how to protect themselves from opportunism, they may in turn use these findings for their own advantage while behaving unfairly toward the partner who may be unaware. So, the model also delivers insight into where and how managers may cheat their alliance partner undetectably. Nevertheless, the model purpose is to reveal insight into how managers may mutually design their learning alliance so that it is a joint success.

Insight from the Feedback Loop Structure and Relating Dynamics Regarding Private Learning

The learning alliance literature mainly states that the balance of competitive to cooperative behavior is grounded in the ratio of prospective private to common benefits. Therefore, we first lay out our findings regarding private learning for areas outside the alliance scope.

In-depth literature analysis, insight from our case study interviews, and analysis with the formalized model revealed that private learning may actually only occur after common learning takes place (Proposition 5a).[1003] This means that alliance partners may learn for areas outside the alliance scope only after they first exchanged their knowledge on the alliance research topic. Common knowledge is thus the basis for private learning. Private learning may also occur with a time delay (Proposition 5b)[1004]: jointly generated knowledge in the alliance first needs to be valued by scientists in the parent firm, then assimilated and applied to new fields.[1005] This cannot happen immediately; it takes time. These two findings contradict the current learning alliance literature, which suggests that private learning is finished before common learning occurs. Alliance scholars further assume that private learning is perceived by the alliance partner which is why firms enter learning races. Yet, our findings once again question current alliance research. We learned from model behavior that private learning may actually be completely concealed from the partner (Proposition 6)[1006]. This is why a partner firm being cheated does not necessarily perceive that the partner is using the jointly created alliance knowledge for its own purposes outside the alliance scope – which might actually be prohibited by the alliance contract.

Moreover, we learned from the model that the cheating firm could make an effort to accelerate private learning (Proposition 7)[1007] to ensure being done with it as soon as possible. If it projects its own behavior on the alliance partner, for example, it may not be sure whether or not its alliance partner is also behaving dishonestly. Consequently, it seeks to ensure that it is done with private learning as soon as possible. Meanwhile, it may only learn privately from what has been learned jointly.

Policy Implications Regarding the Prevention of Private Learning
We learned from the simulation model that an alliance partner firm may apply policies that reveal opportunistic behavior fostering private learning. In Section 7.3 we tested unfair policies with which managers try to take advantage of the alliance for their firms' businesses outside the alliance scope. We found out how a firm may protect itself from being outlearned in such a way. Model runs suggested that strict formal contractual controls may hinder or even prevent private learning from an alliance (Proposition 4)[1008]. Formal controls like gatekeepers, for instance, control the knowledge flows between the partner firms and the alliance. Gatekeepers define which knowledge needs to be marked as alliance confidential and thus must not flow to research or business areas outside the model scope.

We imply from the simulation runs that detaching social from formal controls ensures a successful learning alliance for both partners (Proposition 8)[1009]. Usually, the stronger the bonds between alliance participants become, the more the participants trust each other. The more important these social controls become, the less dominant formal controls become. Less dominant formal controls increase the opportunity to learn privately from the alliance. Hence, if social and formal controls are detached

1003 See Section 7.3.3.
1004 See Section 7.3.3.
1005 According to the definition for absorptive capacity by Cohen and Levinthal (1990), p. 128.
1006 See Section 7.3.3.
1007 See Section 7.4.4.
1008 See Section 7.3.3.
1009 See Section 7.4.4.

from one another, social controls may still increase while formal controls need to stay high, thereby prohibiting knowledge flows from the alliance to the partner firms.

Insight from the Feedback Loop Structure and Relating Dynamics Regarding Common Learning
The current learning alliance literature only considers opportunistic behavior concerning private learning. Yet, we learned from model simulations that competitive behavior not only arises in case of private learning. Collaborative settings also offer opportunities for competitive actions. We learned from the model that at least two further policies exist which enable a parent firm to cheat its partner in a learning alliance: a firm could either desire to free ride (Propositions 2.1a and 2.1b)[1010] or have hidden goals by actually seeking a different number of common goals than agreed on in the contract (Propositions 2.2b and Proposition 2.2c)[1011]. In both cases, moderate cheating is accepted by the alliance partner (Propositions 2.1a and 2.2c)[1012]. Yet, when the cheating partner overacts and allocates too few resources from the partner's point of view, for example, mutual partner trust suffers and the alliance is terminated early (Propositions 2.1b and 2.2b)[1013]. We found that the unfair partner which actually has fewer common goals than agreed and would consequently allocate fewer scientists to the alliance may disguise its insincere behavior by allocating the amount of scientists that is expected by the partner firm (Proposition 2.2d)[1014].

Policy Implications Regarding the Prevention of Opportunism in Common Learning
The opportunities we identified for cheating in the area of common learning provide alliance managers with insight into how a dishonest alliance partner may take advantage of the situation. We did not discover policies to prevent moderate unfair behavior concerning common learning per se. Yet, we learned from the model that if the cheating parent firm overacts and allocates too few resources, for example, the alliance partner should be on its guard and analyze its partner's integrity. If the cheating partner has (hidden) fewer common goals and reaches them early, its partner does not reach the goals agreed on in the alliance contract. Hence, mutual trust suffers. According to the network approach, the cheating firm's reputation as a trustworthy alliance partner suffers within the network. So, even if cheating might be beneficial in the short-term, in the long-term the unfair partner might be confronted with difficulties in finding another partner with complementary knowledge for joint research.

We learned from the model behavior that mutual trust is a critical variable in the context of interorganizational learning in learning alliances. Thus, we found out that a trusting environment facilitates the cooperation and fosters common goal attainment (Proposition 3a)[1015]. Alliance managers should invest enough time to build trust between the alliance participants. Knowledge exchange between competitors is a sensitive task that requires a trustworthy relationship.

[1010] See Section 7.2.4.
[1011] See Section 7.2.4.
[1012] See Section 7.2.4.
[1013] See Section 7.2.4.
[1014] See Section 7.2.4.
[1015] See Section 7.2.4.

Furthermore, we observed that a tipping point determines the shift from a virtuous to a vicious cycle. If the virtuous cycle kicks in, trust increases which results in a stable alliance relationship. If the vicious cycle kicks in, trust depletes and the alliance is terminated. The tipping point implies that one alliance partner trusting the other is not enough to enter a stable alliance (Proposition 3b)[1016]. This means that, if one partner's trust in the other is at a relatively low level, trust-building activities in the early phase of alliance interactions are necessary to push the system above the tipping point and lay the foundation for a trustworthy alliance relationship (Proposition 3c)[1017]. Considering this, according to a study, lack of trust is the reason for alliance failure in 45% of the cases,[1018] these propositions clarify once more how fragile the construct of mutual trust in collaborative relationships is. Alliance managers need to pay attention to trust-building activities between scientists and managers of the participating firms.

We also realized from model behavior that mutual trust does not diminish when the alliance partners state their joint goals frankly. Hence, honesty with respect to the common goals and resource contributions leads to joint success (Propositions 2.2a and 9)[1019]. Besides honesty, it is also necessary for the firms' scientists to be able to share their knowledge with each other openly (Proposition 1)[1020]. Only open knowledge exchange enables the scientists to integrate their complementary knowledge bases and learn jointly.

8.3 Implications for Future Research

In addition to the findings summarized in the sections above, we identify implications for future model-based and feedback-based alliance research. Most of the implications derive from our feedback analysis with the formalized model. They relate to three main issues: policy tests, model boundary, and model structure. We present these in the following. Note that the implications oftentimes arise from shifting the focus of analysis or the aim of a possible analysis.

Policy Tests

Even though we presented a large number of various policy tests in this study the formal model offers a wider range of possible tests. In the following we suggest further promising policy tests. It might be one firm's policy to only start cheating on the alliance partner after the alliance has started successfully, for example. Thus, the partner firm behaves honestly in the relationship until enough trust has been established to support more cheating. Cheating could entail free riding, having different common goals from those agreed on in the contract, or private learning.

Likewise, as the model is capable of visualizing different milestones the partner firms are working on, cheating could also start when the partners reach a new common

[1016] See Section 7.2.4.
[1017] See Section 7.2.4.
[1018] See Section 4.6.4 on trust in alliances.
[1019] See Sections 7.2.4 and 7.4.4, respectively.
[1020] See Section 7.2.4.

milestone. Underlying circumstances here could be that the cheating firm is convinced that free riding, for example, could be done more effectively after reaching a common intermediate goal. Also, when simulating multiple milestones, policies could be modified so that opportunities for private learning only arise after a certain common milestone has been reached. This way, private learning would only occur after the alliance has successfully accomplished important parts of common learning.

Alternatively, further scenarios could be simulated in addition to that presented in Scenario PL2c (see Section 7.3.2). Scenario PL2c tested the effect of relative absorptive capacity on private learning. Firms' knowledge overlaps could be varied, for example, focusing on a variation of the firms' relative scope. This scenario could provide insight into how difficulties might arise when the alliance scope is very small and common learning is delayed. To give another example, the firms' knowledge overlap might be very high, and consequently, there is not much to learn from each other – although the common objectives are high. Alternatively, in another scenario, one could challenge the relevance of the alliance knowledge for private learning. The scenario could, for instance, question the effects of a firm allocating a lot of scientists for private learning that are consequently lacking when it comes to joint knowledge creation (i.e., the firm is free riding). The firm risks its integrity toward its partner firm and then notices that the knowledge is not of great relevance for areas outside the model scope.

These are just a few examples of policies and scenarios. The model provides the possibility of generating even more alternatives.

Model Structure

Future research suggestions also refer to studies on model structure. We present four further areas for analysis. The first suggestion relates to the effect of gatekeepers' tasks. In the current model, gatekeepers' controls of knowledge flows either influence knowledge exchange of the partners' scientists for common learning (represented by the parameter 'Openness of P1's gatekeeper restrictions to P1's knowledge sharing', here specifically denoted for Partner 1; a similar variable exists for Partner 2), or gatekeepers control the knowledge flows from the jointly created alliance knowledge base to the firms' knowledge bases (represented by the stock 'Openness of gatekeeper restrictions to j's private learning – i'; it is denoted in a more general way using indices). So, when common learning is restricted by gatekeepers, then private learning is automatically restricted: joint knowledge does not build up fast, which immediately restricts private learning. We did not explicitly model this relationship. Therefore, the effect of 'Openness of i's gatekeeper restrictions to i's knowledge sharing' on 'Openness of gatekeeper restrictions to j's private learning - i' can be assumed to be equal to one. Yet, further research might examine whether gatekeeper openness for common learning directly affects gatekeeper openness for private learning and/or vice versa in a nonlinear way.

Second, more research could be conducted on examining the fourth-order feedback loop structure on 'Manager trust' presented in Section 7.2.3.4 (see Figure 7-15). Further in-depth analysis of this structure might lead to additional insight into the behavior of 'Manager trust' in this specific example. Yet, besides gaining understanding of this structure for the specific purpose of mutual trust in alliances, further studies could lead to valuable insight into a more general level: the dynamic interrelation of a highly symmetric fourth-order reinforcing feedback loop, two symmetrical second-order reinforcing feedback loops, each consisting of four first-order balancing loops, has not been dealt with in the literature on system archetypes. Though the archetype 'Success to the successful'[1021] consists of two reinforcing loops the underlying story is different. Policy-designers and decision-makers might benefit if it turns out that this structure is a common system structure in the real world that leads to counterintuitive behavior. Hence, this investigation not only advances research on the development of mutual trust but would also enhance insight into the theory of nonlinear dynamics and complex systems.

Third, research on the structure of the fourth-order feedback loop might also include further analysis of the related phase plot depicted in Figure 7-17. Currently, the two-dimensional phase plot illustrates a simplified version of the actual underlying structure of the fourth-order feedback loop. Because of the four-stock system, a more accurate way of representing the system structure in a phase plot would be three-dimensional. It could be that a three-dimensional representation would lead to additional insight for both, the interrelationship of mutual trust and, more generally, the interrelationships of four stocks in a complex system.

Fourth, the model could be calibrated to real world data of a specific learning alliance. If such data were available, the model could be adjusted to an actual alliance, and managers could learn from the model regarding their specific case.[1022]

Finally, the present model structure could be simplified. Simplification is a challenging but promising task regarding further understanding. Substructure analysis of 'Manager trust' (see Section 7.2.3.4) provided valuable insight for a better understanding of the interplay of the interrelated variables and feedback loops leading to the tipping point. Hence, oftentimes, smaller models are more illuminating to people than larger ones.[1023] If the structure generating the essential dynamics of interorganizational learning could be further simplified to maybe two or three feedback loops, insight might be even more comprehensible for learning alliance managers.

Model Boundary

In Section 6.2 we presented and discussed the model boundary. The model boundary always illustrates the scope of the model. Depending on the aim of the study, the formal model should include or exclude variables. An overview of the model bound-

---

1021 The archetype 'Success to the successful' describes two activities that compete for limited resources. The more successful one activity becomes, the more support it receives. The other activity becomes less important. See Senge (1990), p.385. For system archetypes in general, see Senge (1990), pp.93-114 and 378-390 and Wolstenholme (2003).

1022 See Sterman (2000), p. 897 for model calibration.

1023 See also Repenning who illustrates this by the example of reactions to a one-stock model on how organizations react to an ongoing stream of interruptions to normal activities. See Rudolph and Repenning (2002) for the article and Repenning's comments on this publication in Repenning (2003), pp. 311-314.

ary like the model boundary chart in Table 6-1 depicts which areas are left out or which are included in the model. Consequently, depending on the model purpose, the boundary should be enhanced or reduced. Referring to this chart, we present ideas to further model enhancement. As the model is designed in modular substructures, model structure could easily be adjusted.

First, for example, after fully understanding the dynamics of interorganizational learning between two partners, as many alliances represent networks it could be illuminating to include more partners in the simulation. From a technical point of view the current model needs to be adapted to this enhancement by supplementing current subscript indices 'i' and 'j' with further subscripts. Then the equations need to be adjusted accordingly. Yet, this enhancement would increase model complexity considerably.

Second, as indicated in Section 6.2, scholars identify a relationship between learning and a shift of relative bargaining power in an alliance.[1024] According to INKPEN AND BEAMISH, a major change in the partner relationship status occurs when one partner increases its bargaining power over the partner. This may occur when a partner firm acquires "sufficient knowledge and skills to eliminate a partner dependency"[1025] and make the alliance obsolete. Bargaining power is important for alliance negotiations. As we excluded prior negotiations from our model purpose we did not consider bargaining in the model. Yet, if multiple milestones are being simulated, bargaining power could be included. Bargaining plays an important role, for example, when alliance partners negotiate continued joint research after reaching a milestone. Research on alliance negotiations considers game theory, which is why insight from behavioral game theory could provide further insight for modeling the appropriate structure.

Third, bargaining power also plays an important role for firm size. In the current model, it is assumed that firms have an opportunity to allocate equal research inputs to the alliance. Yet, when a large firm cooperates with a small one, firm size not only has an effect on possible bargaining power between the allies but also on resource allocation possibilities.[1026] Larger firms oftentimes are able to allocate more manpower to the alliance than small firms. This might influence the perception of the balance between learning alliance input (like scientists, for instance) and alliance output (e.g., patents), and consequently the partners' perception of fairness.

Fourth, another factor that might be interesting to study is cultural differences between international learning alliances.[1027] Cultural difference might, for example, chal-

---

[1024] See, for example, Hamel (1991), pp. 87-88, Inkpen and Beamish (1997), pp. 183-187, or Larsson et al. (1998), p. 291.

[1025] Inkpen and Beamish (1997), p. 177.

[1026] It is often the case in biotechnology alliances, for example, that a large pharmaceutical company collaborates with a relatively small biotech firm. See, for example, Forrest and Martin (1992), Shan et al. (1994), Powell et al. (1996), DeCarolis and Deeds (1999), Baum et al. (2000), Lerner et al. (2003), or Rothaermel and Deeds (2004).

[1027] See, for example, Nahavandi and Malekzadeh (1988), Levinson and Asahi (1995), Child (1998), and Sukh Pak and Park (2004).

lenge fairness perceptions between the partners, as well as negotiations prior to the start of the alliance.

Fifth, in this study we discussed and interpreted alliance outcome with regard to the firms' reputation in the network in which they are embedded.[1028] It could reveal further insight first to include a variable like 'Parent i's reputation', and second to endogenize it. This could be of interest when considering multiple alliance milestones.

Sixth, a further model structure change could include a relationship between trust-building activities and the desire of a firm to actually behave opportunistically. Trust-building activities strengthen the bonds between alliance participants. Thus, these activities could ultimately convince a partner who is initially prepared to cheat to behave (more) honesty in the relationship: this could affect free riding intentions, sincere goal negotiations, or private learning objectives.

Seventh, changing the current model structure by including a relationship between trust and a perceived need to meet could lead to further insight. When alliance members perceive decreasing mutual trust, they could decide to counteract it by calling meetings or conferences to avoid engaging in the downward spiral of decreasing trust.

Finally, financial aspects could be included in the model. Besides considering meaningful financial metrics indicating the alliance's performance, for instance, long-term returns of the invested resources and their opportunity costs could also be calculated to estimate economic rents as an indication of the appropriateness of entering the learning alliance from a strategic perspective.

Underlying Theory
We learned from the model that private learning may be concealed from the partner firm. Consequently, explorative studies on private learning could reveal further insight into learning race situations in learning alliances.

In this study we illustrated the dilemma of competitive and cooperative learning in alliances. First, we showed the origins of opportunistic behavior in alliances leading to competitive learning. It starts with an insincere attitude toward common goals objectives and it continues with the intention to work on private goals. Second, we proposed policies with the intention of restricting the partner's private learning aspirations with formal controls. Therefore, last but not least, further research could focus on identifying policies to prevent a partner firm from being outlearned at the beginning of the relationship. This could reduce transaction costs to monitor partner behavior and could lead firms to collaborative success. Research insight into this matter would leapfrog alliance research and could save firms monitoring costs.

[1028] See, for example, Granovetter (1985) and Chiles and McMackin (1996).

8.4 Conclusion

With this model we have laid the groundwork for a dynamic perspective on learning alliance research, applying case study driven experimental theory-building in a virtual world. We analyzed the dynamics of learning alliances with a formal model. It captures the behavior of interrelated variables from a feedback perspective. It is a white-box model that is comprehensible. Due to its modular structure, the model boundary could be easily adjusted to other model purposes. Furthermore, the model is validated by a case study and it consists of results of the latest alliance and alliance-related research. Related research entails, for example, behavioral game theory, that reveals insight for the perception of fairness and reciprocity – both of which are important in alliances characterized by the challenge of finding the balance between cooperation and competition. Cooperation and competition are represented by the two types of learning in alliances, common learning and private learning. We suggest implications for how to design learning alliance policies so that they successfully support mutual common learning. At the same time, policies should focus on decreasing the risk of being outlearned by the partner. With this work we call for a focus on finding the right policies that simultaneously support joint learning and prevent private learning. In the long-term, not only would cooperating firms strengthen their competitive position with their partner without taking advantage of the partner, they would also stress that their alliance management focuses on being a loyal alliance partner. Firms considering our propositions to design their alliance policies would increase the quality of their alliance outcomes and thus increase the share of successful alliances.

9. Appendix

9.1 Interview Questions

1. Research Alliance Background
1.1 Questions referring to the personal task in the alliance
- How many research alliances have you joined so far?
- How did get involved in this particular research alliance?
- How long is your expected working period in this research alliance?
- What is your personal task in this research alliance?

1.2 Background to this alliance (Manager's questionnaire only)
- How many research projects is your company involved in at this time?
- Has there been a previous alliance with this partner?
  If yes: What was the alliance about?
- What was the initial trigger for this alliance?
- Who initiated this research alliance?
- Are the parent companies of this alliance still legally independent from one another?
- Is the alliance a legally independent organization?
- What kind of alliance in legal terms is this research alliance? (research alliance, strategic alliance, JV,...)

1.3 General background of this particular research alliance (Manager's questionnaire only)
- What is the name of the joint research project?
- When was the starting date of this project?
- What is the project's duration?
- What is the project's content?
- Do project milestones exist?
- How many milestones are there in this project?
- What are the milestones' contents? (What is the project process?)
- What milestone do you currently work on?
- How would you estimate the project's importance for the company's long-term success?

2. Goals
2.1 Project goals
- What should be developed over the course of the project? How do you measure the alliance's success? (common product/patent?)
- How do you measure alliance success? (Scientist's questionnaire only)
- Do you split up the alliance success at the end of the alliance between your company and the partner company?
- Generally speaking, when would you talk about a "successful alliance"? (Manager's questionnaire only)
- Generally speaking, how would you describe a successful alliance? (Scientist's questionnaire only)

- Can you name a percentage of goal attainment when a alliance could be considered as successful?
- When would you talk about a "failed alliance"? (Manager's questionnaire only)
- Can you name a percentage of goal attainment when a alliance could be considered as unsuccessful or failed? (Manager's questionnaire only)
- Could you please describe how your firm and the alliance partner firm came to the agreement on how to divide the alliance outcome between the two companies? (Manager's questionnaire only), (easy or difficult negotiations, etc.)
- Did you register the cost for the alliance negotiations? (Manager's questionnaire only) If yes: Did you put the cost for the duration of the negotiation into relation to the strived for alliance goals?
  If yes: Do you discount the alliance goals considering the time of the most probable project end?
- How did you record the alliance agreement? (Manager's questionnaire only), (in a contract, verbally, etc.)

2.2 Private and common goals

- Did your company commit to certain goals for this alliance (common goals)?
  If yes: Which are they?
- Do the common goals refer to certain corporate division at your partner with which you would like to combine one of your own corporate divisions?
  If yes:
  Which divisions (knowledge base) of your partner company do the common goals refer to?
- Besides the goals that refer to in the alliance (common goal), do goals exist that could be beneficial to your parent company (private goal)?
  If yes:
  Which are they?
- Which of the partner company's divisions (knowledge base) do these private goals refer to?
- To what extent do common and private goals influence the number your people working in the alliance? (Manager's questionnaire only)

2.3 Change of goals (Manager's questionnaire only)

- Could you please name some examples for effects of increasing the goals for the alliance, both private and common?

2.4 Open/hidden goals

- Do you communicate your alliance goals to the partner firm?
- Why do you/do you not communicate your goals to your partner?
  If yes:
  To what extent do communicated common goals correspond with actual (for example, the goals of the strategic planning division) goals?
  If yes:
  Why do communicated and actual goals (not) correspond with each other?

- Does the number / type of goals that your company has communicated to your employees in the alliance correspond with the actual goals of your company? (Manager's questionnaire only)
- Can the actual goals change over time?
  If yes:
  What does the change of goals depend upon?
- Are the goal changes newly negotiated with the partner? (Manager's questionnaire only)
  If yes:
  When would this be done? (for instance, after reaching a milestone?)
  If yes: Could you please describe how you reach an agreement? (Bargaining Game, playing tricks, honesty in the communication of goals)
- For how important do you estimate openness and honesty in the agreement process on common goals for the long-term success of the learning alliance?

2.5 Own firm's goal attainment

- Do you check your company's goal attainment in the project?
  If yes:
  When do you check your goal attainment? (when reaching a milestone or when working on a milestone)
- How do you measure the goal attainment within a milestone?
- What does the goal attainment influence in the alliance?

2.6 Partner's goal attainment

- Is it important for you to know-how well your partner is doing in reaching his goal?
- Why is it (not) important for you?
- Can you register/record/monitor/notice how your partner is doing on reaching his goals?
  If yes:
  How do you monitor your partner's goal attainment?
- Do you put your goal attainment and your partner's in relation to each other?
- Why do you (not) do it?
  If yes:
  What are possible effects of such a metric?
  What does this relation influence?
- What are the consequences from the comparison of your and your partner's goal attainment for the allocation of your own employees in the alliance?

3. Scientists

- How many employees worked on the project at the beginning of the alliance?
- How many employees work on the alliance at this moment?
- Could you please name the number of your and your partner's employees who have worked on the alliance?
- From which divisions did your employees come from? What are their specific knowledge competences? (corporate division, employee competences, ...)

- What does the decision on how many people work on the common research project depend on? (private and common goals, trust, project manager,...)
- Can the number of people vary over the course of the project?
  If yes:
  Why?
- From what does a possible change in the number of people on the project depend on?
- What is the percentage relation of people of your company to people of your partner's company in the alliance?
- What is the reason for this proportion?
- Have you agreed on this proportion in a contract?
- To what extent does the employee proportion correspond/match with the distribution of reached goals/patents in the end of the partnership?
- What do you think of an unequal share of both parent firms' scientists to the common goals/patents in the alliance?
- How would you react in the case of an unequal number of people of both parents in the alliance considering an equal number of goals/patents to be worked on?
- Consider your partner sends more scientists into the alliance as agreed on in the contract. How would you react?

4. Learning

4.1 Partner learns from own firm's knowledge base

- What kind of special knowledge does your company bring into this partnership?
- Were there situations in which you had to use knowledge of specifically other divisions of your company that originally you would have not counted relevant for the alliance?
  If yes:
  When was that the case?
  If yes:
  From which corporate divisions / knowledge bases did this knowledge originate?
  If yes:
  How did you deal with this knowledge that was originally not project-relevant?
  Have you openly shared it with your alliance partner?
- Why have you (not) shared it with your partner? (Scientist's questionnaire only)
- Do you think that your partner could use this knowledge for other projects than this particular research alliance project? (for private goals – for example, for other markets)
  If yes:
  What could he use this knowledge for?
  (for private use? – for instance, with competitors)

4.2 We learn with our partner for the project

- What kind of specific knowledge-base/ knowledge does your partner bring into this partnership?
- Have you learned from the people of your partner firm?
- From which areas / divisions have you learned from your alliance partner's scientists?
- How important was it for you to fully understand your partner's knowledge contribution?
- Why is it not/little/very important?
- Could you please explain when you have completed the learning of project-relevant knowledge from your partner?
- Why do you think it happened at this particular moment?
- Could you please explain how the project-relevant knowledge you have acquired from your partner has developed over time?

4.3 Private Learning from the partner for areas outside of the alliance scope

- Is the knowledge acquired from your partner also relevant for areas in your organization outside the alliance? (for gaining private benefits)
- In which of your company's divisions could this knowledge be useful?
- Could you please explain how your company's private knowledge has developed due to learning from your partner?
- When did you start and finish private learning from your partner?
- Was it part of your company's goal to learn this "private" information from your partner?
- Did your company inform your partner about this private learning intent?
- For how important do you estimate this private learning for your company's success?
- Was there knowledge in the alliance that was not shared?
  If yes:
  What kind of knowledge was that?

4.4 Learning with each another

- Is common knowledge critical/relevant for successfully completing the project?
- Would you say there has developed a common knowledge base in the meantime of your and your partner's scientists?
- How would you describe the common knowledge base? What is its context?
- Since when does the common knowledge base exist?
- Why does the common knowledge base exist since then?
- Could you please sketch and explain how the common knowledge base has developed since then?
- What does common learning foster?
- Does common learning influence provable influence on success?

5. Trust

- How would you describe the alliance between the members of both companies?

- How do you evaluate the importance of reciprocal trust between the scientists / managers for the project's success

5.1 Trust between managers (Manager's questionnaire only)
- How has trust developed between the managers of both partner companies?
- What fosters trust between the managers of the partner companies? (causes for trust)
- How would you evaluate the importance of degree of goal attainment for fostering reciprocal trust between the managers?
- How does trust in the manager colleagues develop with increasing goal attainment?
- What effects increasing (decreasing) trust between the managers of both partners? (Effect of trust)
- Does reciprocal trust between the managers influence employee allocation to the project?
- Could you please explain and mark the relationship between manager trust and the willingness to allocate resources to the alliance?
- Why does the relationship look like this?

5.2 Trust between scientists (Scientist's questionnaire only)
- Do you trust your partner's scientists?
- How has trust between the scientists developed so far?
- According to your perception, what fosters trust between scientists?
- What kind of importance does the commitment toward the project have on the trust between the scientists?
- How does trust between scientists of your company develop toward scientists of your partner scientists if your company sends more and more scientists in the alliance?
- Why does the relationship develop as indicated?
- What effects increased (decreased) trust between scientists?

6. Project commitment (Scientist's questionnaire only)
6.1 Scientist level
- Do you feel committed to the joint research project?
  If yes:
  How do you feel committed toward the project?
  If yes:
  How do you (as scientist) get committed toward a project?
  What drives your commitment?

6.2 Interaction of project attachment and trust: Commitment influencing trust
- Does project commitment influence scientists' trust toward the scientists of the partner company?

- Is there an effect of project commitment on trust on the scientist level?
  If yes:
  What importance does project commitment play on trust on the scientist level?
  If yes:
  Could you please explain the relationship of commitment toward the project and trust between scientists?

6.3 Interaction of project attachment and trust: Trust influencing commitment

- Does trust between the scientists influence scientists' project commitment?
  Is there an effect of reciprocal trust on project commitment?
  If yes:
  What kind of importance does a balanced number of employees of both partners have on trust between the scientists?
- Could you please explain and mark how the scientists' commitment develops if trust between the scientists increases.

6.4 Further causes for project commitment

- Does belief in project success influence project commitment?
- In your estimation, what importance does the belief in project success have on project commitment?
  Why is there such importance?
- What kind of importance does an increasing goal attainment have on scientists' commitment toward the project?
- Could you please explain this?
- Could you please explain the scientists' commitment toward the project with an increasing degree of goal attainment?
- Could you please sketch and explain how the commitment of scientists toward the project has developed since the start of the project?

7. Personal questions

- Have experiences from previous alliances helped you in managing this alliance?
  Why?
- Were there unsuccessful alliances?
  Why?
- In your estimation, what are the most important factors for a successful management of such learning alliances?
- Who else would you recommend me to talk about these issues?
- What else do you think I should be asking during the interviews to get a better understanding of these issues?
- Other documents
- Other?

9.2 Model Equations

****
.Alliance knowledge base
****

(002) Alliance knowledge base= INTEG (Alliance learning-Alliance unlearning, Init Alliance knowledge)
Units: Knowledge points
The employees' knowledge base is measured in knowledge points. The stock is increased by learning, called alliance learning. The stock is decreased by the outflow called alliance unlearning.

(003) Alliance learning=Normal learning*Alliance research tasks*Effective learning
Units: Knowledge points / week
Alliance learning increases the stock Alliance knowledge base. It is determined by the Alliance research tasks being done, the Normal learning and the Effective learning.

(004) Alliance unlearning= Alliance knowledge base*Normal unlearning rate
Units: Knowledge points / week
This rate decreases the stock Alliance knowledge base through unlearning and forgetting.

(005) Effect of knowledge base on learning=T Effect of knowledge on learning(Relative alliance knowledge base)
Units: Dmnl
The higher the Relative knowledge base, the higher the capacity to absorb new knowledge, or to learn.

(006) Effective learning=Min effective learning+(1-Min effective learning)*Effect of knowledge base on learning*0.1
Units: Dmnl
Effective learning indicates how much is actually learned. If there is no common knowledge the minimum amount is learned.

(007) Normal unlearning rate=0.005
Units: 1/week [0,1]
The parameter Normal unlearning rate refers to the phenomenon that people forget and unlearn things over a certain period of time. Here, it is assumed that people forget 0.5% of their knowledge per week.

(008) Reference alliance knowledge base=150
Units: Knowledge points [0,2000,10]
The Reference knowledge base indicates how difficult it is to nest oneselves inside the matter and networks of a particular research project.

(009) Relative alliance knowledge base=Alliance knowledge base/Reference alliance knowledge base
Units: Dmnl
The Relative knowledge base is a normalizing variable. It is dimensionless and is calculated by dividing the actual Alliance knowledge base by the Reference knowledge base. This variable is used for calculating how many patents the scientists generate.

(010) T Effect of knowledge on learning([(0,0)-(1,1)],(0,0.01),(0.211009,0.0526316),(0.330275,0.149123),(0.446483,0.346491),(0.519878,0.526316),(0.574924,0.657895),(0.636086,0.789474),(0.733945,0.890351),(0.819572,0.947368),(1,1))
Units: Dmnl

This table is an S-shaped function indicating that the more scientists know about a certain topic the easier it is for them to learn new things about it. This goes along with the concept of absorptive capacity.

****
.Commitment to learn and work - scientists
****

(012) "Actual own expected # of alliance patents i"[G1]="Internally communicated # of patents i"[P1]"Actual own expected # of alliance patents i"[G2]="Internally communicated # of patents i"[P2]
Units: Patents
How many patents the scientists expect to be working on depends on the Internally communicated patents.

(013) Change in commitment scientists i[Group]=STEP(Commitment gap scientists i[Group]/ Time to form commitment, Time of alliance start)
Units: Knowledge points/People/week/week
This biflow either increases or decreases the stock of Commitment to learn and work for both parents.

(014) Commitment gap scientists i[Group]=Indicated commitment i[Group]-Commitment to learn and work scientists i[Group]
Units: Knowledge points/People/week
There is a gap between the actual and the Indicated commitment that needs to be closed.

(015) Commitment to learn and work scientists i[Group]= INTEG (Change in commitment scientists i[Group],In Commitment[Group])
Units: Knowledge points/People/week
This stock accumulates the scientists' Commitment to learn and work on the alliance tasks. It is increased and decreased by the biflow Change in commitment group i.

(016) Effect of alliance goal attainment on commitment[Group]=T Effect of alliance goal attainment on perceived alliance success(Goal attainment relative to expected[Group])
Units: Dmnl
It calculates the actual effect of goal attainment on the scientists' commitment.

(017) Effect of Degree of goal attainment on Initial excitement[Group]=T Effect of Degree of goal attainment on Initial excitement(Goal attainment relative to expected[Group])
Units: Dmnl
It calculates the actual effect of goal attainment on initial excitement.

(018) "Expected common # of alliance patents by scientists i"[G1]="Actual own expected # of alliance patents i"[G1]+"Agreed upon # of expected patents i"[P2]"Expected common # of alliance patents by scientists i"[G2]="Actual own expected # of alliance patents i"[G2]+"Agreed upon # of expected patents i"[P1]
Units: Patents
What scientists think on how many patents they work on depends on what the own firm tells them as the internal goals plus the patents that the partner gets according to the contract.

(019) Expected patents based on honeymoon[Group]=DELAY N("Expected common # of alliance patents by scientists i"[Group], Expected time to reach goals[Group], "Expected common # of alliance patents by scientists i"[Group], Order)
Units: Patents
This variable states the expected number of patents by the scientists.

(020) Expected time to reach goals[Group]=ZIDZ("Expected common # of alliance patents by scientists i"[Group], (Normal expected research output[Group]*"Research output per unit of effort (Scaling factor)"))
Units: weeks
The scientists working in the alliance have an expectation regarding the weeks in which they may reach their goals. It can be calculated.

(021) Goal attainment relative to expected[Group]=XIDZ("# of alliance patents", Expected patents based on honeymoon[Group],0)
Units: Dmnl
This variable calculates the degree of goal attainment considering the # of alliance patents divided by the Expected # of alliance patents based on honeymoon.

(022) Indicated commitment i[Group]=(Effect of alliance goal attainment on commitment[Group]+Effect of Degree of goal attainment on Initial excitement[Group])*Normal commitment
Units: Knowledge points/People/week
The Indicated commitment considers the Effect of alliance goal attainment on commitment and the Effect of Degree of goal attainment on commitment and multiplies them with Normal commitment.

(023) Normal expected effective group productivity[Group]=1
Units: task/(People*week)
The Normal expected effective group productivity is assumed to be one in the Base run.

(024) Normal expected effectiveness[Group]=Normal expected effective group productivity[Group]*SUM(Perceived scientists i by j[Parent!]*Unitary matrix parent vs group[Parent!,Group])
Units: tasks/week
This variable calculates the scientists' Normal expected effectiveness.

(025) Normal expected research output[Group]=Normal expected effectiveness[Group]*Knowledge points per tasks multiplier
Units: Knowledge points/week
The Normal expected research output depends on the scientists' Normal expected effectiveness and how much knowledge can be generated per research task.

(026) Order=3
Units: Dmnl
The Order states the type of structural delay.

(027) Perceived scientists i by j[Parent]=Normal expected scientists i by j[Parent]*Fractional scientist bonus per patent i[Parent]
Units: People
This variable states how many of the second parent's scientists the first parent's scientists perceive .

(028) Relative commitment[Group]=Commitment to learn and work scientists i[Group]/Normal commitment
Units: Dmnl
The Relative commitment is a dimensionless variable that puts the respective scientists' Commitment to learn and work into relation to the Normal commitment.

(029) T Effect of alliance goal attainment on perceived alliance success([(0,0)-(2,2)],(0,0.5),(0.262997,0.710526),(0.58104,0.982456),(0.825688,1.11404),(1,1.2),(1.22936,1.29825),(1.51682,1.38596),(1.737,1.40351),(2.00612,1.4))
Units: Dmnl
This table function is increasing at a decreasing rate and states that the closer the goal has been reached, the more the people in the alliance are committed to the alliance.

(030) T Effect of Degree of goal attainment on Initial excitement([(0,0)-(1,1)],(0,0.6),(0.00917431,0.140351),(0.02,0),(1,0))
Units: Dmnl
At alliance start, scientists are very excited about the alliance and feed very committed to the alliance tasks. This initial excitement decreases the longer the alliance is in place.

(031) Time to form commitment=2
Units: week [0,60,0.1]
It takes some time to form the commitment.

****

.Control

****

Simulation Control Parameters

(033) FINAL TIME = 150
Units: week
The final time for the simulation.

(034) INITIAL TIME = 0
Units: week
The initial time for the simulation.

(035) SAVEPER = 1
Units: week [0,?]
The frequency with which output is stored.

(036) TIME STEP = 0.0625
Units: week [0,?]
The time step for the simulation.

****

.Goal attainments

****

(038) Degree of aspiration level attainment i[Parent]=ZIDZ("Parent i # of patents"[Parent], Aspiration level i[Parent])
Units: Dmnl
This variable calculates the parents' Degrees of aspiration level attainment. It is not visible to the other parent as it refers to the non-externally communicated # of patents.

(039) Degree of common and private goal attainment i[Parent]=if then else(Aspiration level i[Parent]>=Aspiration level private j[Parent],Degree of aspiration level attainment i[Parent] , "Degree of private goal attainment - parent j"[Parent])
Units: Dmnl
This variable calculates the Degree of common and private goal attainment.

(040) "Effect of common and private goal attainment i on Desired # of manager interactions"[Parent]=T Effect of i's sensitivity on Desired interactions(Degree of common and private goal attainment i[Parent])
Units: Dmnl
If the parent firms have reached their (common and private) goals, the alliance is seen as terminated. No further interactions are allowed.

(041) Effect of Degree of common and private goal attainment i on Openness scientists[Parent]=T Effect of i's sensitivity on Openness and Scientist allocation to j's actions(Degree of common and private goal attainment i[Parent])
Units: Dmnl

This effect statest that as soon as the parent firm reaches its (common and private) goals, openness between the scientists needs to decrease - the firms are no longer allies.

(042) Effect of Degree of common and private goal attainment i on Scientist allocation j to i[Parent]=T Effect of i's sensitivity on Openness and Scientist allocation to j's actions(Degree of common and private goal attainment i[Parent])
Units: Dmnl
This effect statest that as soon as the parent firm reaches its (common and private) goals, scientists needs to be withdrawn from the alliance - the firms are no longer allies.

(043) Effect of Perceived goal attainment i by j on sensitivity of i to j's actions[Parent]=T Effect of i's sensitivity to j's actions(Perceived goal attainment i by j[Parent])
Units: Dmnl
This variable calculates the Effect of one firm's sensitivity toward its perceived partner's goal attainment on trust.

(044) Perceived goal attainment i by j[Parent]=ZIDZ("Parent i # of patents"[Parent], Aspiration level externally i[Parent])
Units: Dmnl
This variable states the Perceived goal attainment of one parent by the other parent.

(045) T Effect of i's sensitivity on Desired interactions([(0,0)-(1,1)],(0,1),(0.700306,1),(0.862385,1),(0.929664,0.986842),(0.944954,0.798246),(0.95107,0.0263158),(0.966361,0),(1,0))
Units: Dmnl
This table function indicates that a firm gets less sensitive to Desired manager interactions the closer it gets to its (common and private)goals.

(046) T Effect of i's sensitivity on Openness and Scientist allocation to j's actions([(0,0)-(1,1)],(0,1),(0.700306,1),(0.862385,0.995614),(0.911315,0.925439),(0.944954,0.710526),(0.969419,0.0833333),(0.98471,0.0219298),(1,0))
Units: Dmnl
As long as the goals have not been reached, the parent firms' managers effect on Openness and scientist allocation is high. When the firm reaches the goals, openness needs to be immediately decreased and scientists have to withdrawn from the alliance.

(047) T Effect of i's sensitivity to j's actions([(0,0)-(1,1)],(0,1),(0.58,1),(0.73,0.96),(0.81,0.80),(0.817095,0.684211),(0.889908,0.285088),(0.908257,0.0745614),(0.932722,0),(1,0))
Units: Dmnl
This table function indicates that a firm gets less sensitive to the partner's actions the closer it gets to its own goals.

****

.Initial conditions

****

(049) IC Active milestone externally i[Parent]=0
Units: Patents
It states the initial condition of the milestone working on.

(050) IC Active milestone i[Parent]=0
Units: Patents
It states the initial condition for the current milestone the parent firms jointly work on at simulation start.

(051) IC Active milestone private j[Parent]=0
Units: Patents
It states the initial condition of the milestone the parents work on at simulation start.

(052) IC Effect of Manager trust i in j on Openness scientists=1
Units: Dmnl
It states the initial condition of the Effect of Manager trust on Openness scientists.

(053) IC TF Effect of alliance goal attainment on commitment[Group]= INITIAL(0.5)
Units: Dmnl
It states the initial condition of this table function.

(054) IC TF Effect of Degree of goal attainment on Initial excitement=0.5
Units: Dmnl
It states the initial condition of this table function.

(055) IC TF Effect of indicated scientists from reciprocity on scientist allocation i[Parent]=0
Units: Dmnl
It states the initial condition of this table function.

(056) IC TF Effect of trust on scientist allocation i[Parent]=
Units: Dmnl
It states the initial condition of this table function.

(057) IC TF T Effect of Relative manager trust i in j on Openness of gatekeeper restrictions to private learning j=0
Units: Dmnl
The initial condition of the Effect of relative manager trust on openness of gatekeeper restrictions.

(058) In Commitment[Group]= INITIAL(Normal commitment*(IC TF Effect of Degree of goal attainment on Initial excitement+IC TF Effect of alliance goal attainment on commitment[Group]))
Units: Knowledge points/People/week
It calculates the initial condition of the scientists' commitment at simulation start.

(059) In Desired interactions[Parent]= INITIAL(Normal manager interactions-Bias)
Units: Interactions/week
It calculates the initial value for desired interactions.

(060) In Exp Sci[Parent]= INITIAL(IC Active milestone externally i[Parent]*Scientists per patent to be achieved i per agreement[Parent])
Units: People
It calculates the initial value for the Expected scientists working in the alliance.

(061) In Manager trust[P1]=In trust P1
In Manager trust[P2]=In trust P2
Units: Trust points [0,2,0.01]
It states the parents' initial trust levels.

(062) In Open Gate[Parent]= INITIAL(IC TF T Effect of Relative manager trust i in j on Openness of gatekeeper restrictions to private learning j)
Units: Dmnl
It calculates the initial value for the Openness of gatekeeper restrictions.

(063) In Openness Group[G1]= INITIAL(IC Effect of Manager trust i in j on Openness scientists*Normal openness i[G1])
In Openness Group[G2]= INITIAL(IC Effect of Manager trust i in j on Openness scientists*Normal openness i[G2])
Units: Openness points
It states the initial condition for the stock Openness scientists j to i. It depends upon the initial condition of the Effect of Manger trust on Openness and the Normal openness.

(064) in private knowledge[Parent]= INITIAL(Init Alliance knowledge*Relative init parent knowledge[Parent]*if then else(Relative scientist active private j[Parent]*Actual openness of gatekeeper restrictions to private learning i[Parent]*Relevance of alliance knowledge for private needs j[Parent]=0, 0, 1))
Units: Knowledge points
It calculates the initial condition of private knowledge at simulation start.

(065) in pulse=1
Units: 1
This is the initial milestone. It is important to initiate the milestone counter.

(066) In Sci[Parent]= INITIAL(max(IC Active milestone private j[Parent]*Scientists per patent to be achieved i per agreement[Parent], IC Active milestone i[Parent]*Scientists per patent to be achieved i per agreement[Parent])*IC TF Effect of indicated scientists from reciprocity on scientist allocation i[Parent]*IC TF Effect of trust on scientist allocation i[Parent])
Units: People
It calculates the initial condition of the number of scientists working in the alliance at simulation start.

(067) In trust P1=1
Units: Trust points [0,2,0.01]
This parameter states Partner 1's initial trust level.

(069) In trust P2=1
Units: Trust points [0,2,0.05]
This parameter states Partner 2's initial trust level.

(070) Init Alliance knowledge= INITIAL(0)
Units: Knowledge points
It states the initial condition of Alliance knowledge at alliance start.

(071) Inverse Unitary matrix parent vs group[Parent,Group]=1-Unitary matrix parent vs group[Parent,Group]
Units: Dmnl
This variable inverses the Unitary matrix parent vs. group into Group into Parent level subscripts.

(072) Knowledge points per tasks multiplier=1
Units: Knowledge points/task
This multiplier indicates how many knowledge is needed to perform one research task.

(073) Min effective learning=0.1
Units: Dmnl
It indicates that in the case of no initial knowledge, scientists do learn something together.

(074) Normal aspiration level=1
Units: Patents
With varying the normal aspiration level, the externally communicated aspiration level can be altered.

(075) Normal commitment=1
Units: Knowledge points/People/week
This constant indicates the Normal commitment to learn and work on the alliance research tasks per week.

(076) Normal learning=1
Units: Dmnl
Normal learning is a constant that tells us how well people learn under normal conditions. It is assumed to be one.

(077) Normal tasks per scientist per week=1
Units: task/People/week
It is assumed that, generally, one scientists can work on 1 task per week.

(078) Normal trust[P1]=Normal trust manager P1
Normal trust[P2]=Normal trust manager P2
Units: Trust points
It states the parents' normal trust.

(079) Normal trust manager P1=1
Units: Trust points [0,1.9,0.1]
Parent 1's normal trust is 1.

(080) Normal trust manager P2=1
Units: Trust points [0,1.9,0.1]
Parent 2's Normal trust is 1.

(081) Relative init parent knowledge[Parent]=0
Units: Dmnl
The relative initial parent knowledge.

(082) Time of alliance start=5
Units: week [0,10,1]
This variable states the week in which the two partner companies start to cooperate with each other in the learning alliance. Its original value is 5 - hence the alliance starts in week 5.

(083) Unitary matrix parent 1 vs parent 2[Parent from, Parent]=if then else(Parent from=Parent,0,1)
Units: Dmnl
This unitary matrix transforms variables from the 'Parent from' to the 'Parent' subscript.

(084) Unitary matrix parent vs group[Parent,Group]=if then else(Group=Parent,1,0)
Units: Dmnl
This Unitary matrix transforms variables on the parent level to the group level subscript.

****
.Interorganizational Learning Simulation Model - Subscripts
****

(086) Group:G1, G2

(087) MilestoneRange:(m1-m3)one, two, three, four

(088) Parent:P1, P2

(089) Parent from<->Parent

****
.Manager trust
****

(091) Actual manager interactions i with j[Parent]=SUM(Desired manager interactions i with j[Parent!])/2*MIN("Effect of common and private goal attainment i on Desired # of manager interactions"[P1] , "Effect of common and private goal attainment i on Desired # of manager interactions"[P2])
Units: Interactions/week
Whereas the partner's managers may have different Desires to interact with each other, the Actual # of interactions is the average of their desires.

(092) alpha[P1]=alpha P1
alpha[P2]=alpha P2
Units: Dmnl [0,10,0.1]
Alpha indicates how fast it is possible for a partner to increase trust to its maximum. In a trustworthy environment Alpha is small (min: 0). This means that Manager trust may build up easily. However, a research environment in which, i.e., the parents do joint R&D for the first time Alpha would be large and Manager trust would build only slowly.

(093) alpha P1=1
Units: Dmnl
This parameter states Parent 1's Alpha.

(094) alpha P2=1
Units: Dmnl [0,10,0.1]
This parameter states Parent 2's Alpha.

(095) Bias=0.05
Units: Interactions/week [-0.5,0.5,0.01]
The "Bias" states that in an alliance, even if Manager trust is at its normal level, managers meet a little more often than "normal" - here, it is assumed that they meet 5% more often than normal.

(096) Change in desired manager interactions i with j[Parent]=STEP(Desired manager interactions i with j[Parent]*Fractional interaction change[Parent], Time of alliance start)
Units: Interactions/week/week
This biflow increases or decreases the stock Change in desired manager interactions.

(097) Change in manager trust i[Parent]=if then else(Scientists per patent to be achieved i per agreement[Parent]=0, 0, STEP(Fractional manager trust i in j change[Parent]*Manager trust i in j[Parent], Time of alliance start))
Units: Trust points/week
This biflow increases or decreases the stock Manager trust.

(098) Desired manager interactions i with j[Parent]= INTEG (Kick off meeting+Change in desired manager interactions i with j[Parent],In Desired interactions[Parent])
Units: Interactions/week
This stock accumulates the partners' Desired manager interactions with the other partner's managers. It is either increased or decreased by the biflow Change in manager trust. Additional initial meetings could be initiated by the flow Kick off meeting.

(099) Effect of j's relative scientists on i's manager's trust[Parent]=T effect of j's relative scientists on i's manager's trust(Perceived scientist commitment fraction j[Parent])
Units: Dmnl
This variable calculates the Effect of the partner's relative scientist allocation on manager's trust.

(100) Effect of Manager interactions on Manager trust i in j[Parent]="T Effect of # of Manager interactions on Manager trust i in j"("Relative # of manager interactions i with j"[Parent])
Units: Dmnl
This variable calculates the actual Effect of # of Manager interactions on Manager trust.

(101) Effect of max manager interactions on interaction change[Parent]=MIN(0, (Desired manager interactions i with j[Parent]-Normal manager interactions)/(Desired manager interactions i with j[Parent]-"Max # of interactions."))
Units: Dmnl
The more the partner's managers interact per week and the closer interactions get to the max the smaller is any further change to increase.

(102) Effect of openness scientists j to i on fractional manager trust i in j change[Parent]=T Effect of openness scientists j to i on manager trust i in j(Openness i toward j[Parent])
Units: Dmnl
This variable calculates the Effect of openness scientists j to i on manager trust i in j considering the Table function and the Openness of group i toward j.

(103) "Effect of Relative manager trust i in j on # interaction change"[Parent]="T Effect of Relative manager trust i in j on # of interaction change"(Relative manager trust i in j[Parent])
Units: Dmnl
This variable calculates the Effect of Relative manager trust, considering the table function and the Relative manager trust.

(104) Effect of satisfycing on Trust change[Parent]=alpha[Parent]*MIN(0, (Manager trust i in j[Parent]-Normal trust[Parent])/(Manager trust i in j[Parent]-Max trust))
Units: Dmnl
This variable calculates the Effect of satisfycing on Trust change.

(105) Effect of trust on scientist allocation i[Parent]=T Effect of trust on resource allocation i(Relative manager trust i in j[Parent])
Units: Dmnl
This variable calculates the actual effect of trust on scientist allocation, considering the Manager trust level and the table function.

(106) Fractional interaction change[Parent]=Net effect of interaction change[Parent]*Normal fraction interaction adjustment
Units: Dmnl/week
This variable indicates the Fractional change of manager interactions per week, considering the Net effect of interaction change and the Normal fraction interaction adjustment time.

(107) Fractional manager trust i in j change[Parent]=Total effect on trust change[Parent]*Normal fractional change in trust
Units: Dmnl/week
The Fractional manager trust change multiplies the Total effect of trust change with the Normal fractional trust change. This variable states how much trust changes in the hill-climbing process.

(108) "Fractional team-building interactions"=0
Units: Dmnl [0,0.45,0.05]
The Fractional team-building interactions state how many additional team-building interactions the managers participate in at alliance start.

(109) Kick off meeting=((Bias+"Team-building interactions")/TIME STEP)*PULSE(Time of alliance start, TIME STEP)
Units: Interactions/(week*week)
This flow increases the Desired manager interactions during the alliance kick off phase.

(110) Manager trust i in j[Parent]= INTEG (Change in manager trust i[Parent],In Manager trust[Parent])
Units: Trust points
This stock accumulates the trust of one parents' managers toward its partner. It is either increased or decreased by the biflow Change in manager trust.

(111) "Max # of interactions."=2
Units: Interactions/week
This constant indicates the maximum number of interactions per week.

(112) Max trust=2
Units: Trust points [0,10,0.1]
Trust maximally can as high as double the initial amount.

(113) Net effect of interaction change[Parent]=Effect of max manager interactions on interaction change[Parent]+"Effect of Relative manager trust i in j on # interaction change"[Parent]
Units: Dmnl
The Effect of Relative manager trust sums up with the Effect of max # of manager interactions. The smaller this variable, the smaller the change.

(114) Net effect on trust[Parent]=Effect of satisfycing on Trust change[Parent]+Effect of Manager interactions on Manager trust i in j[Parent]+Effect of openness scientists j to i on fractional manager trust i in j change[Parent]+Effect of j's relative scientists on i's manager's trust[Parent]
Units: Dmnl
The Net effect on trust sums up four effects on manager trust - the effects of # of interactions between managers, scientists' openness, reciprocity of scientists allocation, respectively fairness, and satisfycing.

(115) Normal fraction interaction adjustment=0.2
Units: 1/week [0,2,0.01]
The Normal fraction interaction adjustment time indicates that interactions adjust at 20% per week.

(116) Normal fractional change in trust=0.2
Units: 1/week
The Normal fractional change in trust indicates that trust changes at 20% per week.

(117) Normal manager interactions=1
Units: Interactions/week [0,6,0.01]
This constant indicates the Normal # of interactions between the managers per week. Interactions may include physical interacations, phone calls, video conferences, e-mails, etc.

(118) Openness i toward j[Parent]=SUM(Openness scientists j to i relative to normal[Group!]*Inverse Unitary matrix parent vs group[Parent,Group!])
Units: Dmnl
This variable calculates the Openness of one parent's scientists in the alliance to the other parent's scientists.

(119) "Relative # of manager interactions i with j"[Parent]=Actual manager interactions i with j[Parent]/(Normal manager interactions-Bias)
Units: Dmnl
This variable indicates the Relative # of interactions between the managers considering the managers' desire to meet.

(120) Relative manager trust i in j[Parent]=Manager trust i in j[Parent]/Normal trust[Parent]
Units: Dmnl
The Parents' trust in each other is normalized by Normal trust.

(121) "T Effect of # of Manager interactions on Manager trust i in j"([(0,-1)-(3,1)],(0,-1),(1,0),(1.77064,0.780702),(2.04587,0.95614),(2.41284,0.991228),(3,1))
Units: Dmnl
This nonlinear function states that the more managers interact with each other, the more they trust each other. Trust declines if they do not interact regularly. There is no effect on trust if the interactions are equal to the Normal # of interactions.

(122) T effect of j's relative scientists on i's manager's trust([(0,-1)-(3,1)],(0,-1),(1,0),(1.77064,0.780702),(2.04587,0.95614),(2.41284,0.991228),(3,1))
Units: Dmnl
The decreasing slope of this table function indicates that with the partner having less scientists than agreed upon in the agreement, trust decreases. If the numbers are equal to what is expected trust remains. When the partner allocates more scientists to the alliance trust increases slightly to 120%.

(123) T Effect of openness scientists j to i on manager trust i in j([(0,-1)-(3,1)],(0,-1),(1,0),(1.77064,0.780702),(2.04587,0.95614),(2.41284,0.991228),(3,1))
Units: Dmnl
This table function is s-shaped and states that more open the partner's scientists are toward the own scientists, the more the own manager trusts the partner manager. Saturation means that more openness leads to the same fractional increase of trust as a little less.

(124) "T Effect of Relative manager trust i in j on # of interaction change"([(0,-2)-(2,2)],(0,-1),(0.4,-0.802632),(0.7,-0.447368),(1,0),(1.2,0.565789),(1.6,0.855263),(2,1))
Units: Dmnl
With no trust between the managers the change of desired interactions between the managers is negative. In other words, the Desired # of manager interactions decline, everything else equal. When Manager trust is at Normal trust there will be no change to the current number of interactions per week. If managers trust each other more than normal (Manager trust is above Normal trust) they seek to interact with each other more often.

(125) T Effect of trust on resource allocation i([(0,0)-(2,2)],(0,0),(0.211009,0.0877193),(0.556575,0.289474),(0.868502,0.701754),(1,1),(1.07645,1.0614),(1.22324,1.1),(1.42508,1.1),(1.73089,1.1),(2,1.1))
Units: Dmnl
The S-shaped function indicates that when one partner's managers think that the partner is trustworthy, they are willing to send scientists into the alliance. If they don't trust the other, they are not willing to send scientists.

(126) "Team-building interactions"="Fractional team-building interactions"*"Max # of interactions."
Units: Interactions/week [0,0.95,0.05]
This variable multiplies the Fractional team-building interactions with the Maximum number of interactions.

(127) Total effect on trust change[Parent]=Effect of Perceived goal attainment i by j on sensitivity of i to j's actions[Parent]*Net effect on trust[Parent]
Units: Dmnl
Total effect on trust change multiplies the Effect of perceived goal attainment on parent i's sensitivity to its partner's actions with the Net effect on trust. If one partner has nearly reached its goals it is insensitive to its partner's actions like, i.e., unexpected withdraw of scientists or decrease in the partner's scientists' trust.

****
.Milestone counter
****

(129) "# of total milestones to be achieved"=1
Units: Dmnl [0,2,1]
Here, the number of milestones to be worked on are noted. This number has to be in correspondence with the number of aspiration levels indicating the internally and externally communicated aspiration level as well as the number of milestones in the subscript. For example, when both parents seek for 15 patents each, the number of total milestones to be achieved has to be 2x as high - for each parent 15 patents.

(130) Active milestone externally i[Parent]=SUM(if Active externally i[MilestoneRange!,Parent])
Units: Patents
This variable indicates the openly communicated patents that each parent works on during a milestone.

(131) Active milestone i[Parent]=SUM(if Active i[MilestoneRange!,Parent])
Units: Patents
This variable indicates the current number of patents that have to be achieved. To do so, it considers the current milestone. This is the number of patents to be achieved that are com-

L

municated internally. They are the basis for the resource allocation. Also, it determines the trust that the second partner has in the first partner.

(132) "Agreed upon # of expected patents i"[P1]=0+STEP(Aspiration level externally i[P1], Time of alliance start)
"Agreed upon # of expected patents i"[P2]=+STEP(Aspiration level externally i[P2], Time of alliance start)
Units: Patents
The parent firms have agreed upon a certain number of patents to work on cooperatively.

(133) Aspiration level externally i[Parent]=Active milestone externally i[Parent]
Units: Patents
This variable indicates the current number of patents that have to be achieved. To do so, it considers the current milestone. This is the number of patents to be achieved that are communicated externally. They are the basis for the groups' trust toward each other.

(134) Aspiration level i[P1]=Active milestone i[P1]
Aspiration level i[P2]=Active milestone i[P2]
Units: Patents
The Aspiration level is identical to the Active milestone. It is the internal measure that is the basis for the resource allocation and the trust developing on the group level.

(135) Aspiration levels externally communicated i[MilestoneRange,Parent]=Relative Aspiration Level communicated i[MilestoneRange,Parent]*Normal aspiration level
Units: Patents [0,15]
This variable computes the firm's communicated aspiration level by multiplying the relative aspiration level that are externally communicated with the normal aspiration level.

(136) Aspiration levels internally communicated i[MilestoneRange,Parent]=Relative aspiration level internally communicated i[MilestoneRange,Parent]*Normal internal aspiration level
Units: Patents [0,10]
This variable computes the aspiration level by multiplying the relative aspiration level that are internally communicated with the normal aspiration level.

(137) Chng WM externally i[Parent]="is 95% externally i?"[Parent]*1/TIME STEP*if then else(Which Milestone externally communicated i[Parent]="# of total milestones to be achieved",0,1)
Units: 1/week
This flow increases the milestone counter on which milestone the parent works externally.

(138) Chng WM i[Parent]="is 95% i?"[Parent]*1/TIME STEP*if then else(Which Milestone internally communicated i[Parent]="# of total milestones to be achieved",0,1)
Units: 1/week
This flow increases the milestone counter on which milestone the parent works internally.

(139) ComAL1P1=10
Units: Dmnl
This parameter states how many patents need to be achieved for reaching partner 1's first milestone.

(140) ComAL1P2=10
Units: Dmnl
This parameter states how many patents need to be achieved for reaching partner 2's first milestone.

(141) ComAL2P1=20
Units: Dmnl
This parameter states how many patents need to be achieved for reaching partner 1's second milestone.

(142) ComAL2P2=20
Units: Dmnl
This parameter states how many patents need to be achieved for reaching partner 2's second milestone.

(143) ComAL3P1=0
Units: Dmnl
This parameter states how many patents need to be achieved for reaching partner 1's third milestone.

(144) ComAL3P2=0
Units: Dmnl
This parameter states how many patents need to be achieved for reaching partner 1's third milestone.

(145) ComALP1[m1]=ComAL1P1
ComALP1[m2]=ComAL2P1
ComALP1[m3]=ComAL3P1
Units: Dmnl
These are partner 1's communicated milestones.

(146) ComALP2[m1]=ComAL1P2
ComALP2[m2]=ComAL2P2
ComALP2[m3]=ComAL3P2
Units: Dmnl
These are partner 2's communicated milestones.

(147) Fraction of actual internally communicated goals L1P1=1
Units: Dmnl [0,1,0.01]
The fraction of actual internally communicated goals states the fraction of externally communicated patents the partner really seeks to achieve.

(148) Fraction of actual internally communicated goals L1P2=1
Units: Dmnl [0,1,0.01]
The fraction of actual internally communicated goals states the fraction of externally communicated patents the partner really seeks to achieve.

(149) Fraction of actual internally communicated goals L2P1=1
Units: Dmnl [0,6,0.1]
The fraction of actual internally communicated goals states the fraction of externally communicated patents the partner really seeks to achieve.

(150) Fraction of actual internally communicated goals L3P1=1
Units: Dmnl
The fraction of actual internally communicated goals states the fraction of externally communicated patents the partner really seeks to achieve.

(151) if Active externally i[MilestoneRange,Parent]=if then else(MilestoneRange=Which Milestone externally communicated i[Parent],Aspiration levels externally communicated i[MilestoneRange,Parent],0)
Units: Patents
This variable calculates the number of externally communicated common patents to be achieved during a certain milestone.

(152) if Active i[MilestoneRange,Parent]=if then else(MilestoneRange=Which Milestone internally communicated i[Parent],Aspiration levels internally communicated i[MilestoneRange,Parent],0)
Units: Patents
This variable calculates the number of internally communicated common patents to be achieved during a certain milestone

(153) IntComAL1P1=ComAL1P1*Fraction of actual internally communicated goals L1P1
Units: Dmnl
It states how many patents partner 1 internally communicates it need to achieve for reaching its first milestone.

(154) IntComAL1P2=ComAL1P2*Fraction of actual internally communicated goals L1P2
Units: Dmnl
It states how many patents partner 2 internally communicates it need to achieve for reaching its first milestone.

(155) IntComAL2P1=ComAL2P1*Fraction of actual internally communicated goals L2P1
Units: Dmnl
It states how many patents partner 1 internally communicates it need to achieve for reaching its second milestone.

(156) IntComAL2P2=20
Units: Dmnl
It states how many patents partner 2 internally communicates it need to achieve for reaching its second milestone.

(157) IntComAL3P1=ComAL3P1*Fraction of actual internally communicated goals L3P1
Units: Dmnl
It states how many patents partner 1 internally communicates it need to achieve for reaching its third milestone.

(158) IntComAL3P2=0
Units: Dmnl
It states how many patents partner 2 internally communicates it need to achieve for reaching its third milestone.

(159) IntComALP1[m1]=IntComAL1P1
IntComALP1[m2]=IntComAL2P1
IntComALP1[m3]=IntComAL3P1
Units: Dmnl
These are partner 1's internally communicated milestones.

(160) IntComALP2[m1]=IntComAL1P2
IntComALP2[m2]=IntComAL2P2
IntComALP2[m3]=IntComAL3P2
Units: Dmnl
These are partner 2's internally communicated milestones.

(161) "Internally communicated # of patents i"[P1]=0+STEP(Aspiration level i[P1], Time of alliance start)"Internally communicated # of patents i"[P2]=0+STEP(Aspiration level i[P2], Time of alliance start)
Units: Patents
This variables states the number of Internally communicated patents.

(162) "is 95% externally i?"[P1]=if then else("Parent i # of patents"[P1]>Active milestone externally i[P1]*0.9,1,0)
"is 95% externally i?"[P2]=if then else("Parent i # of patents"[P2]>Active milestone externally i[P2]*0.9,1,0)
Units: Dmnl
This variable indicates when 95% of one milestone have been achieved.

(163) "is 95% i?"[P1]=if then else("Parent i # of patents"[P1]>Active milestone i[P1]*0.9 ,1,0)
"is 95% i?"[P2]=if then else("Parent i # of patents"[P2]>Active milestone i[P2]*0.9 ,1,0)
Units: Dmnl
This variable indicates when 95% of the parents' milestones have been achieved. The basis

for this calculation is the internally communicated milestones. The internal milestone of a parent does not count further, if the internal milestone is not reached.

(164) Normal internal aspiration level=
Units: Patents
With varying the normal internal aspiration level, the internally communicated aspiration levels can be altered.

(165) "Parent i # of patents"[Parent]="# of alliance patents"*"Relative assignment of patents with respect to agreed upon # of patents i to j"[Parent]
Units: Patents
This variable states how many of the overall patents are allocated to each of the two parents.

(166) project start= in pulse/TIME STEP*PULSE(Time of alliance start-TIME STEP,TIME STEP)
Units: Dmnl/week
This flow consists of a pulse function. It states that the project the parents work on starts in week 5.

(167) project start 0=in pulse/TIME STEP*PULSE(Time of alliance start-TIME STEP,TIME STEP)
Units: Dmnl/week
This flow consists of a pulse function. It states that the project the parents work on starts in week 5.

(168) Relative Aspiration Level communicated i[MilestoneRange,P1]=ComALP1[MilestoneRange]
Relative Aspiration Level communicated i[MilestoneRange,P2]=ComALP2[MilestoneRange]
Units: Dmnl
Here, the externally communicated aspirations have to be determined. This variable states how many patents have to be achieved to reach a milestone. Depending on whether the parent wants to communicates the patents honestly to the partner, the aspiration level either or not corresponds to the externally communicated aspiration levels. It indicate at how many patents a milestone is reached, i.e., at patent #s 3, 6, 9.

(169) Relative aspiration level internally communicated i[MilestoneRange,P1]=IntComALP1[MilestoneRange]
Relative aspiration level internally communicated i[MilestoneRange,P2]=IntComALP2[MilestoneRange]
Units: Dmnl
Here, the internally communicated aspirations have to be determined. This variable states how many patents have to be achieved to reach a milestone. Depending on whether the parent wants to communicate them honestly to the partner, they either correspond the externally communicated aspiration levels or they do not. Indicate at how many patents a milestone is reached, i.e., at patent #s 3, 6, 9.

(170) "Relative assignment of patents with respect to agreed upon # of patents i to j" [Parent]=ZIDZ ("Agreed upon # of expected patents i"[Parent] , "Tot agreed upon#")
Units: Dmnl
According to the parents' externally communicated aspirations this variable states the relative number of scientists that the parents are seeking for in respect to the overall # of patents to be achieved.

(171) "Tot agreed upon#"=SUM("Agreed upon # of expected patents i"[Parent!])
Units: Patents
This variable states the summed number of agreed upon joint patents.

(172) Which Milestone externally communicated i[Parent]= INTEG (Chng WM externally i[Parent]+project start 0,0)
Units: Dmnl
This stock accumulates the milestones that the parents are working on.

(173) Which Milestone internally communicated i[Parent]= INTEG (Chng WM i[Parent]+project start,0)
Units: Dmnl
This stock accumulates the milestones that the parents are working on.

****
.Openness gatekeeper
****

(175) Change in openness of gatekeeper restrictions[Parent]=STEP(Openness of gatekeeper restrictions gap[Parent]/Time to change openness gatekeeper, Time of alliance start)
Units: Dmnl/week
This variable calculates the change in gatekeeper openness per week.

(176) Effect of Relative manager trust i in j on Openness of gatekeeper restrictions to private learning j[Parent]=T Effect of Relative manager trust i in j on Openness of gatekeeper restrictions to private learning j(Relative manager trust i in j[Parent])
Units: Dmnl
This variable calculates the actual effect of relative manager trust on the importance of the formal safeguard.

(177) Indicated openness of gatekeeper restrictions to private learning i[Parent]=Effect of Relative manager trust i in j on Openness of gatekeeper restrictions to private learning j[Parent]
Units: Dmnl
The indicated openness is used to calculate the gap between it and the Openness to date.

(178) Openness of gatekeeper restrictions gap[Parent]=Indicated openness of gatekeeper restrictions to private learning i[Parent]-"Openness of gatekeeper restrictions to j's private learning - i"[Parent]
Units: Dmnl
The gap is calculated via subtracting the Openness to date from the Indicated openness of gatekeeper restrictions.

(179) "Openness of gatekeeper restrictions to j's private learning - i"[Parent]= INTEG (Change in openness of gatekeeper restrictions[Parent],In Open Gate[Parent])
Units: Dmnl
This stock represents the Openness of the formal safeguard. It becomes less when informal safeguards (i.e., trust) are high and vice versa.

(180) Openness of gatekeeper restrictions to private learning i resumed[P1]=
Openness of i's gatekeeper restrictions to j's private learning from alliance[P1]
Openness of gatekeeper restrictions to private learning i resumed[P2]=Openness of j's gatekeeper restrictions to i's private learning from alliance[P2]
Units: Dmnl [0,1,0.05]
The openness of the gatekeeper restrictions may vary between 0 and 1. Zero means that no private learning allowed. This means that no knowledge spillover from the alliance to unrelated areas besides the alliance is allowed. An openness of 1 indicates that there are no restrictions: whatever is learned in the alliance may be transferred to the partner firm.

(181) Openness of i's gatekeeper restrictions to j's private learning from alliance[P1]= if then else("Switch no Effect of manager trust on openness=0 and Effect of manager trust on openness=1 P1"=0, Openness of P1's gatekeeper restrictions to P2's private learning, "Openness of gatekeeper restrictions to j's private learning - i"[P1])
Units: Dmnl [0,6,0.5]
When one parent's gatekeeper's openness is high, the other parent may learn from the alliance. If it is low, learning is prohibited.

(182) Openness of j's gatekeeper restrictions to i's private learning from alliance[P2]= if then else("Switch no Effect of manager trust on openness=0 and Effect of manager trust on openness=1 P2"=0, Openness of P2's gatekeeper restrictions to P1's private learning , "Openness of gatekeeper restrictions to j's private learning - i"[P2])
Units: Dmnl [0,6,0.5]
When one parent's gatekeeper's openness is high, the other parent may learn from the alliance. If it is low, learning is prohibited.

(183) Openness of P1's gatekeeper restrictions to P2's private learning=0
Units: Dmnl [0,1,0.1]
In case the Openness of gatekeeper restrictions are exogenous, this parameter states Parent 1's openness of gatekeeper restrictions to Parent 2's private learning.

(184) Openness of P2's gatekeeper restrictions to P1's private learning=0
Units: Dmnl [0,1,0.1]
In case the Openness of gatekeeper restrictions are exogenous, this parameter states Parent 2's openness of gatekeeper restrictions to Parent 1's private learning.

(185) "Switch no Effect of manager trust on openness=0 and Effect of manager trust on openness=1 P1" =0
Units: Dmnl [0,1,1]
If the switch is 0, then the loop is deactivated. If it is 1, the loop is activated. The switch decides whether the constant or the variable is taken into consideration for calculating the openness of the gatekeeper.

(186) "Switch no Effect of manager trust on openness=0 and Effect of manager trust on openness=1 P2"=1
Units: Dmnl [0,1,1]
If the switch is 0, then the loop is deactivated. If it is 1, the loop is activated. The switch decides whether the constant or the variable is taken into consideration for calculating the openness of the gatekeeper.

(187) T Effect of Relative manager trust i in j on Openness of gatekeeper restrictions to private learning j([(0,0)-(2,1)],(0,0),(1,0),(1.1682,0.0350877),(1.31498,0.175439),(1.45566,0.802632),(1.55963,0.964912),(1.70031,1),(2,1))
Units: Dmnl
When trust (social safeguard) is low, formal safeguards like contracts (i.e. on gatekeepers) play an important role in the relationship. Until normal trust the gatekeeper does not allow any information or knowledge flows from the alliance to possible private knowledge bases. When trust (social safeguard) increases the formal restrictions become less important and the gatekeeper pays less attention to knowledge and information flows.

(188) Time to change openness gatekeeper=2
Units: weeks
It takes some time to change the gatekeeper's openness.

****
.Openness scientists
****

(190) Change in openness scientists j to i[Group]=0+STEP(Openness discrepancy relative to indicated openness scientists j to i[Group]*Normal fractional change rate j to i[Group], Time of alliance start)
Units: Openness points/week
This flow increases or decreases the stock Openness scientists j to i. It is calculated by multiplying the Normal fractional change rate and the Openness discrepancy.

(191) Company indicated openness scientists j to i from common and private goal attainment[Group]=Effect manager trust i in j on Openness scientists j to i[Group]*Normal openness i[Group]
Units: Openness points
This variable denormalizes the Effect of Manager trust on the Scientists' openness toward each other.

(192) Effect manager trust i in j on Openness scientists j to i[Group]=SUM(Effect of Manager trust i in j on Openness scientists j to i[Parent!]*Unitary matrix parent vs group[Parent!,Group])
Units: Dmnl
This variable transfers the trust from the manager level to the scientist group level.

(193) Effect of Manager trust i in j on Openness scientists j to i[Parent]=T Effect of Manager trust i in j on Openness scientists(Relative manager trust i in j[Parent])
Units: Dmnl
This variable calculates the Effect of Manager trust on Openness between the scientists as the Relative manager trust as an effect of the Table function.

(194) Effect on openness scientists j to i[Group]=SUM(Effect of Degree of common and private goal attainment i on Openness scientists[Parent!]*Unitary matrix parent vs group[Parent!,Group])
Units: Dmnl
This variable transfers the effect from the parent level to the scientist level.

(195) Effective indicated openness scientists j to i[Group]=Weight of company openness to indicated openness*Company indicated openness scientists j to i from common and private goal attainment[Group]+(1-Weight of company openness to indicated openness)*Indicated openness from reciprocity[Group]
Units: Openness points
The Effective indicated openness on the group level is determined by the Indicated openness scientists j to i of the parents and the Indicated openness from reciprocity - weighted.

(196) Indicated openness from reciprocity[Group]=SUM(Openness scientists j to i[Group!])-Openness scientists j to i[Group]
Units: Openness points
This variable states the indicated openness from reciprocity.

(197) Normal fractional change rate j to i[Group]=Normal openness change rate
Units: 1/week
This variable indicates the Normal fractional change rate of openness from one group to the other considering the Normal openness change rate.

(198) Normal openness change rate=0.5
Units: 1/week
The Normal openness change rate is assumed to be constant.

(199) Normal openness G1=1
Units: Openness points [0,6,0.1]
It states scientist group 1's Normal openness.

(200) Normal openness G2=1
Units: Openness points [0,6,0.1]
It states scientist group 2's Normal openness.

(201) Normal openness i[G1]=Normal openness G1
Normal openness i[G2]=Normal openness G2
Units: Openness points
The norm is to be fairly open and thus share a lot of documents, insight, experiences, etc.

(202) Openness decline when finishing alliance[Group]=(1-Effect on openness scientists j to i[Group])*(Openness scientists j to i[Group])/Time for openness to decline
Units: Openness points/week
This flow ensures that Openness between scientists declines once the alliance is terminated. As soon as the alliance is terminated, the prior partners are competitors again. There shall not be any further communication between the scientists.

(203) Openness discrepancy relative to indicated openness scientists j to i[Group]=(Effective indicated openness scientists j to i[Group]-Openness scientists j to i[Group])*Effect on openness scientists j to i[Group]
Units: Openness points
The Openness discrepancy on the group level is equal to the Effective indicated openness minus the actual Openness by the scientists.

(204) Openness scientists j to i[Group]= INTEG (Change in openness scientists j to i[Group]-Openness decline when finishing alliance[Group],In Openness Group[Group])
Units: Openness points
The stock Openness scientists j to i indicates how open the scientists of each group are toward each other. Openness leads to sharing knowledge, experience, documents, etc. The variable is increased and decreased by the flow Change in openness scientists j to i.

(205) Openness scientists j to i relative to normal[G1]=Openness scientists j to i[G1]/Normal openness i[G1]
Openness scientists j to i relative to normal[G2]=Openness scientists j to i[G2]/Normal openness i[G2]
Units: Dmnl
This varialbe normalizes the value for Openness on the scientist level.

(206) T Effect of Manager trust i in j on Openness scientists([(0,0)-(2,2)],(0,0),(2,2))
Units: Dmnl
The more (less) managers trust each other the more (less) scientists trust each other and hence are more (less) open toward each other. This is because trust travels through the organization.

(207) Time for openness to decline=1
Units: week [0,6,0.1]
The time for Openness between scientists to decline is only 1 week.

(208) Weight of company openness to indicated openness=0.5
Units: Dmnl [0,1,0.1]
Currently, it is assumed that openness is equally influenced by the Indicated openness from reciprocity and the Indicated openness from the parent company.

****
.Patent generation
****

(210) "# of alliance patents"= INTEG (Alliance patent generation,0)
Units: Patents
Alliance patents are accumulated and have no outflow. It is measured in # of patents. In the beginning of the cooperation there are no common benefits; its initial value is 0.

(211) Alliance patent generation=Potential research output
Units: Patents / week
What was learnt in the alliance is being applied to products developed by the alliance. This flow increases the stock # of alliance benefits.

(212) Alliance research tasks=SUM("Group research output (per week)"[Group!])
Units: Knowledge points/week
This variable indicates how many research tasks the scientists do per week.

(213) Effect of openness scientists i on effective group tasks i[Group]=T Effect of openness scientists on effective group tasks(Openness scientists j to i relative to normal[Group])
Units: Dmnl
This variable calculates the Effect of openness on the Effective group tasks.

(214) "Effect of relative # of patents on research activity and capacity (Fractional desired workload)"=T Effect of fractional desired workload on research activity and capacity("Relative # of alliance patents")
Units: Dmnl
The higher the Relative # of patents the more difficult it gets for the scientists to generate further patents (diminishing returns) - hence Group productivity would decline.

(215) Effective alliance task output=if then else(Relative alliance knowledge base=0,0,Relative alliance knowledge base^Eta)
Units: Dmnl
This variable calculates the Effective alliance task output considering the Relative alliance knowledge base and how fast the scientists are able to understand the knowledge.

(216) Effective group tasks i[G1]=Group productivity i[G1]*Effective openness i[G1]*Alliance research capacity[P1]
Effective group tasks i[G2]=Group productivity i[G2]*Effective openness i[G2]*Alliance research capacity[P2]
Units: tasks/week
This variable calculates the Effective tasks from each group by multiplying the Group productivity with the Effect of openness and the Research capacity.

(217) Effective openness i[G1]=Effect of openness scientists i on effective group tasks i[G1]*Openness of P1's gatekeeper restrictions to P1's knowledge sharing[G1]
Effective openness i[G2]=Effect of openness scientists i on effective group tasks i[G2]*Openness of P2's gatekeeper restrictions to P2's knowledge sharing[G2]
Units: Dmnl
The Effective openness depends on the Effect of openness scientists on effective group tasks and the parents' Openness of gatekeeper restrictions to knowledge sharing. Though scientists are very open between each other, the openness could be restricted by gatekeeper controls.

(218) Eta=ln(1+Fractional effective knowledge increase at knowledge doubling)/ln(2)
Units: Dmnl
Eta is a sensitivity making a statement about the effectiveness of the knowledge useful for research tasks when the Relative alliance knowledge base doubles.

(219) Fractional effective knowledge increase at knowledge doubling=1
Units: Dmnl
The constant indicates the fractional effective knowledge increase at knowledge doubling. It is assumed to be 1.

(220) Group productivity i[Group]=Relative commitment[Group]*"Effect of relative # of patents on research activity and capacity (Fractional desired workload)"*Normal tasks per scientist per week
Units: task/People/week
Group productivity is a multiplier of the groups' Relative commitment, the Effect of relative # of patents on Group productivity, and the normal tasks per scientists per week.

(221) "Group research output (per week)"[Group]=Normal tasks per week*PROD((ZIDZ(Effective group tasks i[Group!], Normal tasks per week))^0.5)*Knowledge points per tasks multiplier
Units: Knowledge points/week
This variable describes how productive the groups are on performing joint research tasks.

(222) "Max # of alliance patents achievable"=30
Units: Patents [0,60,1]
There exists a maximum number of patents that can be generated at the most. The larger it is, the easier it is for the scientists to generate the first patents - the smaller it is, the more difficult it gets for the scientists to generate the first ones.

(223) Normal tasks per week=SUM(Normal tasks per scientist per week*Normal scientists on project[Parent!])/2
Units: tasks/week
This variable indicates how many research tasks per week the scientists can do under normal conditions. It depends on the Normal tasks per scientist per week and the Normal scientists on the project.

(224) Openness of P1's gatekeeper restrictions to P1's knowledge sharing[G1]=1
Units: Dmnl [0,2,0.01]
Gatekeepers control the knowledge flow for common learning between the scientists.

(225) Openness of P2's gatekeeper restrictions to P2's knowledge sharing[G2]=1
Units: Dmnl [0,2,0.01]
Gatekeepers control the knowledge flow for common learning between the scientists.

(226) Potential research output= Alliance research tasks*Effective alliance task output*"Research output per unit of effort (Scaling factor)"
Units: Patents/week
The potential research output is calculated by multiplying the effective alliance knowledge base with the # of alliance research tasks and the scaling factor.

(227) "Relative # of alliance patents"="# of alliance patents"/"Max # of alliance patents achievable"
Units: Dmnl
The relative # of patents is a dimensionless variable that puts the actual # of alliance patents into perspective with what is possible for the alliance to generate at most (Max # of alliance patents achievable).

(228) "Research output per unit of effort (Scaling factor)"=0.1
Units: Patents/Knowledge points
The scaling factor indicates how many patents are generated per knowledge point. The higher it is, the more patents can be generated per knowledge point; the smaller it is, the less patents.

(229) T Effect of fractional desired workload on research activity and capacity([(0,0)-(1,1)],(0,1),(0.238532,0.982456),(0.351682,0.934211),(0.415902,0.859649),(0.498471,0.684211),(0.556575,0.464912),(0.623853,0.232456),(0.69419,0.100877,(0.801223,0.0350877),(0.911315,0.0131579),(1,0))
Units: Dmnl
This table function indicates that the higher the Relative # of patents the more difficult it gets for the scientists to generate further patents (diminishing returns). It is inverse S-shaped and goes from [(0,1] to [1,0]).

(230) T Effect of openness scientists on effective group tasks([(0,0)-(6,2)],(0,0),(0.183486,0.267544),(0.440367,0.570175),(0.691131,0.785088),(1,1),(2.00612,1.2193),(2.98471,1.3),(3.97554,1.3),(6,1.3))
Units: Dmnl
The Effect of openness of the scientists on Effective group tasks increases digressively from

[(0,0)-(1,1)]. It means that the more (less) open the scientists are, the more (less) Effective group tasks they can work on.

****
.Private benefits
****

(232) "# of private patents j"[Parent]= INTEG (Private patent generation j[Parent],0)
Units: Patents
This stock indicates the # of private patents by each parent firm. It is increased by the flow Private patent generation j.

(233) Actual effective private and alliance knowledge j[Parent]=Relative private knowledge j[Parent]^Eta
Units: Dmnl
This variable calculates the Effective private and alliance task output considering the Relative alliance knowledge base and how fast the scientists are able to understand the knowledge.

(234) "Effect of relative # of private patents on research activity and capacity (Fractional desired workload) j"[Parent]=T Effect of fractional desired workload on research activity and capacity ("Relative # of private patents j"[Parent])
Units: Dmnl
The higher the relative # of private patents the more difficult it gets for the scientists to generate further patents (diminishing returns).

(235) Effective private group tasks j[Parent]=Private group productivity j[Parent]*Private research capacity j[Parent]
Units: tasks/week
This variable indicates how many tasks each parent group does research on privately. It is calculated via multiplying the Private group productivity with the Private research capacity.

(236) "Maximum # of private patents achievable j"[Parent]=15
Units: Patents [0,20,1]
There exists a maximum number of patents that can be generated at the most. The larger it is, the easier it is for the scientists to generate the first patents - the smaller it is, the more difficult it gets for the scientists to generate the first ones.

(237) Normal private tasks per week[Parent]=Normal tasks per scientist per week*"Scientists active on private learning - parent j"[Parent]
Units: tasks/week
This variable indicates the normal tasks per week that scientists can work on generating private benefits.

(238) Parent relative scaling factor[Parent]=1
Units: Dmnl
The Parent relative scaling factor indicates how close the two knowledge areas (alliance knowledge and private knowledge) are to each other.

(239) Potential private research output j[Parent]="Private group research task (per week) j"[Parent]*Actual effective private and alliance knowledge j[Parent]*"Scaling factor for private patents (output per unit of effort)"[Parent]
Units: Patents/week
The Potential private research output is calculated by multiplying the Actual effective private and alliance knowledge with the Private group research tasks and the Scaling factor for private patents.

(240) Private group productivity j[Parent]="Effect of relative # of private patents on research activity and capacity (Fractional desired workload) j"[Parent]*Relative commitment to learn and work private j[Parent]*Normal tasks per scientist per week
Units: task/(week*People)
The Private group productivity is a multiplier of the groups' relative commitment to learn and work privately, the fractional desired workload, and the Normal tasks per scientists per week.

(241) Private group research output j[Parent]=Normal private tasks per week[Parent]*ZIDZ(Effective private group tasks j[Parent],Normal private tasks per week[Parent])^0.5*Knowledge points per tasks multiplier
Units: Knowledge points/week
This variable describes how productive the groups are on performing private research.

(242) "Private group research task (per week) j"[Parent]=Private group research output j[Parent]
Units: Knowledge points/week
This variable indicates how many private research tasks are being done per week.

(243) Private patent generation j[Parent]=Potential private research output j[Parent]
Units: Patents / week
This flow increases the stock # of private patents.

(244) Private research capacity j[Parent]=0+STEP("Scientists active on private learning - parent j"[Parent], Time of alliance start)
Units: People [0,5]
This variable indicates how many scientists work in the parent firm on another project that is not directly related to the alliance, but which requires insight from alliance learning for the own research enhancement.

(245) "Relative # of private patents j"[Parent]=ZIDZ("# of private patents j"[Parent],"Maximum # of private patents achievable j"[Parent])
Units: Dmnl
The relative # of private patents is a dimensionless variable that puts the actual # of private patents into perspective what is possible for the parent to generate at most.

(246) Relative commitment to learn and work private j[Parent]=1
Units: Dmnl [0,2]
The Relative commitment to learn and work privately is a dimensionless variable. For private learning it is assumed to be constant at 1. This means that the scientists are fully committed to learn and work privately.

(247) "Scaling factor for private patents (output per unit of effort)"[Parent]="Research output per unit of effort (Scaling factor)"*Parent relative scaling factor[Parent]
Units: Patents/Knowledge points
The productivity is important for knowing how many private patents each scientist can generate per week. The variable considers the Scaling factor and the Parent relative scaling factor.

****

.Private knowledge and knowledge spillover

****

(249) Actual knowledge spillover rate[Parent]=Effect of relative private knowledge j on private learning j[Parent]*Relative scientist active private j[Parent]/Normal time for knowledge to spillover[Parent]
Units: Dmnl/week
The Actual knowledge spillover rate depends on the number of scientists working on private tasks, the Normal time for knowledge to spillover and the Effect of relative private knowledge on private learning.

(250) Actual openness of gatekeeper restrictions to private learning i[Parent]= if then else("Switch no PL=O and PL=1"=0, 0 , Openness of gatekeeper restrictions to private learning i resumed[Parent])
Units: Dmnl [0,1]
This is the switch variable for Openness of gatekeeper restrictions to common learning i PL.

(251) Effect of relative private knowledge j on private learning j[Parent]=T Effect of knowledge on learning(Relative private knowledge j[Parent])
Units: Dmnl
The higher the Relative private knowledge base, the higher the capacity to absorb new knowledge, or to learn.

(252) Indicated private knowledge j from alliance[P1]=Alliance knowledge base*Relevance of alliance knowledge for private needs j[P1]*Actual openness of gatekeeper restrictions to private learning i[P2]
Indicated private knowledge j from alliance[P2]=Alliance knowledge base*Relevance of alliance knowledge for private needs j[P2]*Actual openness of gatekeeper restrictions to private learning i[P1]
Units: Knowledge points
This variable indicates how relevant the alliance knowledge is for private purposes, considering the openness of the gatekeeper.

(253) Normal scientists on project[Parent]=Normal aspiration level*Scientists per patent to be achieved i per agreement[Parent]
Units: People
This variable indicates how many scientists should be working on the alliance considering the Normal aspiration level and the Scientists per patent to be achieved.

(254) Normal time for knowledge to spillover[Parent]=1
Units: week
It takes the scientists a certain number of weeks to have the required knowledge spilled over from the alliance.

(255) Private knowledge base parent j[Parent]= INTEG (Private learning j from alliance[Parent],in private knowledge[Parent])
Units: Knowledge points
The stock Private knowledge base indicates the level of private knowledge that each parent generates from the common knowledge generated by the alliance. The stock is increased by the flow Private learning from alliance.

(256) Private learning j from alliance[Parent]=(Indicated private knowledge j from alliance[Parent]-Private knowledge base parent j[Parent])*Actual knowledge spillover rate[Parent]
Units: Knowledge points/week
The flow Private learning from alliance increases the stock Private knowledge base from each parent.

(257) Reference private knowledge[Parent]=Reference alliance knowledge base*Reference private knowledge relative to private knowledge[Parent]
Units: Knowledge points
It states each firm's reference private knowledge.

(258) Reference private knowledge relative to private knowledge[Parent]=Reference private knowledge relative to private knowledge PL[Parent]
Units: Dmnl [0,2]
This variable equals the Reference private knowledge relative to private knowledge PL.

(259) Reference private knowledge relative to private knowledge PL[Parent]=1
Units: Dmnl [0,2]
If the Reference private knowledge relative to the private knowledge equals 2, the knowledge that is required for private purposes is twice as deep.

(260) Relative private knowledge j[Parent]=Private knowledge base parent j[Parent]/Reference private knowledge[Parent]
Units: Dmnl
This variable indicates how much of the Reference private knowledge the parent has already achieved.

(261) Relative scientist active private j[Parent]=if then else("Switch no PL=O and PL=1"=0, 0 , Relative scientist active private j PL[Parent])
Units: Dmnl [0,1,0.1]
This is the switch variable for Relative scientists active private j.

(262) Relative scientist active private j PL[Parent]=1
Units: Dmnl [0,10,0.1]
If there are more scientists active on absorbing the knowledge from the alliance into private areas, the value of this variable must be larger than 1; if there are less scientists, it must be smaller. In the Base run this variable is 1 which means that there are as many scientists active for private learning as for common learning.

(263) Relevance of alliance knowledge for private needs j[P1]=if then else("Switch no PL=O and PL=1"=0, 0 , Relevance of alliance knowledge for private needs j PL[P1])
Relevance of alliance knowledge for private needs j[P2]=if then else("Switch no PL=O and PL=1"=0, 0 , Relevance of alliance knowledge for private needs j PL[P2])
Units: Dmnl [0,1]
This is the switch variable for Relevance of alliance knowledge for private needs j PL.

(264) Relevance of alliance knowledge for private needs j PL[P1]=1
Relevance of alliance knowledge for private needs j PL[P2]=1
Units: Dmnl [0,1]
Knowledge relevance indicates how relevant or important the knowledge is that is transferred from the alliance to the parent for pushing private research forward. Zero means that the alliance knowledge is of no relevance; one means that the alliance is of significant relevance to move private projects forward.

(265) "Scientists active on private learning - parent j"[Parent]=Scientists per patent to be achieved i per agreement[Parent]*Relative scientist active private j[Parent]*Aspiration level private j[Parent]
Units: People [0,4]
This variable indicates how many scientists work on the generation of private benefits. It is assumed that this number is constant; or that the private project goes on for a longer time than the indicated alliance running time. The variable may range between 0 and 4 scientists. It considers the Normal scientists on the common project and is varied through the variable Relative scientists active on the private research tasks.

(266) "Switch no PL=O and PL=1"=1
Units: Dmnl [0,1,1]
If the switch is 0, then the private learning loop is deactivated. If it is 1, the private learning loop is activated.

****

.Private milestone counter

****

(268) "# of expected private patents j"[P1]=0+STEP(Aspiration level private j[P1], Time of alliance start)
"# of expected private patents j"[P2]=0+STEP(Aspiration level private j[P2], Time of alliance start)
Units: Patents
This variable calculates the # of expected private patents in each milestone. It starts to calculate when the alliance starts.

(269) "# of private milestones to be achieved"=if then else("Switch no PL=O and PL=1"=0, 0 , "# of private milestones to be achieved PL")
Units: Dmnl [0,3,1]
This is the switch variable for # of private milestones to be achieved PL.

(270) "# of private milestones to be achieved PL"=1
Units: Dmnl [0,3,1]
Here, the number of private milestones to be worked on are noted. This number has to be in correspondence with the number of private aspiration levels. The closer this number is in respect to the "Aspiration levels goals j", the less likely it is for the alliance to get all the patents it seeks for as it gets harder and harder to use the knowledge for working on the last patents.

(271) Active milestone private j[Parent]=SUM(if Active private j[MilestoneRange!,Parent])
Units: Patents
This variable indicates the private patents that each parent works on during a milestone.

(272) Aspiration level private j[Parent]=Active milestone private j[Parent]
Units: Patents
This variable indicates the current number of patents that are achieved. To do so, it considers the current milestone (the number of private patents to be achieved) the alliance works on.

(273) Aspiration levels private goals j[MilestoneRange,P1]=if then else("Switch no PL=O and PL=1"=0, 0 , Aspiration levels private goals j PL[MilestoneRange,P1])
Aspiration levels private goals j[MilestoneRange,P2]=if then else("Switch no PL=O and PL=1"=0, 0 , Aspiration levels private goals j PL[MilestoneRange,P2])
Units: Patents [0,15]
This is the switch variable for Aspiration levels private goals j PL.

(274) Aspiration levels private goals j PL[MilestoneRange,P1]=PrivALP1[MilestoneRange]
Aspiration levels private goals j PL[MilestoneRange,P2]=PrivALP2[MilestoneRange]
Units: Patents [0,15,1]
Here, the private aspirations are determined. This variable states how many private patents need to be achieved to reach a private milestone.

(275) Chng WM private j[Parent]="is 95% private j?"[Parent]*1/TIME STEP*if then else(Which Private Milestone j[Parent]="# of private milestones to be achieved",0,1)
Units: 1/week
This flow increases the milestones the parents work on as soon as the prior milestone has been reached.

(276) "Degree of private goal attainment - parent j"[Parent]=ZIDZ("# of private patents j"[Parent],"# of expected private patents j"[Parent])
Units: Dmnl
This variable just calculates the Degree of private goal attainment by dividing the actual # of private patents by the # of expected private patents.

(277) if Active private j[MilestoneRange,Parent]=if then else(MilestoneRange=Which Private Milestone j[Parent],Aspiration levels private goals j[MilestoneRange,Parent],0)
Units: Patents
This variable calculates the number of private patents to be achieved during a certain milestone.

(278) In pulse private milestones=if then else("Switch no PL=O and PL=1"=0, 0, In pulse private milestones PL)
Units: 1
The pulse is activated by the switch to privately learn.

(279) In pulse private milestones PL=1
Units: 1 [1,1]
This pulse initializes the first private milestone the parents work on.

(280) "is 95% private j?"[P1]=if then else("# of private patents j"[P1]>Active milestone private j[P1]*0.9,1,0)
"is 95% private j?"[P2]=if then else("# of private patents j"[P2]>Active milestone private j[P2]*0.9,1,0)
Units: Dmnl
This variable indicates when 95% of one milestone have been achieved. If 95% have been achieved, the goal is considered as accomplished.

(281) PrivAL1P1=10
Units: Patents [0,15,1]
It states how many private patents equal parent 1's first private milestone.

(282) PrivAL1P2=0
Units: Patents [0,6,1]
It states how many private patents equal parent 2's first private milestone.

(283) PrivAL2P1=0
Units: Patents [0,12,1]
It states how many private patents equal parent 1's second private milestone.

(284) PrivAL2P2=0
Units: Patents [0,10,1]
It states how many private patents equal parent 2's second private milestone.

(285) PrivAL3P1=0
Units: Patents
It states how many private patents equal parent 1's third private milestone.

(286) PrivAL3P2=0
Units: Patents
It states how many private patents equal parent 2's third private milestone.

(287) PrivALP1[m1]=PrivAL1P1
PrivALP1[m2]=PrivAL2P1
PrivALP1[m3]=PrivAL3P1
Units: Patents
PrivALP1 states the various private patents that Parent 1 seeks to achieve in the various milestones.

(288) PrivALP2[m1]=PrivAL1P2
PrivALP2[m2]=PrivAL2P2
PrivALP2[m3]=PrivAL3P2
Units: Patents
PrivALP1 states the various private patents that Parent 2 seeks to achieve in the various milestones.

(289) Project start private learning=In pulse private milestones/TIME STEP*PULSE(Time of alliance start-TIME STEP,TIME STEP)
Units: Dmnl/week
This flow consists of a pulse function. It states that the project the parents work on starts in the week determined by the Time of alliance start.

(290) Which Private Milestone j[Parent]= INTEG (Chng WM private j[Parent]+Project start private learning,0)
Units: Dmnl
This stock accumulates the milestones that the parents are privately working on.

****
.Scientist allocation
****

(292) Actual goal of scientist allocation i for common learning[Parent]=Aspiration level i[Parent]*(Scientists per patent to be achieved i per agreement[Parent]*Fractional scientist bonus per patent i[Parent])
Units: People
The actual, internally communicated common goals determine how many scientists a partner firm assigns to the learning alliance.

(293) Actual goal of scientist allocation j for private benefits[Parent]=Aspiration level private j[Parent]*Scientists per patent to be achieved i per agreement[Parent]
Units: People
In the case of private benefits the firms adjust their scientist allocation to the number of private goals. Even though these scientists do not directly work on generating private knowledge the firms allocates more scientists for common learning when they expect higher knowledge spillovers.

(294) Alliance research capacity[Parent]=0+STEP("Scientists active in alliance - parent i"[Parent], Time of alliance start)
Units: People [0,10]
Both parents' scientists are summed up in the research capacity.

(295) Desired scientists level i[Parent]=Indicated max scientist level i[Parent]*Effect of indicated scientists from reciprocity on scientist allocation i[Parent]*Effect of trust on scientist allocation i[Parent]
Units: People
The variable indicates the desired # of scientists in the alliance. It is a multiplier of three inputs: the Indicated max scientist level by the respective common or private aspiration levels, the Effect of indicated scientists from reciprocity, and the Effect of manager trust on scientist allocation.

(296) Effect of indicated scientists from reciprocity on scientist allocation i[Parent]=T Effect of indicated scientists from reciprocity on scientist allocation i(Relative commitment j vs i[Parent])
Units: Dmnl
This variable calculates the effect of the relative scientist commitment on the own scientist allocation.

(297) Expected scientist allocation based on honeymoon[Parent]= INTEG (Scientist change rate[Parent],In Exp Sci[Parent])
Units: People
This stock calculates how many scientists should be working in the alliance. It is acknowledged that scientists cannot work in the alliance immediately after the beginning of the alliance (here called honeymoon). They have to be chosen, asked, prepared, etc. Also, the stock acknowledges that firms assign more scientists the closer the alliance gets to its goal due to increasing expectations.

(298) Fractional scientist bonus P1=1
Units: Dmnl [0,10,0.01]
If it is greater than one, the firm allocates more scientists per patent to the alliance than agreed upon. If it is smaller than one, the firm allocates fewer scientists per patent to the alliance than agreed upon.

(299) Fractional scientist bonus P2=1
Units: Dmnl
If it is greater than one, the firm allocates more scientists per patent to the alliance than agreed upon. If it is smaller than one, the firm allocates fewer scientists per patent to the alliance than agreed upon.

(300) Fractional scientist bonus per patent i[P1]=Fractional scientist bonus P1
Fractional scientist bonus per patent i[P2]=Fractional scientist bonus P2
Units: Dmnl
Varying this fraction leads to a change in the firm's actual goal of scientist allocation for joint learning.

(301) Indicated max scientist level i[Parent]=max(Actual goal of scientist allocation j for private benefits[Parent] , Actual goal of scientist allocation i for common learning[Parent])
Units: People
This variable calculates the firms' max indicated level of scientists, considering common and private goals.

(302) Net scientist allocation i[Parent]=STEP(Effect of Degree of common and private goal attainment i on Scientist allocation j to i[Parent]*Scientist gap i[Parent]/Time for allocation decision , Time of alliance start)
Units: People/week
Scientist allocation is a biflow that increases or decreases the number of Scientists active in the alliance. Mathematically this flow is determined by the Scientist gap divided by the Time of the allocation decision. Furthermore, it states when the alliance begins. Also, there might be adjustments by the Effect of Degree of common and private goal attainment.

(303) Normal expected scientists i by j[Parent]=Aspiration level externally i[Parent]*Scientists per patent to be achieved i per agreement[Parent]
Units: People
The firm's Normal # of scientists that are expected by the partner firm is calculated by multiplying the externally communicated aspiration level from the firm with the # of scientists assigned to the alliance by the firm depending on the # of patents to be achieved.

(304) Perceived scientist commitment fraction i[Parent]=SMOOTH(Scientist commitment fraction i[Parent], Perception delay)
Units: Dmnl
The Scientist commitment fraction is only perceived after a delay.

(305) Perceived scientist commitment fraction j[Parent]=SUM(Perceived scientist commitment fraction i[Parent!])-Perceived scientist commitment fraction i[Parent]
Units: Dmnl
This variable indicates the Perceived partner firm's scientist commitment fraction.

(306) Perception delay=6
Units: week
The perception delay is 6 weeks.

(307) Relative commitment j vs i[Parent]=ZIDZ(Perceived scientist commitment fraction j[Parent], Perceived scientist commitment fraction i[Parent])
Units: Dmnl
This variables calculates the Perceived relative scientist commitment from the partner company to the own firm.

(308) Scientist change rate[Parent]=(Normal expected scientists i by j[Parent]-Expected scientist allocation based on honeymoon[Parent])/Time for allocation decision
Units: People/week
The Scientist change rate changes the stock Expected scientist allocation. It does so by subtracting the Expected scientist allocation from the firm's Normal expected scientists by the partner. This requires time.

(309) Scientist commitment fraction i[Parent]=XIDZ("Scientists active in alliance - parent i"[Parent], Expected scientist allocation based on honeymoon[Parent], 1)
Units: Dmnl
The # of Scientists active in the alliance by the partner firm is put into relation to the total # of Expected scientists allocated to the alliance.

(310) Scientist gap i[Parent]=Desired scientists level i[Parent]-"Scientists active in alliance - parent i"[Parent]
Units: People
This is the gap between the Desired and the actual Scientists active in the alliance. The gap is closed via the Net scientist allocation.

(311) Scientist withdrawal when finishing alliance[Parent]=(1-Effect of Degree of common and private goal attainment i on Scientist allocation j to i[Parent])*("Scientists active in alliance - parent i"[Parent])/Time for scientist withdrawal in case of alliance dissolution
Units: People/week
When a parent reaches its goals, the scientists need to be withdrawn from the alliance as fast as possible as the former partner is no longer an ally.

(312) "Scientists active in alliance - parent i"[Parent]= INTEG (Net scientist allocation i[Parent]-Scientist withdrawal when finishing alliance[Parent],In Sci[Parent])
Units: People
This variable indicates how many scientists from each partner work in the alliance. The stock is adjusted to the scientist gap by the biflow not scientist allocation. At the end of the alliance, the stock is depleted quickly by a second outflow. After withdrawing them they don't work any longer on alliance research tasks.

(313) Scientists per patent to be achieved i per agreement[P1]=Scientists per patent to be achieved P1
Scientists per patent to be achieved i per agreement[P2]=Scientists per patent to be achieved P2
Units: People/Patents
The parent companies allocate a certain number of people to the alliance according to their common and private goals.

(314) Scientists per patent to be achieved P1=1
Units: People/Patents [0,4,0.1]
This constant indicates how many Scientists per patent to be achieved parent 1 allocates to the alliance.

(315) Scientists per patent to be achieved P2=1
Units: People/Patents [0,4,0.1]
This constant indicates how many Scientists per patent to be achieved parent 2 allocates to the alliance.

(316) T Effect of indicated scientists from reciprocity on scientist allocation i([(0,0)-(1,1)],(0,0),(0.834862,0.960526),(0.9,1),(1,1))
Units: Dmnl
This table function is a slightly saturating curve that indicates the scientist allocation reaction from one firm toward its partner. If the partner spends 90% of the resources indicated in the contract the firm's managers do not worry about its partner's integrity - following tit-for-tat. However, if the partner allocates less than 90% of the scientists indicated, the firm withdraws resources to end up on an equivalent level of contribution. The firm does not worry of the partner decides to allocate more scientists than agreed upon in the contract.

(317) Time for allocation decision=4
Units: week
It takes the managers on average 4 weeks to think about the allocation or withdrawal of scientists: deciding on this topic, looking for the appropriate scientists and to actually assigning them to the alliance. It also takes 4 weeks to reintegrate them back into another project when withdrawn.

(318) Time for scientist withdrawal in case of alliance dissolution=1
Units: week
Once the alliance is terminated it only takes one week to assign people from the alliance to new tasks.

10. References

A.T.-Kearney (2003), The Partnering Paradox, in: AT Kearney Executive Agenda, 6, 2003, 2, pp. 39-49

Ackoff, R.L. (1994), Systems Thinking and Thinking Systems, in: System Dynamics Review, 10, 1994, 2-3, pp. 175-189

Albers, W., Born, K.E., Dürr, E., Hesse, H., Kraft, A., Lampert, H., Rose, K., Rupp, H.-H., Scherf, H., Schmidt, K., and Wittmann, W. (Eds., 1977), Handwörterbuch der Wirtschaftswissenschaften, 7th Volume, Stuttgart, New York, and others 1977

Alchian, A. (1965), Some Economics of Property Rights, in: Il Politico, 30, 1965, 1, pp. 816-829

Aloysius, J.A. (2002), Research Joint Ventures: A Cooperative Game for Competitors, in: European Journal of Operational Research, 136, 2002, 3, pp. 591-602

Amann, E. (1999), Evolutionäre Spieltheorie: Grundlagen und neue Ansätze, Heidelberg 1999

Amburgey, T.L., Dacin, T., and Singh, J.V. (2000), Learning Races and Dynamic Capabilities, Working Paper of the Wharton School, University of Toronto, Working Paper 2000-13, Toronto 2000

Amit, R. and Schoemaker, P.J.H. (1993), Strategic Assets and Organizational Rent, in: Strategic Management Journal, 14, 1993, 1, pp. 33-46

Anand, B.N. and Khanna, T. (2000), Do Firms Learn to Create Value? The Case of Alliances, in: Strategic Management Journal, 21, 2000, 3, pp. 295-315

Anand, J. and Delios, A. (2002), Absolute and Relative Resources As Determinants of International Acquisitions, in: Strategic Management Journal, 23, 2002, 2, pp. 119-134

Anderson, J.C. and Narus, J.A. (1990), A Model of Distributor Firm and Manufacturer Firm Working Partnerships, in: Journal of Marketing, 54, 1990, 1, pp. 42-58

Apelt, M. (1999), Vertrauen in der zwischenbetrieblichen Kooperation, Wiesbaden 1999

Arend, R.J. and Seale, D.A. (2005), Modeling Alliance Activity: An Iterated Prisoners' Dilemma with Exit Option, in: Strategic Management Journal, 26, 2005, 11, pp. 1057-1074

Argote, L., Ingram, P., Levine, J.M., and Moreland, R.L. (2000), Knowledge Transfer in Organizations: Learning from the Experience of Others, in: Organizational Behavior and Human Decision Processes, 82, 2000, 1, pp. 1-8

Argyris, C. and Schön, D.A. (1978), Organizational Learning: A Theory of Action Perspective, Reading, Mass., Menlo Park, and others 1978

Ariño, A. (2003), Measures of Strategic Alliance Performance: An Analysis of Construct Validity, in: Journal of International Business Studies, 34, 2003, 1, pp. 66-79

Ariño, A. and de la Torre, J. (1998), Learning from Failure: Towards an Evolutionary Model of Collaborative Ventures, in: Organization Science, 9, 1998, 3, pp. 306-325

Arrow, K.J. (2003), Introductory Remarks on the History of Game Theory, in: Games and Economic Behavior, 45, 2003, 1, pp. 15-18

Atkins, P.W.B., Newell, E.B., and Wood, R.E. (2001), Developing a Measure of System Dynamics Understanding, in: Proceedings of the 19th International Conference of the System Dynamics Society, 2001

Aulakh, P.S. and Madhok, A. (2002), Cooperation and Performance in International Alliances: The Critical Role of Flexibility, in: Contractor, F.J. and Lorange, P. (Eds., 2002a), pp. 25-48

Axelrod, R.M. (1984), The Evolution of Cooperation, New York 1984

Axelrod, R.M. (1997a), Advancing the Art of Simulation in the Social Sciences, in: Conte, R., Hegselmann, R. and Terna, P. (Eds., 1997), pp. 21-40

Axelrod, R.M. (1997b), The Complexity of Cooperation: Agent-Based Models of Competition and Collaboration, Princeton and Chichester 1997

Bachmann, R. (1998), Conclusion: Trust-Conceptual Aspects of a Complex Phenomenon, in: Lane, C. and Bachmann, R. (Eds., 1998), pp. 298-322

Bachmann, R. and Lane, C. (1997), Vertrauen und Macht in zwischenbetrieblichen Kooperationen - zur Rolle von Wirtschaftsrecht und Wirtschaftsverbänden in Deutschland und Großbritannien, in: Schreyögg, G. and Sydow, J. (Eds., 1997), pp. 79-110

Baetge, J. (1977), Systemtheorie, in: Albers, W., Born, K.E., Dürr, E., Hesse, H., Kraft, A., Lampert, H., Rose, K., Rupp, H.-H., Scherf, H., Schmidt, K. and Wittmann, W. (Eds., 1977), pp. 510-534

Bain, J.S. (1956), Barriers to New Competition: Their Character and Consequences in Manufacturing Industries, Cambridge, Mass. 1956

Bamberger, I. and Wrona, T. (1996), Der Ressourcenansatz und seine Bedeutung für die Strategische Unternehmensführung, in: Zeitschrift für betriebswirtschaftliche Forschung, 48, 1996, 2, pp. 130-153

Bandura, A. (1976), Lernen am Modell: Ansätze zu einer sozial-kognitiven Lerntheorie, Stuttgart 1976

Bandura, A. (1979), Sozial-kognitive Lerntheorie, Stuttgart 1979

Barlas, Y. (1996), Formal Aspects of Model Validity and Validation in System Dynamics, in: System Dynamics Review, 12, 1996, 3, pp. 183-210

Barlas, Y. and Carpenter, S. (1990), Philosophical Roots of Model Validation: Two Paradigms, in: System Dynamics Review, 6, 1990, 2, pp. 148-166

Barney, G.O., Kreutzer, W.B., and Garrett, M.J. (Eds., 1991), Managing a Nation: The Microcomputer Software Catalog, 2nd Edition, Boulder, San Francisco, and Oxford 1991

Barney, J.B. (1991), Firm Resources and Sustained Competitive Advantage, in: Journal of Management, 17, 1991, 1, pp. 99-120

Barney, J.B. (1996), The Resource-Based Theory of the Firm, in: Organization Science, 7, 1996, 5, p. 469

Barney, J.B. (2001), Resource-Based *Theories* of Competitive Advantage: A Ten Year Retrospective on the Resource-Based View, in: Journal of Management, 27, 2001, 6, pp. 643-650

Barney, J.B., Wright, M., and Ketchen Jr., D.J. (2001), The Resource-Based View of the Firm: Ten Years After 1991, in: Journal of Management, 27, 2001, 6, pp. 625-641

Batt, P.J. and Purchase, S. (2004), Managing Collaboration within Networks and Relationships, in: Industrial Marketing Management, 33, 2004, 3, pp. 169-174

Baum, J.A.C., Calabrese, T., and Silverman, B.S. (2000), Don't Go It Alone: Alliance Network Composition and Startups' Performance in Canadian Biotechnology, in: Strategic Management Journal, 21, 2000, 3, pp. 267-294

Becker, M., Kloock, J., Schmidt, R., and Wäscher, G. (Eds., 1998), Unternehmen im Umbruch und Wandel: Transformation, Evolution und Neugestaltung privater und öffentlicher Institutionen, Stuttgart 1998

Bellmann, K. (Ed., 2001), Kooperations- und Netzwerkmanagement, Berlin 2001

Benner, M.J. and Tushman, M.L. (2003), Exploitation, Exploration, and Process Management: The Productivity Dilemma Revisited, in: Academy of Management Review, 28, 2003, 2, pp. 238-256

Berg, J., Dickhaut, J., and McCabe, K. (1995), Trust, Reciprocity, and Social History, in: Games and Economic Behavior, 10, 1995, 1, pp. 122-142

Berman, S.L., Down, J., and Hill, C.W.L. (2002), Tacit Knowledge As a Source of Competitive Advantage in the National Basketball Association, in: Academy of Management Journal, 45, 2002, 1, pp. 13-31

Berninghaus, S.K., Ehrhart, K.-M., and Güth, W. (2002), Strategische Spiele: Eine Einführung in die Spieltheorie, Berlin, Heidelberg, and others 2002

Bhagat, R.S., Kedia, B.L., Karveston, P.D., and Triandis, H.C. (2002), Cultural Variations in the Cross-Border Transfer of Organizational Knowledge: An Integrative Framework, in: Academy of Management Review, 27, 2002, 2, pp. 204-221

Bies, B., Sheppard, B., and Lewicki, R.J. (Eds., 1995), Research on Negotiation in Organizations, Greenwich, Conn. 1995

Black, L.J. (2002), Collaboration across Boundaries: Theoretical, Empirical, and Simulated Explorations, Thesis (Ph.D.) at the Sloan School of Management, Massachusetts Institute of Technology, Cambridge, Mass. 2002

Black, L.J., Carlile, P.R., and Repenning, N.P. (2004), A Dynamic Theory of Expertise and Occupational Boundaries in New Technology Implementation: Building on Barley's Study of CT Scanning, in: Administrative Science Quarterly, 49, 2004, 4, pp. 572-607

Blau, P.M. (1964), Exchange and Power in Social Life, New York 1964

Bontis, N., Crossan, M.M., and Hulland, J. (2002), Managing an Organizational Learning System by Aligning Stocks and Flows, in: Journal of Management Studies, 39, 2002, 4, pp. 437-469

Booth Sweeney, L. and Sterman, J.D. (2000), Bathtub Dynamics: Initial Results of a Systems Thinking Inventory, in: System Dynamics Review, 16, 2000, 4, pp. 249-286

Börner, C.J. (2000), Die Integration marktorientierter und ressourcenorientierter Strategien, in: Das Wirtschaftsstudium, 29, 2000, 6, pp. 817-821

Bowman, E.H. (1974), Epistemology, Corporate Strategy, and Academe, in: MIT Sloan Management Review, 15, 1974, 2, pp. 35-50

Bradach, J.L. and Eccles, R.G. (1989), Price, Authority, and Trust: From Ideal Types to Plural Forms, in: Annual Review of Sociology, 15, 1989, 1, pp. 97-118

Brandenburger, A.M. and Nalebuff, B.J. (1995), The Right Game: Use Game Theory to Shape Strategy, in: Harvard Business Review, 73, 1995, 4, pp. 57-71

Brandenburger, A.M. and Nalebuff, B.J. (1996), Coopetition, New York 1996

Brandt Husman, T. (2001), Efficiency in Inter-Organisational Learning: A Taxonomy of Knowledge Transfer Costs, Working Paper of the Copenhagen Business School, Working Paper 2001-4, Copenhagen 2001

Brehm, J.W. (1966), A Theory of Psychological Reactance, New York 1966

Bromiley, P. and Cummings, L.L. (1995), Transaction Costs in Organizations with Trust, in: Bies, B., Sheppard, B. and Lewicki, R.J. (Eds., 1995), pp. 219-247

Büchel, B. (2000), Framework of Joint Venture Development: Theory-Building through Qualitative Research, in: Journal of Management Studies, 37, 2000, 5, pp. 637-661

Büchel, B. (2003), Managing Partner Relations in Joint Ventures, in: MIT Sloan Management Review, 44, 2003, 4, pp. 91-95

Büchs, M.J. (1991), Zwischen Markt und Hierarchie: Kooperationen als alternative Koordinationsform, in: Zeitschrift für Betriebswirtschaft, 61, 1991, 1 (Additional Issue), pp. 1-36

Burks, A.W., Goldstine, H.H., and von Neumann, J. (1963), Preliminary Discussion on the Logical Design of an Electronic Computing Instrument, in: von Neumann, J. (Ed., 1963), pp. 34-79

Calantone, R.J., Cavusgil, S.T., and Zhao, Y. (2002), Learning Orientation, Firm Innovation Capability, and Firm Performance, in: Industrial Marketing Management, 31, 2002, 6, pp. 515-524

Camerer, C.F. (1997), Progress in Behavioral Game Theory, in: Journal of Economic Perspectives, 11, 1997, 4, pp. 167-188

Camerer, C.F. (1999), Behavioral Economics: Reunifying Psychology and Economics, in: Proceedings of the National Academy of Sciences of the United States of America, 96, 1999, 19, pp. 10575-10577

Camerer, C.F. (2003a), Behavioral Game Theory: Experiments in Strategic Interaction, Princeton and New York 2003

Camerer, C.F. (2003b), Behavioural Studies of Strategic Thinking in Games, in: Trends in Cognitive Sciences, 7, 2003, 5, pp. 225-231

Camerer, C.F. (2003c), Strategizing in the Brain, in: Science, 300, 2003, 5626, pp. 1673-1675

Camerer, C.F., Babcock, L., Loewenstein, G., and Thaler, R. (1997), Labor Supply of New York City Cabdrivers: One Day at a Time, in: Quarterly Journal of Economics, 112, 1997, 2, pp. 407-441

Camerer, C.F. and Thaler, R.H. (1995), Anomalies: Ultimatums, Dictators and Manners, in: Journal of Economic Perspectives, 9, 1995, 2, pp. 209-219

Carayannis, E.G. and Alexander, J. (2002), Is Technological Learning a Firm Core Competence, When, How and Why? A Longitudinal, Multi-Industry Study of Firm Technological Learning and Market Performance, in: Technovation, 22, 2002, 10, pp. 625-643

Carley, K.M. (1992), Organizational Learning and Personnel Turnover, in: Organization Science, 3, 1992, 1, pp. 20-46

Carlile, P.R. (2004), Transferring, Translating, and Transforming: An Integrative Framework for Managing Knowledge Across Boundaries, in: Organization Science, 15, 2004, 5, pp. 555-568

Carpenter, J.P. (2003), Bargaining Outcomes As the Result of Coordinated Expectations, in: The Journal of Conflict Resolution, 47, 2003, 2, pp. 119-139

Castanias, R.P. and Helfat, C.E. (1991), Managerial Resources and Rents, in: Journal of Management, 17, 1991, 1, pp. 155-171

Castanias, R.P. and Helfat, C.E. (2001), The Managerial Rents Model: Theory and Empirical Analysis, in: Journal of Management, 27, 2001, 6, pp. 661-678

Child, J. (1998), Trust and International Strategic Alliances: The Case of Sino-Foreign Joint Ventures, in: Lane, C. and Bachmann, R. (Eds., 1998), pp. 241-272

Child, J. (2001a), Learning through Strategic Alliances, in: Dierkes, M., Antal, A.B., Child, J. and Nonaka, I. (Eds., 2001), pp. 657-680

Child, J. (2001b), Trust - The Fundamental Bond in Global Collaboration, in: Organizational Dynamics, 29, 2001, 4, pp. 274-288

Child, J. and Faulkner, D. (1998), Strategies of Cooperation: Managing Alliances, Networks, and Joint Ventures, Oxford, New York, and others 1998

Chiles, T.H. and McMackin, J.F. (1996), Integrating Variable Risk Preferences, Trust, and Transaction Cost Economics, in: Academy of Management Review, 21, 1996, 1, pp. 73-99

Chmielewicz, K. (1994), Forschungskonzeptionen der Wirtschaftswissenschaft, 3rd Edition, Stuttgart 1994

Coase, R.H. (1937), The Nature of the Firm, in: Economica, 4, 1937, 16, pp. 386-405

Coffey, A. and Atkinson, P. (1996), Making Sense of Qualitative Data: Complementary Research Strategies, Thousand Oaks 1996

Cohen, W.M. and Levinthal, D.A. (1990), Absorptive Capacity: A New Perspective on Learning and Innovation, in: Administrative Science Quarterly, 35, 1990, 1, pp. 128-152

Coleman-Kammula, S., Burton, L.P.J., Sterman, J.D., Andersen, D.F., and Richardson, G.P. (2005), A System Dynamics Study of a Commodity Plastics Industry, in: Proceedings of the 23rd International System Dynamics Conference, 2005

Colman, A.M. (2003), Cooperation, Psychological Game Theory, and Limitations of Rationality in Social Interaction, in: Behavioral and Brain Sciences, 26, 2003, 2, pp. 139-198

Combs, J.G. and Ketchen, D.J. (1999), Explaining Interfirm Cooperation and Performance: Toward a Reconciliation of Predictions from the Resource-Based View and Organizational Economics, in: Strategic Management Journal, 20, 1999, 9, pp. 867-888

Conner, K.R. (1991), A Historical Comparison of Resource-Based Theory and Five Schools of Thought within Industrial Organization Economies: Do We Have a New Theory of the Firm?, in: Journal of Management, 17, 1991, 1, pp. 121-154

Conner, K.R. and Prahalad, C.K. (1996), A Resource-Based Theory of the Firm: Knowledge versus Opportunism, in: Organization Science, 7, 1996, 5, pp. 477-501

Conte, R., Hegselmann, R., and Terna, P. (Eds., 1997), Simulating Social Phenomena, Berlin, Heidelberg, and others 1997

Contractor, F.J., Kim, C.-S., and Beldona, S. (2002), Interfirm Learning in Alliance and Technology Networks: An Empirical Study in the Global Pharmaceutical and Chemical Industries, in: Contractor, F.J. and Lorange, P. (Eds., 2002a), pp. 493-516

Contractor, F.J. and Lorange, P. (Eds., 1988a), Cooperative Strategies in International Business, Lexington and Toronto 1988

Contractor, F.J. and Lorange, P. (1988b), Why Should Firms Cooperate? The Strategy and Economics Basis for Cooperative Ventures, in: Contractor, F.J. and Lorange, P. (Eds., 1988a), pp. 3-30

Contractor, F.J. and Lorange, P. (Eds., 2002a), Cooperative Strategies and Alliances, Amsterdam, Boston, and others 2002

Contractor, F.J. and Lorange, P. (2002b), The Growth of Alliances in the Knowledge-Based Economy, in: Contractor, F.J. and Lorange, P. (Eds., 2002a), pp. 3-22

Cook, K.S. (Ed., 2001), Trust in Society, New York 2001

Coyle, R.G. (1996), System Dynamics Modelling: A Practical Approach, London, Glasgow, and others 1996

Crawford, V.P. (2002), Introduction to Experimental Game Theory, in: Journal of Economic Theory, 104, 2002, 1, pp. 1-15

Crossan, M.M. and Berdrow, I. (2003), Organizational Learning and Strategic Renewal, in: Strategic Management Journal, 24, 2003, 11, pp. 1087-1105

Cummings, L.L. and Staw, B.M. (Eds., 1985), Research in Organizational Behavior, Greenwich, Conn. 1985

Currall, S.C. and Epstein, M.J. (2003), The Fragility of Organizational Trust: Lessons from the Rise and Fall of Enron, in: Organizational Dynamics, 32, 2003, 2, pp. 193-206

Currall, S.C. and Inkpen, A.C. (2002), A Multilevel Approach to Trust in Joint Ventures, in: Journal of International Business Studies, 33, 2002, 3, pp. 479-495

Currall, S.C. and Judge, T.A. (1995), Measuring Trust between Organizational Boundary Role Persons, in: Organizational Behavior and Human Decision Processes, 64, 1995, 2, pp. 151-170

Das, T.K. and Rahman, N. (2002), Opportunism Dynamics in Strategic Alliances, in: Contractor, F.J. and Lorange, P. (Eds., 2002a), pp. 89-118

Das, T.K. and Teng, B.-S. (1996), Risk Types and Inter-Firm Alliance Structures, in: Journal of Management Studies, 33, 1996, 6, pp. 827-843

Das, T.K. and Teng, B.-S. (1998), Between Trust and Control: Developing Confidence in Partner Cooperation in Alliances, in: Academy of Management Review, 23, 1998, 3, pp. 491-512

Das, T.K. and Teng, B.-S. (2000), Instabilities of Strategic Alliances: An Internal Tensions Perspective, in: Organization Science, 11, 2000, 1, pp. 77-101

Das, T.K. and Teng, B.-S. (2001), Trust, Control, and Risk in Strategic Alliances: An Integrated Framework, in: Organization Studies, 22, 2001, 2, pp. 251-283

Das, T.K. and Teng, B.-S. (2002), Alliance Constellations: A Social Exchange Perspective, in: Academy of Management Review, 27, 2002, 3, pp. 445-456

D'Aunno, T.A. and Zuckerman, H.S. (1987), A Life Cycle Model of Organizational Federations: The Case of Hospitals, in: Academy of Management Review, 12, 1987, 3, pp. 534-545

Davis, M.D. (1993), Spieltheorie für Nichtmathematiker, 2nd Edition, München 1993

Day, G.S., Reibstein, D.J., and Gunther, R. (Eds., 1997), Wharton on Dynamic Competitive Strategy, New York 1997

de Holan, P.M., Phillips, N., and Lawrence, T.B. (2004), Managing Organizational Forgetting, in: MIT Sloan Management Review, 45, 2004, 2, pp. 45-51

de Man, A.-P. and Duysters, G. (2002), The State of Alliance Management: Special ASAP Report of Research into Alliance Capability, Working Paper of the University of Maastricht, Working Paper, Maastricht 2002

de Rond, M. and Bouchikhi, H. (2004), On the Dialectics of Strategic Alliances, in: Organization Science, 15, 2004, 1, pp. 56-69

DeCarolis, D.M. and Deeds, D.L. (1999), The Impact of Stocks and Flows of Organizational Knowledge on Firm Performance: An Empirical Investigation of the Biotechnology Industry, in: Strategic Management Journal, 20, 1999, 10, pp. 953-968

Deering, A. and Murphy, A. (2003), The Partnering Imperative: Making Business Partnerships Work, West Sussex 2003

Demsetz, H. (1967), Toward a Theory of Property Rights, in: The American Economic Review, 57, 1967, 2, pp. 347-359

Dengel, H.M. and Milling, P.M. (2002), Aspects of the Dynamics of Cooperations in a Supply Chain under Consideration of Trust, in: Proceedings of the 20th International Conference of the System Dynamics Society, 2002

Dierickx, I. and Cool, K. (1989), Asset Stock Accumulation and Sustainability of Competitive Advantage, in: Management Science, 35, 1989, 12, pp. 1504-1511

Dierkes, M., Antal, A.B., Child, J., and Nonaka, I. (Eds., 2001), Handbook of Organizational Learning and Knowledge, Oxford 2001

Dörner, D. (2002), Die Logik des Misslingens, 15th Edition, Hamburg 2002

Dosi, G. (1988), Sources, Procedures, and Microeconomic Effects of Innovation, in: Journal of Economic Literature, 26, 1988, 3, pp. 1120-1171

Doyle, J.K. and Ford, D.N. (1998), Mental Models Concepts for System Dynamics Research, in: System Dynamics Review, 14, 1998, 1, pp. 3-29

Doz, Y.L. (1996), The Evolution of Cooperation in Strategic Alliances: Initial Conditions or Learning Processes?, in: Strategic Management Journal, 17, 1996, 7, pp. 55-83

Doz, Y.L. and Hamel, G. (1998), Alliance Advantage: The Art of Creating Value through Partnering, Boston 1998

Durand, R. (2002), Competitive Advantages Exist: A Critique of Powell, in: Strategic Management Journal, 23, 2002, 9, pp. 867-872

Dussauge, P., Garrette, B., and Mitchell, W. (2000), Learning from Competing Partners: Outcomes and Durations of Scale and Link Alliances in Europe, North America and Asia, in: Strategic Management Journal, 21, 2000, 2, pp. 99-126

Dussauge, P., Garrette, B., and Mitchell, W. (2002), The Market Share Impact of Inter-Partner Learning in Alliances: Evidence from the Global Auto Industry, in: Contractor, F.J. and Lorange, P. (Eds., 2002a), pp. 707-727

Duysters, G., Kok, G., and Vaandrager, M. (1999), Crafting Successful Strategic Technology Partnerships, in: R&D Management, 29, 1999, 4, pp. 343-351

Dyer, J.H. (1997), Effective Interfirm Collaboration: How Firms Minimize Transaction Costs and Maximize Transaction Value, in: Strategic Management Journal, 18, 1997, 7, pp. 535-556

Dyer, J.H., Kale, P., and Singh, H. (2001), How to Make Strategic Alliances Work, in: MIT Sloan Management Review, 42, 2001, 4, pp. 37-43

Dyer, J.H. and Nobeoka, K. (2000), Creating and Managing a High-Performance Knowledge-Sharing Network: The Toyota Case, in: Strategic Management Journal, 21, 2000, 3, pp. 345-367

Dyer, J.H. and Singh, H. (1998), The Relational View: Cooperative Strategy and Sources of Interorganizational Competitive Advantage, in: Academy of Management Review, 23, 1998, 4, pp. 660-679

Eisenhardt, K.M. (1989), Agency Theory: An Assessment and Review, in: Academy of Management Review, 14, 1989, 1, pp. 57-74

Eisenhardt, K.M. and Martin, J.A. (2000), Dynamic Capabilities: What Are They?, in: Strategic Management Journal, 21, 2000, 10-11, pp. 1105-1121

Engel, A. and Möhring, M. (1995), Der Beitrag sozialwissenschaftlicher Informatik zur sozialwissenschaftlichen Modellbildung und Simulation, in: Gsänger, M. and Klawitter, J. (Eds., 1995), pp. 39-60

Espejo, R. (1994), What Is Systemic Thinking?, in: System Dynamics Review, 10, 1994, 2-3, pp. 199-212

Fang, C., Kimbrough, S.O., Pace, S., Valluri, A., and Zheng, Z. (2002), On Adaptive Emergence of Trust Behavior in the Game of Stag Hunt, in: Group Decision and Negotiation, 11, 2002, 6, pp. 449-467

Fehr, E. and Schmidt, K.M. (1999), A Theory of Fairness, Competition, and Cooperation, in: The Quarterly Journal of Economics, 114, 1999, 3, pp. 817-868

Fehr, E. and Schmidt, K.M. (2001), Theories of Fairness and Reciprocity: Evidence and Economic Applications, Working Paper of the Institute for Empirical Research in Economics of the University of Zürich, Working Paper No. 75, Zürich 2001

Feinberg, S.E. and Gupta, A.K. (2004), Knowledge Spillovers and the Assignment of R&D Responsibilities to Foreign Subsidiaries, in: Strategic Management Journal, 25, 2004, 8-9, pp. 823-845

Fichman, M. (2003), Straining towards Trust: Some Constraints on Studying Trust in Organizations, in: Journal of Organizational Behavior, 24, 2003, 2, pp. 133-157

Finnie, W.C. (1998), Strategic Partnering: Three Case Studies, in: Strategy & Leadership, 26, 1998, 4, pp. 18-22

Fiol, C.M. (2001), Revisiting an Identity-Based View of Sustainable Competitive Advantage, in: Journal of Management, 27, 2001, 6, pp. 691-699

Fiol, C.M. and Lyles, M.A. (1985), Organizational Learning, in: Academy of Management Review, 10, 1985, 4, pp. 803-813

Fishwick, P.A. and Luker, P.A. (Eds., 1991), Qualitative Simulation Modeling and Analysis, New York, Berlin, and Heidelberg 1991

Flam, H. (1990), Emotional 'Man': I. The Emotional 'Man' and the Problem of Collective Action, in: International Sociology, 5, 1990, 1, pp. 39-56

Flam, H. (2000), The Emotional *Man* and the Problem of Collective Action, Frankfurt am Main, Berlin, and others 2000

Ford, D.N. (1995), The Dynamics of Project Management: An Investigation of the Impacts of Project Process and Coordination on Performance, Thesis (Ph.D.) at the Sloan School of Management, Massachusetts Institute of Technology, Cambridge, Mass. 1995

Ford, D.N. (1999), A Behavioral Approach to Feedback Loop Dominance Analysis, in: System Dynamics Review, 15, 1999, 1, pp. 3-36

Forrest, J.E. and Martin, M.J.C. (1992), Strategic Alliances between Large and Small Research Intensive Organizations: Experiences in the Biotechnology Industry, in: R&D Management, 22, 1992, 1, pp. 41-53

Forrester, J.W. (1961), Industrial Dynamics, Cambridge, Mass. 1961

Forrester, J.W. (1969), Urban Dynamics, Portland 1969

Forrester, J.W. (1971), World Dynamics, Cambridge, Mass. 1971

Forrester, J.W. (1972), Grundzüge einer Systemtheorie, Wiesbaden 1972

Forrester, J.W. (Ed., 1975a), Collected Papers of Jay W. Forrester, Cambridge, Mass. 1975

Forrester, J.W. (1975b), Counterintuitive Behavior of Social Systems, in: Forrester, J.W. (Ed., 1975a), pp. 211-244

Forrester, J.W. (1980), System Dynamics - Future Opportunities, in: Legasto, A.A., Forrester, J.W. and Lyneis, J.M. (Eds., 1980), pp. 7-21

Forrester, J.W. (1985), "The" Model versus a Modeling "Process", in: System Dynamics Review, 1, 1985, 1, pp. 133-134

Forrester, J.W. (1994a), Learning through System Dynamics As Preparation for the 21st Century, Working Paper of the Massachusetts Institute of Technology, Sloan School of Management, Working Paper D-4434-1, Cambridge, Mass. 1994

Forrester, J.W. (1994b), Policies, Decisions, and Information Sources for Modeling, in: Morecroft, J.D.W. and Sterman, J.D. (Eds., 1994), pp. 51-84

Forrester, J.W. (1994c), System Dynamics, System Thinking, and Soft OR, in: System Dynamics Review, 10, 1994, 2-3, pp. 245-256

Forrester, J.W. and Senge, P.M. (1980), Tests for Building Confidence in System Dynamics Models, in: Legasto, A.A., Forrester, J.W. and Lyneis, J.M. (Eds., 1980), pp. 209-228

Foss, N.J. (1996a), Knowledge-Based Approaches to the Theory of the Firm: Some Critical Comments, in: Organization Science, 7, 1996, 5, pp. 470-476

Foss, N.J. (1996b), More Critical Comments on Knowledge-Based Theories of the Firm, in: Organization Science, 7, 1996, 5, pp. 519-523

Frank, R.H. (2002), Passions within Reason: The Strategic Role of the Emotions, New York and London 2002

Frank, U. (Ed., 2004), Wissenschaftstheorie in Ökonomie und Wirtschaftsinformatik: Theoriebildung und -bewertung, Ontologien, Wissensmanagement, Wiesbaden 2004

Freiling, J. (2000), Entwicklungslinien und Perspektiven des Strategischen Kompetenz-Managements, in: Hammann, P. and Freiling, J. (Eds., 2000), pp. 13-45

Freiling, J. (2004), Competence-Based View der Unternehmung, in: Die Unternehmung, 58, 2004, 1, pp. 5-25

Friedrichs, J. (1990), Methoden empirischer Sozialforschung, 14th Edition, Opladen 1990

Galunic, D.C. and Rodan, S. (1998), Resource Recombinations in the Firm: Knowledge Structures and the Potential for Schumpeterian Innovation, in: Strategic Management Journal, 19, 1998, 12, pp. 1193-1201

Gambetta, D. (1988a), Can We Trust Trust?, in: Gambetta, D. (Ed., 1988b), pp. 213-237

Gambetta, D. (Ed., 1988b), Trust: Making and Breaking Cooperative Relations, New York and Oxford 1988

Garcia, R., Calantone, R.J., and Levine, R.L. (2003), The Role of Knowledge in Resource Allocation to Exploration versus Exploitation in Technologically Oriented Organizations, in: Decision Sciences, 34, 2003, 2, pp. 323-349

Gary, M.S. (2005), Implementation Strategy and Performance Outcomes in Related Diversification, in: Strategic Management Journal, 26, 2005, 7, pp. 643-664

Gass, S.I. and Harris, C.M. (Eds., 1996), Encyclopedia of Operations Research and Management Science, Boston, Dordrecht, and London 1996

Gass, S.I. and Harris, C.M. (Eds., 2001), Encyclopedia of Operations Research and Management Science, 2nd Edition, Boston, Dordrecht, and London 2001

Gebrekidan, D.A. and Awuah, G.B. (2002), Interorganizational Cooperation: A New View of Strategic Alliances. The Case of Swedish Firms in the International Market, in: Industrial Marketing Management, 31, 2002, 8, pp. 679-693

Gerard-Varet, L.A., Kirman, A.P., and Ruggiero, M. (Eds., 1999), Economics Beyond the Millennium, Oxford 1999

Gerrard, B. (1993), The Economics of Rationality, Padstow 1993

Geschka, H. (1999), Die Szenariotechnik in der strategischen Unternehmensplanung, in: Hahn, D. and Taylor, B. (Eds., 1999), pp. 518-545

Ghemawat, P. (1986), Sustainable Advantage, in: Harvard Business Review, 64, 1986, 5, pp. 53-58

Ghemawat, P. and del Sol, P. (1998), Commitment versus Flexibility?, in: California Management Review, 40, 1998, 4, pp. 26-42

Ghoshal, S. and Moran, P. (1996), Bad for Practice: A Critique of the Transaction Cost Theory, in: Academy of Management Review, 21, 1996, 1, pp. 13-47

Gintis, H., Bowles, S., Boyd, R., and Fehr, E. (2003), Explaining Altruistic Behavior in Humans, in: Evolution and Human Behavior, 24, 2003, 3, pp. 153-172

Gladwell, M. (2000), The Tipping Point: How Little Things Can Make a Big Difference, New York and Boston 2000

Glaister, K.W. and Buckley, P.J. (1996), Strategic Motives for International Alliance Formation, in: Journal of Management Studies, 33, 1996, 3, pp. 301-332

Glaser, B.G. (1978), Theoretical Sensitivity. Advances in the Methodology of Grounded Theory, Mill Valley 1978

Glaser, B.G. and Strauss, A.L. (1967), The Discovery of Grounded Theory: Strategies for Qualitative Research, Chicago and New York 1967

Glückler, J. and Armbrüster, T. (2003), Bridging Uncertainty in Management Consulting: The Mechanism of Trust and Networked Reputation, in: Organization Studies, 24, 2003, 2, pp. 269-297

Goldstine, H.H. (1972), The Computer from Pascal to von Neumann, Princeton 1972

Goldstine, H.H. and von Neumann, J. (1963), On the Principles of Large Scale Computing Machines, in: von Neumann, J. (Ed., 1963), pp. 1-32

Gonçalves, P.M. (2003), Demand Bubbles and Phantom Orders in Supply Chains, Thesis (Ph.D.) at the Sloan School of Management, Massachusetts Institute of Technology, Cambridge, Mass. 2003

Gonçalves, P.M. and Sterman, J.D. (2005), Overordering Games in Supply Chains, in: Proceedings of the 23rd International Conference of the System Dynamics Society, 2005

Gorobets, A. and Nooteboom, B. (2004), Agent Based Computational Model of Trust, Working Paper of the Erasmus Research Institute of Management, Erasmus University Rotterdam, Working Paper ERS-2004-108-ORG, Rotterdam 2004

Goussevskaia, A. and Swan, J. (2003), The Role of Inter-Firm Learning in the Constructive Process of Organizational Change, Working Paper of the Warwick Business School, University of Warwick, Working Paper July 2003, Coventry 2003

Gramelsberger, G. (1996), Theorie-Simulation - Experiment, Thesis (Diploma) at the Lehrstuhl für Philosphie mit Schwerpunkt Analytische Philosophie / Wissenschaftstheorie, Universtität Augsburg, Augsburg 1996

Gramelsberger, G. (2001), Semiotik und Simulation: Fortführung der Schrift ins Dynamische, Thesis (Ph.D.) at the Fachbereich Philosophie und Geisteswissenschaften, Freie Universität Berlin, Berlin 2001

Granovetter, M. (1985), Economic Action and Social Structure: The Problem of Embeddedness, in: American Journal of Sociology, 91, 1985, 3, pp. 481-510

Granovetter, M. (1992), Problems of Explanation in Economic Sociology, in: Nohria, N. and Eccles, R.G. (Eds., 1992), pp. 25-56

Grant, R.M. (1991), The Resource-Based Theory of Competitive Advantage: Implications for Strategy Formulation, in: California Management Review, 33, 1991, 3, pp. 114-135

Grant, R.M. (1996), Toward a Knowledge-Based Theory of the Firm, in: Strategic Management Journal, 17, 1996, Winter Special Issue, pp. 109-122

Grant, R.M. and Baden-Fuller, C. (1995), A Knowledge-Based Theory of Inter-Firm Collaboration, in: Academy of Management Best Papers Proceedings, No Volume, 1995, No Issue Number, pp. 17-21

Grant, R.M. and Baden-Fuller, C. (2004), A Knowledge Accessing Theory of Strategic Alliances, in: Journal of Management Studies, 41, 2004, 1, pp. 61-84

Gray, B. (1989), Collaborating: Finding Common Ground for Multiparty Problems, San Francisco and London 1989

Griliches, Z. (1990), Patent Statistics As Economic Indicators: A Survey, in: Journal of Economic Literature, 28, 1990, 4, pp. 1661-1707

Größler, A. (2004), A Content and Process View on Bounded Rationality in System Dynamics, in: Systems Research and Behavioral Science, 21, 2004, 4, pp. 319-330

Größler, A. and Thun, J.-H. (2004), Die Diffusion von Netzwerkgütern: Eine systemdynamische Betrachtung, in: Das Wirtschaftswissenschaftliche Studium, 33, 2004, 12, pp. 700-705

Grossman, G.M. and Helpman, E. (1994), Endogenous Innovation in the Theory of Growth, in: Journal of Economic Perspectives, 8, 1994, 1, pp. 23-44

Grossman, G.M. and Shapiro, C. (1986), Optimal Dynamic R&D Programs, in: Rand Journal of Economics, 17, 1986, 4, pp. 581-593

Grossman, G.M. and Shapiro, C. (1987), Dynamic R&D Competition, in: The Economic Journal, 97, 1987, 386, pp. 372-387

Grunwald, R. (2003), Inter-organisationales Lernen: Eine empirische Analyse von Lernprozessen in Unternehmenskooperationen, Wiesbaden 2003

Grunwald, R. and Kieser, A. (2003), Lernen, nicht zu lernen, in: Harvard Business Manager, 25, 2003, 7, pp. 35-43

Gsänger, M. and Klawitter, J. (Eds., 1995), Modellbildung und Simulation in den Sozialwissenschaften, Dettelbach 1995

Gulati, R. (1995a), Does Familiarity Breed Trust? The Implications of Repeated Ties for Contractual Choice in Alliances, in: Academy of Management Journal, 38, 1995, 1, pp. 85-112

Gulati, R. (1995b), Social Structure and Alliance Formation Patterns: A Longitudinal Analysis, in: Administrative Science Quarterly, 40, 1995, 4, pp. 619-652

Gulati, R. (1998), Alliances and Networks, in: Strategic Management Journal, 19, 1998, 4, pp. 293-317

Gulati, R. (1999), Network Location and Learning: The Influence of Network Resources and Firm Capabilities on Alliance Formation, in: Strategic Management Journal, 20, 1999, 5, pp. 397-420

Gulati, R., Khanna, T., and Nohria, N. (1994), Unilateral Commitments and the Importance of Process in Alliances, in: MIT Sloan Management Review, 35, 1994, 3, pp. 61-69

Güth, W., Schmittberger, R., and Schwarze, B. (1982), An Experimental Analysis of Ultimatum Bargaining, in: Journal of Economic Behavior and Organization, 3, 1982, 4, pp. 367-388

Hagedoorn, J., Link, A.N., and Vonortas, N.S. (2000), Research Partnerships, in: Research Policy, 29, 2000, 4-5, pp. 567-586

Hagedoorn, J. and Osborn, R., N. (2002), Interfirm R&D Partnerships: Major Theories and Trends Since 1960, in: Contractor, F.J. and Lorange, P. (Eds., 2002a), pp. 517-542

Hagreaves Heap, S. (1993), Post-Modernity and New Conceptions of Rationality in Economics, in: Gerrad, B. (Ed., 1993), pp. 68-90

Hahn, D. and Taylor, B. (Eds., 1999), Strategische Unternehmensplanung - Strategische Unternehmensführung, 8th Edition, Heidelberg 1999

Håkansson, H. (1987), Industrial Technological Development: A Network Approach, London, Sydney, and Dover, N.H. 1987

Håkansson, H., Havila, V., and Pedersen, A.-C. (1999), Learning in Networks, in: Industrial Marketing Management, 28, 1999, 5, pp. 443-452

Hamel, G. (1991), Competition for Competence and Interpartner Learning within International Alliances, in: Strategic Management Journal, 12, 1991, Summer Special Issue, pp. 83-103

Hamel, G., Doz, Y.L., and Prahalad, C.K. (1989), Collaborate with Your Competitors - and Win, in: Harvard Business Review, 67, 1989, 1, pp. 133-139

Hamel, G. and Prahalad, C.K. (1994), Competing for the Future, Boston 1994

Hammann, P. and Freiling, J. (Eds., 2000), Die Ressourcen- und Kompetenzperspektive des Strategischen Managements, Wiesbaden 2000

Hampton, W.J. and Norman, J.R. (1987), General Motors: What Went Wrong, in: Business Week, 16 March 1987, pp. 102-110

Hannan, M.T. and Freeman, J. (1977), The Population Ecology of Organizations, in: American Journal of Sociology, 82, 1977, 5, pp. 929-964

Hansen, M.T. and Nohria, N. (2004), How to Build Collaborative Advantage, in: MIT Sloan Management Review, 46, 2004, 1, pp. 22-30

Harbison, J.R. and Pekar Jr., P. (1997), Smart Alliances, San Francisco 1997

Harrigan, K.R. (1988), Strategic Alliances and Partner Asymmetries, in: Contractor, F.J. and Lorange, P. (Eds., 1988a), pp. 205-226

Harrison, J.S., Hitt, M.A., Hoskisson, R.E., and Ireland, R.D. (2001), Resource Complementarity in Business Combinations: Extending the Logic to Organizational Alliances, in: Journal of Management, 27, 2001, 6, pp. 679-690

Hayward, M.L.A. (2002), When Do Firms Learn from Their Acquisition Experience? Evidence from 1990-1995, in: Strategic Management Journal, 23, 2002, 1, pp. 21-39

Hedberg, B. (1981), How Organizations Learn and Unlearn, in: Nystrom, P.C. and Starbuck, W.H. (Eds., 1981), pp. 3-27

Heine, B.-O. and Kunz, J. (2003), Die Computersimulation als Methode in der betriebswirtschaftlichen Forschung, in: Controlling & Management, 47, 2003, 6, pp. 374-378

Hennart, J.-F. (1988), A Transaction Cost Theory of Equity Joint Ventures, in: Strategic Management Journal, 9, 1988, 4, pp. 361-374

Hennart, J.-F. (1991), The Transaction Costs Theory of Joint Ventures: An Empirical Study of Japanese Subsidiaries in the United States, in: Management Science, 37, 1991, 4, pp. 483-497

Henrich, J., Boyd, R., Bowles, S., Camerer, C.F., Fehr, E., Gintis, H., and McElreath, R. (2001), In Search of Homo Economicus: Behavioral Experiments in 15 Small-Scale Societies, in: American Economic Review, 91, 2001, 2, pp. 73-78

Herbst, C. (2002), Interorganisationales Schnittstellenmanagement: Ein Konzept zur Unterstützung des Managements von Transaktionen, Frankfurt am Main 2002

Hill, C.W.L. (1988), Differentiation versus Low Cost or Differentiation and Low Cost - A Contingency Framework, in: Academy of Management Review, 13, 1988, 3, pp. 401-412

Hill, C.W.L. (1990), Cooperation, Opportunism, and the Invisible Hand: Implications for Transaction Cost Theory, in: Academy of Management Review, 15, 1990, 3, pp. 500-513

Hines, J. (2004), Course Material: Guidelines for Kickoff Meeting and First Breakout Group Presentation: Definition of Concern and Momentum Policies, MIT Sloan School of Management, Cambridge, Mass. 2004

Hinterhuber, H.H. and Friedrich, S.A. (1999), Markt- und ressourcenorientierte Sichtweise zur Steigerung des Unternehmenswertes, in: Hahn, D. and Taylor, B. (Eds., 1999), pp. 990-1018

Ho Park, S., Chen, R., and Gallagher, S. (2002), Firm Resources As Moderators of the Relationship between Market Growth and Strategic Alliances in Semiconductor Start-Ups, in: Academy of Management Journal, 45, 2002, 3, pp. 527-545

Ho Park, S. and Ungson, G.R. (2001), Interfirm Rivalry and Managerial Complexity: A Conceptual Framework of Alliance Failure, in: Organization Science, 12, 2001, 1, pp. 37-53

Ho, T.-H., Camerer, C., and Weigelt, K. (1998), Iterated Dominance and Iterated Best Response in Experimental "p-Beauty Contests", in: The American Economic Review, 88, 1998, 4, pp. 947-969

Ho, T.-H. and Weigelt, K. (1997), Game Theory and Competitive Strategy, in: Day, G.S., Reibstein, D.J. and Gunther, R. (Eds., 1997), pp. 127-150

Höfer, S. (1997), Strategische Allianzen und Spieltheorie: Analyse des Bildungsprozesses strategischer Allianzen und planungsunterstützender Einsatzmöglichkeiten der Theorie der strategischen Spiele, Köln 1997

Hofstadter, D.R. (1998), Tit for Tat: Kann sich in einer Welt voller Egoisten kooperatives Verhalten entwickeln?, in: Spektrum der Wissenschaft, 21, 1998, 1, pp. 60-67

Holmqvist, M. (1999), Learning in Imaginary Organizations: Creating Interorganizational Knowledge, in: Journal of Organizational Change Management, 12, 1999, 5, pp. 419-438

Holmqvist, M. (2003), A Dynamic Model of Intra- and Interorganizational Learning, in: Organization Studies, 24, 2003, 1, pp. 95-123

Hoßfeld, F. (1993), Wissenschaftliches Rechnen - Motor der Rechnerentwicklung, in: Weberpals, H. (Ed., 1993), pp. 5 -17

Huber, G.P. (1991), Organizational Learning: The Contributing Processes and the Literatures, in: Organization Science, 2, 1991, 1, pp. 88-115

Hullmann, A. (2001), Internationaler Wissenstransfer und technischer Wandel: Bedeutung, Einflussfaktoren und Ausblick auf technologiepolitische Implikationen am Beispiel der Nanotechnologie in Deutschland, Heidelberg 2001

Hungenberg, H., Wulf, T., and Maack, B. (2002), Erfolgsmessung in strategischen Allianzen, in: Zeitschrift für Planung, 13, 2002, 3, pp. 263-283

Hutt, M.D., Stafford, E.R., Walker, B.A., and Reingen, P.H. (2000), Defining the Social Network of a Strategic Alliance: A Case Study, in: MIT Sloan Management Review, 41, 2000, 2, pp. 51-62

Inkpen, A.C. (1995), The Management of International Joint Ventures: An Organizational Learning Perspective, London and New York 1995

Inkpen, A.C. (1996), Creating Knowledge through Collaboration, in: California Management Review, 39, 1996, 1, pp. 123-140

Inkpen, A.C. (2000a), Learning through Joint Ventures: A Framework of Knowledge Acquisition, in: Journal of Management Studies, 37, 2000, 7, pp. 1019-1043

Inkpen, A.C. (2000b), A Note on the Dynamics of Learning Alliances: Competition, Cooperation, and Relative Scope, in: Strategic Management Journal, 21, 2000, 7, pp. 775-779

Inkpen, A.C. (2002), Learning, Knowledge Management, and Strategic Alliances: So Many Studies, so Many Unanswered Questions, in: Contractor, F.J. and Lorange, P. (Eds., 2002a), pp. 267 -289

Inkpen, A.C. and Beamish, P.W. (1997), Knowledge, Bargaining Power, and the Instability of International Joint Ventures, in: Academy of Management Review, 22, 1997, 1, pp. 177-202

Inkpen, A.C. and Crossan, M.M. (1995), Believing Is Seeing: Joint Ventures and Organization Learning, in: Journal of Management Studies, 32, 1995, 5, pp. 595-618

Inkpen, A.C. and Currall, S.C. (2004), The Coevolution of Trust, Control, and Learning in Joint Ventures, in: Organization Science, 15, 2004, 5, pp. 586-599

Inkpen, A.C. and Dinur, A. (1998), Knowledge Management Processes and International Joint Ventures, in: Organization Science, 9, 1998, 4, pp. 454-468

Inkpen, A.C. and Tsang, E.W.K. (2005), Social Capital, Networks, and Knowledge Transfer, in: Academy of Management Journal, 30, 2005, 1, pp. 146-165

Ireland, R.D., Hitt, M.A., and Vaidyanath, D. (2002), Alliance Management As a Source of Competitive Advantage, in: Journal of Management, 28, 2002, 3, pp. 413-446

Janowicz, M. and Noorderhaven, N. (2002), The Role of Trust in Interorganizational Learning in Joint Ventures, Working Paper of the Center for Economic Research, University of Tilburg, Working Paper No. 2002-119, Tilburg 2002

Jensen, M.C. and Meckling, W.H. (1976), Theory of the Firm - Managerial Behavior, Agency Costs and Ownership Structure, in: Journal of Financial Economics, 3, 1976, 4, pp. 305-360

Johnson, E.J., Camerer, C.F., Sen, S., and Rymon, T. (2002), Detecting Failures of Backward Induction: Monitoring Information Search in Sequential Bargaining, in: Journal of Economic Theory, 104, 2002, 1, pp. 16-47

Jorde, T.M. and Teece, D.J. (1989), Competition and Cooperation: Striking the Right Balance, in: California Management Review, 31, 1989, 3, pp. 25-37

Jost, P.-J. (1998), Strategisches Konfliktmanagement in Organisationen: Eine spieltheoretische Einführung, Wiesbaden 1998

Kainz, D. (2002), Can Students Learn Stock-Flow-Thinking? An Empirical Investigation, in: Proceedings of the 20th International Conference of the System Dynamics Society, 2002

Kale, P., Dyer, J.H., and Singh, H. (2002), Alliance Capability, Stock Market Response, and Long-Term Alliance Success: The Role of the Alliance Function, in: Strategic Management Journal, 23, 2002, 8, pp. 747-767

Kale, P., Singh, H., and Perlmutter, H. (2000), Learning and Protection of Proprietary Assets in Strategic Alliances: Building Relational Capital, in: Strategic Management Journal, 21, 2000, 3, pp. 217-237

Kaluza, B. and Blecker, T. (Eds., 2000), Produktions- und Logistikmanagement in Virtuellen Unternehmen und Unternehmensnetzwerken, Berlin, Heidelberg, and others 2000

Kanter, R.M. (1994), Collaborative Advantage: The Art of Alliances, in: Harvard Business Review, 72, 1994, 4, pp. 96-108

Kapmeier, F. (2002), Dynamics of Interorganizational Learning, in: Proceedings of the 20th International Conference of the System Dynamics Society, 2002

Kapmeier, F. (2003), Dynamics of Common Learning in Learning Alliances, in: Proceedings of the 21st International Conference of the System Dynamics Society, 2003

Kapmeier, F. (2004), Findings from Four Years of Bathtub Dynamics at Higher Management Education Institutions in Stuttgart, in: Proceedings of the 22nd International Conference of the System Dynamics Society, 2004

Kapmeier, F. (2005), Private and Common Goals in Learning Alliances, in: Proceedings of the 23rd International Conference of the System Dynamics Society, 2005

Keough, M. and Doman, A. (1992), The CEO As Organization Designer: An Interview with Professor Jay W. Forrester, the Founder of System Dynamics, in: The McKinsey Quarterly, 28, 1992, 2, pp. 3-30

Kerr, S. and Landauer, S. (2004), Using Stretch Goals to Promote Organizational Effectiveness and Personal Growth: General Electric and Goldman Sachs, in: Academy of Management Executive, 18, 2004, 4, pp. 134-138

Keynes, J.M. (1936), General Theory of Employment, Interest, and Money, London 1936

Khanna, T. (1998), The Scope of Alliances, in: Organization Science, 9, 1998, 3, pp. 340-355

Khanna, T., Gulati, R., and Nohria, N. (1998), The Dynamics of Learning Alliances: Competition, Cooperation, and Relative Scope, in: Strategic Management Journal, 19, 1998, 3, pp. 193-210

Khanna, T., Gulati, R., and Nohria, N. (2000), The Economic Modeling of Strategy Process: 'Clean Models' and 'Dirty Hands', in: Strategic Management Journal, 21, 2000, 7, pp. 781-790

Kim, D.H. (1993), The Link between Individual and Organizational Learning, in: MIT Sloan Management Review, 35, 1993, 1, pp. 37-50

Kim, K. and Park, J.-H. (2002), The Determinants of Value Creation for Partner Firms in the Global Alliance Context, in: Management International Review, 42, 2002, 4, pp. 361-384

King, A.W. and Zeithaml, C.P. (2001), Competencies and Firm Performance: Examining the Causal Ambiguity Paradox, in: Strategic Management Journal, 22, 2001, 1, pp. 75-99

Klein, B., Crawford, R.G., and Alchian, A.A. (1978), Vertical Integration, Appropriable Rents, and the Competitive Contracting Process, in: Journal of Law and Economics, 21, 1978, 2, pp. 297-326

Kleinaltenkamp, M. and Wolters, H. (1997), Die Gestaltung von Systempartnerschaften zwischen Automobilherstellern und ihren Zulieferern – eine spieltheoretische Analyse, in: Schreyögg, G. and Sydow, J. (Eds., 1997), pp. 45-78

Kogut, B. (1988a), Joint Ventures: Theoretical and Empirical Perspectives, in: Strategic Management Journal, 9, 1988, 4, pp. 319-332

Kogut, B. (1988b), A Study of the Life Cycle of Joint Ventures, in: Contractor, F.J. and Lorange, P. (Eds., 1988a), pp. 169-185

Kogut, B. (1989), The Stability of Joint Ventures: Reciprocity and Competitive Rivalry, in: The Journal of Industrial Economics, 38, 1989, 2, pp. 183-198

Kogut, B. and Zander, U. (1992), Knowledge of the Firm, Combinative Capabilities, and the Replication of Technology, in: Organization Science, 3, 1992, 3, pp. 383-397

Kogut, B. and Zander, U. (1993), Knowledge of the Firm and the Evolutionary Theory of the Multinational Corporation, in: Journal of International Business Studies, 24, 1993, 4, pp. 625-645

Kogut, B. and Zander, U. (2003), A Memoir and Reflection: Knowledge and an Evolutionary Theory of the Multinational Firm 10 Years Later, in: Journal of International Business Studies, 34, 2003, 6, pp. 505-515

Kopainsky, B. (2005), A System Dynamics Analysis of Socio-Economic Development in Lagging Swiss Regions, Aachen 2005

Koza, M.P. and Lewin, A.Y. (1998), The Co-Evolution of Strategic Alliances, in: Organization Science, 9, 1998, 3, pp. 255-264

Kramer, R.M. and Tayler, T.R. (Eds., 1996), Trust in Organizations: Frontiers of Theory and Research, Thousand Oaks, London, New Delhi 1996

Krystek, U. (1997), Vertrauen als vernachlässigter Erfolgsfaktor der Internationalisierung, in: Krystek, U. and Zur, E. (Eds., 1997), pp. 543-562

Krystek, U. and Zur, E. (Eds., 1997), Internationalisierung: Eine Herausforderung für die Unternehmensführung, Berlin, Heidelberg, and others 1997

Kühl, S. (2003), Die Grenzen des Vertrauens, in: Harvard Business Manager, 25, 2003, 4, pp. 112-113

Kumar, R. and Nti, K.O. (1998), Differential Learning and Interaction in Alliance Dynamics: A Process and Outcome Discrepancy Model, in: Organization Science, 9, 1998, 3, pp. 356-367

Küpper, H.-U. and Wagenhofer, A. (Eds., 2002), Handwörterbuch des Rechnungswesens, 4th Edition, Stuttgart 2002

Lado, A.A., Boyd, N.G., and Hanlon, S.C. (1997), Competition, Cooperation, and the Search for Economic Rents: A Syncretic Model, in: Academy of Management Review, 22, 1997, 1, pp. 110-141

Lado, A.A., Boyd, N.G., and Wright, P. (1992), A Competency-Based Model of Sustainable Competitive Advantage: Toward a Conceptual Integration, in: Journal of Management, 18, 1992, 1, pp. 77-91

Lamb, R.B. (Ed., 1984), Competitive Strategic Management, Englewood Cliffs 1984

Lamnek, S. (1995), Qualitative Sozialforschung: Methoden und Techniken, 2nd Volume, 3rd Edition, Weinheim 1995

Lane, C. (1998), Introduction: Theories and Issues in the Study of Trust, in: Lane, C. and Bachmann, R. (Eds., 1998), pp. 1-30

Lane, C. and Bachmann, R. (Eds., 1998), Trust within and between Organizations: Conceptual Issues and Empirical Applications, Oxford, New York, and others 1998

Lane, D.C. (1999), Friendly Amendment: A Commentary on Doyle and Ford's Proposed Re-Definition of 'Mental Model', in: System Dynamics Review, 15, 1999, 2, pp. 185-194

Lane, P.J. and Lubatkin, M. (1998), Relative Absorptive Capacity and Interorganizational Learning, in: Strategic Management Journal, 19, 1998, 5, pp. 461-477

Lane, P.J., Salk, J.E., and Lyles, M.A. (2001), Absorptive Capacity, Learning, and Performance in International Joint Ventures, in: Strategic Management Journal, 22, 2001, 12, pp. 1139-1161

Lang, J.W. (1997), Leveraging Knowledge across Firm Boundaries: Achieving Strategic Flexibility through Modularization and Alliances, in: Sanchez, R. and Heene, A. (Eds., 1997), pp. 209-227

Langerfeldt, M. (2003), Das Gefangenendilemma: "Der Beißknochen der Spieltheorie", in: Das Wirtschaftswissenschaftliche Studium, 32, 2003, 4, pp. 226-230

Lant, T.K. and Mezias, S.J. (1990), Managing Discontinuous Change: A Simulation Study of Organizational Learning and Entrepreneurship, in: Strategic Management Journal, 11, 1990, Summer Special Issue, pp. 147-179

Larsson, R., Bengtsson, L., Henriksson, K., and Sparks, J. (1998), The Interorganizational Learning Dilemma: Collective Knowledge Development in Strategic Alliances, in: Organization Science, 9, 1998, 3, pp. 285-305

Lazerson, M.H. and Lorenzoni, G. (1999), The Firms that Feed Industrial Districts: A Return to the Italian Source, in: Industrial and Corporate Change, 8, 1999, 2, pp. 235-266

Legasto, A.A., Forrester, J.W., and Lyneis, J.M. (Eds., 1980), System Dynamics: Studies in the Management Science, Amsterdam, New York, and Oxford 1980

Leonard-Barton, D. (1992), Core Capabilities and Core Rigidities: A Paradox in Managing New Product Development, in: Strategic Management Journal, 13, 1992, Summer Special Issue, pp. 111-125

Lerner, J., Shane, H., and Tsai, A. (2003), Do Equity Financing Cycles Matter? Evidence from Biotechnology Alliances, in: Journal of Financial Economics, 67, 2003, 3, pp. 411-446

Levinson, N.S. and Asahi, M. (1995), Cross-National Alliances and Interorganizational Learning, in: Organizational Dynamics, 24, 1995, 2, pp. 50-63

Levinthal, D.A. (1997), Adaptation on Rugged Landscapes, in: Management Science, 43, 1997, 7, pp. 934-950

Levinthal, D.A. and March, J.G. (1993), The Myopia of Learning, in: Strategic Management Journal, 14, 1993, Winter Special Issue, pp. 95-112

Lewicki, R.J. and Bunker, B.B. (1996), Developing and Maintaining Trust in Work Relationships, in: Kramer, R.M. and Tayler, T.R. (Eds., 1996), pp. 114-139

Lewis, C.T. and Short, C. (1966), A Latin Dictionary, Oxford 1966

Lewis, J.D. and Weigert, A. (1985), Trust As a Social Reality, in: Social Forces, 63, 1985, 4, pp. 967-985

Liebeskind, J.P. (1996), Knowledge, Strategy, and the Theory of the Firm, in: Strategic Management Journal, 17, 1996, Winter Special Issue, pp. 93-107

Liebeskind, J.P. (1997), Keeping Organizational Secrets: Protective Institutional Mechanisms and Their Costs, in: Industrial and Corporate Change, 6, 1997, 3, pp. 623-663

Lippman, S.A. and Rumelt, R.P. (1982), Uncertain Imitability: An Analysis of Interfirm Differences in Efficiency under Competition, in: The Bell Journal of Economics, 13, 1982, 2, pp. 418-438

Lippman, S.A. and Rumelt, R.P. (2003), The Payments Perspective: Micro-Foundations of Resource Analysis, in: Strategic Management Journal, 24, 2003, 10, pp. 903-927

Lubatkin, M., Florin, J., and Lane, P.J. (2001), Learning Together and Apart: A Model of Reciprocal Interfirm Learning, in: Human Relations, 54, 2001, 10, pp. 1353-1382

Luhmann, N. (1979), Trust and Power, Chichester 1979

Luhmann, N. (1988), Familiarity, Confidence, Trust: Problems and Alternatives, in: Gambetta, D. (Ed., 1988b), pp. 94-107

Luna-Reyes, L.F. and Andersen, D.L. (2003), Collecting and Analyzing Qualitative Data for System Dynamics: Methods and Models, in: System Dynamics Review, 19, 2003, 4, pp. 271-296

Luo, Y. (2002), Contract, Cooperation, and Performance in International Joint Ventures, in: Strategic Management Journal, 23, 2002, 10, pp. 903-919

Luo, Y. and Tan, J. (2003), Structuring International Joint Ventures: How Should Contractual Design Be Aligned with Environmental Conditions?, in: Management International Review, 43, 2003, 2, pp. 185-211

Lyles, M.A. (1988), Learning among Joint Venture-Sophisticated Firms, in: Contractor, F.J. and Lorange, P. (Eds., 1988a), pp. 301-316

Lyles, M.A. and Salk, J.E. (1996), Knowledge Acquisition from Foreign Parents in International Joint Ventures: An Empirical Examination in the Hungarian Context, in: Journal of International Business Studies, 27, 1996, 5, pp. 877-903

Lyles, M.A., von Krogh, G., and Aadne, J.H. (2003), Knowledge Acquisition and Knowledge Enablers in International Joint Ventures and Their Foreign Parents, in: Management International Review, 43, 2003, 3, pp. 111-129

Lyneis, J.M. (1999), System Dynamics for Business Strategy: A Phased Approach, in: System Dynamics Review, 15, 1999, 1, pp. 37-70

Maani, K.E. and Cavana, R.Y. (2002), Systems Thinking and Modelling: Understanding Change and Complexity, Auckland 2002

Madhok, A. (1995), Revisiting Multinational Firms' Tolerance for Joint Ventures: A Trust-Based Approach, in: Journal of International Business Studies, 26, 1995, 1, pp. 117-137

Madhok, A. (1996), The Organization of Economic Activity: Transaction Costs, Firm Capabilities, and the Nature of Governance, in: Organization Science, 7, 1996, 5, pp. 577-590

Madhok, A. and Tallman, S.B. (1998), Resources, Transactions and Rents: Managing Value through Interfirm Collaborative Relationships, in: Organization Science, 9, 1998, 3, pp. 326-339

Mahoney, J.T. (2001), A Resource-Based Theory of Sustainable Rents, in: Journal of Management, 27, 2001, 6, pp. 651-660

Makadok, R. (2001), Toward a Synthesis of the Resource-Based and Dynamic-Capability Views of Rent Creation, in: Strategic Management Journal, 22, 2001, 5, pp. 387-401

Malueg, D.A. and Tsutsui, S.O. (1997), Dynamic R&D Competition with Learning, in: Rand Journal of Economics, 28, 1997, 4, pp. 751-772

March, J.G. (1991), Exploration and Exploitation in Organizational Learning, in: Organization Science, 2, 1991, 1, pp. 71-87

March, J.G. and Sutton, R.I. (1997), Organizational Performance As a Dependent Variable, in: Organization Science, 8, 1997, 6, pp. 698-706

Margolis, H. (1982), Selfishness, Altruism, and Rationality: The Theory of Social Choice, Cambridge, Mass. 1982

Mason, E.S. (1939), Price and Production Policies of Large-Scale Enterprise, in: The American Economic Review, 29, 1939, 1, Supplement, pp. 61-74

McAllister, D.J. (1995), Affect- and Cognition-Based Trust As Foundations for Interpersonal Cooperation in Organizations, in: Academy of Management Journal, 38, 1995, 1, pp. 24-59

McCutchen Jr., W.W., Swamidass, P.M., and Teng, B.-S. (2004), R&D Risk-Taking in Strategic Alliances: New Explanations for R&D Alliances in the Biopharmaceutical Industry, in: Management International Review, 44, 2004, 1, pp. 53-67

Meadows, D.H. (1980), The Unavoidable A Priori, in: Randers, J. (Ed., 1980), pp. 23-57

Meadows, D.H. (1982), Whole Earth Model and Systems, in: The CoEvolution Quarterly, 34, 1982, Summer, pp. 98-108

Meadows, D.H., Meadows, D.L., Randers, J., and Behrens III, W.W. (1972), The Limits to Growth, New York 1972

Meadows, D.H., Randers, J., Meadows, D.L. (2004), Limits to Growth – The 30-Year Update, White River Junction 2004

Meadows, D.L. (1989), Gaming to Implement System Dynamics Models, in: Milling, P.M. and Zahn, E.O.K. (Eds., 1989), pp. 635-640

Meadows, D.L., Behrens III, W.W., Meadows, D.H., Naill, R.F., Randers, J., and Zahn, E.O.K. (1974), Dynamics of Growth in a Finite World, Cambridge, Mass. 1974

Messick, D.M. and Kramer, R.M. (2001), Trust As a Form of Shallow Morality, in: Cook, K.S. (Ed., 2001), pp. 89-117

Miles, M.B. and Huberman, A.M. (1994), Qualitative Data Analysis: An Expended Sourcebook, 2nd Edition, Thousand Oaks, London, and New Delhi 1994

Miller, K.D. (2002), Knowledge Inventories and Managerial Myopia, in: Strategic Management Journal, 23, 2002, 8, pp. 689-706

Milling, P.M. (1984), Leitmotive des System-Dynamics-Ansatzes, in: Das Wirtschaftswissenschaftliche Studium, 13, 1984, 10, pp. 507-513

Milling, P.M. and Zahn, E.O.K. (Eds., 1989), Computer-Based Management of Complex Systems, Berlin, Heidelberg, and others 1989

Mittelstrass, J. (Ed., 1995), Enzyklopädie Philosophie und Wissenschaftstheorie, 3rd Volume, Stuttgart and Weimar 1995

Mody, A. (1993), Learning through Alliances, in: Journal of Economic Behavior and Organization, 20, 1993, 2, pp. 151-170

Mojtahedzadeh, M., Andersen, D.F., and Richardson, G.P. (2004), Using *Digest* to Implement the Pathway Participation Method for Detecting Influential System Structure, in: System Dynamics Review, 20, 2004, 1, pp. 1-20

Morecroft, J.D.W. (1983), System Dynamics: Portraying Bounded Rationality, in: OMEGA - The International Journal of Management Science, 11, 1983, 2, pp. 131-142

Morecroft, J.D.W. (1985), Rationality in the Analysis of Behavioral Simulation Models, in: Management Science, 31, 1985, 7, pp. 900-916

Morecroft, J.D.W. (1988), System Dynamics and Microworlds for Policymakers, in: European Journal of Operational Research, 35, 1988, 3, pp. 301-320

Morecroft, J.D.W. (1994), Executive Knowledge, Models, and Learning, in: Morecroft, J.D.W. and Sterman, J.D. (Eds., 1994), pp. 3-28

Morecroft, J.D.W., Sanchez, R., and Heene, A. (Eds., 2002), Systems Perspective on Resources, Capabilities, and Management Processes, Amsterdam, London, and others 2002

Morecroft, J.D.W. and Sterman, J.D. (Eds., 1994), Modeling for Learning Organizations, Portland 1994

Morrison, B.J. (2005), Implementation As Learning: An Extension of Learning Curve Theory, in: 23rd International System Dynamics Conference, 2005

Mowery, D.C., Oxley, J.E., and Silverman, B.S. (1996), Strategic Alliances and Interfirm Knowledge Transfer, in: Strategic Management Journal, 17, 1996, Winter Special Issue, pp. 77-91

Mowery, D.C., Oxley, J.E., and Silverman, B.S. (2002), The Two Faces of Partner-Specific Absorptive Capacity: Learning and Co-Specialization in Strategic Alliances, in: Contractor, F.J. and Lorange, P. (Eds., 2002a), pp. 291-319

Moxon, R.W., Roehl, T.W., and Truitt, J.F. (1988), International Cooperative Ventures in the Commercial Aircraft Industry: Gains, Sure, But What's My Share?, in: Contractor, F.J. and Lorange, P. (Eds., 1988a), pp. 255-277

Mullainathan, S. and Thaler, R.H. (2001), Behavioral Economics, in: Smelser, N.J. and Baltes, P.B. (Eds., 2001), pp. 1094-1100

Müller, S. (2004), Programm für eine neue Wissenschaftstheorie, Würzburg 2004

Müller-Stewens, G. and Osterloh, M. (1996), Kooperationsinvestitionen besser nutzen: Interorganisationales Lernen als Know-How-Transfer oder Kontext-Transfer?, in: Zeitschrift Führung + Organisation, 65, 1996, 1, pp. 18-24

Mumby, D.K. and Putnam, L.K. (1992), The Politics of Emotion: A Feminist Reading of Bounded Rationality, in: Academy of Management Review, 17, 1992, 3, pp. 465-486

Murray Jr., E.A. and Mahon, J.F. (1993), Strategic Alliances: Gateway to the New Europe?, in: Long Range Planning, 26, 1993, 4, pp. 102-111

Muthusamy, S.K. and White, M.A. (2005), Learning and Knowledge Transfer in Strategic Alliances: A Social Exchange View, in: Organization Studies, 26, 2005, 3, pp. 415-441

Nahavandi, A. and Malekzadeh, A.R. (1988), Acculturation in Mergers and Acquisitions, in: Academy of Management Review, 13, 1988, 1, pp. 79-90

Nalebuff, B.J. and Brandenburger, A.M. (1996), Coopetition - kooperativ konkurrieren: Mit der Spieltheorie zum Unternehmenserfolg, Frankfurt am Main and New York 1996

Nalebuff, B.J. and Brandenburger, A.M. (1997), Co-opetition: Competitive and Cooperative Business Strategies for the Digital Economy, in: Strategy & Leadership, 25, 1997, 6, pp. 28-35

Nelson, R.R. and Winter, S.G. (1982), An Evolutionary Theory of Economic Change, Cambridge, Mass. and London 1982

Nicolai, A.T. and Kieser, A. (2002), Trotz eklatanter Erfolglosigkeit: Die Erfolgsfaktorenforschung weiter auf Erfolgskurs, in: Die Betriebswirtschaft, 62, 2002, 6, pp. 579-596

Nielsen, R.P. (1988), Cooperative Strategy, in: Strategic Management Journal, 9, 1988, 5, pp. 475-492

Nohria, N. and Eccles, R.G. (Eds., 1992), Networks and Organizations: Structure, Form, and Action, Boston 1992

Nonaka, I. (1994), A Dynamic Theory of Organizational Knowledge Creation, in: Organization Science, 5, 1994, 1, pp. 14-37

Nonaka, I. and Takeuchi, H. (1995), The Knowledge Creating Company. How Japanese Companies Create the Dynamics of Innovation, Oxford 1995

Nooteboom, B. (1996), Trust, Opportunism and Governance: A Process and Control Model, in: Organization Studies, 17, 1996, 6, pp. 985-1010

Nooteboom, B. (2000), Learning and Innovation in Organizations and Economics, Oxford, New York, and others 2000

Norman, P.M. (2004), Knowledge Acquisition, Knowledge Loss, and Satisfaction in High Technology Alliances, in: Journal of Business Research, 57, 2004, 6, pp. 610-619

Nystrom, P.C. and Starbuck, W.H. (Eds., 1981), Handbook of Organizational Design, 1st Volume: Adapting Organizations to Their Environment Volume, Oxford, London, and others 1981

Oesterle, M.-J. (2003), Kooperation in Forschung und Entwicklung, in: Zentes, J., Swoboda, B. and Morschett, D. (Eds., 2003), pp. 631-658

Oliva, R. and Sterman, J.D. (2001), Cutting Corners and Working Overtime: Quality Erosion in the Service Industry, in: Management Science, 47, 2001, 7, pp. 894-914

Olk, P. (2002), Evaluating Strategic Alliance Performance, in: Contractor, F.J. and Lorange, P. (Eds., 2002a), pp. 119-162

Oriesek, D.F. and Friedrich, R. (2003), Blick in die Zukunft, in: Harvard Business Manager, 25, 2003, 5, pp. 65-71

Ossimitz, G. (2002), Stock-Flow-Thinking and Reading Stock-Flow-Related Graphs: An Empirical Investigation in Dynamic Thinking Abilities, in: Proceedings of the 20th International Conference of the System Dynamics Society, 2002

Osterloh, M. and Grand, S. (1995), Modellbildung versus Frameworking: Die Positionen von Williamson und Porter, in: Wächter, H. (Ed., 1995), pp. 1-26

Otto, P. and Richardson, G.P. (2004), Interorganizational Learning: A Dynamic View on Knowledge Development in Strategic Alliances, in: Proceedings of the 22nd International Conference of the System Dynamics Society, 2004

Oxley, J.E. and Sampson, R.C. (2004), The Scope and Governance of International R&D Alliances, in: Strategic Management Journal, 25, 2004, 8-9, pp. 723-749

Parker, D.C., Berger, T., and Manson, S.M. (Eds., 2001), Agent-Based Models of Land-Use and Land-Cover Change: Report and Review of an International Workshop, Irvine, Calif. 2001

Parkhe, A. (1993), Strategic Alliance Structuring: A Game Theoretic and Transaction Cost Examination of Interfirm Cooperation, in: Academy of Management Journal, 36, 1993, 4, pp. 794-829

Pausenberger, E. (1989), Zur Systematik von Unternehmenszusammenschlüssen, in: Das Wirtschaftsstudium, 18, 1989, 11, pp. 621-626

Pausenberger, E. and Nöcker, R. (2000), Kooperative Formen der Auslandsmarktbearbeitung, in: Zeitschrift für betriebswirtschaftliche Forschung, 52, 2000, 6, pp. 393-412

Penner-Hahn, J. and Shaver, J.M. (2005), Does International Research and Development Increase Patent Output? An Analysis of Japanese Pharmaceutical Firms, in: Strategic Management Journal, 26, 2005, 2, pp. 121-140

Penrose, E.T. (1959), The Theory of the Growth of the Firm, Oxford 1959

Perlmutter, H.V. and Heenan, D.A. (1986), Cooperate to Compete Globally, in: Harvard Business Review, 64, 1986, 2, pp. 136-152

Peteraf, M.A. (1993), The Cornerstones of Competitive Advantage: A Resource-Based View, in: Strategic Management Journal, 14, 1993, 3, pp. 179-191

Peteraf, M.A. (1994), Commentary: The Two Schools of Thought in Ressource-Based Theory: Definitions and Implications for Research (W.S.Schulze), in: Shrivastava, P., Huff, A.S. and Dutton, J.E. (Eds., 1994), pp. 153-158

Peteraf, M.A. and Bergen, M.E. (2003), Scanning Dynamic Competitive Landscapes: A Market-Based and Resource-Based Framework, in: Strategic Management Journal, 24, 2003, 10, pp. 1027-1041

Peterson, D. and Eberlein, R. (1994), Reality Check: A Bridge between Systems Thinking and System Dynamics, in: System Dynamics Review, 10, 1994, 2-3, pp. 159-174

Pfähler, W. and Wiethaus, L. (2004), Forschung und Entwicklung: Wettbewerb oder Kooperation, in: Das Wirtschaftsstudium, 33, 2004, 5, pp. 682-690

Picot, A., Dietl, H., and Frank, E. (1997), Organisation: Eine ökonomische Perspektive, Stuttgart 1997

Pless, N. (1999), Von der Dominanz zur Partnerschaft – Erfolgreiches Diversitätsmanagement erfordert einen Paradigmenwechsel, in: Die Unternehmung, 53, 1999, 3, pp. 159-175

Polanyi, M. (1967), The Tacit Dimension, London 1967

Polanyi, M. (1983), The Tacit Dimension (Reprint), Gloucester, Mass. 1983

Polanyi, M. (1997), The Tacit Dimension, in: Prosak, L. (Ed., 1997), pp. 135-146

Porter, M.E. (1985), Competitive Advantage: Creating and Sustaining Superior Performance, New York and London 1985

Porter, M.E. (Ed., 1986), Competition in Global Industries, Cambridge, Mass. 1986

Porter, M.E. (1991), Towards a Dynamic Theory of Strategy, in: Strategic Management Journal, 12, 1991, Winter Special Issue, pp. 95-117

Porter, M.E. and Fuller, M.B. (1986), Coalitions and Global Strategy, in: Porter, M.E. (Ed., 1986), pp. 315-344

Porter, M.E. and Stern, S. (2001), Innovation: Location Matters, in: MIT Sloan Management Review, 42, 2001, 4, pp. 28-36

Powell, T.C. (2002), The Philosophy of Strategy, in: Strategic Management Journal, 23, 2002, 9, pp. 873-880

Powell, W.W. (1987), Hybrid Organizational Arrangements: New Form or Transitional Development?, in: California Management Review, 30, 1987, 1, pp. 67-87

Powell, W.W., Koput, K.W., and Smith-Doerr, L. (1996), Interorganizational Collaboration and the Locus of Innovation: Networks of Learning in Biotechnology, in: Administrative Science Quarterly, 41, 1996, 1, pp. 116-145

Prahalad, C.K. and Bettis, R.A. (1986), The Dominant Logic: A New Linkage between Diversity and Performance, in: Strategic Management Journal, 7, 1986, 6, pp. 485-501

Prahalad, C.K. and Hamel, G. (1990), The Core Competence of the Corporation, in: Harvard Business Review, 68, 1990, 3, pp. 79-91

Prange, C. (1996), Interorganisationales Lernen: Lernen in, von und zwischen Organisationen, in: Schreyögg, G. and Conrad, P. (Eds., 1996), pp. 163-189

Prange, C., Probst, G.J.B., and Rüling, C.-C. (1996), Lernen zu kooperieren - Kooperieren, um zu lernen, in: Zeitschrift Führung + Organisation, 65, 1996, 1, pp. 10-16

Priem, R.L. and Butler, J.E. (2001), Is the Resource-Based "View" a Useful Perspective for Strategic Management Research?, in: Academy of Management Review, 26, 2001, 1, pp. 22-40

Prosak, L. (Ed., 1997), Knowledge in Organizations, Boston, Oxford, and others 1997

Rabin, M. (1993), Incorporating Fairness into Game Theory and Economics, in: The American Economic Review, 83, 1993, 5, pp. 1281-1302

Rahmandad, H. (2004), Heterogeneity and Network Structure in the Dynamics of Contagion: Comparing Agent-Based and Differential Equation Models, in: Proceedings of the 22nd International Conference of the System Dynamics Society, 2004

Rahmandad, H. (2005), Dynamics of Platform-Based Product Development, in: Proceedings of the 23rd International Conference of the System Dynamics Society, 2005

Randers, J. (Ed., 1980), Elements of the System Dynamics Method, Cambridge, Mass. and London 1980

Reagans, R. and McEvily, B. (2003), Network Structure and Knowledge Transfer: The Effects of Cohesion and Range, in: Administrative Science Quarterly, 48, 2003, 2, pp. 240-267

Reich, R.B. and Mankin, E.D. (1986), Joint Ventures with Japan Give Away Our Future, in: Harvard Business Review, 64, 1986, 2, pp. 78-86

Reid, D., Bussiere, D., and Greenaway, K. (2001), Alliance Formation Issues for Knowledge-Based Enterprises, in: International Journal of Management Reviews, 3, 2001, 1, pp. 79-100

Repenning, N.P. (2001), Understanding Fire Fighting in New Product Development, in: Journal of Product Innovation Management, 18, 2001, 5, pp. 285-300

Repenning, N.P. (2002), A Simulation-Based Approach to Understanding the Dynamics of Innovation Implementation, in: Organization Science, 13, 2002, 2, pp. 109-127

Repenning, N.P. (2003), Selling System Dynamics to (Other) Social Scientists, in: System Dynamics Review, 19, 2003, 4, pp. 303-327

Repenning, N.P., Gonçalves, P.M., and Black, L.J. (2001), Past the Tipping Point: The Persistence of Firefighting in Product Development, in: California Management Review, 43, 2001, 4, pp. 44-63

Repenning, N.P. and Sterman, J.D. (2002), Capability Traps and Self-Confirming Attribution Errors in the Dynamics of Process Improvement, in: Administrative Science Quarterly, 47, 2002, 2, pp. 265-295

Reus, T.H. and Ritchie III, W.J. (2004), Interpartner, Parent, and Environmental Factors Influencing the Operation of International Joint Ventures: 15 Years of Research, in: mir Management International Review, 44, 2004, 4, pp. 369-395

Richardson, G.P. (1986), Problems with Causal-Loop Diagrams, in: System Dynamics Review, 2, 1986, 2, pp. 158-170

Richardson, G.P. (1991a), Feedback Thought in Social Science and System Theory, Philadelphia 1991

Richardson, G.P. (1991b), System Dynamics: Simulation for Policy Analysis from a Feedback Perspective, in: Fishwick, P.A. and Luker, P.A. (Eds., 1991), pp. 144-169

Richardson, G.P. (1995), Loop Polarity, Loop Dominance, and the Concept of Dominant Polarity (1984), in: System Dynamics Review, 11, 1995, 1, pp. 67-88

Richardson, G.P. (1996), System Dynamics, in: Gass, S.I. and Harris, C.M. (Eds., 1996), pp. 656-660

Richardson, G.P. (2001), System Dynamics, in: Gass, S.I. and Harris, C.M. (Eds., 2001), pp. 807-810

Richardson, G.P. and Andersen, D.F. (1995), Teamwork in Group Model Building, in: System Dynamics Review, 11, 1995, 2, pp. 113-137

Richardson, G.P. and Pugh III, A.L. (1981), Introduction to System Dynamics Modeling with DYNAMO, Cambridge, Mass. and London 1981

Ring, P.S. and van de Ven, A.H. (1992), Structuring Cooperative Relationships between Organizations, in: Strategic Management Journal, 13, 1992, 7, pp. 483-498

Ring, P.S. and van de Ven, A.H. (1994), Developmental Processes of Cooperative Interorganizational Relationships, in: Academy of Management Review, 19, 1994, 1, pp. 90-118

Roberts, E.B. (Ed., 1999a), Managerial Applications of System Dynamics, Waltham, Mass. 1999

Roberts, E.B. (1999b), A Simple Model of R&D Project Dynamics (Reprint), in: Roberts, E.B. (Ed., 1999a), pp. 293-314

Robson, M.J., Leonidou, L.C., and Katsikeas, C.S. (2002), Factors Influencing International Joint Venture Performance: Theoretical Perspectives, Assessment, and Future Directions, in: Management International Review, 42, 2002, 4, pp. 385-418

Rockart, S.F. (2001), Calling Spirits from the Deep: Competing for and through Sophisticated Customers, Thesis (Ph.D.) at the Sloan School of Management, Massachusetts Institute of Technology, Cambridge, Mass. 2001

Rotering, J. (1993), Zwischenbetriebliche Kooperation als alternative Organisationsform: Ein transaktionskostentheoretischer Erklärungsansatz, Stuttgart 1993

Rothaermel, F.T. and Deeds, D.L. (2004), Exploration and Exploitation Alliances in Biotechnology: A System of New Product Development, in: Strategic Management Journal, 25, 2004, 3, pp. 201-221

Rotter, J.B. (1954), Social Learning and Clinical Psychology, Englewood Cliffs 1954

Rouwette, E.A.J.A. (2003), Group Model Building as Mutual Persuasion, Nijmegen 2003

Rouwette, E.A.J.A., Größler, A., and Vennix, J.A.M. (2004), Exploring Influencing Factors on Rationality: A Literature Review of Dynamic Decision-Making Studies in System Dynamics, in: Systems Research and Behavioral Science, 21, 2004, 4, pp. 351-370

Rudolph, J. and Repenning, N.P. (2002), Disaster Dynamics: Understanding the Role of Quantity in Organizational Collapse, in: Administrative Science Quarterly, 47, 2002, 1, pp. 1-30

Rugman, A.M. and Verbeke, A. (2002), Edith Penrose's Contribution to the Resource-Based View of Strategic Management, in: Strategic Management Journal, 23, 2002, 8, pp. 769-780

Rumelt, R.P. (1984), Towards a Strategic Theory of the Firm, in: Lamb, R.B. (Ed., 1984), pp. 556-570

Rupprecht-Däullary, M. (1994), Zwischenbetriebliche Kooperation: Möglichkeiten und Grenzen durch neue Informations- und Kommunikationstechnologien, Wiesbaden 1994

Ryle, G. (1949), The Concept of Mind, New York 1949

Sakakibara, M. (1997), Heterogeneity of Firm Capabilities and Cooperative Research and Development: An Empirical Examination of Motives, in: Strategic Management Journal, 18, 1997, Summer Special Issue, pp. 143-164

Sally, D. (1995), Conversation and Cooperation in Social Dilemmas: A Meta-Analysis of Experiments from 1958 to 1992, in: Rationality and Society, 7, 1995, 1, pp. 58-92

Sally, D. (2003), Dressing the Mind Properly for the Game, in: Philosophical Transactions of The Royal Society of London Series B - Biological Sciences, 358, 2003, 1431, pp. 583-592

Sanchez, R. (1997), Managing Articulated Knowledge in Competence-Based Competition, in: Sanchez, R. and Heene, A. (Eds., 1997), pp. 163-187

Sanchez, R. and Heene, A. (Eds., 1997), Strategic Learning and Knowledge Management, Chichester, New York, and others 1997

Sanchez, R. and Mahony, J.T. (1996), Modularity, Flexibility, and Knowledge Management in Product and Organization Design, in: Strategic Management Journal, 17, 1996, Winter Special Issue, pp. 63-76

Sandler, T. (1992), Collective Action: Theory and Applications, Ann Arbor, Mich. 1992

Sastry, M.A. (1997), Problems and Paradoxes in a Model of Punctuated Organizational Change, in: Administrative Science Quarterly, 42, 1997, 2, pp. 237-275

Schleichert, H. (1995), Simulation, in: Mittelstrass, J. (Ed., 1995), pp. 807-809

Schnell, R., Hill, P.B., and Esser, E. (1999), Methoden der empirischen Sozialforschung, 6th Edition, München, Wien, and Oldenburg 1999

Schramm, W. (1971), Notes on Case Studies of Instructional Media Projects, Working Paper of the Academy for Educational Development, Working Paper, Washington, D.C. 1971

Schreyögg, G. and Conrad, P. (Eds., 1996), Managementforschung 6: Wissensmanagement, Berlin and New York 1996

Schreyögg, G. and Sydow, J. (Eds., 1997), Managementforschung 7: Gestaltung von Organisationsgrenzen, Berlin and New York 1997

Schumpeter, J.A. (1934), The Theory of Economic Development: An Inquiry into Profits, Capital, Credit, Interest, and the Business Cycle, Cambridge, Mass. 1934

Schumpeter, J.A. (1949), The Theory of Economic Development: An Inquiry into Profits, Capital, Credit, Interest, and the Business Cycle, 3rd Edition, Cambridge, Mass. 1949

Schumpeter, J.A. (1950), Kapitalismus, Sozialismus und Demokratie, 2nd Edition, München 1950

Schwerk, A. (2000), Dynamik von Unternehmenskooperationen, Berlin 2000

Selten, R. (1965), Spieltheoretische Behandlung eines Oligopolmodells mit Nachfrageträgheit, in: Zeitschrift für die gesamte Staatswissenschaft, 121, 1965, 2, pp. 301-324

Selten, R. (1975), Reexamination of the Perfectness Concept for Equilibrium Points in Extensive Games, in: International Journal of Game Theory, 4, 1975, 1, pp. 25-55

Selten, R. (1978), The Chain Store Paradox, in: Theory and Decision, 9, 1978, 2, pp. 127-159

Selten, R. (2001), Die konzeptionellen Grundlagen der Spieltheorie einst und jetzt, Working Paper of the Department of Economics, Universität Bonn, Working Paper bgse2_2001, Bonn 2001

Sen, A. (1985), Goals, Commitment, and Identity, in: Journal of Law, Economics, and Organization, 1, 1985, 2, pp. 341-355

Senge, P.M. (1990), The Fifth Discipline: The Art and Practice of the Learning Organization, New York, London, and others 1990

Shan, W., Walker, G., and Kogut, B. (1994), Interfirm Cooperation and Startup Innovation in the Biotechnology Industry, in: Strategic Management Journal, 15, 1994, 5, pp. 387-394

Shannon, C.E. and Weaver, W. (1949), The Mathematical Theory of Communication, Urbana 1949

Shrivastava, P., Huff, A.S., and Dutton, J.E. (Eds., 1994), Advances in Strategic Management: Interorganizational Relations and Interorganizational Strategies, Greenwich, Conn. and London 1994

Simon, H. (1988), Management strategischer Wettbewerbsvorteile, in: Zeitschrift für Betriebswirtschaft, 58, 1988, 4, pp. 461-480

Simon, H.A. (1955), A Behavioral Model of Rational Choice, in: The Quarterly Journal of Economics, 69, 1955, 1, pp. 99-118

Simon, H.A. (1957), Models of Man, New York and London 1957

Simon, H.A. (1969), The Sciences of the Artificial, Cambridge, Mass. and London 1969

Simon, H.A. (1994), Die Wissenschaften vom Künstlichen, 2nd Edition, Wien and New York 1994

Simonin, B.L. (1999), Ambiguity and the Process of Knowledge Transfer in Strategic Alliances, in: Strategic Management Journal, 20, 1999, 7, pp. 595-623

Smelser, N.J. and Baltes, P.B. (Eds., 2001), International Encyclopedia of the Social & Behavioral Sciences, Amsterdam, Paris, and others 2001

Spanos, Y.E. and Lioukas, S. (2001), An Examination into the Causal Logic of Rent Creation: Contrasting Porter's Competitive Strategy Framework and the Resource-Based Perspective, in: Strategic Management Journal, 22, 2001, 10, pp. 907-934

Spender, J.-C. (1996), Making Knowledge the Basis of a Dynamic Theory of the Firm, in: Strategic Management Journal, 17, 1996, Winter Special Issue, pp. 45-62

Spöhring, W. (1989), Qualitative Sozialforschung, Stuttgart 1989

Stachowiak, H. (1973), Allgemeine Modelltheorie, Wien and New York 1973

Stein, V. (2003), Kooperation: Erklärungsperspektive der strategischen Managementforschung, in: Zentes, J., Swoboda, B. and Morschett, D. (Eds., 2003), pp. 167-182

Sterman, J.D. (1985), Preface to "'The" Model versus a Modeling "Process'" by Jay W. Forrester, in: System Dynamics Review, 1, 1985, 1, p. 133

Sterman, J.D. (1987), Testing Behavioral Simulation Models By Direct Experiment, in: Management Science, 33, 1987, 12, pp. 1572-1592

Sterman, J.D. (1991), A Skeptic's Guide to Computer Models, in: Barney, G.O., Kreutzer, W.B. and Garrett, M.J. (Eds., 1991), pp. 209-229

Sterman, J.D. (1994), Learning in and about Complex Systems, in: System Dynamics Review, 10, 1994, 2-3, pp. 291-330

Sterman, J.D. (2000), Business Dynamics: Systems Thinking and Modeling for a Complex World, Boston, Madison, and others 2000

Sterman, J.D. (2001), System Dynamics Modeling: Tools for Learning in a Complex World, in: California Management Review, 43, 2001, 4, pp. 8-25

Sterman, J.D. (2002), All Models Are Wrong: Reflections on Becoming a Systems Scientist, in: System Dynamics Review, 18, 2002, 4, pp. 501-531

Sterman, J.D., Henderson, R., Beinhocker, E.D., and Newman, L.I. (1995), A Behavioral Analysis of Learning Curve Strategy, Working Paper of the Massachusetts Institute of Technology, Sloan School of Management, Working Paper D-4354, Cambridge, Mass. 1995

Struben, J. (2004), Technology Transitions: Identifying Challenges for Hydrogen Vehicles, in: Proceedings of the 22nd International Conference of the System Dynamics Society, 2004

Struben, J. (2005), Space Matters Too! Mutualistic Dynamics between Hydrogen Fuel Cell Vehicle Demand and Fueling Infrastructure, in: Proceedings of the 23rd International Conference of the System Dynamics Society, 2005

Sukh Pak, Y. and Park, Y.-R. (2004), A Framework of Knowledge Transfer in Cross-Border Joint Ventures: An Empirical Test of the Korean Context, in: mir Management International Review, 44, 2004, 4, pp. 417-434

Surowiecki, J. (2003), The Coup de Grasso, in: The New Yorker, 6 October 2003, p. 50

Swoboda, B. (2003), Kooperation: Erklärungsperspektiven grundlegender Theorien, Ansätze und Konzepte im Überblick, in: Zentes, J., Swoboda, B. and Morschett, D. (Eds., 2003), pp. 34-64

Sydow, J. (1992), Strategische Netzwerke: Evolution und Organisation, Wiesbaden 1992

Sydow, J. (1998), Understanding the Constitution of Interorganizational Trust, in: Lane, C. and Bachmann, R. (Eds., 1998), pp. 31-63

Sydow, J. and Windeler, A. (Eds., 1994), Management interorganisationaler Beziehungen. Vertrauen, Kontrolle und Informationstechnik, Opladen 1994

Szulanski, G. (1996), Exploring Internal Stickiness: Impediments to the Transfer of Best Practice within the Firm, in: Strategic Management Journal, 17, 1996, Winter Special Issue, pp. 27-43

Tajfel, H. (1982), Social Identity and Intergroup Relations, New York 1982

Tallman, S. (2003), The Significance of Bruce Kogut's and Udo Zander's Article, 'Knowledge of the Firm and the Evolutionary Theory of the Multinational Cooperation', in: Journal of International Business Studies, 34, 2003, 6, pp. 495-497

Tallman, S. and Jenkins, M. (2002), Alliances, Knowledge Flows, and Performance in Regional Clusters, in: Contractor, F.J. and Lorange, P. (Eds., 2002a), pp. 163-187

Taylor, T., Ford, D.N., and Johnson, S.T. (2005), Why Good Projects Go Bad: Managing Development Projects Near Tipping Points, in: Proceedings of the 23rd International Conference of the System Dynamics Society, 2005

Teece, D.J. (1992), Competition, Cooperation, and Innovation: Organizational Arrangements for Regimes of Rapid Technological Progress, in: Journal of Economic Behavior and Organization, 18, 1992, 1, pp. 1-25

Teece, D.J. (Ed., 1998), Economic Performance and the Theory of the Firm, Cheltenham, Glos, and Northampton, Mass. 1998

Teece, D.J. and Pisano, G. (1994), The Dynamic Capabilities of Firms: An Introduction, in: Industrial and Corporate Change, 3, 1994, 3, pp. 537-556

Teece, D.J. and Pisano, G. (1998), The Dynamic Capabilities of Firms: An Introduction, in: Teece, D.J. (Ed., 1998), pp. 56-75

Teece, D.J., Pisano, G., and Shuen, A. (1997), Dynamic Capabilities and Strategic Management, in: Strategic Management Journal, 18, 1997, 7, pp. 509-533

Telser, L.G. (1980), A Theory of Self-Enforcing Agreements, in: Journal of Business, 53, 1980, 1, pp. 27-44

Thaler, R.H. (1988), Anomalies: The Ultimatum Game, in: Journal of Economic Perspectives, 2, 1988, 4, pp. 195-206

Thorelli, H.B. (1986), Networks: Between Markets and Hierarchies, in: Strategic Management Journal, 7, 1986, 1, pp. 37-51

Tidd, J. and Izumimoto, Y. (2002), Knowledge Exchange and Learning through International Joint Ventures: An Anglo-Japanese Experience, in: Technovation, 22, 2002, 3, pp. 137-145

Tilebein, M. (2005), Nachhaltiger Unternehmenserfolg in turbulenten Umfeldern: Die Komplexitätsforschung und ihre Implikationen für die Gestaltung wandlungsfähiger Unternehmen, Frankfurt am Main 2005

Troitzsch, K.G. (2004), Simulationsverfahren, in: Das Wirtschaftsstudium, 33, 2004, 10, pp. 1256-1268

Tröndle, D. (1987), Kooperationsmanagement: Steuerung interaktioneller Prozesse bei Unternehmenskooperationen, Bergisch Gladbach and Köln 1987

Tsai, W. (2002), Social Structure of "Coopetition" within a Multiunit Organization: Coordination, Competition, and Intraorganizational Knowledge Sharing, in: Organization Science, 13, 2002, 2, pp. 179-190

Tsang, E.W.K. (2002), Acquiring Knowledge by Foreign Partners from International Joint Ventures in a Transition Economy: Learning-By-Doing and Learning Myopia, in: Strategic Management Journal, 23, 2002, 9, pp. 835-854

Tully, S. (1996), Northwest and KLM: The Alliance from Hell, in: Fortune, 24 June 1996, pp. 44-50

Tushman, M.L. and Katz, R. (1980), External Communication and Project Performance: An Investigation into the Role of Gatekeepers, in: Management Science, 26, 1980, 11, pp. 1071-1085

Tushman, M.L. and O'Reilly III, C.A. (1996), Ambidextrous Organizations: Managing Evolutionary and Revolutionary Change, in: California Management Review, 38, 1996, 4, pp. 8-30

Tushman, M.L. and Romanelli, E. (1985), Organizational Evolution: A Metamorphosis Model of Convergence and Reorientation, in: Cummings, L.L. and Staw, B.M. (Eds., 1985), pp. 171-222

Ulrich, H. (1970), Die Unternehmung als produktives soziales System, 2nd Edition, Bern and Stuttgart 1970

van Damme (1999), Game Theory: The Next Stage, in: Gerard-Varet, L.A., Kirman, A.P. and Ruggiero, M. (Eds., 1999), pp. 184-214

van de Ven, A.H. and Poole, M.S. (1995), Explaining Development and Change in Organizations, in: Academy of Management Review, 20, 1995, 3, pp. 510-540

Veliyath, R. and Fitzgerald, E. (2000), Firm Capabilities, Business Strategies, Customer Preferences, and Hypercompetitive Arenas: The Sustainability of Competitive Advantages with Implications for Firm Competitiveness, in: Competitiveness Review, 10, 2000, 1, pp. 56-82

Vennix, J.A.M. (1998), Group Model Building: Facilitating Team Learning Using System Dynamics, New York, Brisbane, and others 1998

Vennix, J.A.M. (1999), Group Model Building: Tackling Messy Problems, in: System Dynamics Review, 15, 1999, 4, pp. 379-401

von Bertalanffy, L. (1932), Theoretische Biologie, Berlin 1932

von Bertalanffy, L. (1949), Zu einer allgemeinen Systemtheorie, in: Biologia Generalis, 24, 1949, 1, pp. 114-129

von Hippel, E. (1994), "Sticky Information" and the Locus of Problem Solving: Implications for Innovation, in: Management Science, 40, 1994, 4, pp. 429-439

von Neumann, J. (Ed., 1963), Collected Works, V: Design of Computers, Theory of Automata and Numerical Analysis Volume, Oxford, London, and others 1963

von Neumann, J. and Morgenstern, O. (1953), Theory of Games and Economic Behavior, 3rd Edition, Princeton 1953

Wächter, H. (Ed., 1995), Selbstverständnis betriebswirtschaftlicher Forschung und Lehre: Tagung der Kommission Wissenschaftstheorie, Wiesbaden 1995

Warren, K. (2002), Competitive Strategy Dynamics, Chichester 2002

Warren, K. (2004), Why Has Feedback Systems Thinking Struggled to Influence Strategy and Policy Formulation? Suggestive Evidence, Explanations and Solutions, in: Systems Research and Behavioral Science, 21, 2004, 4, pp. 331-347

Weber, K. (2004), Der wissenschaftstheoretische Status von Simulationen, in: Frank, U. (Ed., 2004), pp. 171-187

Weberpals, H. (Ed., 1993), Das wissenschaftliche Rechenzentrum der Zukunft, München, New Providence, and others 1993

Wernerfelt, B. (1984), A Resource-Based View of the Firm, in: Strategic Management Journal, 5, 1984, 2, pp. 171-180

Wernerfelt, B. (1995), The Resource-Based View of the Firm: Ten Years after, in: Strategic Management Journal, 16, 1995, 3, pp. 171-174

Whipple, J.M. and Frankel, R. (2000), Strategic Alliance Success Factors, in: The Journal of Supply Chain Management, 36, 2000, 3, pp. 21-28

Wiener, N. (1948), Cybernetics: Or Control and Communication in the Animal and the Machine, New York 1948

Williamson, O.E. (1975), Markets and Hierarchies: Analysis and Antitrust Implications, New York and London 1975

Williamson, O.E. (1983), Credible Commitments: Using Hostages to Support Exchange, in: The American Economic Review, 73, 1983, 4, pp. 519-540

Wolstenholme, E.F. (2003), Towards a Definition and Use of a Core Set of Archetypal Structures in System Dynamics, in: System Dynamics Review, 19, 2003, 1, pp. 7-26

Wurche, S. (1994), Vertrauen und ökonomische Realität in kooperativen Interorganisationsbeziehungen, in: Sydow, J. and Windeler, A. (Eds., 1994), pp. 142-159

Wyssusek, B. (2004), Plädoyer für ein soziopragmatisch-konstruktivistisches Verständnis der Organisationsmodellierung in der Wirtschaftsinformatik, in: Frank, U. (Ed., 2004), pp. 358-392

Yin, R.K. (1994), Case Study Research: Design and Models, 2nd Edition, Thousand Oaks, London, and New Delhi 1994

Zagonel, A.A. (2004), Developing an Interpretative Dialogue for Group Model Building, in: Proceedings of the 22nd International Conference of the System Dynamics Society, 2004

Zaheer, A., Lofstrom, S., and George, V., P. (2002), Interpersonal and Interorganizational Trust in Alliances, in: Contractor, F.J. and Lorange, P. (Eds., 2002a), pp. 347-377

Zahn, E.O.K. (1998), Wettbewerbsfähigkeit durch strategische Erneuerung, in: Becker, M., Kloock, J., Schmidt, R. and Wäscher, G. (Eds., 1998), pp. 383-410

Zahn, E.O.K. (1999), Strategizing Needs Systems Thinking, in: Proceedings of the 17th International Conference of the System Dynamics Society & Australian New Zealand Systems Conference, 1999

Zahn, E.O.K. (2001), Lernen in Allianzen, in: Bellmann, K. (Ed., 2001), pp. 11-29

Zahn, E.O.K. and Foschiani, S. (2000), Wettbewerbsfähigkeit durch interorganisationale Kooperation, in: Kaluza, B. and Blecker, T. (Eds., 2000), pp. 494-532

Zahn, E.O.K., Foschiani, S., and Tilebein, M. (2000), Wissen und Strategiekompetenz als Basis für die Wettbewerbsfähigkeit von Unternehmen, in: Hammann, P. and Freiling, J. (Eds., 2000), pp. 47-68

Zahn, E.O.K. and Kapmeier, F. (2002), Systemanalyse, in: Küpper, H.-U. and Wagenhofer, A. (Eds., 2002), pp. 1919-1932

Zahn, E.O.K. and Tilebein, M. (1998), Führung wandlungsfähiger Unternehmen - eine Herausforderung in neuen Dimensionen, in: Industrie Management, 14, 1998, 6, pp. 49-52

Zahra, S.A. and George, G. (2002), Absorptive Capacity: A Review, Reconceptualization, and Extension, in: Academy of Management Review, 27, 2002, 2, pp. 185-203

Zajac, E.J. and Olsen, C.P. (1993), From Transaction Cost to Transactional Value Analysis: Implications for the Study of Interorganizational Strategies, in: Journal of Management Studies, 30, 1993, 1, pp. 131-145

Zand, D.E. (1972), Trust and Managerial Problem Solving, in: Administrative Science Quarterly, 17, 1972, 2, pp. 229-239

Zeng, M. and Chen, X.-P. (2003), Achieving Cooperation in Multiparty Alliances: A Social Dilemma Approach to Partnership Management, in: Academy of Management Review, 28, 2003, 4, pp. 587-605

Zeng, M. and Hennart, J.-F. (2002), From Learning Races to Cooperative Specialization: Towards a New Framework for Alliance Management, in: Contractor, F.J. and Lorange, P. (Eds., 2002a), pp. 189-210

Zentes, J. and Schramm-Klein, H. (2003), Exogene und endogene Einflussfaktoren der Kooperation, in: Zentes, J., Swoboda, B. and Morschett, D. (Eds., 2003), pp. 257-276

Zentes, J., Swoboda, B., and Morschett, D. (Eds., 2003), Kooperationen, Allianzen und Netzwerke, Wiesbaden 2003

Zhang, Y. and Rajagopalan, N. (2002), Inter-Partner Credible Threat in International Joint Ventures: An Infinitely Repeated Prisoner´s Dilemma Model, in: Journal of International Business Studies, 33, 2002, 3, pp. 457-478

Zielasek, G. (1995), Projektmanagement: Erfolgreich durch Aktivierung aller Unternehmensebenen, Berlin, Heidelberg, and others 1995

Zott, C. (2003), Dynamic Capabilities and the Emergence of Intraindustry Differential Firm Performance: Insights from a Simulation Study, in: Strategic Management Journal, 24, 2003, 2, pp. 97-125

Zucker, L.G. (1986), Production of Trust: Institutional Sources of Economic Structure, 1840-1920, in: Research in Organizational Behavior, 8, 1986, 1, pp. 53-111

SCHRIFTEN ZUR UNTERNEHMENSPLANUNG

Band 1 Bernhard Früh: Entscheidungsträgermodelle bei Planungstechniken. 1984.

Band 2 Ekbert Hering: Planung neuer Produkt-Marktbereiche unter besonderer Berücksichtigung der Realisierung in Klein- und Mittelbetrieben. 1984.

Band 3 Thomas Hintsch: Geschäftsfeldsteuerung in Kreditinstituten. Eine Konzeption für die strategische Planung in Banken. 1984.

Band 4 Rainer Mager: Investitions- und Steuerplanung mit Systemsimulation. 1984.

Band 5 August Zimmermann: Evolutionsstrategische Modelle bei einstufiger, losweiser Produktion. Simultane Programm-, Losgrößen- und Lossequenzplanung mit Hilfe der Simulation auf der Basis biologischer Evolutionsfaktoren. 1985.

Band 6 Paul Bäuerle: Finanzielle Planung mit Hilfe heuristischer Kalküle. Ein Beitrag zur Methodologie modellgestützter Entscheidungsfindung, konkretisiert am Beispiel der Investitions- und Finanzplanung in Klein- und Mittelbetrieben. 1987.

Band 7 Hans-Jürgen Hillmer: Planung der Unternehmensflexibilität. Eine allgemeine theoretische Konzeption und deren Anwendung zur Bewältigung strategischer Flexibilitätsprobleme. 1987.

Band 8 Wilfried H. Schwarz: Systeme der Entscheidungsunterstützung im Rahmen der strategischen Planung. 1987.

Band 9 Horst Michael: Steigerung der Effektivität betriebswirtschaftlicher Planungsprozesse durch das Leitbild des kritischen Rationalismus. Zu den Möglichkeiten eines Methodentransfers zwischen realwissenschaftlicher Forschung und betriebswirtschaftlicher Planung. 1988.

Band 10 Reiner Beutel: Unternehmensstrategien international tätiger mittelständischer Unternehmen. 1988.

Band 11 Andreas Bunz: Strategieunterstützungsmodelle für Montageplanungen. System Dynamics-Modelle zur Analyse und Gestaltung der Flexibilität von Montagesystemen. 1988.

Band 12 Lienhard Hopfmann: Flexibilität im Produktionsbereich. Ein dynamisches Modell zur Analyse und Bewertung von Flexibilitätspotentialen. 1989.

Band 13 Andreas M. Kleinhans: Wissensverarbeitung im Management. Möglichkeiten und Grenzen wissensbasierter Managementunterstützungs-, Planungs- und Simulationssysteme. 1989.

Band 14 Klaus J. Enßlin: Technologische Spin-off-Effekte aus der Raumfahrt. Vom staatspolitischen Anspruch zum unternehmenspolitischen Problem. 1989.

Band 15 Günther Unterkofler: Erfolgsfaktoren innovativer Unternehmensgründungen. Ein gestaltungsorientierter Lösungsansatz betriebswirtschaftlicher Gründungsprobleme. 1989.

Band 16 Wolfgang Kömpf: Unternehmensführung in erfolgreichen Klein- und Mittelbetrieben. Eine empirische Untersuchung. 1989.

Band 17 Wolfgang Brandt: Strategien für Rundfunkanstalten. Strategische Entwicklungsmöglichkeiten der öffentlich-rechtlichen Rundfunkanstalten. 1989.

Band 18 Uwe Schmid: Umweltschutz - Eine strategische Herausforderung für das Management. 1989.

Band 19 Josef Röhrle: Unternehmensführung und Unternehmensentwicklung. Ein Führungskonzept zur ganzheitlichen Steuerung der Unternehmensentwicklung. 1990.

Band 20 Harald W. Sondhof: Finanzdienstleistungsmärkte im Wandel. Eine industrieökonomische Branchenanalyse für strategische Zwecke. 1990.

Band 21 Ulrich Kreutle: Die Marketing-Konzeption in deutschen Chemieunternehmen – eine betriebswirtschaftlich-historische Analyse am Beispiel der BASF Ludwigshafen. 1992.

Band 22 Dieter Schmidt: Strategisches Management komplexer Systeme. Die Potentiale computergestützter Simulationsmodelle als Instrumente eines ganzheitlichen Managements – dargestellt am Beispiel der Planung und Gestaltung komplexer Instandhaltungssysteme. 1992.

Band 23 Heinrich Huber: Wettbewerbsorientierte Planung des Informationssystem (IS)-Einsatzes. Theoretische und konzeptionelle Grundlagen zur Entwicklung eines integrierten Planungsmodells. 1992.

Band 24 Wolfram Anders: Strategische Einkaufsplanung. Kernbereich eines strategischen Einkaufsmanagements. 1992. 2. Aufl. 1994.

Band 25 Maria Barth-Renz: Planungs- und Kontrollsysteme öffentlich-rechtlicher Rundfunkanstalten. Anpassung des Planungsverhaltens an neue strategische Herausforderungen. 1992.

Band 26 Ottmar Schneck: Finanzmanagement von Rundfunkanstalten. Ein Finanzplanungs-, -kontroll- und -organisationskonzept für öffentlich-rechtliche Rundfunkanstalten. 1993.

Band 27 Ralf Bertram: Informations- und Kommunikationsmanagement im Marketing mittelständischer Unternehmen der Investitionsgüterindustrie. Eine empirische Untersuchung. 1993.

Band 28 Thomas Keiser: Absatzprognosen für modeabhängige Unternehmen. Ein zweistufiges Absatzprognosesystem für Unternehmen mit modisch orientiertem Sortiment. 1993.

Band 29 Thomas Gumsheimer: Informationspartnerschaften. Konzeptionelle Grundlagen für die Gestaltung von Partnerschaften im Informationsmanagement. 1994.

Band 30 Dino Ivan Dogan: Strategisches Management der Logistik. Der logistische Kreis als Antwort auf die neuen logistischen Herausforderungen 'Umweltschutz' und 'Zeit'. 1994.

Band 31 Stefan Foschiani: Strategisches Produktionsmanagement. Ein Modellsystem zur Unterstützung produktionsstrategischer Entscheidungen. 1995.

Band 32 Jan Schäfer-Kunz: Strategische Allianzen im deutschen und europäischen Kartellrecht. 1995.

Band 33 Frank-Jürgen Richter: Die Selbstorganisation von Unternehmen in strategischen Netzwerken. Bausteine zu einer Theorie des evolutionären Managements. 1995.

Band 34 Udo Wupperfeld: Management und Rahmenbedingungen von Beteiligungsgesellschaften auf dem deutschen *Seed-Capital*-Markt. Empirische Untersuchung. 1996.

Band 35 Hartmut Feucht: Implementierung von Technologiestrategien. 1996.

Band 36 Hans-Jürgen Reichardt: Sachstand und Probleme umweltorientierter Unternehmensführung in der mittelständischen Industrie. Ergebnisse und Lösungsansätze aus einer empirischen Untersuchung. 1996.

Band 37 Jürgen Bruck: Entwicklung einer Gesamtkonzeption für das Management strategischer Allianzen im F&E-Bereich. 1996.

Band 38 Jürgen Greschner: Lernfähigkeit von Unternehmen. Grundlagen organisationaler Lernprozesse und Unterstützungstechnologien für Lernen im strategischen Management. 1996.

Band 39 Stefan Hagemann: Strategische Unternehmensentwicklung durch Mergers & Acquisitions. Konzeption und Leitlinien für einen strategisch orientierten Mergers & Acquisitions-Prozeß. 1996.

Band 40 Uwe Schmid: Ökologiegerichtete Wertschöpfung in Industrieunternehmungen. Industrielle Produktion im Spannungsfeld zwischen Markterfolg und Naturbewahrung. 1996.

Band 41 Bernhard Leitermann: Wahl der Zusammenschlußform von Unternehmen. Eine transaktionsökonomische Entscheidungskonzeption. 1996.

Band 42 Andreas Seebach: Betriebswirtschaftliche Systemanalyse des Fahrzeug-Recyclings in der Bundesrepublik Deutschland. Eine System-Dynamics-Studie. 1996.

Band 43 Nicole Karle-Komes: Anwenderintegration in die Produktentwicklung. Generierung von Innovationsideen durch die Interaktion von Hersteller und Anwender innovativer industrieller Produkte. 1997.

Band 44 Andreas Weidler: Entwicklung integrierter Innovationsstrategien. 1997.

Band 45 Frank Braun: Strategische Wettbewerbsforschung. Ein Simulationsmodell zur Erforschung der möglichen Wirkungen des EG-Binnenmarktes auf den Wettbewerb in der PKW-Branche. 1997.

Band 46 Jürgen Haas: Die Entwicklungsfähigkeit von Unternehmungen. Eine theoretische und pragmatische Analyse. 1997.

Band 47 Franz Xaver Bea / Alfred Kötzle / Kuno Rechkemmer / Alexander Bassen: Strategie und Organisation der Daimler-Benz AG. Eine Fallstudie. 1997.

Band 48 Klaus Zehender: Unternehmensführung in fraktalen Unternehmungen. Aufgaben, Architektur und Funktionsweise. 1998.

Band 49 Markus Göltenboth: Global Sourcing und Kooperationen als Alternativen zur vertikalen Integration. 1998.

Band 50 Richard M. Hesch: Das Management der Verlagerung von Wertschöpfungsstufen. Ein phasenorientiertes Modell, dargestellt am Beispiel Deutschland und Mittelosteuropa. 1998.

Band 51 Ralf Dillerup: Strategische Optionen für vertikale Wertschöpfungssysteme. 1998.

Band 52 Rainer Schmidbauer: Konzeption eines unternehmenswertorientierten Beteiligungs-Controlling im Konzern. 1998.

Band 53 Lars Gierke: Instrumentarium zur Planung und Umsetzung von Zulieferer-Hersteller-Netzwerken. 1999.

Band 54 Florian Kall: Controlling im Turnaround-Prozeß. Theoretischer Bezugsrahmen, empirische Fundierung und handlungsorientierte Ausgestaltung einer Controlling-Konzeption für den Turnaround-Prozeß. 1999.

Band 55 Klemens Berktold: Strategien zur Revitalisierung von strategischen Geschäftseinheiten. Eine empirische Untersuchung zur Ermittlung einer Typologie von Unternehmenskrisen und von typischen Strategien zu deren Bewältigung. 1999.

Band 56 Claus J. Kathke: Handlungsziele und Gestaltungsmöglichkeiten des Insolvenzverwalters im neuen Insolvenzrecht. 2000.

Band 57 Susanne Thissen: Strategisches Desinvestitionsmanagement. Entwicklung eines Instrumentariums zur Bewertung ausgewählter Desinvestitionsformen. 2000.

Band 58 Iris K. Weber: Das Planungs- und Kontrollsystem der mittelständischen Unternehmung. Gestaltungsmöglichkeiten in Abhängigkeit von der Unternehmensentwicklungsphase. 2000.

Band 59 Hermann Schnaitmann: Prozeßorientierte Unternehmensführung. 2000.

Band 60 Ulrike Suhr: Gestaltungsempfehlungen für interne Dienstleistungs-Anbieter. 2002.

Band 61 Claus Herbst: Interorganisationales Schnittstellenmanagement. Ein Konzept zur Unterstützung des Managements von Transaktionen. 2002.

Band 62 Andreas Hertweck: Strategische Erneuerung durch integriertes Management industrieller Dienstleistungen. 2002.

Band 63 Cyrus B. Bark: Integrationscontolling bei Unternehmensakquisitionen. Ein Ansatz zur Einbindung der Post-Merger-Integration in die Planung, Steuerung und Kontrolle von Unternehmensakquisitionen. 2002.

Band 64 Bernd Gagsch: Wandlungsfähigkeit von Unternehmen. Konzept für ein kontextgerechtes Management des Wandels. 2002.

Band 65 Tilmann Barth: Outsourcing unternehmensnaher Dienstleistungen. Ein konfigurierbares Modell für die optimierte Gestaltung der Wertschöpfungstiefe. 2003.

Band 66 Steffen Kinkel: Dynamische Standortbewertung und strategisches Standortcontrolling. Erfolgsmuster, kritische Faktoren, Instrumente. 2003.

Band 67 Jochen Schellinger: Konzeption eines wertorientierten strategischen Personalmanagements. 2004.

Band 68 Martin Weinmann: Wertorientiertes Management von Unternehmenszusammenschlüssen. 2004.

Band 69 Meike Tilebein: Nachhaltiger Unternehmenserfolg in turbulenten Umfeldern. Die Komplexitätsforschung und ihre Implikationen für die Gestaltung wandlungsfähiger Unternehmen. 2005.

Band 70 Björne Raetzell: Logistische Netzwerke. Ein Modell zur Ermittlung strategischer Handlungsempfehlungen. 2006.

Band 71 Andreas Falkinger: Riskomanagement im strategischen Fit. 2006.

Band 72 Anja Kern: The Use of Key Figures and its Impact on Activity. The Case of a Hospital. 2007.

Band 73 Michael Nowak: Führungsrelevante Prozesse. Systematisierung und Gestaltung. 2006.

Band 74 Florian Kapmeier: Dynamics of Interorganizational Learning in Learning Alliances. 2007.

www.peterlang.de

Kolibri 360 GmbH
Ferdinand-Jühlke-Straße 7
99095 Erfurt, Deutschland
produktsicherheit@kolibri360.de

Druck:
CPI Druckdienstleistungen GmbH
im Auftrag der
Kolibri 360 GmbH
Ferdinand-Jühlke-Str. 7
99095 Erfurt